The Cambridge Companion to Conducting

In this wide-ranging inside view of the history and practice of
conducting, analysis and advice come directly from working
conductors, including Sir Charles Mackerras on opera, Bramwell
Tovey on being an artistic director, Martyn Brabbins on modern
music, Leon Botstein on programming, and Vance George on choral
conducting, and from those who work closely with conductors: a
leading violinist describes working as a soloist with Stokowski,
Ormandy, and Barbirolli, while Solti and Abbado's studio producer
explains orchestral recording, and one of the world's most powerful
managers tells all.

The book includes advice on how to conduct different types of
groups (choral, opera, symphony, early music) and provides a
substantial history of conducting as a study of national traditions. It is
an unusually honest book about a secretive industry, and managers,
artistic directors, soloists, players, and conductors openly discuss their
different perspectives for the first time.

The Cambridge Companion to

CONDUCTING

....

EDITED BY
José Antonio Bowen
Georgetown University

CAMBRIDGE
UNIVERSITY PRESS

PUBLISHED BY THE PRESS SYNDICATE OF THE UNIVERSITY OF CAMBRIDGE
The Pitt Building, Trumpington Street, Cambridge, United Kingdom

CAMBRIDGE UNIVERSITY PRESS
The Edinburgh Building, Cambridge CB2 2RU, UK
40 West 20th Street, New York, NY 10011–4211, USA
477 Williamstown Road, Port Melbourne, VIC 3207, Australia
Ruiz de Alarcón 13, 28014 Madrid, Spain
Dock House, The Waterfront, Cape Town 8001, South Africa

http://www.cambridge.org

First published 2003
Reprinted 2005

Printed in the United Kingdom at the University Press, Cambridge

Typeface Minion 10.75/14pt.   *System* LATEX 2$_\varepsilon$ [TB]

A catalogue record for this book is available from the British Library

ISBN 0 521 82108 8 hardback
ISBN 0 521 52791 0 paperback

Contents

Illustrations

Figures

Music examples

Notes on the contributors

Charles F. Barber is a conductor active in concert, opera, and recording, and received a DMA in conducting from Stanford University. He has conducted for Stan Getz, Weslia Whitfield, Sarah Vaughn, and Francis Ford Coppola. With Marty Paich he worked on recording projects with Mel Tormé, Linda Ronstadt, Carly Simon, and on the films *Prince of Tides*, *Alive*, and *Grand Canyon*. In classical music he has co-produced CDs for Naxos/Marco Polo, led over forty works of musical theatre and opera, and guest-conducted in the United States, Canada, Japan, South Korea, Singapore, and Morocco. In 1992 he established the "Conductors on Film Collection" at Stanford. Barber is author of *Lost in the Stars: The Forgotten Musical Life of Alexander Siloti* (Scarecrow Press, 2002). "I never write letters of recommendation, so this is an exception. Charles Barber is a scholar and a conductor who adores and understands music. We have become friends, and he pretends to believe that I have taught him something" – Carlos Kleiber.

Leon Botstein is the President and Leon Levy Professor in the Arts and Humanities at Bard College. He is music director of the American Symphony Orchestra, as well as co-artistic director of the Bard Music Festival. His international conducting engagements have included performances in London, Prague, Budapest, São Paulo, Bucharest, Manila, Seoul, Vienna, Edinburgh, and Hong Kong. He has worked with Rudolf Firkusny, Benny Goodman, Yo-Yo Ma, Blanca Uribe, Leon Fleischer, Yefim Bronfmann, and Janos Starker. A champion of new music, Leon Botstein has performed works by Richard Wilson, Robert Moevs, Peter Schickele, Joan Tower, Sofia Gubaidulina, and many others. His recordings include a series on CRI featuring works by Richard Wilson, Robert Starer, Richard Wernick, and Meyer Kupferman, and two recordings with the London Philharmonic on the Telarc label. Dr. Botstein is also editor of *The Musical Quarterly*. He has published books in both English and German. He was a National Arts Club Gold Medal recipient in 1995, and in 1996 he was awarded the Centennial Medal of the Harvard Graduate School of the Arts and Sciences.

José Antonio Bowen is the Caestecker Chair and Director of Music at Georgetown University. He founded the Centre for the History and Analysis of Recorded Music (CHARM) at the University of Southampton, and his articles have appeared in many books and journals and in the *New Grove Dictionary of Music and Musicians*. He was awarded a National Endowment for the Humanities Fellowship to work on his forthcoming book, *The Conductor and the Score: A History of the Relationship between Interpreter and Text from Beethoven to Wagner*, and he is the editor of *A Guide to Discography* (University of California Press, forthcoming). His compositions and playing are featured on numerous recordings, and in over twenty-five years as a conductor and jazz performer, he has appeared with Stan Getz, Dave Brubeck, Liberace, and many others. He is a fellow of the Royal Society of Arts (FRSA) in England and Founding Member of the National Recordings Preservation Board at the Library of Congress.

Martyn Brabbins studied in London and with Ilya Musin in Leningrad. He has since conducted most of the major symphony orchestras in Britain: he has been Associate Principal Conductor of the BBC Scottish Symphony Orchestra and Principal Conductor of Sinfonia 21 since 1994 and is the conductor for the Philharmonia Orchestra's "Music of Today" Series. He conducts at the BBC Proms every year, and his international experience ranges from the orchestras of Bayerischer Rundfunk and St. Petersburg, to the Ensemble InterContemporain. In recent years he has championed the music of James Dillon, Jonathan Lloyd, Harrison Birtwistle, Steve Reich, James MacMillan, Minna Keal, Mark-Anthony Turnage, and Robin Holloway. Known for his performances of British concert music, he is equally at home at the Kirov Opera or English National Opera; he recently conducted the world premiere of Alexander Knaifel's *Alice in Wonderland* with the Netherlands Opera. He records for Hyperion with the BBC Scottish and has also recorded works by Birtwistle, David Bedford, and Finnissy for NMC. His recording of Korngold's *Die Kathrin* with the BBC Concert Orchestra for CPO won the Opera Award at the Cannes International Music Festival.

David Cairns CBE was music critic of the *Sunday Times* from 1983 to 2002, having previously written for the *Spectator*, the *Financial Times*, and the *New Statesman*. From 1967 to 1972 he worked as classical program co-ordinator for Philips Records and was involved in some of the company's major recording projects, including operas by Mozart, Berlioz, and Tippett. He has always been actively involved in music-making: he was co-founder of the Chelsea Opera Group in 1950, and sang solo roles under the group's first conductor, Colin Davis. He is conductor of the Thorington Players, an amateur orchestra which gives regular concerts for charity. He has written several books including a prize-winning two-volume biography of Berlioz (University of California Press).

J. Michele Edwards, conductor and musicologist, is professor emerita of music at Macalester College and was Director of the Macalester Festival Chorale (1992–9) and programmed innovative repertoire including *Mass in D* by Ethyl Smyth, commissioned and premiered Libby Larsen's *Like a Needle Guide Us in our Weaving*, prepared a backup chorus for Rosemary Clooney's holiday show at Orchestra Hall, and recorded Marta Ptaszyńska's *Holocaust Memorial Cantata.* She has appeared as guest conductor of the St. Paul Chamber Orchestra and the Shreveport Symphony and conducts the Calliope Women's Chorus. Her many publications include the book *Women and Music: A History* (second edn., 2001).

Harold Farberman graduated from Juilliard before joining the Boston Symphony Orchestra as a percussionist/timpanist. He moved to full-time conducting in 1963, becoming Principal Guest Conductor of the Denver Symphony Orchestra in 1963, Music Director of the Colorado Springs Symphony in 1967 and of the Oakland Symphony Orchestra from 1971–9. He has conducted the London Symphony Orchestra, the Philharmonia, the BBC Symphony, the Stockholm Philharmonic, the Danish Radio Orchestra, the RAI in Rome, the Hong Kong Philharmonic, the Seoul Philharmonic, the Sydney and Melbourne Symphonies, and was Principal Guest Conductor of the Bournemouth Sinfonietta. He is the founder and director of the Conductors' Institute at Bard College. He is a prolific composer and in addition to acclaimed versions of Mahler symphonies he has recorded most of Charles Ives's works, and was awarded the Ives Medal.

Vance George is internationally recognized as one of America's leading choral conductors. Under his direction the San Francisco Symphony Chorus has been hailed as one of the finest in the world. On their behalf he has accepted three Grammy awards: for Best Performance of a Choral Work (Orff's *Carmina Burana*, 1993, and Brahms's *Ein Deutsches Requiem*, 1996) and Best Classical Album of the Year (Stravinsky's *Perséphone*, 2000). He has also conducted them in works ranging from Bach's Mass in B minor to *Carmina Burana*. TV and film credits include an Emmy (*Sweeney Todd*, 2002) and soundtracks for *Amadeus, The Unbearable Lightness of Being*, and *Godfather III*. Vance George's work embodies the legacy of the great maestros he has known as protégé and colleague, especially Robert Shaw, Julius Herford, Margaret Hillis, Robert Page, Otto Werner-Mueller, and Mary Oyer. He has received great acclaim for his unique knowledge of musical styles, languages, vocal colors, and his synthesis of the choral–orchestral tradition. He was awarded an honorary doctorate by Kent State University, and a Lifetime Achievement Award by Chorus America.

Raymond Holden studied in Sydney, Cologne, and London. After a period of study with Sir John Pritchard CBE, he was invited to act as his assistant. In this role, he performed with Sir John throughout the UK and Europe, working as his associate conductor at the Royal Festival Hall (BBCSO Winter Season, 1980–9), the Royal Albert Hall (Proms, 1981–9), the City of London Festival (Philharmonia Orchestra, 1980), and the Edinburgh Festival (BBCSO, 1986). He has also conducted many leading British and European ensembles and was the Australian representative at the Seventh Malko International Conducting Competition (Copenhagen) with the Danish Radio Orchestra. He later conducted an all-Beethoven concert with the Philharmonia Orchestra, and a concert with the BBC Symphony Orchestra. Since completing his Ph.D. at the University of London, Dr. Holden has investigated the performing activities of Richard Strauss. He is writing a book on conducting and its traditions for Yale University Press.

Michael Haas has more than twenty years' experience as producer for both Decca/London and the Sony Classical labels. He has won a number of Grammys and was producer for Sir Georg Solti for over ten years, before leaving to work with Claudio Abbado and the Berlin Philharmonic; in 1994 he was Vice President of A&R for Sony Classical in New York. He now runs his own production company, Coralfox Ltd. Since 1978, he has produced prize-winning recordings with many important conductors, including Christoph von Dohnányi, Zubin Mehta, Riccardo Chailly, David Zinman, Charles Dutoit, Sir Charles Mackerras, Bernard Haitink, Mstislav Rostropovich, Valery Gergiev, and Sir Simon Rattle. His most regarded work has been in the rediscovery of music lost during the Nazi years as creator of Decca's series, *Entartete Musik*. This was a groundbreaking project which was the first major attempt to bring a critical examination of many works assumed lost, or dismissed as irrelevant, after 1945.

Stephen Johnson was born in Lancashire in 1955. He studied at the Northern
School of Music, Manchester, under Alexander Goehr at Leeds University, then
at Manchester University. Since then he has written regularly for *The
Independent* and *The Guardian*, and was Chief Music Critic of *The Scotsman*
(1998–9). He has also broadcast frequently for BBC Radios 3, 4, and World
Service, major projects including a series of fourteen programmes about the
music of Bruckner for the centenary of the composer's death (1996). He is the
author of *Bruckner Remembered* (Faber, 1998).

David Mermelstein is editorial director of KUSC, a classical radio station in Los
Angeles. He regularly writes about music for the Sunday edition of *The New York
Times*. His feature articles and criticism have also appeared in *Gramophone*,
ICRC, *The New Criterion*, *Opera News*, the *Los Angeles Times*, the *San Francisco
Chronicle*, the *Washington Post*, *LA Weekly* and *Variety*. In addition, he is a
contributor to the revised edition of the *New Grove Dictionary of Music and
Musicians*.

Sir Charles Mackerras studied in Sydney and Prague before making his debut with
Sadler's Wells Opera. He has since been Principal Conductor of the BBC Concert
Orchestra (1954–6), the First Conductor at the Hamburg State Opera
(1966–70), Music Director at the Sadler's Wells Opera (1970–77, becoming the
English National Opera in 1974), Artistic Director of the Welsh National Opera
(1987–92), and a constant Guest Conductor at the Royal Opera House since
1964. His Metropolitan Opera debut was made in 1972 with Gluck's *Orfeo et
Euridice*. He continues to conduct at the Met and is Conductor Emeritus with
the San Francisco Opera and the Scottish Chamber Orchestra, as well as
Principal Guest Conductor of the Czech Philharmonic Orchestra. He is
President of Trinity College, London.

David Nice is a writer, lecturer, and broadcaster on music. As a regular contributor
to monthly publications including the *BBC Music Magazine* and *Gramophone*, he
has interviewed all the major living Russian conductors. His many broadcasts in
the BBC Radio 3 series *Building a Library* have included detailed comparisons of
all the available interpretations of major works by Prokofiev, Shostakovich, and
Tchaikovsky. He lectures on Russian music for the Music Club of London, the
City Literary Institute, and several of the major London orchestras. He has
written short studies of Elgar, Richard Strauss, Tchaikovsky, and the history of
opera, and is currently working on a biography of Prokofiev for Yale University
Press.

Robert L. Ripley was brought up in a musical home, where his mother was a voice
teacher and pianist. He started the cello at age nine and attended the Curtis
Institute of Music upon finishing high school. After two summers at the
Berkshire Music Center (now the Tanglewood Music Center), he became a
member of the Cleveland Orchestra in 1942, but this was quickly terminated by
World War II, when he found himself in the string section of the Glenn Miller
Air Force Band. Following the war, he rejoined the Cleveland Orchestra, playing
under George Szell for his first nine years there. In 1955, he moved to the Boston
Symphony Orchestra and remained there until his retirement in 1995.

Michael Rose read French and Italian at Oxford and studied composition with Bernard Stevens. With the late Hanns Hammelmann he wrote the radio series *Birth of an Opera* for the BBC Third Programme (1954–76). From 1961 to 1981 he lived in Italy, where he arranged scripts and music for television art documentaries, collaborated with Emanuele Luzzati on a cartoon film of *The Magic Flute*, and contributed articles and advice to *The New Grove*. He provided the music entries for the new *Oxford Companion to English Literature*, contributed to the *Viking* (now New Penguin) *Opera Guide*, and with John Amis compiled an anthology, *Words about Music* (Faber, 1989). He was general editor of the Everyman–EMI Music Companions, wrote the commentary for Erich Auerbach's photographs in *Images of Music*, and has most recently published *Berlioz Remembered* (Faber, 2001).

Bernard D. Sherman is the author of *Inside Early Music* (Oxford University Press, 1997), and co-editor of *Performing Brahms* (Cambridge University Press, forthcoming). He wrote an essay on "Authenticity in Musical Performance" for *The Encyclopedia of Aesthetics* (Oxford University Press, 1998), and contributes regularly to *The New York Times*. His writings have also appeared in *Early Music, The Los Angeles Times, Historical Performance, Schwann/Opus, Early Music Quarterly*, and many other publications.

Joseph Silverstein has appeared as both conductor and violin soloist with more than a hundred orchestras in the United States, Europe, Israel, and the Far East. He began his conducting career as assistant conductor of the Boston Symphony in 1971, after having been concertmaster with that orchestra for nine years. In 1983 he became the Music Director of the Utah Symphony Orchestra, becoming Conductor Laureate in 1998. He has conducted the Berlin Symphony in Germany and on tour in North America in the winter of 1998. He remains an active soloist, chamber music performer, and teacher. He organized the Boston Symphony Chamber Players in 1962 and has been on the faculties of Boston University, the Tanglewood Music Center, Susquehanna University, and Yale University. Currently he is on the string faculty of the Longy School of Music in Cambridge, Massachusetts. He has recorded as both conductor and violin soloist with the Utah Symphony on the Pro Arte label and his Telarc recording of Vivaldi's *Four Seasons* with the Boston Symphony received a Grammy nomination.

Bramwell Tovey is Music Director of the Vancouver Symphony and Chief Conductor and Music Director of L'Orchestre Philharmonique du Luxembourg. In 2004 and 2005 he will direct and conduct a new series of concerts at the Lincoln Center for the New York Philharmonic. From 1989 to 2001 he was artistic director of the Winnipeg Symphony Orchestra where he founded the du Maurier New Music Festival in 1992. He has given world or North American premieres by Corigliano, Pärt, Tower, Schafer, Turnage, and many other distinguished composers. He has directed every major British orchestra, including the LSO, CBSO, LPO, and the RSNO. In North America his appearances include the Toronto and Montreal Symphonies and the New York and Los Angeles Philharmonic. He made his Canadian Opera Company debut in

1994 and in 2003 conducted the world premiere of Estacio's *Filumena* for Calgary Opera and the Banff Centre. As a composer his works include concertos for viola and cello. His *Requiem for a Charred Skull* won the 2003 Juno Prize for best classical composition. In 1999 he won the $25,000 Chalmers Award for artistic direction of a major Canadian arts organization. He studied at the Royal Academy of Music and London University.

Stephen Wright studied law and modern languages at Cambridge University where he co-founded the Oxford and Cambridge Shakespeare Company. In 1971 he set up and ran the European office of an American concert management agency, Shawconcerts Ltd. Then in 1975 he joined Harold Holt Ltd., later becoming joint Managing Director and looking after a group of thirty artists (including Mariss Jansons, Sir Neville Marriner, and Seiji Ozawa) and touring a wide range of international orchestras (including St. Petersburg, Oslo, and the Leipzig Gewandhaus). He left Harold Holt with his division to form IMG Artists Europe in 1991; he took on his current role of Managing Director of IMG Artists in 1995, where he has managed or worked for Seiji Ozawa, Rafael Kubelík, Sergiv Celibidache, Yuri Temirkanov, Antonio Pappano, Michael Tilson Thomas, and many others. IMG has also established a new international television/video arm which has, with the BBC, produced BBC Legends and made *The Art of Conducting* and *The Art of Singing.*

Preface

Every contributor to this book is either a conductor or has had considerable professional experience with conductors. A few are also academics, but many continue to make their livelihood as conductors and most of us had to juggle the task of writing with the daily routines of rehearsals, concerts, recordings and tours. This book was a truly collaborative effort and I am grateful to all of the contributors not only for such probing insights into the art of conducting, but also for being so willing to engage in discussion about who would say what, and how we would manage the various styles and perspectives of contributors. I apologize for taking you away from the music, but it was my privilege to work with such great musicians.

Asking so many professional musicians to contribute, of course, was a risk. Many were first-time writers and nervous about tone, referencing systems, and, most importantly, about what to say. As working conductors, there was little academic detachment. While this resulted in a variety of voices and many disagreements, it has the tremendous advantage of truly illuminating the history and role of the conductor. In the end, I resisted the editor's natural urge to make every chapter sound the same; I could not make the orchestral player, the soloist, the studio producer, the manager, and the choral conductor all speak with the same voice. What remains is not one, but many unique views into the world of conductors and conducting.

Many topics came up repeatedly. Everyone agreed that most of a conductor's work occurs in rehearsal and there was remarkable agreement about best practice, although the regular reminders that conductors should speak up, learn a few names and end on time suggests that none of these is yet common practice. There was little agreement, however, about marking parts for the performers. Positions at the extremes ranged from travelling with your own set of performance parts (including a back-up set) to allowing the orchestra to bow their own parts. These, and all the positions in between, were rooted in practical experience. Arriving with parts for each player which already contain the conductor's preferred bowings and dynamics saves time in a tight schedule. Others, though, questioned the psychology of telling a group of professionals, generally more skilled on their own instrument than the conductor, how to create a sound: individual players (especially when performing in their own hall for a guest conductor) may know best. This issue came up in nine different chapters in all manner of guises and nothing better illuminates how practice can reveal important cultural and historical differences; recommendations about marking parts intersect with discussions of studio and live recordings, guest conducting, whether the soloist should directly address the orchestra, and how European and American orchestras differ. (American orchestras are more likely to use and keep new sets of parts for each new conductor while many European orchestras still use the parts they used in the nineteenth century – Mengelberg's blue pencil markings can still be found on Concertgebouw music stands.) I have, in many cases, included cross-references to other chapters where the same topic is discussed, often from a different perspective.

The book is divided into three sections, but all of them mix practical insight with some historical perspective. While the first section deals with practice per se, it mixes information about rehearsals and studio seating with discussion of how rehearsal techniques have changed and how different conductors approach studio work. There is plenty of advice, but also discussion of why conductors do the things they do.

The middle historical section is not a who's who of conducting. While most of the major figures are mentioned, the aim is to tell the stories of how conducting developed in different places and how this influenced national and even individual practice. While it is certainly true that modern jet travel and recordings have gradually homogenized the world's orchestras, there are still differences in practice and sound and there is little question that through the middle of the twentieth century many orchestras (Berlin, Leningrad, and Philadelphia, for example) played with a sound tied to both the region and the conductor. The aim here is not to define schools, but to analyze the history of conducting in a new way.

The final section concentrates on a range of issues confronting modern conducting, from how to create a coherent concert program to what a manager does. Again the practical is mixed with the historical. While there is disagreement about whether conducting technique has "improved" and whether or not it is easier to conduct an orchestra now than it was for Berlioz, all agree that technique has changed. Should modern conducting technique be used when leading players holding eighteenth-century instruments? While this is a model of the typical academic question (as it is relatively easy to argue either side), conductors, in the end, must make decisions that have interpretative consequences. Academics, pundits, and critics can contemplate various options from the safety of the aisle seat, but a performer can only commit to one approach at a time. Other challenges to modern conducting include a radically different relationship with contemporary music, the job of Artistic Director, and the marginal acceptance of women as conductors.

While there are plenty of textbooks on conducting and biographies of conductors, this book attempts to bridge that gap. It is my hope that the combination of practical details (how *not* to start a rehearsal with a major orchestra) with a fresh look at the musical, social, and economic history of conducting will together provide students and anyone interested in conducting with new insight.

Despite all of the excellent contributions, I am responsible for all shortcomings and errors, and only hope my efforts have done justice to the work assembled here. I am grateful to Penny Souster and her team at Cambridge and to Dorothy Biondi, at Georgetown, who somehow managed to keep the wolves at bay long enough for me to finish. My thanks to everyone who contributed and supported me during this effort, especially Nancy, Naomi and Molly.

Acknowledgments

Acknowledgment for kind permission to reproduce illustrations and music examples is due to the following:

The Richard-Strauss-Institut, in Garmisch-Partenkirchen: Fig. 1.2
The personal archives of Robert Ripley: Figs. 7.1, 12.2
Meininger Museen: Figs. 9.1, 9.2
British Museum, Prints and Drawings: Fig. 11.1
BBC Research Collection, Written Archives, News Information:
Fig. 15.1
New York Public Library: Fig. 16.2
21C Media Group: Fig. 16.3
Oxford University Press: Ex. 19.2

The music examples were set by Mark Gruen of Enterprise Musical Arts and Sciences, Bethesda, MA, with the exception of chapter 16, where Vance George's annotated examples and figures were created by Dennis Dieterich of Music Publications Technologies in San Francisco.

Thank you also to Elizabeth MacLeod, of Central Michigan University, for help finding figures, and to Frank Villella of the Chicago Symphony Orchestra's Rosenthal Archives.

PART ONE

Practice

1 The technique of conducting

RAYMOND HOLDEN

Any discussion of conducting technique can be problematic. The potential for disagreement over what constitutes a conductor's technique is huge, so this chapter will be limited to the ways in which conductors express their thoughts and ideas through physical movements, the tools they use, and the skills that they employ.[1] The film footage of conductors like Willem Mengelberg, Wilhelm Furtwängler, Klaus Tennstedt, and Pierre Boulez demonstrates that there are as many styles of conducting as there are conductors, and to attempt to codify, to dissect, and to analyze fully the variety of gestures used by conductors is beyond the scope of this, or perhaps any, chapter. Although the gesticulations that they use seem to vary widely, all conductors' techniques have a basic task in common: to act as a kind of conduit through which their ideas are transmitted to the musicians. Of course, body movements are not all they use: a conductor also communicates verbally in rehearsal and makes eye contact with fellow performers throughout the performance process. A member of the Sydney Symphony Orchestra once remarked laconically to the present author that "it matters not whether a conductor stands on his head and wiggles his toes or beats time like a metronome as long as his intentions are clear." While the first position described has more in common with yoga than music, the player's basic thesis has merit; clarity of intention is paramount for any conductor.

The baton

The tool that is most often associated with the conductor is the baton. Today, batons are still used commonly and their length and materials vary according to the requirements of the individual conductor. Generally, they are made of light wood with a point at one end and tapered to a grip, usually made of cork, at the other. Conductors who use batons often have them made to their own specifications, insisting on a stick that suits their physical demands and the nature of their performance style. Sir Henry Wood, for example, had his batons made by Palmer's of Great Yarmouth, and his requirements were set out precisely:

WEIGHT: Slightly under 1 ounce
LENGTH of exposed Shaft: 19 inches
    of Handle: 5 [inches]
TOTAL LENGTH: 24 [inches]
SHAFT made of seasoned straight-grain poplar wood, carefully rived by hand to ensure that the grain runs straight. Painted white with two coats of water paint. The shaft runs right through the handle.
HANDLE of cork 5 inches long, diameter at base $1\frac{1}{4}$ inches, diameter at shaft end 1 inch.[2]

Sir Henry's preference for long batons was not shared universally. Herbert von Karajan preferred a short baton, while Sir John Barbirolli opted for a stick of moderate length, arguing that "it is as absurd to use a baton which resembles a diminutive lead pencil as it is to wave a weapon of exceeding length and frailty."[3]

The baton is usually held in the right hand, though some left-handed conductors hold it in the left. The ways in which batons are held vary as widely as the styles of batons used, but many conductors hold the grip between the thumb and the first two fingers. This was the approach suggested by Max Rudolf who wrote that "the most advisable way to hold the baton is with the thumb, first and second fingers, and with the butt against the palm of the hand."[4] Ideally, the method of holding the baton should ensure that the stick acts as an extension of the arm, and that the point of the baton is the focal point of the beat.

Some conductors, however, prefer not to use a baton. Pierre Boulez, who beats time with his bare hands, argues that with smaller contemporary ensembles, "the more one is inclined toward contemporary music, the less one needs this particular extension."[5] Other eminent conductors who did not use a baton included Leopold Stokowski and Dimitri Mitropoulos, both of whom were leading figures in the performance of twentieth-century music. Stokowski's use of bare hands gained wide exposure with the release of Walt Disney's film, *Fantasia.* It has often been argued that his abandonment of the baton was an act of showmanship, a notion that should be treated with caution. In his book, *Music for Us All,* Stokowski explained his reasons for conducting with bare hands, arguing that "whether or not a conductor uses a baton is of little importance. Personally I find a baton unnecessary – I am convinced that unessentials should be eliminated."[6] Choral conductors also tend to conduct without a baton. This is particularly common for conductors who perform in churches and cathedrals. As the singers often stand close to the conductor and have rehearsed extensively with him or her, the use of subtle hand gestures can be interpreted more easily. But conducting without a baton has provoked a hostile response from those who prefer to use a stick. Bruno Walter, for example, argues that "the renunciation of the baton . . . carries the seeds of decay."[7] For him, the baton extends "the obviously restricted beat of the bare hand, magnifying it to distantly visible proportions" and enhancing the "clarity and plausibility of its movements, a better aid to precise orchestral playing."[8] While it is hard to reconcile the notion of decay with the practices of Stokowski, Mitropoulos, and Boulez, Walter's advice is generally sagacious.

Whether or not a conductor uses a baton is a matter of personal choice, but whichever method is chosen, it must have direct relevance to the music being performed. Leonard Bernstein believed this to be true and stated: "if [the conductor] uses a baton, the baton itself must be a living thing, charged with a kind of electricity, which makes it an instrument of meaning in its tiniest movement. If [the conductor] does not use a baton, his hands must do the job with equal clarity. But baton or no baton, his gestures must be first and always meaningful in terms of the music."[9]

Beating patterns and tempo

One of the primary functions of the baton, or the hand in which it is customarily held, is the indication of the music's beat with both vertical and lateral movements. While gestures vary, the basic beating patterns are relatively standard. In general, the baton should move in a fluid manner, with the beats being outlined at the point of the stick. Fig. 1.1 illustrates the various patterns that are commonly used today. If the music is to be rendered fast, slow, staccato or legato, the conductor must manipulate the stick accordingly, using short, long, jerky and smooth gestures that are in direct proportion to the effect required.

The preliminary beat, commonly known as the upbeat, is one of the conductor's most important gestures. Otto Klemperer remarked that "it's the upbeat and not the downbeat that makes an orchestra attentive,"[10] a notion that is shared, at least in part, by Wilhelm Furtwängler who argued that "it is not the instant of the downbeat itself that produces the precision with which the orchestra enters, nor is it the precision of the conductor's gesture but the way he prepares for it."[11] To achieve a clear upbeat, Bernstein suggested that a conductor should treat it "exactly like breathing: the preparation is like an inhalation, and the music sounds as an exhalation."[12] Although this might sound peculiar, a short, silent, rhythmic intake of breath often helps to communicate the conductor's intentions to the players. Whichever approach is used, clarity of movement is essential. As the upbeat directly precedes the first sound rendered, the speed, character and direction of the movement has a direct bearing on the initial tempo of the work.

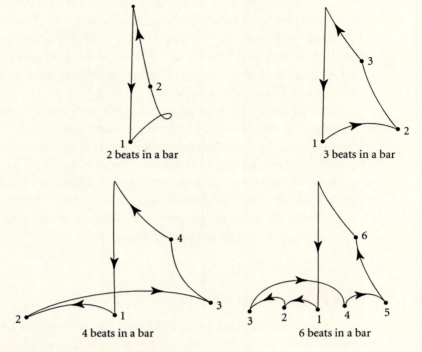

Figure 1.1 Beat diagrams for music in 2, 3, 4, and 6

Example 1.1 Mozart: Symphony No. 35, first movement, opening measures

The conductor's preliminary beat acts as a kind of code for the musicians and singers being led, and the direction and speed adopted are related directly to the rhythmic disposition of the bar performed. For example, the preliminary beat is a vertical upbeat when the music begins on the first beat of a bar (Ex. 1.1), a vertical downbeat when it begins on the second beat (Ex. 1.2), or a lateral movement to either the left or the right when it begins on the third or fourth beats (Exx. 1.3 and 1.4).

The preparatory beat becomes more complicated when a work begins with rests. If the first bar is written out fully, the preliminary beat will vary according to a number of factors. Some conductors argue that all the beats must be indicated, even if they are silent; others maintain that it is only necessary to give a single, preliminary beat. The rules, however, are not defined clearly and the gestures used depend upon the tempo

Example 1.2 Liszt: A *Faust Symphony*, third movement, opening measures

Example 1.3 Mozart: *Eine kleine Nachtmusik*, second movement, opening measures

Example 1.4 Liszt: A *Faust Symphony*, first movement, opening measures

and the character of the music to be directed. In Ex. 1.5, a vertical down-beat is usual; in Ex. 1.6, a vertical downbeat followed by a lateral movement to the left is common; while, in Ex. 1.7, a vertical downbeat followed by lateral movements to the left and then the right are customary. Ex. 1.8 can be approached in two different ways. If the Andante is played by a competent, professional orchestra, a single vertical upbeat is sufficient, but, if the

Example 1.5 Liszt: *Tasso*, opening measures

Example 1.6 Liszt: *Les Préludes*, opening measures

Example 1.7 Liszt: *Die Ideale*, opening measures

Example 1.8 Rossini: Overture to *Il barbiere di Siviglia*, opening measures

Example 1.9 Haydn: Symphony No. 54, first movement, opening measures

Example 1.10 Beethoven: Symphony No. 1, fourth movement, opening measures

ensemble is inexperienced, two preliminary beats might be necessary: first, a lateral movement to the right, followed by a vertical upbeat.

Indicating the continuation of the music after a pause can be difficult. In Ex. 1.9, a vertical upbeat followed by a vertical downbeat to mark the resumption of the normal pulse at the start of the next bar is appropriate; while, in Ex. 1.10, a lateral movement to the right followed by a vertical upbeat would serve the same purpose. In passages that are either rhythmically difficult or subject to rubato, the beat might need to be subdivided. But subdivisions can often be misleading and unnecessary, and should only be used in a controlled manner. If used indiscriminately, they can interrupt the flow and direction of the music.

Setting and holding a suitable tempo is one of the conductor's primary functions. Indicating the desired tempo can only be done by giving a clear and precise preliminary beat; therefore, the conductor must have the tempo firmly in mind before making this gesture. Sergiu Celibidache argued that the best method of doing this was to subdivide the pulse mentally before making the preliminary beat.[13] This approach is particularly useful when conducting a slow tempo, where a broad upbeat can be problematic. When conducting a work that contains metronome marks, the performer is confronted with ethical, historical, and aesthetic problems. If a work has metronome marks that suggest very quick tempi and if the orchestra is amateur, it might be necessary to modify the speeds accordingly. In the case of compositions such as Beethoven's Symphony No. 4, where the tempi of the first (Allegro vivace) and last movements are linked, any adjustment to the printed speeds should reflect these relationships.

For ballet conductors, the needs of both the dancers and the composer must be considered. As dancers rely heavily on an organized pulsal plan, the conductor must ensure that the various performance tempi correspond to any prearranged scheme. When conducting opera or choral music, the conductor must allow time for the singers to breathe and should pace the phrasing accordingly. Similarly, wind players also need to breathe and the tempo and pacing of the phrasing must be judged according to the needs and abilities of the ensembles being directed.

Often, young professional conductors will act as an assistant conductor, directing off- and on-stage bands. As these groups are generally placed at some distance from the main orchestra, the assistant conductor, when following the speed and beat of the senior colleague, might use a television monitor. From this monitor, the assistant can relay the tempo to the off- or on-stage band. In some circumstances, when the distance between the main and the subsidiary ensembles is particularly great, the assistant should beat slightly in advance of the conductor, so as to compensate for any time delay; this delay will vary according to the exact distance between the two groups and the venue's acoustics.

When accompanying in concertos, the conductor must be prepared to anticipate the soloist's reading and be ready to respond quickly to any unexpected acts of *rubato*. In passages where the orchestra is silent, the conductor should mark these bars with a single downbeat; this helps the orchestral players count the empty bars. When working with singers, the conductor needs to be especially vigilant, and when accompanying recitatives, the pacing of the drama is paramount. By indicating the recitative's isolated chords in a clear and unequivocal manner, the conductor can control the speed and direction of the stage action. These chords can be indicated by the following methods: first, they can be beaten only as they occur; or, second, the conductor can continue to beat metrically throughout the course of the recitative, giving a more decisive gesture when a chord has to be played.

The left hand

Richard Strauss (1864–1949) famously dismissed the importance of the left hand arguing that it "has nothing to do with conducting." For him, "Its proper place is in the waistcoat pocket from which it should only emerge to restrain or to make some minor gesture for which in any case a scarcely perceptible glance would suffice." He felt that it is "better to conduct with the ear instead of the arm . . . [then] the rest follows automatically."[14] As if to underline his argument, Strauss posed for a photograph (Fig. 1.2) in 1898 in which he is shown facing the camera with the baton held high in the right hand and the left-hand thumb inserted into his waistcoat pocket. What Strauss

Figure 1.2 Photograph of Richard Strauss in 1898

objected to most was replicating the motion of the right hand with the left, a practice that is both confusing and superfluous. Hermann Scherchen (1891–1966) also objected to this approach and warned that "the student [should] avoid the duplicating, simultaneous use of both arms, which never renders his motions clearer for the orchestra, more expressive, or more relevant. On the contrary, the practice robs a conductor of an important resource as regards expressive, representative conducting." Moreover, when the left hand "remains independent of the right arm's motions . . . the use of the left hand is a splendid method of articulating, intensifying, reinforcing, emphasizing, hushing, and refining."[15] The left hand should be used, therefore, to indicate entries, to shape the dynamics and the phrasing, and to gesture warnings.

Eye contact

For the conductor, eye contact with the performers is of particular importance. The eye has the power to indicate entries, to alert the players and the singers to possible difficulties, and to act as an expressive device, complementing the motion of the arms and the stick. Throughout the nineteenth and twentieth centuries, conductors stressed the importance of the eye. Richard Wagner recalled that Gasparo Spontini relied heavily on eye contact to achieve his results and refused to wear spectacles when conducting;[16] Richard Strauss held the baton at eye level to ensure the complete attention of the players and singers; Stokowski argued that "conducting is only to a small extent beating of time – it is done far more through the eyes,"[17] while Walter emphasised the importance of "seeing *eye to eye*" with the musicians.[18] Probably the most famous example of a conductor using eye contact to achieve his musical objectives was Arthur Nikisch. Throughout his career, commentators often mentioned his "mesmeric" style, which was related directly to his use of the eye. Nikisch's reliance on eye contact is immediately apparent from film footage of him conducting in 1913.[19] Though the film is silent, his physical gestures are seen clearly, with his arms held high and the beat placed firmly at the point of the baton. By having the end of the stick function at eye level, the players were drawn into closer eye contact with him, and this, some commentators argue, was the source of Nikisch's mesmerism. Sir Adrian Boult also commented on Nikisch's use of the eye, but suggested that his ability to "mesmerise" was a consequence of sound musical practices, rather than an act of hypnosis. Boult recalled that "the curious slow gaze with which [Nikisch] seemed to take in the whole orchestra at the beginning of most rehearsals and of every concert gave him an opportunity of noticing everything and at the same time of getting on terms with everyone. Under such conducting it is easy for players to 'feel unlike themselves' and for observers to think they are being mesmerised."[20] In contrast, Herbert von Karajan regularly conducted with his eyes closed, arguing that it helped him "concentrate on the inner content of the music."[21] But, when performing choral music, he, too, performed with his eyes open because "sometimes it is a matter of establishing a direct human contact; and in choral music this must always be the case. With me the choirs never use music, which has the double effect: their eyes are not fixed on the page in front of them and they can communicate directly with me."[22]

The podium

While the podium has been linked with the popular notion that the conductor is the ruler of all he or she surveys, the box on which the conductor stands has little to do with the respect commanded.[23] Generally, the podium is a square, plinth-like platform that remained popular throughout the nineteenth and twentieth centuries. While there is no fixed height for the podium, it should be high enough for all the members of the orchestra and/or choir to see the conductor's beat. While many conductors continue to direct the music from an elevated position, some, like Nikolaus Harnoncourt, when working with early music groups or smaller ensembles, prefer to stand on the floor of the stage. Others, when performing music from the eighteenth century or earlier, direct from either the keyboard or the front desk of the violins. Though the above are the most common positions from which to lead a performance, some musicians are less orthodox. Peter Schreier, for example, conducts while singing in early vocal and choral music. Whether a conductor chooses to stand on a podium or prefers to remain on the floor of the stage is of little importance. Whichever method is chosen, it is essential that the beat is visible to all. For a conductor like Sir John Barbirolli, who was little more than five foot tall, the podium was an absolute necessity but, for others who are taller, it is of little consequence. The decision whether or not to use a podium, however, should be based on purely practical criteria and not by the notion that elevation is synonymous with talent and ability.

Preparation and interpretation

Thorough preparation is essential for any conductor. A conductor must be able to read and to analyse a full orchestral score, have good communication skills, and be able to detect imperfections easily. In the late twentieth century, some aspiring conductors have turned to recordings as a study tool. While recordings are of value, they should not replace traditional methods of preparation. Of particular importance are good keyboard skills and an understanding of string technique. These allow the conductor to study the score at the piano and to make decisions about bowing. Where possible the conductor should use his or her own marked parts. If this is not possible, it is advisable to check the orchestral and vocal parts in advance, as they often contain textual errors. Although printed mistakes can be corrected in rehearsal, these encounters can sometimes be stressful and, when working under such conditions, imperfections can pass unnoticed, undermining the musicians' confidence in the conductor.

The conductor's role in interpreting the work has a long and complex history (see chapter 8). Realizing the composer's intentions is considerably easier when the composer is available for consultation and becomes more difficult as performance traditions and styles change. Current scholarly research is making some attempt to recover older methods and techniques of performing, but juxtaposing these concepts within a coherent musical whole can prove difficult. On the most basic level, the conductor must make decisions regarding tempi, dynamics, and balance. Often these are complementary and are influenced by the architectonics of the work being performed. Such judgments, though, can only be made after a period of intense preparation. For many conductors, their interpretations are the result of a long affinity with a particular composer, or school of composers. During their early years, both Wilhelm Furtwängler and Arturo Toscanini championed the music of their contemporaries, but later restricted their activities to Mozart, Beethoven, Brahms, and Wagner. By restricting themselves in this way, these conductors argued they were better able to explore a limited repertoire in detail. For the average, jobbing conductor, however, the styles and types of music to be directed are often determined by practical imperatives. For example, a conductor in a German opera house must have a broad understanding of the standard operatic repertoire. As these performers are regularly asked to deputize for a colleague at short notice, the interpretation of a work is often determined by existing "house" trends. A chorus master, when preparing a chorus for a symphonic or operatic performance, must ensure that the singers are rehearsed in accordance with the musical demands of the main conductor. Similarly, when directing off- or on-stage ensembles, an assistant conductor must relay the intentions of the senior colleague to the stage band.

Conducting from memory

Conducting from memory should only be attempted after extensive preparation. Walter, who began to conduct from memory late in his career, stated that, by performing without a score, he "realized . . . what it had been that had so strangely impeded [him] in the past."[24] By freeing himself of the score, he believed that "nothing stood any longer between [his] internal image of the music and [his] communication with the orchestra." For him, "independence of the score" was important in achieving "intensity and spontaneity in music-making" and was helpful in obtaining a "close spiritual contact with the orchestra." He warned, however, that "anyone who cannot trust his memory with absolute certainty . . . [should] have no qualms about putting the score on his desk." Moreover, "in rehearsals . . . the score is indispensable . . . because it has to be consulted when an orchestral part gives room for doubt . . . [this, then, enables] conductor and players to resume their work after interruptions without delay."[25] Mitropoulos took a different stance. He regularly rehearsed from memory using a method that, for some, seemed complex. Apparently, he used slips of papers on which he wrote letters and numbers that related to rehearsal letters and bar numbers found in the scores that he was preparing. When asked to clarify a query or to correct an error in rehearsal, he would close his eyes, tap his head, and mentally turn the pages of score he was conducting until he reached the relevant passage.[26] Mitropoulos justified his abandonment of the score by arguing "I feel the need to liberate myself from the printed score just as an actor does from the script. You would not expect someone to play Hamlet in front of a paying audience with the script in his hands – it's the same thing with me and music."[27]

Mitropoulos's ability to memorize complex scores at will was not, and is not, shared by most conductors. Whether a conductor performs with or without the music is of little importance, a view shared by Barbirolli who stated "it is foolish to imagine that a man knows less about a work because he uses a score. On the other hand, it is just as foolish to accuse all those who dispose of them of being bluffers and charlatans. The prime duty of any conductor is to secure the best possible performance of any work with which he is entrusted, and to use such means as he conscientiously believes will ensure the best possible results."[28]

Training and career opportunities

Conductors, unlike instrumentalists, rely on others when practising their craft. Walter observed that the

> conductor is denied [the] years of quiet, preparatory exercise, in which he could become familiar with his many-sided instrument and develop his technical mastery of it . . . To him alone, of all executant musicians, is denied the inestimable advantage of being able to try out matters in the quiet of his study . . . It is the complicated character of his instrument and indirect way in which it has to be played, and above all, the unavailability of the instrument at the time of his training, that prevent the conductor from setting out on his professional career with a degree of assurance and technical proficiency akin to that obtained by other musicians.[29]

It is clear, then, that for students of conducting, the route to a professional career can be both circuitous and difficult. While many conservatories, colleges of music, and universities offer courses in conducting, they often lack the facilities necessary for aspiring conductors. Traditionally, professional conductors begin their careers by either working as orchestral players; rising through the ranks of the opera-house system; becoming choral conductors; or acting as assistants to major, international conductors. Many leading artists, including Hans Richter, Arthur Nikisch, Bernard Haitink and Nikolaus Harnoncourt, gained valuable early experience by playing in professional orchestras. In an opera house, young conductors, when employed as répétiteurs, work with professional singers, orchestral players, and conductors on a daily basis. The répétiteur's function as a rehearsal pianist provides first-hand experience of the music being performed. If the necessity arises, the répétiteur might deputize for the chorus master and, on some occasions, direct the stage bands. For conductors of larger choral groups, the opportunities to direct either amateur or professional ensembles occur according to the demands of the repertoire performed. While some choral conductors have made the transition from choirs to symphony orchestras, they rarely join the front rank of professional orchestral conductors; the skills necessary for each discipline are not transferred easily.

Most major international conductors employ an assistant. The assistant's role varies according to the needs of the individual conductor and the ensemble being directed. The assistant might conduct preliminary rehearsals, edit performing material, function as a rehearsal pianist and/or conduct off- and on-stage bands. This type of post is a useful way for an aspiring conductor to learn the profession. While the opportunities for a permanent appointment are limited, young conductors can also gain experience by forming and directing vocal and instrumental ensembles. Another means by which to become a professional conductor is to participate in conducting competitions. The criteria for acceptance into these events can be rigorous, and it is common for the competitors to have had considerable experience before being chosen.

Barbirolli argued "without any qualification whatever, that a conductor is born and not made."[30] While this thesis might sound harsh, it has merit. The physical gesticulations and tools that a conductor uses are merely the external manifestations of a wider artistic vision and are of little consequence without the innate ability to inspire, to motivate, and to educate. More important, a conductor is responsible to the composer, and the conductor's readings must reflect that responsibility. Bernstein believed this to be true, arguing that "perhaps the chief requirement of [the conductor] is that he be humble before the composer; that he never interpose himself between the music and the audience; that all his efforts, however strenuous or glamorous, be made in the service of the composer's meaning – the music itself, which, after all, is the whole reason for the conductor's existence."[31]

2 Conductors in rehearsal

CHARLES F. BARBER

Great conductors tend to follow the imperatives of their teachers and apprenticeship, their national musical cultures, and above all the special requirements of their repertoire. Close study of their work reveals no code, conformity, nor Ten Commandments to be found across their individual approaches to rehearsal.

The Conductors on Film Collection at Stanford University has over two thousand hours of some two hundred and fifty conductors in concert, conversation, and rehearsal. From Abbado to Zender, they reveal an extraordinary canvas of action and aesthetic. This chapter will examine the elements of their work that seem to be most successful, vital, and enduring, although much of the (no doubt biased) advice also comes from the author's experience in concert, opera, and recordings. These comments are meant both for young conductors just setting out and for those trying to understand where the real work gets done with an orchestra.

Preparing for the first rehearsal

No serious work is possible without consideration of the performing edition to be employed. Especially since the rise in the mid-twentieth century of the scholar-conductor, it is no longer acceptable simply to hire a full score and go at it. It is essential first to acquire a copy of the manuscript and its variants, and to look into its published history.[1] Many first-class university or conservatory music libraries will have microfilm or microfiche of mainstream repertoire in autograph and first edition. Study these sources closely.

On the largest scale, conductors must learn about the kinds of changes made by composers to their own work over time, in light of critical reception, and in consequence of practical circumstances. There are numerous examples of scores which have been revised wholesale by their own composers (think of Bruckner or Brahms), or by others assuming the duty to "help" them (think of Musorgsky or Borodin helped across the street by Rimsky or Shostakovich). There are examples as well of scores which were altered by political diktat (*Un ballo in maschera*) or by economics (too many to count, plus Stravinsky) – and in a dozen other ways. One must choose knowledgeably.

Discrepancies between the full score and the parts are the most common printed error. Honorable publishers now make available lists of errata. Professional conductors share these lists among themselves. Numerous journals publish such errata as well, and a good music librarian can direct you to all of them.[2]

On a smaller scale, there is a body of error that must be discovered, and fixed. For example, some years ago I served as assistant in a very fine production of *Der Rosenkavalier* and was reading the score as the orchestra rehearsed the end of Act I. Its last chord contains a B-flat in the first bassoon. I didn't hear it. Looking up, I saw the bassoonist had already taken the instrument from his mouth, while the orchestra continued the fermata. The note was missing from his part. I made the correction, and so did he. This was in a part-set which had been used for more than seventy years, under numerous first-rate conductors, and was published by a first-rate house. This error of omission had passed for generations. Every working conductor can tell you similar stories.[3] Ask them.

Other errors are more tricky, and have to do with first purposes and second thoughts. For example, the end of the second movement of Beethoven's Symphony No. 7 poses a serious problem. As commonly published, the strings are instructed to play pizzicato at m. 255, and then resume arco in the fourth, or third, measure from the end. This creates a potent change in sonority, mood and rhetoric. But is this what Beethoven really wanted? In the manuscript, the arco in the first violins plainly begins on the F sharp, as it does in the Steiner first edition. But in the Dover score, reprinted from Eulenberger and widely used by modern conductors, it begins on the preceding E. Some conductors (Klemperer, Strauss, Carlos Kleiber) have taken the view that the *whole* arco passage is a mistake, and they have performed it pizzicato to the end. The startling austerity which results is a disturbing new voice. I have come to do it this way myself, and much prefer the exactness and emotional *secco* which results. The manuscript here is virtually unreadable and it may simply be a question of Beethoven changing his mind, and of a conductor determining whether the composer's first instinct was, in fact, superior to his second. Either way, informed choices must be made.

Tempos

Metronome marks did not exist in the eighteenth century or prior. Even from the nineteenth century on they cannot be taken as gospel. And though Beethoven in 1817 kindly (and retrospectively) provided metronome markings for his first eight symphonies,[4] only very young (or literal-minded) conductors will simply reproduce them without further thought. No less importantly, beginning conductors are usually horrified to discover that Andante and Largo are imprecise terms.

Tempo comes from the historical context and genre of the work itself. It is governed by the acoustics of the hall. It must reflect the actual playing level of your musicians.[5] It must accord to an overarching pulse for the *entire* work, and to relationships among movements, and between subjects and phrases. Tempo cannot be arbitrary and mechanistic. It must breathe the line and concentrate the form and reveal the spirit. In many ways, it must accord to the human voice. Finding truly *musical* tempos is the next working obligation of the conductor before entering the first rehearsal.

When accompanying a soloist in concerto, or a singer in opera, tempos will of course be worked out in private coaching sessions long before first rehearsal. These negotiations are usually not difficult, especially if the conductor has a clear and well-informed conception of the work. However, politics can intervene. If the soloist is a senior and well-regarded musician, the wise junior will always defer. (If the soloist is simply an egomaniac, call the Metropolitan Opera. Ask for Joe Volpe.)

For music written before the metronome, George Houle has suggested a way to discover tempo: learn the actual dance from which the music and its rhythms are drawn.[6] Learn to discern a gigue or a passepied, a Ländler or a gavotte, from within the music. These dance topics are everywhere. Then, learn the dance itself and dance it. Literally. Once you internalize the outer limits – and inner necessities – of the originating dance, you will find a workable tempo. This is how conductors make useful discoveries, and avoid ignorant presumption. Learn the dance form, and you have the heart of it.

Tempos may also be discovered by looking at the black notes. When first studying a piece which opens slowly and in white notes, it is often very difficult to find a compelling pulse. Look ahead and see if the work is building to *passaggio* in 16ths or 32nds, for example, and see what tempo succeeds in this speedier material. Once you are settled, work backward and the opening tempo will now present itself. The opening of Beethoven's second symphony serves to make this point.

A caution: many conductors learn scores at the keyboard. This is a useful tool for analysis, but I have seen it happen that young conductors also learn tempos this way. Especially when their keyboard skills are inadequate, they have often discovered that keyboard tempos become laughable when presented to an orchestra.

Consider fortifying your analysis, post-keyboard, with solfège. Numerous rehearsal films of Riccardo Muti, for example, show a polyglot conductor speedily conveying the line through instant solfège. His intentions are thereby unmistakable.[7] In time, you will hear the whole work in your head.

Employing dance and other aesthetic considerations, you are more likely to be satisfied with the pulse and proportions you find before and during rehearsal.

Learn to think proportionally. The greatest conductors move us not by special effects and dazzling surprise, but by a quality of cohesion and insight which lives within and above the entire work. There is no better exemplar than Wilhelm Furtwängler. Although one does not want to recommend listening to recordings as a substitute for analysis, there is much to be learned from genius of his calibre.[8] Fritz Sedlak, late concertmaster of the Vienna Philharmonic, once wisely observed that

> we liked to call Furtwängler the Master of Form, because he so masterfully understood how to build and work intuitively toward the climax of a score . . . he was a master of transitions, and worked with us again and again to unite tempo changes within a movement with the smoothness that prevented the dissolution of the movement's structure . . . "smooth" was an especially favorite word of his during rehearsals. It was because of his art of handling transitions . . . that he could weld often problematic finales into a unified whole.[9]

This quality of *unification* is one of the features of his gift. It should be part of our own. For Furtwängler and a few others, it functions from the widest to the smallest horizons. The distinguished Austro-American conductor Josef Krips saw it the same way: "Furtwängler knew about the 'eternal line' in a great piece; when he started the first bar, in his mind he was already in the last."[10]

Marking parts

In Europe, it is generally the case that there are "house" parts. These – and only these – are used by the conductor, visiting or otherwise. In North America, orchestras often have more than one set of parts available. (Some visiting conductors supply their own.) By pre-arrangement, a working set can be altered prior to first rehearsal in order to bring it into conformity with the conductor's purposes. Assuming that the latter circumstance holds, begin by marking your own score. It is best to see the whole effect, laid out on the page. In this way one can juggle, adjust, and make sounds balance in every quarter. Thereafter, transfer these markings to the parts themselves. Be particularly clear about repeats and cuts.

If you do not have the privilege of working with your own marked parts, inspect rehearsal numbers in the house parts in advance. Make sure yours are the same as the players'. Especially in opera this is a terrible problem, usually the result of working from different editions. Always amend *your* score to incorporate *their* rehearsal figures. Never dream of going to first rehearsal without having done this.

If you are able to mark parts in advance of first rehearsal, make your intentions starkly evident in regard to such devices as staccato, *notes inégales*, trills, other ornaments, and the like. Enter them in the parts only after careful study of the composer's intentions and the realities of the era in which the music was written. A baroque trill in a Bizet *tarantelle* is absurd.

Start with the strings. If you are not a well-trained string player, get the best advice you can find. The concertmaster, if skilled, should always be able to help. Some concertmasters will do all the marking for you. Section leaders may also have useful advice. (Cellos do not always bow the same way as violins, and basses are different again.) Bowings are, by far, the most elaborate markings with which you must contend. Again, there are many extant sources for information on these matters.[11] Your knowledge of these sources is essential.

Bowings must accord to tempos. They must reflect phrase and line. In some instances, they should also reflect tradition. Many Central European composers specify the use of recurring up-bows, for example, to give lightness and character to their music. Where one could simply allow alternating bows, awareness of this special tradition should be reflected in the parts. It will sound in your music, and you will have served it well.

Bowing must accord to sound. Conductors must know the differences between *portato* and *portamento*, and where to start on the bow, and when and how to re-draw, and when hooked bowings are best, and when to gloss the bows among the string sections in order to obtain greater homogeneity. If you are not professionally competent as a string player, take advice from the best one you can find. (Or, feign belief in Stokowski and insist on free bowing altogether.)

Breath marks in winds and brass must also cohere to the phrase and line overall. Although not usually as elaborate as for the strings, such markings are also vital to your work. As always, consult professional players. Recognize that instruments with inherently high back-pressure (any double reed will do) can hold notes much longer than, say, trombones or tubas. Your markings should reflect these facts of musical life.

Remember that dynamics are not universal. *Forte* in the bass drum is a completely different *forte* from that in the violas. Mark accordingly. And be prepared to make changes according to the acoustic.

Even when you have been disciplined and careful about markings, changes will inevitably be required in rehearsal. Make them, do so quickly, and take advice from good ears in the hall to help you adjust balances. Be sure to enter those changes in your score.[12]

Know the instruments

No one expects the conductor to come to rehearsal able to play every part on every instrument. However, it is expected that you have studied each part separately, and that you know the basics of every instrument. In this way you can make sensible requests of your players. If you ask for double-tonguing where none is possible, you will lose respect. If you ask a timpanist to change sticks and work closer to the rim, you may get not only the sound you want but also the respect you have earned.

I once attended a rehearsal of a Mahler symphony led by a "maestro" whose work was full of gimmick and pizzazz. Nonetheless, things were going reasonably well until he stopped the orchestra to demand more sound from the pair of harps. They played louder. He stopped, now a bit impatiently, and asked for more. They played even louder, their instruments falling flat and flatter with every grab. He stopped a third time, and demanded to know why they still weren't playing loud enough. (It apparently hadn't occurred to him to reseat the harps, or to adjust the orchestra's dynamics.) "But maestro," the first harp replied, "if we play louder our calluses will come off." "Well then," he said, in a voice trembling with exasperation, "push down *all* the pedals!"

"Maestro" was nearly hooted off the stage. The quality of sound you can obtain, and its blend and balance, derives materially from your working knowledge of the properties of every instrument. No one knew this better than Szell. Study his rehearsal films with Cleveland to see how he did it.[13]

Memorize all the names in standard languages for standard instruments. Your score may be in Italian, and their parts in German. Do not enter a rehearsal – ever – without this working practical knowledge. Otherwise, you may one day be embarrassed to discover that "tambour" is not an abbreviation for "tambourine."

The issue of "authentic" performance on early instruments at low pitch, and so on, must be the subject of another discussion. However, if you have a choice in the matter, you will want to consider whether or not to use piston or valve trumpets, small or modern-bore trombones, wooden or metal flutes (if flutes at all), leather or plastic drum-heads, real ophicleides in the *Symphonie fantastique*, and the rest of it. These are questions of color. If you do have options in this regard, consider them carefully.[14]

Seating

Prior to first rehearsal, you will need to decide on seating – if the orchestra permits. If you do have consent, seat according to the sound you wish to conjure. If you don't have prior knowledge of the hall, ask. If you do, consider the following.

The most basic decision today lies in placement of the strings. It is increasingly common to split firsts and seconds across the stage, and thereafter to seat the other strings as space and voice-leading requires. Seating must always derive from repertoire.

Especially in music where, for example, fugue and its cousins are a propellant, it is advantageous to seat in stereo. Let your audience *see* what Bach or Haydn meant them to *hear*. Such seating also helps your players identify with voice and line, and strive to make it more audibly and musically distinct. Contrarily, in certain Romantic repertoire you might find it better to mass firsts, seconds and violas together. The brass might best be boxed together in small and deep ranks, rather than being spread out across the back in an ant-line. As ever, be guided by repertoire. And, if circumstance permits and repertoire requires, plan your program to allow reseating at intermission. It can be done, with adequate notice and legitimate purpose (although stage crews may cringe at the suggestion).[15]

When I conduct musicals in the pit, or record in the studio, I like to have the percussionist(s) immediately in front of me. This allows complete control of tempos and transitions. The battery is the motor of such music, and one has better control when these instrumentalists are sitting close by. Players will feel the difference when they can hear the engine turning over, rhythmically speaking, in their very midst. This is powerfully helpful in Sondheim and similar scores.

In Italian opera, I like to have the cellos sitting *en masse* immediately in front of the podium – and the audience. The soaring Italian melodies in this style illuminate themselves. Much of the special timbre of this music, and the grace and voice of the strings, comes from the cellos. (I am generalizing, of course.) I find that such seating warms and directs string sonorities in a very pleasing way – especially if your players have no prior experience with its advantages.

Finally, and also in opera, many houses have substandard pits. If they are carpeted (it happens), consider putting plywood around and under the strings. This strengthens and brightens their sound. Conversely, put absorbent materials around the brass, winds and percussion, occasionally even draping these materials from their music stands.

And in pit or concert, always insist before first rehearsal that players who sit in front of winds and brass have their hearing protected. Today, many orchestras take this into account, but some do not. Respect your players' hearing, insist on acoustic blocks or guards on their behalf, and you will earn their gratitude and protect their careers.

Tuning

Assuming there is no question as to tuning pitch, make sure that you are satisfied with tuning procedures in advance of the first downbeat. First-rate orchestras will take care of this for you. When working with less able orchestras, tuning is a constant question. I prefer the following procedure.

Tell your concertmaster how you wish to tune. Insist on absolute quiet from the outset; tune the woodwinds and brass separately; then tune the strings, and do so with cellos and basses first, and then violas and violins. Demand that they tune as quietly as possible so that they may hear the beats and overtones. *Precise hearing is impossible when people tune loudly.* Do not hesitate to demand perfection in tuning. No good work can begin without it. And don't hesitate to ask for re-tuning whenever you think it required.

Starting the rehearsal

The players must be told what you are rehearsing, and in what order. No one should ever be surprised. If you can arrange to excuse people early from a given orchestral choir, in order to focus on another, do so. Strings always expect to have to stay the whole time.

Learn the names of all your principals in advance. Ideally, learn *all* of your players' names. Many European and Asian orchestras prefer more formal terms of address, and those in the Americas less formal. This includes how you wish to be addressed. You should make your preferences clear, so as to avoid clumsiness. However, naming individuals being "corrected" is always risky. Many fine conductors, especially of the old school, always corrected players in rehearsal by naming the instrument, and not the individual. This saved face, humanely. Praise by personal name, and criticize by instrument name.

After you are introduced to the orchestra, the fewer words spoken the better. The most remarkable conductor I know once told me of rehearsing with the Vienna Philharmonic. "Around here, every word you speak is another nail in your coffin." Players come to play. Unless it is an all-Jesuit orchestra, they are rarely interested in metaphysical discussion, number theory, or the Fibonacci series. If it is not absolutely essential to comprehension of the music, leave these matters to the program notes.[16]

Players come to listen to one another. Make that possible. I know of two unmatched rehearsal films. In them, we see superb conductors helping their players hear one another in ways that are simply astonishing. I cannot recommend highly enough Karajan's film rehearsing the Schumann fourth symphony with the Vienna Symphony.[17] Watch him assist the strings and flutes to match timbre, overtones, and expression. Von Karajan knows what he wants and how to get it, and does so with efficiency and absolute respect for his players.

The other film is of Carlos Kleiber rehearsing the overture to *Die Fledermaus*.[18] In forty-five minutes we see how he leads, cajoles, sings the text and addresses its personality, adjusts balance, clarifies rhythm, makes jokes, attends to detail and structure, never yields, and transforms the work utterly. He uses verbal imagery to convey tonal objective. His images and metaphors, though brief, are immensely vivid and instantly understood by his players. At the beginning, an orchestra of bored civil servants visibly resents Kleiber's demands. At the end, they play with total commitment, as if present at the work's creation.

Players come to serve the music. You come to serve them, *and* the music. If you have learned the score deeply and reliably, the players will know it. If you are faking, they will know it. Many of them have played the standard repertoire twenty times more often than you have. Respect their learning, and don't condescend to discuss the obvious. They've heard it all before. They would rather hear Britten than hear you talk about Britten.

Rehearsal strategies

Rehearsal strategies vary widely. All are imprisoned by the clock. Many conductors will play a work from beginning to end, and then return to correct deficiencies. Beecham always favored this approach.[19] Some will correct error and phrase from the first measure. Many will call out errors as the work is under way, and some will stop and alter at every instance. Stokowski, later in life especially, worked with a ferocious intensity from the outset, demanding final-quality results from the first.[20]

In our time, it is almost always best to begin by simply playing through, stopping only in the case of absolute train-wrecks.[21] Keep mental (or actual) notes of problem areas, and prepare to return to them after the first pass is complete. Kleiber is famous for writing notes his players have come to call "Kleibergrams," which he goes around and leaves on their stands after each rehearsal.

At the second rehearsal, highly skilled conductors often work from a list of problems revealed at the first. In the process, they will select important templates from within the music, the solution of whose problems will then apply broadly across the work. In that process they establish a model, conserve time, and create musical coherence. This sort of modelling is only possible if you know the score immaculately, and if you are clear about its purposes. Simply declaring that "this is sonata form" is largely useless information. Knowing when and how to show structural downbeats helps a good deal more.

Sir Charles Mackerras is particularly effective in opera rehearsal when he tells his players (briefly) who they are accompanying, and what they are singing, and why.[22] Erich Kleiber famously did much the same thing, and in writing, when preparing the premieres of new opera.

If time and contract permit, use sectionals. They allow close and detailed attention to every note in every choir of the orchestra. Such a master as Václav Talich in Prague often spent half his rehearsal time in sectional, and frequently even took violin sectionals, viola sectionals, and the like. If one wonders how the Czech Philharmonic sounded so astoundingly united, know that it resulted from Talich's genius – and his sectionals.

Use "rehearsal-only" tempi: take slow passages quickly, and vice versa. This often helps to reveal form and structure. And use "rehearsal-only" dynamics. Playing loud passages very, very quietly does wonders for articulation and voice-leading. If everyone plays everything *blastissimo* all the time, who can hear anything? Not only will you protect your players' hearing, arms, and embouchure, but by playing quietly you may also reveal detail obscured by mere volume. Thus revealed, it may also thrive in performance.

Be sensitive to your players. If you watch faces, you will know when your work has become tedious. If you've made your point, move on.

Make jokes. Self-deprecation never hurts. Jokes release tension, save feelings, shape the music, and have often saved the rehearsal. If you want to glad-hand, however, save it for the break and never waste time in rehearsal trying to be lovable. It is resented.

Be clear. Speak loudly. Lead and govern with your eyes. Be direct. A simple and eloquent baton is more than adequate.[23] Bouncing up and down like the ballet dancer you will never be is, especially for younger conductors, simply risible.

Be alert to your players' inspiration. You may discover the pleasure of hearing a phrase turned in an unexpected and beautiful way. It may well serve to blueprint something you hadn't planned. Use it, and credit the author. I have many times stopped rehearsals in order to single out a player who did something remarkably well. This honor is always welcome. At a recent rehearsal of the Los Angeles Philharmonic it was delightful to see how the players interacted among themselves, smiling, breathing, acknowledging, communicating, and then shuffling their feet in mutual respect. If one is lucky enough to work with such players, smile no less. This is a rare and moving collegiality. It reminds us why we make orchestral music in the first place.

At the end

Never run out of time. Even though it can happen, try desperately to avoid it and never expect management to bail you out with overtime. Unless you want the money to come out of your fee, it isn't going to happen.

If you do find that you've still got two hours' work left, and only one hour in which to do it, use the final rehearsal break to plan accordingly. Focus on the material that simply will not play itself, and leave the rest aside. Although this seems obvious, I have many times watched inexperienced conductors panic when faced with this problem, and in their anxiety make matters much worse. If necessary, consult with the concertmaster and use the remaining time as she or he recommends. Veteran members of your orchestra will know better than you how to take care of the problem.

When assisting the late Marty Paich at the Hollywood Bowl years ago, I found we had only one morning's rehearsal with Sarah Vaughn. She was cranky and coughing the whole time, and the rehearsal ended with one number untouched. Marty was unworried. "If they learned our style in everything else, they'll get that number. No problem. Trust me." Come the concert the orchestra played superbly, her singing was wondrous, and the audience was none the wiser. He knew the music, the singer, and the solution.

Save something for the performance. Conductors like Munch, Abendroth, Matačić, Talich, and Mitropoulos always knew how to hold something in reserve for the concert. A special fire, a drama, a release – whatever it might be, it serves to ignite the players to levels of sound and meaning which they had never achieved in rehearsal. This is invariably a reward for the orchestra, a delight for the audience, and a triumph for the conductor.

And finally, a word about bows. I have conducted opera for years, and have never taken a stage bow. When one has neither sung nor played a note, it can look like mere self-aggrandizement to be up there, swaying. It is a much better idea to have your players rise instead, even though no one can see them. In concert, bowing is probably unavoidable. However, there is a very nice way to show respect: get off the podium, enter the horse-shoe of your players, and share bows with them on the floor. It makes clear to the audience whom you serve, and clear to your players that you are honored to be among them. Let Beethoven take the bow.

3 Studio conducting

MICHAEL HAAS

A studio is not a concert hall and a recording is not a concert. A recording is music made objective. The experience of setting an interpretation into stone in a recording is a humbling one for even the most ego-crazed, over-coiffed, mega-multi-media-jet-setting superstar. It creates a multitude of unique problems which often require immediate decisions that have lasting and sometimes costly consequences. Much debate is focused on the battle between "live" and studio (by implication, "dead"!) performances, where intellectual laziness has exaggerated the claims for "live" recording. As with "live" theatre and film, the differences (in both means and ends) between recordings and concerts are so vast, that they are hardly the same art form, but we can enjoy both without needing to set one above the other. How do conductors adjust to these challenges and what does the producer do? The conductor in the studio, particularly for an opera recording, can be compared with a train driver on a journey from A to Z, but travelling from R to Z first, and A to B last, with all of the bits in between jumbled together, sometimes twice or three times over, to allow for passengers who missed the train the first time. At the end, one literally does not know if one is coming or going, or if all the passengers have been safely delivered. Not so far removed from the opera conductor is the conductor with a soloist. The studio magnifies the pressure on the conductor and presents an interesting opportunity to examine this exotic creative ego.

"Live" vs. "dead"

Music is always drama. As with theatre, music propels the listener along a narrative. When theatre moved into the studio, it created the new genres of film and television. So separate have the genres become, that there is now no debate about the advantages of live theatre over film and television, or vice versa. In the transition from concert hall to studio, the nature of musical narrative would seem not to change to the same extent as that of theatrical narrative, if only because stage plays that transfer to the screen are rewritten to accommodate the move. But a casual listen to any concerto recording instantly proves that an artificial element has been allowed to enhance the relationship between soloist and accompaniment; the soloist can now soar over the orchestra even when all trumpets are blaring. More analytical listening will discover a multitude of points and details that would have been visible only in the score. Indeed, if the most obvious difference between film and theatre is the ability to change perspectives, than the most obvious difference between concerts and studio recordings is the ability to hear a work unfold from different positions within the ensemble. To appreciate this point, it is important to recognize how little the conductor can hear from the podium; it may be the best position in the hall, but the conductor is still surrounded by an ocean of strings, with woodwinds more visible than audible in loud passages.

Sir Georg Solti (1912–97), perhaps the most abundantly gifted studio conductor with whom I have worked, made most of his recordings after performances. (Many were made in Chicago where the American Musicians Union makes prior performances a condition.) The first morning in the studio would deliver the shock of discovering that great effects in the concert hall would not necessarily come across in the studio. Tempos, the engines that drive musical narrative, were found to produce vastly different results. Orchestral balance, which can be compared to the placement and perspective of actors and scenery in our musical narrative, was found to be undifferentiated and unclear, with unimportant background action upstaging crucial soliloquies.

The first thing Solti did in the studio was to put down a take that was free of the sudden surges of momentum that audiences seemed to elicit from him. This more "objective" view of the score may have been less hair-raising, but was truer to the composer's script. Smoothing out these spots allowed more room for organic rhythmic and dynamic development.

In the studio, a crescendo can begin from total silence. In concert, a pianissimo requires more sound to be heard. In the studio there is the ability to highlight the plaintive counterpoint of a single oboe, even in a full Brucknerian orchestral climax. The most crucial rule in the studio is that *maximum effect is achieved by extremes of the achievable*. In other words, it is impossible to record the loudest *forte* an orchestra can play, but it is not impossible to record the softest pianissimo. The ultimate *forte* is more convincing when it is not as loud, but is arrived at organically with a more evenly paced crescendo. The studio also offers a more secure sounding board for sudden dynamic shifts such as a loud tutti followed by a single quiet instrumental solo, which is lost in the orchestral resonance of a concert hall. Solti's genius was the instant recognition that an inaudible instrumental voice meant something else was too loud. Despite his reputation for brassy showmanship, he was ruthless if a sustained trombone or timpani covered a woodwind solo. His solution was never to ask the soloist to "play up." Solti understood that moving a work from the concert platform into the studio is not so different from translating a play into cinema.

The opposite conductor in the studio was Claudio Abbado (b. 1926). Rarely could someone have been more designed for "live" performances rather than "manufactured" studio recordings. The men had different talents. Where Solti had total musical authority, Abbado's approach was more democratic. While Solti took his already energetic view of a work and could be driven to extremes by the engagement of the audience, Abbado arrived with a more measured view of a work that was ignited only by the audience's presence. As Abbado's musical energy was dependent on the public, he was unable to recreate and control it in the studio. He was comfortable only with multi-tracking that allowed weird and often near impossible alterations later in post-production. Solti had a magnificent ear and had once been a pianist. Wrong notes were easily and efficiently dispatched. Abbado would agonize with every clash. Whispered and often aggressive telephone calls in the sessions to the control room, calculated so that nobody from the orchestra could hear, only emphasized how unhappy and unsuited he was to the studio. Yet his live concerts were truly alive and his ability to pace a performance in concert compensated for Solti's ability to chart and conduct a performance in the studio. Solti was the equivalent of the theatre director who mastered both stage and screen. I viewed Abbado as the master director for stage who felt powerless to achieve the results he wanted in the studio. The fact that both have made important and indeed, historic recordings, only underlines the fundamental differences between the studio and concert hall. To say one is "better" is as nonsensical as saying that Max Reinhardt is better than Billy Wilder.

There was only a short evolution from Louis Spohr's first attempt to keep the musical narrative together with his baton, to the conductor becoming the actual conduit of that narrative. This demonstrates how plastic our concept of musical performance is. If we think nothing of using baton conductors for works which predate Spohr, why do we balk at conductors taking their craft into the studio where the music can be viewed from a myriad of angles? In part, perhaps because it seems that live performances have more energy; but the opposite should be the case. The recordings of the last twenty to thirty years represent an unhealthy mixture of commerce with art. Recording companies and artists' agents have required recordings *before* a work was performed, so that the recording could then be available for the performances. The absurdity of this was a tidal wave of works learned in the studio rather than making recordings after a run of performances.

Figure 3.1 Michael Haas with Claudio Abbado in rehearsal for a "live" recording of Schumann's "Scenes from Goethe's *Faust*," but with further patched sessions

The studio should be a tool to achieve more fully the composers' musical concepts. It is not a witches' cauldron where mad, one-eyed experimenters emerge to hoodwink an innocent public. A conductor should be able to use the studio as an expressive aid. But to do this, one needs to start from the score. Composers are usually flexible and relatively fatalistic. Mahler was constantly reorchestrating his works to achieve a desired musical effect in different venues. The balance of voices in music is as complex as the placement of actors in any play or film. A raised eyebrow from a minor character in response to a long monologue by a major character requires a very different sort of placement, lighting and focus in a film than it does on stage. Incredibly, the same holds true in music. Perhaps because they did not anticipate the studio, composers often set up devices within their orchestrations to keep important details from going unnoticed. Once in the studio, however, the devices become the equivalent of the actor in the background who potentially upstages the lead's most dramatic moments. Often such strange shifts in perspective are the result of modern orchestral instruments developing at different rates. At other times, slight adjustments to the score simply aim to achieve what the composer wished for at the expense of what he wrote. I have hardly worked with a conductor who has not at some point or another dropped a piccolo by an octave or left it out altogether, in the studio. This is just one example of where a side attraction can endanger the central unfolding drama. The principle must be established of *achieving the intentions of the composer by allowing the music's leading voices to settle into their natural perspectives.* This principle must be understood, as it opens fully the potential of the studio. It is also why it is near folly to record before performances. In recordings of works learned in the studio, the most common request in post-production is the lifting and/or suppression of exactly these details.

Seating

Suggesting that composers always wrote with studio conditions in mind may seem a bit like arguing that Bach would have written for the modern grand piano if he had one, but every score performed contains masses of indications to highlight the musical narration in the face of acoustic challenges. Different dynamics or accents are often applied only to one voice, but many of these indications remain unachievable on the concert platform. Seating, which is intimately tied to balance and the perspective of voices, is one area where the studio offers more ideal conditions.

In the studio, balance refers to both the perspective of leading voices and the weight of sound coming out of each speaker. On stage, orchestral layout is a compromise between the practical (allowing instruments that play together to sit together) and the ideal (putting the weakest voices in places they will be heard). So the brass and percussion sit together on one side and are always too loud for half the audience. The harps and celeste are soft instruments, but they play with the piano which is too large to go anywhere but the back. But in countless cases – brass and horns in Wagner, harps and piano in Korngold, and trumpets and timpani in Haydn – composers want antiphony, or the spatial effect where the sound comes from two different places. Just as cinema can incorporate space in a way that theatre cannot, the recording studio can often better achieve the composer's desires. In recordings we can more evenly spread the sound between speakers.

In the studio, we can reseat the players (with horns and brass on opposite sides), isolate harps and special instruments, or even allow players the security of sitting where they want, while mixing the sound to achieve the acoustic effects indicated in the score. Changing the seating, however, creates more work for the conductor. More instrumental entries have to be given and beats possibly subdivided for the sake of clarity. Further, musicians are almost always more confident of their technical abilities in a concert acoustic, so a conductor must provide even clearer gestures in the studio and must hear internally what the results should be.

Acoustics

In the late 1980s, Solti decided that he was too old to do any more studio-recordings. He wanted "live" recordings because he felt that performances followed by studio work were exhausting. This process took vast amounts of time out of his schedule, and he found making all of the adjustments from concert to studio wearing. Decca/London had always made expensive and extensive changes to Chicago's Orchestra Hall for Solti's studio recording and we would now have to adjust. For recording, the stage was extended from under the proscenium to across the top of the seats in the public. This resulted in the open acoustic of the hall being used for the recording, and not the acoustic behind the proscenium, which was tighter and drier. Things came apart, however, when we embarked on a live recording of Bruckner's Symphony No. 8. Here the proscenium acoustic was simply too dead. The die-away of the vast chords was almost instantaneous, which resulted in the music being pushed along to fill the resultant gaps. Upon hearing the final master tape, the result was clear. The tempos were too fast, the scale of the work too compact and the overall effect too dead. The recording was discarded and re-recorded in St Petersburg in 1990 under studio conditions in the wonderful acoustic of the Philharmonie.

The idea that live acoustics are better is a falsehood. The reason the Chicago proscenium acoustic is dry is to allow the players to hear each other more easily. This saves time in rehearsals, allows for the tightest possible ensemble and makes even the largest works feel like chamber music. Upon leaving the proscenium, the sound enters the hall and in theory, opens out. In studio recording, viewing the work from a cinematic perspective, one can "open the orchestra up." This means the acoustic is richer and more reverberant, which makes it more difficult for the players to follow and hear each other. If the acoustic of the studio affects the tempo, and thus the structure of a performance, the conductor may have to make major and instant adjustments to his or her concept and beat patterns. Some conductors have even used the acoustic of their recording venue to enhance the sound of their orchestras. Ernest Ansermet and the Suisse Romande Orchestra achieved results in recording that would have been impossible live. To a lesser extent, the recordings of the Montreal Orchestra with Charles

Dutoit have also benefited from the luxurious ambience of their recording venue, the church of St. Eustache.

The conductor in the studio

The rules for recording are simple: the producer needs *one* take of the musical material right in all of the fundamentals. Another cosmetically good take is useful in case the first take reveals something unnoticed at the time of recording. These can be nasty little bugs like tape or disc faults, a mistake that is not noticed until the calmer environment of post-production, a watch peeping or the buzz of a building's generator that shows up only when inter-splicing. Beyond needing two "clean" takes, basic orchestral balance should also be right. It is difficult to take down heavy brass or percussion afterwards. Other balance points can usually be accommodated afterwards if necessary.

Conductors handle these challenges in different ways. Sometimes a difficult entry is repeated endlessly; one conductor I worked with made musical decisions based on his skill at bringing in groups of instruments in painfully slow tempi. There are also conductors, particularly those learning a work in the studio, who change the way they beat a particular passage. Having decided their new beat division obtains more efficient results, they wish to re-record entire passages though there is no audible difference on tape between the takes. Other conductors, like Abbado, give you one good take and resent recording a note more than necessary. There are numerous accounts of recording teams returning to the studio to mend such basic negligence. Indeed, of all the conductors in the studio, it is the one who thinks everything can be fixed in post-production who is the most frightening. In theory, most things can be improved, though "fixed" is often too strong a word if covering material is not available.

The most confident and experienced was Solti, who ironically disliked post-production "messing about" more than others. He wanted to put down what he had heard and controlled. He might ask that here and there an entrance be lifted for the sake of greater clarity, but in general, he was loath to remix following the recording session.

The producer

The relationship of the conductor with a recording producer is an unusual one. The producer can either be the sad little man in a suit who must be charmed or bullied to make the results sound better than they really are, or he (still rarely she) is a companion in arms.

The producer has a very basic job: translating an artist's performance to disc or tape. The job often starts in the office, with the producer technically hiring musicians, recording venues, technical staff and sound engineers. In some cases, he has to find the financing as well. In old-fashioned recording companies, this "Executive Producer" was meant to protect the investment of the company and oversee recording commitments made to various artists. In today's more competitive market, executive producers will often fund every element of a recording and license it for sale to a recording label.

"Recording Producers" are more akin to theatre directors. They have the score in front of them and they direct operations from a control box. While it seems that a producer can offer little musical advice to a "great artist," translating a performance into a recording requires special skills. Unlike an actor using a script uniquely tailored for the cinema (a screenplay) conductors come to the studio having usually performed a work only on stage. They need help adjusting the audio perspective and shaping tempos, balance, and dynamics to match the recording medium.

In other cases, where a conductor has never performed the work, the producer becomes more of a director with a view on expression and inter-pretation. The producer is a facilitator, translating the "stage-drama" to the aural equivalent of cinema, but a good producer is also a sounding board with musical views and experience in all stages of the process.

Opera in the studio

Opera is an even more complex undertaking in the studio. If music has its own dramatic narrative, than opera imposes another theatrical narrative on top. These narratives, musical and theatrical, exist in different time scales, with the libretto as the principal text and music as the subtext. Unlike in straight theatre, layers of thought can be shown concurrently, but there is a logistical problem; speech takes little or no time for its meaning to be clear, while the musical narrative unfolds at a slower rate. Usually, this discrepancy is evened out on the opera stage with gestures, props, costumes, and scenery, but other means must be found in the studio.

In performance, the conductor must work with a stage director. In the studio, sections are often rehearsed and recorded in the order that singers are available. In extreme cases, the principal roles may be recorded much later. One can either synchronize a singer on top of the accompaniment or reconvene months or even years later to cover the missing part. Scenes with chorus are always recorded in adjoining sessions to record as much in as little time as possible. Opera choruses are extremely expensive and have caused the grand finales to be recorded in the first sessions, followed by all other scenes surgically removed and run together like parts on a conveyor belt. To make sense of something that looks so messy, it is important to keep several principles firmly in mind.

1. Opera has a structure

The conductor who views the musical architecture only in relation to the sections carved out in the daily recording pensum (allotment of time) will render a performance without a clear center of gravity. The musical and theatrical narratives of an opera eventually meet, and this determines the pacing of the work. The architecture of a traditional opera is a string of numbers that leads to a grandiose conclusion. The center of gravity can be anywhere from the first scene to the finale, but *there will always be a point of arrival that must be set up perfectly.* Indeed, "building" an opera is truly the best way to describe a conductor and recording team in the studio. The conductor must keep the structures incrementally increasing or decreasing in tension, dynamic and tempo, but it is not uncommon to break the daily recording pensum in the middle of such a musical "build-up," or "wind-down." It is important that the pace, tension, and dynamics are matched to dovetail into the sections recorded before, and it cannot be done by feel. Today's Maestoso may sound either too slow or too fast next week when recording the transitional sections on either side. Metronomes are of great importance, but equally important is constant listening to takes from previous sessions which join in to passages being newly recorded.

2. Opera is theatre

The result of an opera recording must still be theatre. Opera involves storytelling, people pretending to be someone else, and a suspension of reality. In addition to the musical structures, the conductor and producer need to understand the libretto and the relationship of every character. Without the aid of a stage director, the conductor carries full responsibility for integrating the musical and theatrical narratives. If an opera is unfamiliar, the responsibility of the conductor and the producer is doubled, as rarely will singers arrive in rehearsal having read the text from beginning to end. The conductor should take it as understood (as this producer has often experienced) that singers will arrive without a clue as to their dramatic role and their relationships to the people around them. More than once in rehearsal have I heard someone shout with delight the equivalent of "Oh *now* I get it! You're supposed to be my *father*!" The surprising point to make is that musical ambiguities are often cleared when the play is understood. Likewise, ambiguities in the dramatic text are often cleared when the music is added. (It is interesting that some conductors choose to be involved in the recitatives and spoken dialogue, while others leave it to the producer, or hired language coach.) The drama of opera can only be realized with total command of both the theatrical and musical narratives.

3. There are no costumes, gestures, or props in recording

The lack of gestures, props, and devices demands both over- and under-compensation from the participants. They are actually in a similar position to actors in a radio drama; the whole panoply of emotions that demands facial expression has to be translated into sound. The solution is tied to the following principle, so the two are treated together.

4. The text is illustrated in the score

In the studio, singers are sometimes called to sing less beautifully than they would on stage. Bitterness, on stage, is often conveyed with unpleasant faces in addition to unpleasant sounds. Presenting a simpleton on stage might be accompanied by physical buffoonery; on tape we often have singers singing strategically sharp or flat to make the same point. Voices come pre-equipped with all manner of devices that make it possible to carry off a dramatic persona: crooning, singing without vibrato, singing between clenched teeth, and "creative" intonation are only the most obvious. Again, without a stage director, it falls to the conductor and producer to explain to the singers what expression is required when singing individual words. For example, singing "Guten Morgen mein Schatz" (Good morning my treasure) can be done in numerous ways. With singers learning roles between other engagements, they usually arrive at rehearsals with no idea whether their *Schatz* is loved or despised. Piano scores, unlike orchestral ones, give little away. A clue is almost always found in the score. The word *Schatz* may be underscored with either harp arpeggios or a sour harmonic in the violin. The text is illuminated by the orchestration of the opera. Translations should be careful not to move a key word from its appointed orchestral color.

The underscoring of sung texts is, as a device, more readily suited to recording than the stage! The lifting of instruments (increasing the volume of that instrument relative to the others around it) can be enough to high-light the text while not disrupting the general balance. This shift in orchestral emphasis is absolutely crucial in the transfer from theatre to studio. Orches-tration is a subtle device, originally used as a subconscious means of hinting at situations and circumstances, but often lost in large opera houses. In the recording studio, without props, costumes and gestures, it becomes the most important means of allowing the drama to unfold naturally without recourse to manipulating the tempo.

Concertos

While recording a talented young pianist recently, I was struck by the strength of her tirade against conductors. It went roughly as follows:

> I resent working with someone who isn't as good a musician as I am, and who can't hear the things I hear. He, it's almost always a he, is the embodiment of ego and believes it's me who's got to adjust to his inability to solve problems. I can't even tell him what's wrong, even though it's obvious that there's either a wrong note in the parts, or he's beating in an unhelpful or even unmusical way. I have to stay quiet and listen to his incompetence so that I don't undermine his authority. Otherwise, he might not invite me to play with the orchestra again.

This young pianist has everything necessary for a major career. She is able to memorize music at a glance, play it note-perfectly, and is extremely attractive (a requirement in today's pin-up marketplace). Despite having heard similar remarks before, the depth of feeling in one so young and gifted shocked me and challenged my own experience of twenty-five years with conductors in the recording studio.

The beauty of concertos is the fact that room is allowed for two musical beasts to roam the same territory. Yet, the balance between instrumental solo and orchestra is so unnatural on virtually any recording, that it would be difficult to justify as anything other than proof that recording is another genre altogether from concert performance. The forward balance of the instrument defies every natural law. The composer would never have imagined it, nor does the public hear this balance in the concert hall. Not even the instrumentalist hears the balance as presented on recordings. As with singers, the solo instrument is recorded virtually solo with the orchestra existing in a parallel universe of equal intensity. The separation between orchestra and instrument in the studio enables maximum control over both units, while allowing them to be integrated at the same time.

The difficulties encountered between soloist and conductor in concert are compounded in recording. The conductor may consider it of secondary importance to accompany a soloist in concert and only save the last minutes of a rehearsal to remove any potential flies in the performance ointment. He (or she) is caught out on recording, however. The matter of being together with a soloist, who naturally wants to go faster or slower at unpredictable moments is made infinitely worse in recording. Trying to find a solution quickly can be a major challenge. "Being together" has to be more than arriving at the downbeat together; it needs to sound as if the parallel universes of orchestra and soloist have been in strict synchronization since the beginning. An artificial sense of playing together, where the obvious moments of ensemble are together but the overall flow is disjointed, is most often achieved in the editing suite after the recording. It accounts for an inorganic performance.

Many conductors see accompanying as something that gives them a poor image. Most treat it as a necessary evil to be dispatched before intermission and the major feature of the evening's concert, but in the studio there is only the soloist trying to collaborate with another strong musical personality. What matters is the ability to maintain a strong, active performance alongside the soloist.

From the other side, the studio creates new challenges for the soloist. I have noticed how great soloists rely on mind over matter when solving certain technical problems. This to me would seem to be the secret of great performers. It is the ability to hear so clearly what one wishes to achieve that the physical effort needed is somehow realized without fully understanding how. Most soloists rely on this "magic" but feel that in the studio, without the audience to sharpen their perception, they are somehow exposed. The conductor needs to arrive with the orchestral contribution equally organically conceived, which is difficult if soloist, conductor, and orchestra are meeting for the first time in the studio! The conductor's view of the work needs to accommodate the soloist's, but this should never mean that the role is only supportive.

The business of recording

The industry is adjusting to financial limitations and trying to produce hybrid projects of "live" recordings as a composite of several performances with "patch sessions" to allow for mistakes or special effects that are impossible in performance. The days of allowing an orchestra and conductor to create in the studio are slowing down and could conceivably disappear altogether. Sales of orchestral repertoire are lower than virtually any other genre, yet remain the most expensive to make (apart from opera). Conductors no longer have the power they enjoyed during the days of Karajan and Solti as recording sales do not justify the money spent. With the advent of Surround Sound and Super Audio, the possibilities for new developments in the art of studio performance continue to expand, but if there is no change in the commercial environment, will conductors will be able to exploit them?

4 The conductor and the soloist

JOSEPH SILVERSTEIN

As a soloist, conductor, orchestra member, and conductor/soloist, I have had a unique opportunity to examine the relationship between the soloist and the conductor. During a long career, I have experienced collaborations between soloist and conductor that ranged from performances of great ensemble sensitivity and finesse to some that bordered on musical sabotage.

Conducting with a soloist differs in many ways from the norm, the most obvious difference being the expectations of the soloist and the orchestra. The soloist expects the conductor to embrace his or her interpretation without question. Discussions of differences should take place only in the privacy of the pre-rehearsal, as any evidence of disapproval by the conductor is very upsetting to the orchestra. The orchestra expects the conductor to be familiar with the soloist's interpretation and be technically prepared to indicate clearly any tempo changes or dynamic adjustments required. Any suggestions from the soloist should be given to the orchestra by the conductor! On one occasion a soloist chose to communicate directly with a wind player in the Boston Symphony Orchestra and this breach of etiquette caused an angry confrontation that required public apologies before we could resume the rehearsal. Vocal soloists expect the conductor to balance dynamics carefully so that they will not have to strain the voice. Singing full voice on the day of a concert is not to be expected of a vocal soloist. Keeping these expectations in mind, what follows is some of what I have learned from three legendary conductors, Ormandy, Barbirolli, and Stokowski, all of whom were splendid accompanists, followed by some further advice on rehearsal procedures and preparing for soloists.

Eugene Ormandy

I am proud to be one of the many musicians who enjoyed the sensitive support of Eugene Ormandy (1899–1985). The extraordinary discography of the Philadelphia Orchestra during his long tenure as its Music Director bears strong witness to his gifts as a superb accompanist.

Ormandy's chief assets on the podium were the ability to elicit a rich string sonority from any orchestra, student or professional, and a fine sense of balance between the various choirs of the orchestra. His concept of balance always included the soloist. This beautiful string sonority was always controlled at a dynamic level that permitted the soloist to be free of the need to force his or her sound in order to be heard.

He was always gracious in his acceptance of the soloist's interpretation. Ormandy took great pride in his ability to give warm support to an approach that might not agree with his own. His response to the soloist created an atmosphere of comfort, which certainly enhanced the playing of all participants.

Several features of his conducting technique stand out in my memory as being particularly effective. His right hand stopped moving only in a silence and he rarely, if ever, employed subdivision, relying instead on his ability to use large rhythmic units without losing the pulse. His left hand was constantly employed in controlling balance; without needing to stop the orchestra, he simply indicated the desire for more or less of a part with a simple hand motion. As a member of the orchestra, I found that I listened to the soloist with greater interest when Ormandy conducted, because he seemed so deeply involved with the soloist's playing. As a soloist, both in concertos and within the orchestra in the symphonic repertoire, I felt positive reinforcement from Ormandy's habit of breathing with me. The constantly flowing right hand, the balancing effect of the left hand, and the total acceptance of the soloist's approach are characteristics of Ormandy's approach that can serve any conductor well.

Listen to the Chopin piano concertos with Emmanuel Ax as good example of Ormandy's craft. In the free-recitative passages of the slow movements, he shapes the long notes with the phrasing of the piano so that each harmonic change is precisely together with the soloist. Ormandy's very active left hand suppresses anything that might cover the soloist.

John Barbirolli

Sir John Barbirolli (1899–1970) was known for his ability to build a performance around a soloist. Unlike Ormandy, Barbirolli did not provide a luxurious surrounding. Instead, he took the initiative with a strong statement of the soloist's style in the orchestral tuttis. When working with a soloist for the first time, Sir John would arrange a private meeting to go over the concerto, and also to hear some additional repertoire to help him get a sense of the soloist's style. This process would enable him to start the orchestra rehearsal in a way that made the soloist feel very much at home. His splendid recording of Elgar's Cello Concerto with Jacqueline Du Pré gives evidence of his ability to emphasize the soloist's approach rather than stay in the background.

I loved the enveloping lyricism of his conducting style. A man of rather delicate stature, he used a long baton in a manner that always reminded us (in the Boston Symphony Orchestra) that his instrument had been the cello. He had great rhythmic intensity that he conveyed with a small impulse at the point of each long, flowing beat while the baton moved towards the next rhythmic event. He varied the speed of his baton to conform to the phrase, as shaped by the inflections of the soloist. It was the subtle way he pantomimed the contour of the soloist's phrasing with his stick that enhanced and encouraged the soloist to greater levels of expression. Some of the recently re-released recordings of Barbirolli with Jascha Heifetz and Jacqueline Du Pré, among others, are prime specimens of the art of accompaniment. As in the case of Ormandy, Barbirolli seemed to thrive in the role of a supporting actor.

Leopold Stokowski

Highly successful in a very different manner, Leopold Stokowski (1882–1977) was a flexible and inspiring accompanist. Unlike Ormandy and Barbirolli, with their acceptance of the role of the subordinate partner, Stokowski took the soloist's ideas and made them his own, employing his uniquely commanding podium presence to control the performance. Playing a concerto or incidental orchestral solos with Stokowski was like being a comfortable passenger in a vehicle he was driving. I use this example to illustrate that a soloist can be co-opted by the conductor to great advantage in some cases. The second movement of the Brahms Violin Concerto became a piece of intimate chamber music with Stokowski. He made the orchestra aware of the interweaving parts by directing his attention to the specific voice that related to the solo line. As the soloist, I could then react to those elements with heightened expression. The flamboyant style of interpretation that was one of his trademarks in orchestral repertoire was always under complete control when accompanying a soloist. Louis Krasner spoke glowingly of Stokowski's support in the premiere of Schoenberg's Violin Concerto in 1936: he said that at the first piano rehearsal, Stokowski seemed unfamiliar with the work, and yet, by the time the orchestra rehearsals began he not only grasped this complex work, but was able to rehearse it in great detail, displaying an enormous enthusiasm for the concerto that won over the rather sceptical orchestra players.

All three of these conductors adopted the soloist's approach (to different degrees) but maintained a strong control of the orchestra. Other conductors do as well, and my choice of these three is in no way a criticism of the many fine conductors with whom I have performed. Despite the differences in their musical styles, however, these three maestros shared a special ability to convey an enjoyment of the process of supporting a soloist while using their conducting techniques to obtain perfect ensemble. I offer their recordings, made in the pre-splicing era, as evidence of their virtuosity.

Preparing for the soloist

I would strongly advise young conductors to rehearse some accompaniments prior to the soloist's arrival. The orchestral exposition of Mozart piano concertos, the first and second concertos of Beethoven, and a number of passages in the Brahms piano concertos come to mind as music that can be well served by some work before the artist appears on the stage. It is rather frustrating for a soloist to have to sit quietly on the stage while the orchestra spends time rehearsing music that precedes his or her first entrance, as in the Mozart piano concertos. I remember the orchestra's embarrassment when the octogenarian Arthur Rubenstein had to sit patiently while we rehearsed the opening tutti of the Brahms D minor piano concerto for what seemed at least thirty minutes prior to his first entrance. Concertos with heavy orchestration, such as the violin concertos of Bartók, Berg, Glazunov, and Walton, benefit greatly from a reading without soloist. The orchestra will follow dynamics far better with the familiarity of a second or third reading of the music. It is cost-efficient and will improve the performance. The soloist will also be greatly pleased that you have taken this time to prepare.

With new works, I frequently have string and wind soloists face towards the orchestra in the first reading, as it makes the orchestra more aware of the soloist in a shorter time and solves many balance problems without stopping repeatedly. This can also be useful with singers, particularly when there is music in an unflattering range. One must be careful not to imply that there is any weakness on the part of the singer!

Conductors should be prepared to deal with many different types of soloists. String players need greater dynamic sensitivity than pianists as they are more easily covered. Singers are generally more unpredictable and can be more demanding than instrumentalists. As a soloist, I have found that playing with a community or student orchestra requires an approach that allows for the weaknesses of the ensemble to dictate tempi and nuances. By following the orchestra in those situations and not making demands of them that were beyond their capacities, I achieved a much better performance even though I had to sacrifice some of my interpretation.

Do not have the library change dynamics! Use your left hand rather than the librarian's pencil to balance the orchestra with the soloist. Some conductors love to add supplementary dynamic markings to orchestra parts.

As a long-time orchestra player, I can tell you of the annoyance expressed by my colleagues when confronted with a standard concerto part which has been overly edited. A conductor whom I admired a great deal was responsible for re-orchestrating the accompaniment of the Brahms D minor piano concerto in such an excessive manner that the librarian had to paste inserts into all of the string parts! This otherwise admirable conductor simply did not understand how offensive this was to the players, who found this level of editing patronizing and gratuitous. This lack of confidence in the conductor's ability to convey dynamics found its most egregious moment with the marking of "poco meno grazioso" in a Mozart serenade.

In my role as concertmaster, I was always interested in guest conductors' attitudes to bowings. Some supplied their own materials, which saved time in rehearsals if they had specific ideas that would have made it necessary to change our own parts. Some were happy with our previously "bowed" parts. A few would send me a clean part with a request for me to add bowings. In all cases, the proper gesture is to call the librarian to express your preference: i.e. your own materials (in which case they had better be well marked and matching), the orchestra's own parts (if you want to change them, ask politely *after* the first rehearsal), or a clean part to be marked. Nowadays, most orchestras maintain a good library with well-marked parts of much of the repertoire. I like to use my own parts in Haydn, Mozart, and Beethoven, because my bowings are an important ingredient in my approach to this repertoire. I must add, however, the comment of the wise Richard Burgin (concertmaster of the Boston Symphony Orchestra for a mere forty-two years) who said, "There are no bad bowings, only poor execution." In short, you must develop the technique to communicate these nuances clearly and efficiently to the orchestra.

Finally, I would suggest that those of you who enjoy a fine memory restrain your desire to work without a score. The presence of the score on the conductor's stand is a good source of added security for a slightly nervous soloist. Leonid Kogan was seriously unnerved at his American debut with the Boston Symphony Orchestra when Pierre Monteux conducted the Brahms Violin Concerto from memory.

Never forget that the comfort level of the soloist should always be the prime concern of the conductor. A happy soloist will give a better performance and will have nice things to say about you and your orchestra at their next engagement.

5 Choral conducting

VANCE GEORGE

Sir Georg Solti said, "Singing is the basis of all music making."[1] In this spirit, any aspiring conductor should learn to sing; the better you understand your voice, the better you will train a choir and demonstrate for the orchestra. Sing in a choir, apprentice with another conductor, form a group, attend concerts, listen to recordings, do anything to gain experience and learn how the voice works.

The choral tradition

There is a burgeoning choral movement in the world today. Opportunities for conductors range from children's choirs, collegiate, church and community choirs, and lesbian and gay choruses, to symphony choruses, chamber choirs, and other professional groups. This incredible diversity stems from nineteenth-century singing societies, the great cathedral tradition, the rise of orchestra choruses, chamber choirs, and musicological research resulting in an avid interest in early music. The greatest influence, perhaps, has been technology's role in disseminating an immense variety of choral performances throughout the world.

Through the media, many conductors established their reputations with a specific chorus, notably Sir David Willcocks (b. 1919, The Bach Choir), Sir Roger Norrington (b. 1934, Schütz Choir of London), Robert Shaw (1916–99, Robert Shaw Chorale), Sir John Eliot Gardiner (b. 1943, Monteverdi Choir), Helmut Rilling (b. 1933, Gächinger Kantorei and Bach-Collegium Stuttgart), Eric Ericson (b. 1919, Swedish Radio Choir), and Nicholas Harnoncourt (b. 1929, Concentus Musicus Wien).[2] Major British orchestras, like the Philharmonia and the London Symphony Orchestra, began sponsoring their own choirs mid-century. In the United States, Arturo Toscanini (1867–1957) recognized Robert Shaw's genius, prompting George Szell (1897–1970) to invite him to Cleveland in 1956 to create the first American symphony chorus. One year later Fritz Reiner (1888–1963) invited Margaret Hillis (1921–98) to Chicago to do the same. Then in 1964 Roger Wagner (1914–92) created a new genre, the Los Angeles Master Chorale, a group with their own concert series that also collaborated with the Los Angeles Philharmonic. The next generation, which was equally influential in advancing choral/orchestral performances, included Thomas Dunn (b. 1925), John Nelson (b. 1941) and Robert Page (b. 1927).

Since then, there has been an explosion of excellent chamber groups and conductors: Bach Choir (David Hill, b. 1957), Kammerchor Stuttgart (Frieder Bernius, b. 1943), Cambridge Singers (John Rutter, b. 1945), Chanticleer (Joseph Jennings, b. 1954), Estonian Philharmonic Chamber Choir (Tõnu Kaljuste, b. 1953), Santa Fe Desert Chorale (Dennis Shrock, b. 1944), The Sixteen (Harry Christophers, b. 1953), Kansas City Chorale (Charles Bruffy, b. 1958), Quink, and Netherlands Chamber Choir.

Radio listeners enjoy the BBC Singers, the Swedish Radio Choir and the Danish National Radio Choir and a new audience is listening on the Internet. These avid audiences recall the response to Fred Waring's twice-daily broadcasts of the 1940s and 1950s, which so profoundly influenced Robert Shaw. At this time opportunities in the choral field far exceed those in orchestral work, and the quality of today's choirs has created new respect for choral conducting.

Analysis is architecture

If "singing is the basis of all music-making" then structural analysis is the basis of musicianship. Analysis opens the door to the composer's ideas of form, "order, coherence, and proportion,"[3] and allows you to stretch the sound fabric of text, harmony, melody, and rhythm, over this structure. Honoring the composer's structural design will keep your music making honest by getting inside the piece and allowing it to sound, which guards against the temptation to "interpret."

The great Berlin theorist and musicologist, Julius Herford (1901–81), taught many of us, including Leonard Bernstein, Robert Shaw, and Margaret Hillis, to grapple with musical structure as a source of music's spiritual energy.[4]

Your first step of study in preparation for performance is to create a graph form of your analysis noting major sections, tonal areas, cadences and phrase groups, tempo changes and compositional procedures. Figure 5.1 shows what such an analysis might look like for the fourth movement of Brahms's *Ein deutsches Requiem*. Write the phrase lengths at the top of your score. This is the simplest building block for teaching musicianship, shape and structure for use in rehearsal. From detailed analysis of each movement you can then create a one-page overview for the chorus, illustrating text, keys, mood, tempo and form (Fig. 5.2).[5]

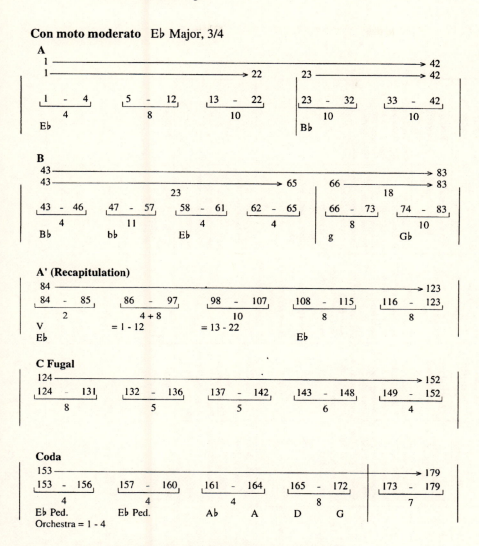

Figure 5.1 Brahms, *Ein deutsches Requiem*, analysis of fourth movement

Analysis in action

You need not play every orchestral instrument, but you must know the score thoroughly section by section, and part by part. Solfège and/or play each part. This is a slow process but it will help internalize the music's structure and proportion. Once you have sung, played and analyzed every note, you are ready to begin building a repertoire of short pieces that will allow you to develop both musical and technical skills.

Bach's "O Sacred Heart Now Wounded," for example, is comprised of four phrase groups of 2 + 2 = 4 bars. (Ex. 5.1) Have your choir sing each

	I	II	III	IV	V	VI	VII
FORCES	Chorus Orchestra	Chorus Orchestra	Chorus Baritone Orchestra	Chorus Orchestra	Chorus Soprano Orchestra	Chorus Baritone Orchestra	Chorus Orchestra
MOOD	Somber pp. 3-11	Dark and brooding pp. 11-27	Introspective pp. 28-43	Restful and confident pp. 44-53	Contemplative pp. 54-60	Mysterious then triumphant pp. 61-83	Ecstatic, heavenly pp. 84-95
TEXT	New Testament Matthew 5:4 *Blessed are they that mourn for they shall be comforted* Old Testament Psalm 126:5, 6 *They who sow in tears shall reap in joy.*	New Testament Peter 1:24, 25 *Consider the frailty of the flesh.* James 5:7 *Be patient for the coming of the Lord, as the farmer is with the land.* Peter 1:25 *But the Lord's word endures forever.*	Old Testament Psalm 39: 4-7 *The futile and temporal nature of man. What is the nature of life? What hope is there? My hope is in thee in my spiritual being.*	Old Testament Psalm 84:1, 2 *How lovely is thy dwelling place. Man longs for perfection and a state of spiritual grace.*	Apocrypha Ecclesiasticus 51:27 *Ye labor, yet I have found rest.* Old Testament Isaiah 66:13 *I will comfort you as your mother might.* New Testament John 16:22 *Ye now have sorrow but will be given consolation and grace.*	New Testament Hebrews 13:14 Corinthians 15:51, 52, 54, 55 *Summary of the Requiem texts: Man is temporal but seeks the eternal. Death delineates the temporal. The eternal nature of the spirit is yet to come.*	New Testament Revelation 14:13 *Blessed are the dead The spirit saith they live on in their works.*
FUGUES		Joyous fugue pp. 20-27 Old Testament Isaiah 35:9, 10 *For the eternal lies in God and therein is man's joy.*	Joyous Praise fugue pp. 38-43 Apocrypha Wisdom of Solomon 3:1 *Our souls are in the hand of God.*	Joyous Praise imitative pp. 51, 52 Old Testament Psalm 84:4 *They praise Thee for evermore.*		Joyous Praise dbl.fugue, pp. 73-83 New Testament Revelations 4:11 *For your omnipotence we praise You.*	
KEYS/TEMPI	F Major 4 Rather slow with expression c.58-66 [75] p.14 somewhat faster Gb, c.100-104	Bb minor—Bb major 3 moderately c.50-60 [H] Bb Major c.65 [206] 4 fast, but not too fast p.20, c.120 [N] Tranquil c.104, p.26	D minor—D Major 4 moderate c.52-64 [173] D Major pedal c.54-60	Eb Major 3 moderate c.92-104	G Major 4 slowly c.48-52	C minor—C Major 4 walking tempo c.80-92 [82] C minor p.65 3 lively c.128-144 [208] C Major 4 fast, dbl. fugue ¼ = ½ c.100-108	F Major 4 festive c.60-72

F ← p4 → bbBb ← M3 → d:D ← ½ → Eb ← M3 → G ← p4 → c:C ← p4 → F

Figure 5.2 Brahms, *Ein Deutsches Requiem*, overview

Example 5.1 "O Sacred Heart Now Wounded" (Hans L. Hassler [1601] harmonized by
J. S. Bach, *St. Matthew Passion*, 1729)

voice part, emphasizing the circled words. A slight leaning or crescendo–
decrescendo into each phrase will reflect Bach's textual and harmonic em-
phases on measure 1 (beat 1) and measure 3 (beats 3–4).

The circling of the important words will help the sopranos emphasize "wounded" (a low note) rather than "sacred" (a high note). Singers
will naturally sing high notes louder than low notes. The basses should
be especially careful to sing lighter as they near the top of the staff and
heavier towards the bottom of the staff, dropping the jaw and brighten-
ing below C. The tenor's wide range contrasts with the alto which lies in
a narrow midrange. Therefore ask altos to crescendo and grind their dis-
sonant D against the sopranos' E in measure 2, emphasizing the seventh

of the chord. Make them feel special by impressing upon them how important they are to the harmonic structure, since they get all the leftover notes in a triad and are usually cast in opera as witches, mothers or handmaids.

Inner parts are the most difficult to hear when rehearsing. Use a medial syllable "loo" [lu] or solfège syllables; have basses and sopranos sing together, followed by low voices (bass/alto) then high voices (soprano/tenor). Each combination will reveal a different listening and tuning experience for singers and conductor. Lastly add the text.

The amplitude of your conducting gestures should reflect your structural analysis. Each phrase shape should grow slightly larger and more intense, culminating in phrase 4. Begin with a small beat pattern from the wrist, growing in amplitude to beat 3, measure 2. Use a snap of the wrist, down-up on beat 3, to indicate a catch-breath for the next phrase.

Every choir should sing Bach, but William Byrd's *Ave verum corpus* provides the chorus with the experience of singing polyphony in Latin, each part moving as an independent melody. Count the internal note values while singing the pitches and hear the polyphonic phrase shapes unfold; count "one" for quarter notes, "one-two" for half notes, and "one-two-three-four" for whole notes. Conduct quarter-note pulses in the early rehearsals, shifting later to half-note pulses. However, conduct a bar with sixteenths in steady quarter pulses to provide a firm framework for the fast notes. Singing the lines with an underlying quarter pulse honors Byrd's manner of writing without barlines. Disregard the barlines found in modern editions.[6]

Samuel Barber's arrangement of "Sure on this shining night" (Op. 13, No. 3) explores the subtleties of singing in English. Train your singers to express the text like a soloist performing an art song. Model after your favorite singer savoring the consonants s, h, w and r; "sure, this-shining, this-side, star-made, shadows, healed, health, high, holds, hearts, whole, weep, wonder, and wand'ring."

Text

Language is the only difference between conducting a chorus and an orchestra. Conducting is conducting, but in choral music the text is the catalyst for a composer's creative impulse and your access to his or her inspiration. Stravinsky's vision of Elijah's chariot ascending into the heavens, for instance, inspired *Symphony of Psalms*, leading to his choice of texts.[7]

Table 5.1 *Teaching a foreign language*

- Speak the text slowly, syllable by syllable, then whole words and finally sentences. Read the poetic translation to reconnect with the meaning.
- Speak the text in rhythm. Read the literal translation again.
- Count-sing pitches in rhythm, substituting "tee" for three for ease in counting.[8]
- Have half the singers count-sing and the other half sing pitches on "doo."
- Sing the text on pitch. Read the poetic translation.
- Sing the language while thinking the English meaning.
- At a rehearsal break, ask the singers to converse in their own language, but in the accent of the language you are singing. It is good ear-training and amusing.

A chorus must understand what they are singing. Train your singers to work from both a poetic and literal translation, writing the literal translation under each line of music. (See Table 5.1.) Then have a native speaker, live or recorded, model the text. Bringing inner life to a text requires work, but if you both understand and mean what you sing, you will touch the hearts of your audience, a quality that is absent in many performances today.

Choirs should use stage speech and an even more exaggerated declamation for choral/orchestral works and opera. A singer should be able to pronounce and understand the Romance languages according to stage practice plus Latin. Consonants, diphthongs, and triphthongs are especially difficult in English, German, Czech, and Russian. You should become conversant with the International Phonetic Alphabet (IPA), a phonetic shorthand for language sounds.[9] Be aware that English is difficult to sing; cabaret and Broadway singers like Joan Morris, Barbara Cook, and Frank Sinatra are great models.

Choral colors and registration

Color and style are a matter of taste. Form your own ideas of what best serves the music, be true to your singers' vocal gifts and do not impose either straight tone or vibrato on them. The voices you choose will make your group and your sound unique. A substantive musical expression will move your audience more than a superficial concern for blend and sonority. Perfection does not lie in sonority but in musical expression.

To create instant depth and maturity, have the singers gently push their index fingers inward at the corners of the mouth to form a square, puckered mouth "aw" [ɔ]. Maintain this puckered embouchure to unify sonority. Both embouchure and vowel adjustments help maintain a consistent dynamic level and vocal color throughout high and low ranges. As you add text be sure that the vowels remain uniform; i.e. relate all vowels in a sentence to the first vowel. Thus using ee [i], "Since by man came death," becomes "Seence-bee-meen-keem-deeth." This looks strange on the page but creates vowel uniformity.

Eliminating text will also help in registration, thereby extending the range of your singers. This is accomplished by textless vocalizing on "aw" [ɔ] at the top of the staff and "ah" [a] as you near the top or bottom of the staff. I panicked when sopranos in a Japanese choir could not sing a high G in Beethoven's Symphony No. 9. After eliminating the text above the staff we reduced jaw tension and they soon sang with ease. Men singing above the staff should also change the vowel to an "aw" [ɔ]. Experiment with high registration by asking the men to speak in a high, pleading, teenage voice: "Gee Dad, I'm sorry I wrecked the car last night." This always gets a chuckle and gives the sensation of shifting between middle and high registers where the tenors live most of their lives.[10] Gene Kelly, in his rendition of "Singing in the Rain," accomplished this with an "ee" or "ih" [I] tongue position.

Explore the spectrum of vocal colors of opera and art song from Broadway and popular personalities like Ethel Merman, Gene Kelly, and Bing Crosby, Margaret Thatcher, and Julia Childs (the latter are examples of an elevated soft palate). Be playful and encourage your singers to create vocal effects that reflect the music ranging from brassy and bright to dark and light, even baring the teeth.

Composers score most music for four-part chorus, SATB, but five-part, six-part or eight-part chords necessitate revoicing. The score may read SSA or TTB but, to provide better balance, assign your singers to high, middle and low parts (HML). Be sure to rehearse the middle part alone to help them habituate reading between staves. Strengthen a part that lies too high or too low by "railroad tracking"; i.e. having sopranos double altos, altos and basses double tenors or tenors double basses.

Breaking the orchestral sound barrier

Historically the chorus was seated in front or at the side of the orchestra.[11] Today it is necessary to project *over* them. To be expressive you must first be heard, but expression also requires understanding the text, involving uniform entrances, cut-offs, consonants, vowels, and registration. A chorus spends 95 percent of the time singing beautiful sounds. Sometimes, however, unorthodox techniques (see Ex. 5.2) will help project the text and character of a work over the orchestra.

Example 5.2 Operatic colors in "Libera me" from Verdi's *Requiem*

In addition to allowing text to be understood, articulation will also help your choir be heard. "Uh" [ʌ] before weak consonants like "w," "f," or "l," for example, helps delineate entrances; a grace-note "uh" in Beethoven's Ninth "uh-Freude" adds point to the men's entrance. "Uh" is great for uniform cut-offs like "Amen": "Ah-meh-nuh"! It also gives pitch to "muh," "nuh," "puh," "luh," and "kuh." To accomplish this simply snap the abdomen toward the backbone in an "abdominal thrust."

Substituting "k"s for "g"s also strengthens entrances ("Gloria" becomes "klaudia"). "D" consonants help articulate fast notes; sixteenth notes in "Cum sancto spiritu" from Bach's *Mass in B Minor* become "koo-sa-to-spee-dee-dee–too, een-klaw-dee-aw-day-dee-dee-pah-t'dis." and Beethoven's "Et ascendit in coelum" from the *Missa Solemnis* becomes "Et ah-shay-day-day-day-day-day."

Weak consonants like "h" and "p" require silence or space, which the audience will comprehend through silence. Delineate awkward or buried pitches with an unorthodox scoop from above or below in an almost un-pitched, spoken *parlando*. "R"s may be dropped, flipped, trilled or sounded. Singers who cannot trill an "r" should substitute a "d"; "Kyrie" becomes "kee-dee-ay," and "Credo" "k'day-do." To flip the "r" in "spirit" say "spit it." Sound "r" when singing American English.

To clarify thick textures in Beethoven, Verdi, Mahler, and John Adams, strike out ties and slurs. Shaw paraphrased Szell saying "Don't sing the dots." For example, a short note following a dotted note will gain rhythmic life and clarity by lifting on the dot. Likewise, lifting before two sixteenths or a grace note provides space for re-articulation. This space creates energy on the next entrance and saves the voice from fatigue when singing with an orchestra.

Soft singing

The last thing a singer learns is soft singing. But if you can hum, you can sing softly. Here is a four-step routine for singing Byrd's *Ave verum* or "Since by man came death" from *Messiah* softly: (1) sing a comfortable *mf*, (2) hum *piano* on "mm," (3) match the hum singing "ee" [i], and (4) sing the text inside the mouth, *pianissimo*, through barely parted lips.[12] This routine will create uniform vowels and provides a mesmerizing, veiled sonority that is only "one step up from silence."[13]

Support all soft singing on a fine breath-stream, thinking a long vertical vowel at the back of the throat. A raised soft palate and a loose jaw will result in a warm vocal color created by greater pharyngeal space. Experiment with embouchure and vowels but don't exaggerate so your choir sounds like Papageno with a padlock on his mouth.

A *ppp* entrance after sitting for seventy minutes presents a special challenge in Mahler's Symphony No. 2. A silent warm-up routine for body, breath and voice will prepare the chorus for this intense and scary entrance.

> *Body:* start with isometric exercises tensing ankle, calf, thigh, and hip in both legs. Elevate the spine and think space between each vertebra stretching shoulders back and down.
> *Breath:* press the abdomen to expel the breath and hold. Release the abdominal tension and inhale tucking the abdomen up under the ribcage. Repeat three times.
> *Voice:* swallow, and licking the lips, stick the tongue to the back teeth, left and hold, then repeat on the right. Bite the tongue gently for saliva, breathe through the nose, flare the nostrils, pop your ears and lift your eyebrows to lift the soft palate sending warm air to the back of the throat. Practice in rehearsal to habituate the routine.

At one performance while the chorus warmed up silently a guest artist expressed surprise at feeling warm winds on the back of her neck.

Rehearse this passage (Ex. 5.3) on a hum building the chords like a pyramid from the bass up. Basses and tenors should modify "auferstehen" to "muh-fuh-stehn," the text barely enunciating through almost closed lips "in the hum". Encourage the low basses to open, rattle and buzz on the extremely low notes. Even in performance, sopranos and altos should hum without text until measure 13, so that they do not overbalance the basses.

Example 5.3 "Aufersteh'n" from fifth movement of Mahler, Symphony No 2

Example 5.4 "Yo-oh," pulsing for articulation

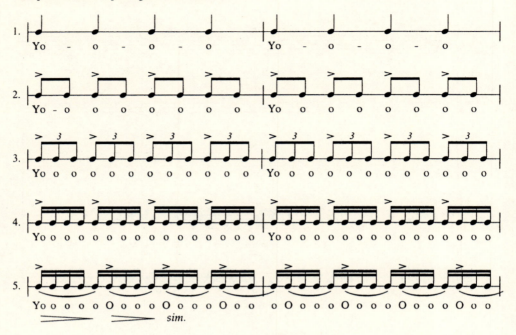

Baroque idioms

Baroque music was conceived instrumentally and requires extreme vocal agility. These exercises will help your choir articulate with the ease of Barbara Bonney or Cecilia Bartoli. Begin by pulsing "yo-oh" for eight quarter- note pulses (Ex. 5.4). "Yoh" engages the abdomen, which should tuck slightly up and under, rolling on each pulse.

Now adapt this to Handel by singing the bracketed pitches in Ex 5.5 on the syllable "daw" [ɔ], in any octave. Observe the crescendos and decrescendos indicated in (a) then (b). Now put them together in (c). "Born" provides the vowel and "d" the articulation. Increase the energy of the sixteenths with each sequence. Decrescendo to lighten the registration of the last four pitches. The "d" concept may be adapted for any rapid sequence and discarded later if you like.[14]

In that same movement "And the government shall be, shall be upon his shoulder" may be given greater crispness and rhythmic energy using "Aw-duh-guh-vuh-meh-chuh-be-chuh-be-uh-paw-nih-sho-o-o-o-o-ol-duh."

The last movement of Bach's Magnificat is very difficult to make sound. No one tempo seems right for the grand opening chords of the "Gloria"

Example 5.5 "For unto us a child is born" from Handel's *Messiah*

and the swirling triplets bursting into "Patri." One day while listening to the Buxtehude Fantasia in C it occurred to me that the "Gloria" is in the style of a keyboard fantasy beginning with slow, homophonic chords followed by an accelerando of upward-sweeping triplets. Could voices translate keyboard rubato? I rushed to rehearsal to find that it translated and worked perfectly. Try it.

Table 5.2 *Warm-up exercises*

- Body:
  Stand tall, hands touching side seams, shoulders dropped.
  Reach upward picking apples, or clasp fingers, invert, and stretch skyward.
  Tap face and neck with fingertips to awaken facial muscles.
- Breath:
  Inhale, one hand on the abdomen, the other on the chest
  Exhale with a quick thrust of the abdomen.
  Stand tall, feel the head float off the tip of the spine, slowly turn left then right without force.
  To experience "support" put your index finger in your mouth and blow against it. Pop your finger
    out allowing air to escape. Now, do the same but when you remove your finger do not allow air to
    escape. The abdomen will tense and that is what support means.
- Voice:
  Pucker: using both index fingers lightly push inward to form a square mouth.
  Lip trills: buzz your lips together like a baby blowing bubbles.
  Press from the abdomen, burbling the lips on pitch sliding from C up to G and back.
  Sing "zee" descending scale-wise G to C, now ascend scale-wise to D with a decrescendo adjusting
    the vowel from "ee" to "aw" (this is called covering or registration and is an aid in teaching high
    voice). As you descend brighten and crescendo returning to "ee."
  Ascend by half steps C to F.
- Ear/mind:
  Sing an ascending series of triads: major, minor, diminished, major, augmented.[15]
  Count-sing a passage on pitch for greater accuracy, counting eighth notes inside each quarter note,
    substituting "tee" for three.[16]
  Raise the pitch half a step while humming and counting from one to sixteen.[17] This is excellent for
    pitch sensitivity and intonation.

The choral rehearsal

Audition your singers for natural vocal potential and for reading experience.[18] Choose warm, rich voices with a fine range and capable of singing a straight tone as well as with full vibrato.

Warm-ups are a great way to build a group's sound, but are a waste of time if you do not understand the voice. Begin each rehearsal with attention to body, breath and voice in that sequence. (See Table 5.2.) Experiment with a few exercises that make sense to you, given your ensemble and training.[19] Teach your singers to mark their music (Fig. 5.3) indicating phrase lengths by numbering or drawing bold barlines. Markings will make subsequent rehearsals more efficient.[20] These simple devices are fundamental in building musicianship, ensemble, and spinning a line on breath.

The orchestral rehearsal

Check your materials; the measure numbers and letters in your score must match those in the choral scores and orchestra parts. Write piano-vocal score page numbers into your score at structural points and tempo changes to facilitate rehearsals: "Four measures before letter Q, chorus – page 221," pause, make eye contact, give the upbeat, and go on. The orchestra will appreciate your efficiency.

1.   √   Breath mark

2.   (Kyrie) *f* *p*   Circle important words, meter and tempo changes, or pitch errors, a pitch in another part to help you, or important dynamics

3.   Place an arrow to indicate cueing or doubling another part

     1 2 3 4   Place an arrow to indicate cut-off the 4th beat

4.   Kyri-e e e e   Articulate eighth notes with extra vowels, accent, staccato, or tenuto marks

5.   Love = lo ve   Place a final consonant on the eighth rest

6.   dear = de- ar   Dividing a note value for a dipthong, each half receiving a separate vowel

     fear = fe - uh

7.   Give ___ = Gi - ve   Strike out tied notes to place a consonant and provide space

8.   A pair of glasses, watch for suprise entrance, tempo change

9.   Kein | auge   Slash for a glottal stroke

10.   Where no accent is to be made that would seem natural, as in a downbeat or the top of an ascending scale passage (anacrusis)

11.   Stress or tenuto to hightlight text or an important pitch (thesis)

12.   Staccato, very separated

13.   Bach staccato or half staccato

14.   Accent, stronger than a stress. Requiring more abdominal kick and support

Figure 5.3 Common conventions for marking parts

Table 5.3 *Exercise for scaling patterns*

Right hand:
- Conduct a choir of 100 from the shoulder (large ball and socket)
- Conduct a choir of 50 from the elbow (large hinge)
- Conduct a chamber group of 24 from the wrist (small ball and socket)
- Conduct a chamber group of 12 from the fingers (small hinges)

Left hand:
- Move your left hand, out left and back, then up and down, counting 4 pulses for each direction. Repeat these movements for choirs of 100, 50, 24 and 12 as above.
- When not using the left hand simply allow the arm to rest on an imaginary shelf just above the hip, poised halfway between the wrist and elbow.

Hands together:
- Now 4/4 with the right hand and the left hand out/back/up/down.

Bowings act as punctuation and should reflect the text. Bowings also prevent players from making changes just for convenience. Many professional conductors mark their own parts aided by an experienced violinist. Conduct from your own marked parts and always carry a set of emergency backup parts.[21]

Adjust dynamics between strings, winds and brasses and between the chorus and orchestra. Bruckner marks *ff* in all parts, but balance the winds and brasses by marking them one or two dynamic levels lower. You may ask them to play under the voices, but dynamics have a way of creeping back up. Bracket and mark fugue themes *f*, marking countersubjects and episodes one dynamic level lower. In a final rehearsal of Brahms's *Requiem* I reminded the orchestra to play the brackets in the foreground and the remainder in the background. It took hours to mark but those few words rescued the fugal textures and the structure of the *Requiem*.

Provide marked scores for soloists, chorus director and coach the arias and recitatives as early as possible to allow time to work your ideas into the voice. You need not conduct recitatives accompanied by continuo, but you must conduct all recitatives accompanied by orchestra.

Mastering the baton

At first the baton may feel strange to a choral conductor, but it will discipline your gestures and make you more efficient in reflecting the music. The great Russian conductor, Igor Markevich, said, "Use only the amount of energy necessary for the desired result."[22] One remedy for overconducting is to scale your choreography for an imaginary group (Table 5.3); use a mirror, conduct a pianist, or videotape yourself. You are less apt to over-conduct away from the group. Remember to look like you want the music to sound. Whether you use or ultimately reject it, you will never regret your work with a baton.

Use a baton, with or without orchestra, no matter the size of the group. Economy of gesture may provide greater depth of music making. Remember: less is always more. And you will conserve energy, which is important when conducting concert repertoire or a three-hour oratorio or opera.

Conductors who do not use a baton have usually made a conscious choice for physical not musical reasons. Their baton training still shows in the economy of their gestures. Conductors without baton experience tend towards overly rounded gyrations of wrists, elbows and shoulders that blur the rhythmic pulse. Some conductors put the baton down when conducting an unaccompanied passage thinking they are creating a special choral effect. This is a good theatrical device, but affects neither the choir's sonority nor musicianship.

Balancing the orchestra and chorus

The ratio of singers to strings should take into account the number of performers available, their experience and the hall's capacity.

> Renaissance: 1–24 singers, strings 1, 1, 1, 1, 1.
> Baroque: 40–60 singers, strings 4, 4, 3, 3, 2.
> Classical: 80–100 singers, strings 8, 8, 5, 4, 2.
> Romantic: 125 to 180 singers, strings 16, 16, 8, 8, 6.
> Mahler Symphony No. 8: 200 adults and 75 children.

Experiment with placement.[23] Allow the width of one person between each singer for a richer sonority, blend and better hearing. The first row of singers should be twenty inches above the orchestra level with a lift of ten inches for succeeding rows. Separate distinct vibratos and edgy voices to mix vocal colors. When recording, move wide vibratos and edgy voices away from the microphones. If the men are few in number position them in the middle flanked by the women.

When nearing performance, rehearse the choir in the performance hall to adjust to the new acoustic. Warn against over-singing; the hall will feel strange and you may seem far away. Singing half-voice or "marking" (speaking the text and singing staccato) will save the voice and is helpful when making corrections.

Establish a conducting horizon, making eye contact with the chorus above the horizon and the orchestra below the horizon.[24] And warn your chorus that your focus will be on the orchestra in the combined rehearsal. As you near the performance, use the full score, singing a movement without stopping and focusing on conducting. Acknowledge this moment of growth verbally. You are building ensemble and your own conducting skills.

Request three to five orchestra/chorus rehearsals for a major work. Plan rehearsals by checking CDs for timings; include rehearsals for soloists, continuo and obbligato players. Submit a seating plan for the stage manager.[25] Never count on overtime (it may be forbidden by union rules). A well-known conductor ran out of time in a *Messiah* rehearsal. On opening night, five choral movements were performed unrehearsed, the performers rescuing the conductor (who was not re-engaged).

The first orchestra rehearsal

You are usually given one rehearsal with a professional orchestra to solve any issues of bowings, balance and style prior to the combined rehearsals. Begin *tutti*, rehearse the movements out of order and excuse the players as they finish. Rehearse only difficult spots. You need not run entire movements. Play the beginning of each movement to establish character, play the final bars with cadence and immediately give the downbeat in the tempo and character of the next movement. These are words to live by. I cannot stress this enough because it instantly creates and establishes that split-second shift between movements for orchestra, chorus and conductor.

Combined chorus/orchestra rehearsals

Welcome everyone, introduce the soloists, and give the downbeat. Vocal soloists should face the choir, providing a voice lesson and the orchestra's only chance to hear them. At some point you may find it valuable to make comments to the orchestra concerning text or tempo. Be succinct and do not sermonize. Run the rehearsal, listen, repair, and maintain a sense of well-being.

Play a movement or segment without stopping. Address the orchestra, check with the concertmaster for string issues and then with your assistant for balances. Appoint an assistant, a colleague or student, to act as "ears" in the rehearsal. The orchestra may correct itself the second time. Learning what will self-correct and what will not is an art. Make mental notes, insert "stickies" or turn the corner of a page down for later correction. Remind the chorus to follow the baton and not to over-sing.

Learn to listen differently from the podium. Things may sound strange and out of balance when facing the orchestra and chorus for the first time. The orchestra will be too close and overplaying and the chorus distant and lagging behind. Be calm in the midst of chaos; it is simply the nature of the beast, and one to which you will become accustomed as you master your craft.

Messiah performances often include only one rehearsal each for orchestra, soloists and chorus. A reality: your first complete runthrough is the first performance. Community and church choirs often rehearse and perform on the same day; schedule separate rehearsals for soloists with piano, soloists with chorus and meet with your concertmaster beforehand to discuss any stylistic or bowing issues. Run the rehearsal, then make corrections, talk to individual players after rehearsal or leave notes on the players' stands.

Be yourself

With better training and baton experience, attitudes towards the choral conductor are slowly changing. Orchestras may be sceptical until you prove you have knowledge of the score, can wave the stick, run the rehearsal, and make music. Don't take yourself too seriously: it is not about you so do not take it personally.

A few words of appreciation are appropriate at the end of a rehearsal. Remember everyone wants to go home. After a final rehearsal, express how much this performance means to you, the chorus, and the community. The joy and adventure of making music together builds rapport, establishes your reputation, and helps redefine "choral conductor."

In 1984, Robert Shaw came to San Francisco to conduct *Ein deutsches Requiem*. It was my first season and I was full of apprehension as the great mentor stepped off the podium, dripping with sweat, and stammered, "Vance, this is a fine chorus . . . and in five years it can be a great chorus." It does, indeed, take five years to build a musical community and a lifetime to learn the myriad aspects of conducting a chorus and orchestra. Do not hesitate to ask questions and glean information from colleagues, players, and singers. It can be daunting to conduct a great work for the first time confronted by those who have performed it often, but their skill and experience are a gift.

Through the process of analysis, singing, playing, and rehearsing you have completed the cycle that began with the composer's original inspiration and are ready to experience the mystery of the music. Remember that your work, for all its challenges and labor, is a privilege and a joy.

Choral director resources

Support organizations have been created to support this growth of choral music. Chorus America was formed in 1977 to promote the professional interests of paid and volunteer singers. In 1982 the International Federation for Choral Music was formed to foster exchange between choral musicians throughout the world. ChoralNet, a website co-sponsored by Chorus America and IFCM, provides information and can put you in touch with groups throughout the UK, Europe, Asia, and the Americas. In addition IFCM publishes an International Choral Bulletin and sponsors concerts and festivals, notably the triennial World Symposium on Choral Music. Chorus America publishes *The Voice*, holds workshops on organization and conducting, offers assistance to US and Canadian member choruses, and sponsors an annual conference.

ACDA
American Choral Director Association, 502 SW 38th Street, Lawton OK 73505, USA
Telephone: +1 580 355 8161
www.acdaonline.org

ABCD
Association of British Choral Directors, 15 Granville Way, Sherborne, Dorset DT9 4AS, UK
Telephone: +44 (0) 1935 389482
www.abcd.org.uk

CA
Chorus America, 1156 15th Street NW, Suite 310, Washington DC 20005–1704, USA
Telephone +1 202 331 7599
www.chorusamerica.org

CHORALNET
The Internet Center for Choral Music
www.choralnet.org

IFCM
International Federation for Choral Music, Centro Internacional de la Música de la UNESCO, Villa Gadea, E-03590 Altea, Spain
Telephone: +34 96 584 5213 0353
www.ifcm.net

6 Opera conducting

SIR CHARLES MACKERRAS

A good orchestra, fully trained, will be able to play most symphonic works of the classical period without any conductor at all. It might not have the stamp or the personality of an enlightened musician on it, but the performance would not actually come to a halt. However, an opera cannot even *begin* to be performed without a proper conductor directing the whole proceedings. It has always been a great mystery to me how complicated passages like, say, the second finale of *Così fan tutte*, or many scenes in *Idomeneo*, could have been done without a baton-waving conductor. But of course, it may not have been all that well together in those days. As Mozart said himself of the first performance of *Don Giovanni*, "a lot of notes fell under the desks."

There is, therefore, a feeling among orchestras that, although they do not really admire symphony conductors so much, they have a grudging respect for opera conductors, because they realize that opera conducting is so much more difficult and complicated. The general suspicion that orchestra players have of conductors is a great deal more prevalent in the concert hall than in the opera house, where the smallest mistake can show up the conductor.

Working with singers

The actual training of an opera conductor is, in a way, much more stringent than that of a symphony conductor. The opera conductor must be able to play the piano, and give the listener a good impression of the sound of the orchestral score. He must know a great deal about singing and the problems that singers face. He has to learn how to breathe with them. He has to understand that, although there are singers who are highly educated musicians, just as cultured as any solo violinist or pianist, many successful singers can hardly read music at all and have to be taught their roles by rote, have them bashed into them by a répétiteur.

Opera conducting is akin to concerto conducting in the symphony world. The singers are all soloists, even if there are ten of them singing together. There are many complicated ensembles which are extremely difficult to coordinate between the stage and the orchestra, especially in productions with a lot of rushing about. A lot of action means that the singers cannot actually look at the conductor all the time, and must produce

Example 6.1 "Hier soll ich dich denn sehen, Konstanze" from Mozart's *Die Entführung aus dem Serail*. All annotations (everything but the notes) are the performance markings of the author

their own rhythm. One moment you are giving a strict beat and making all these soloists, with their different personalities, follow you. The next minute you are following them, sensitive to when they need to take a breath.

Let me illustrate this with some problematic bars from Mozart's *Die Entführung aus dem Serail*. Its opening aria, Belmonte's "Hier soll ich dich denn sehen, Konstanze," is of beautiful simplicity (Ex. 6.1). To sing it

Example 6.1 (*cont.*)

Example 6.1 (*cont.*)

correctly is not so simple. In fact, because of its uncomfortable tessitura it is regarded by tenors as being very difficult. It requires extremely sympathetic conducting.

The tempo should be approximately 80 eighth-notes per minute. Measures 18 and 19 are quite difficult. Here, the singer must take a final breath after the word "*zurück.*" The conductor must wait not only for the breath, but also for the upbeat to the next phrase, "gib mir." By his or her gestures in measure 18 the conductor must arrange that between the first and second chords there is air and space, and by a cut-off gesture must ensure that the bass does not hang on longer than the upper parts, despite the apparent difference of note values.

Measure 19 has several more difficulties. First, one must come to an agreement with the singer as to how he sings the grace notes at the beginning of the bar. These are usually sung as two thirty-second-notes, and one sixteenth. The conductor must make the orchestra coincide *exactly* with that second sixteenth beat. To do this the conductor must be very sensitive to the length of time the singer holds the fermata on the word "*mir*" and not bring the orchestra in late, after the singer glides down into measure 19. The conductor needs to be extremely clear in measure 19 because in that bar the phrase begins, exceptionally, with a sixteenth. All other times that theme appears, e.g. bars 8 and 58, as well as in the Overture, the first note is given as a thirty-second-note.

Having successfully jumped the hurdle of the first fermata, in measure 28 we come to the second. In this bar the orchestra will not expect to wait too long, because they play only one note (whereas the tenor has to sing two, and then take a long breath). Consequently, quite a long gap has to be indicated by the conductor before the second beat.

In measure 34 once again the conductor has to wait a very long time before giving the second beat, because of the singer's need to breathe and take time on the octave jump to the top G. The fermata on the second beat of measure 34 should not be too long, as the singer finds it difficult to get through this *and* the next bar in one breath. Time must be given to make the G sharp tell, and for him to sing the triplet at the beginning of measure 35 broadly. Because he is nearly running out of breath, he will need to sing the last three words "mich ans Ziel" in tempo. Consequently, for the conductor it means conducting measure 35 with the first beat clearly separated from the second and third beats.

The above problem is magnified in measures 41 to 47, because here the singer needs a still longer breath in measure 41 in order to get through the long top note and finish the phrase in one breath. The conductor, having waited before the second beat in measure 41 for the singer to breathe and to sing the octave clearly, must then hurry the next four bars, faster than the main tempo, so that the singer can get to the end of the phrase without gasping. In measure 47 the singer needs a really long time to recover from the difficulties of the previous phrase. The conductor must induce the orchestra to wait that duration before bringing in the second beat. The same is true, to a lesser extent, in measure 50.

Perhaps the most difficult phrase of all, for both singer and conductor, occurs in measures 53 to 55. The phrase is so long, high, and difficult that it is virtually impossible to meet Mozart's requirement of not only a fermata but also a diminuendo. Most singers need measures 53 and 54 to be conducted *faster* than the main tempo. In measure 55, the wise conductor will allow the singer a long time to accomplish the triplet on the first beat, returning to the main tempo for the words "mich ans Ziel."

The above analysis shows how an apparently simple aria can pose huge problems for the conductor. My old boss in Hamburg, Professor Rolf Liebermann, used to say that he could judge a person's feeling for operatic conducting by hearing him do this one short aria.

Training for the opera house

Symphony and opera conducting are similar to this extent: the beat has to be clear. The way you make a rallentando or an accelerando is, of course, virtually the same for both. But, stick technique aside, they are quite different arts.

In the late nineteenth and early twentieth centuries, young conductors usually got their first experience in the opera house. They learned their trade by playing for rehearsals, coaching the singers in their roles, and playing for staging rehearsals, thus being able to learn the importance of the production and the gestures and movements that singers have to make while singing and keeping in tempo. The young répétiteur turning conductor also learned to conduct off-stage. Even now with television monitors it is important that répétiteurs know how to anticipate the beat from a distance when choruses sing off-stage, or when there are brass fanfares off-stage. In my first job at the Sadler's Wells Opera I played oboe in the orchestra, was a répétiteur, assistant conductor, and finally a fully-fledged conductor. One of my first experiences conducting backstage was relaying the beat by means of looking through a hole in the scenery in the Te Deum at the end of the first act of *Tosca*. This opera has a *huge* amount of off-stage activity, and needs a direct link between pit and off-stage. Before the arrival of television monitors, I was that link.

Having acquired some experience conducting off-stage, the young conductor in the old days used to take over repertoire performances which had been fully rehearsed by more experienced conductors. The young apprentice simply took the work over, beating the same number of beats in every bar as his master, but through his personality managed to put his own stamp on the performance. This situation obtains today. Younger conductors take over from the older in later performances. Sometimes the conductor may be ill, or may not be available for all the performances. That is the time when the young conductor gets his (and too rarely her) chance. The young conductor learns from the reaction of the performers, singers, or players, what works and what does not. When the singer is rhythmically not quite together with the orchestra, the conductor must *adjust the tempo* rather than beat harder, faster and more forcefully. One adapts to singers very, very discreetly so that the performance goes on, in general, in fully perfect ensemble, and the audience is none the wiser.

Making the debut

I had conducted a couple of operas as a teenager in Australia, but they were very small fry, such as Mozart's *Bastien und Bastienne*, which I conducted and also orchestrated, there being no original orchestration in Australia at that time. My first professional opera performance, conducting as an apprentice, was *Die Fledermaus* in 1948 at Sadler's Wells, after I had come back from studying conducting in Prague. This masterpiece of operetta is full of passages which are tricky to get together. When you think of the overture to *Die Fledermaus*, with its sudden changes of tempo, its starts, stops and rubato, its polka tunes and waltzes, it is quite a challenge for the young conductor. After *Die Fledermaus* I was given other operas to conduct, some at very short notice. One of the principal conductors in the Sadler's Wells company, Michael Mudie, had a terrible illness, disseminated sclerosis, and was apt to collapse now and then during a performance. I took over *Cavalleria rusticana* and *Pagliacci* at extremely short notice. Sometimes you have to be able to conduct without any rehearsal. When you can do that, you're on your way.

Operas are, in general, *much* more difficult to conduct from a technical point of view than symphonies, and that is why (as explained above) the best conductors in the old days came from the opera. I still feel that, even though many symphonic conductors are obviously extremely talented and successful people, those who start in opera and then move on to the concert podium are the ones who *really* have mastery of their trade. The emanations that a conductor produces, the demeanor and way of performance, will be the same in opera or symphony. However, many of the apparently simplest operas require far more conducting technique and knowledge of players' and singers' reactions than most symphonies. *Tosca*, *La bohème*, and *Pagliacci* are far more difficult to conduct than any Beethoven or Brahms symphony (with the possible exception of the first movement of Beethoven's Symphony No. 5, which has similar problems to the opening of *La bohème*).

Premieres

I've done the first performances of two operas: Britten's *Noye's Fludde* (1958), and Alexander Goehr's *Arden Must Die*, in Hamburg (1967). It is quite difficult to sift out how the music is supposed to go when it has never been done before, but one gets to know it best through the experiences of working with the singers and the orchestra. In the case of *Noye's Fludde*, it was a very special score because it was mainly written for amateurs. Many members of the orchestra and choirs were schoolchildren, playing recorders, bugles and all kinds of things not normally used in an opera. Britten was a superb musician and had firm opinions on how his music should be performed, and was very strict about adherence to what he had written. He said, "I do not wish to be interpreted. I have written what I mean very clearly." He meant it. Britten was wonderful to work with because of his great musicianship, and the fact that he really knew what he wanted. Conducting the music of Shostakovich, in his presence, was a somewhat different experience because I didn't know him as well as I knew Britten, and he was not so dogmatic as to how his music was to be performed.

Manuscripts and editions

Many operas, particularly when first performed, were very carelessly edited and often full of mistakes. Today there is a drive to find out exactly what the composer wrote, even if many of us differ as to how he should be interpreted. In the case of Mozart, Handel, and the older composers, it is always interesting to see the original manuscript. One cannot actually work from facsimiles of the composer's autograph, of course. You have to pick an edition and stick to it. I have prepared my own editions for certain works of Janáček, Mozart, and Handel, but that is because of my particular experience in that field. It is not absolutely necessary for one to have produced an edition of an old masterpiece, but it does help speed up the learning process for the singers if they're told, for example, exactly which appoggiaturas or embellishments to sing. From the mid-nineteenth century onwards, composers were more specific in what they wrote down. This, however, has not prevented singers giving widely different interpretations of well-known roles.

It is a good idea that young conductors themselves delve into singing tutors and performance-practice books of the past. Certain matters, like the ever-present question in eighteenth- and nineteenth-century music of the appoggiatura and its use, *must* be studied by conductors because there is still, unfortunately, a very great deal of ignorance regarding this subject – not because the conductors themselves are unmusical, but because they simply haven't read enough.

Recordings

It is important for a young conductor to listen to recordings when getting to know an opera. How otherwise can he possibly know such performance traditions in Verdi and Puccini as, for instance, the big allargandos and fermatas on top notes? The young conductor is well advised to listen to older traditional performances, even if he decides eventually that the traditions are to be ignored. I know a tremendous number of young musicians today, and even young singers, who don't know these traditions and thus actually take longer to learn the style than they should.

Period performance

I have conducted several operas with period instruments; however, one still has to *conduct* in the modern way in order to get things together. There have been experiments in conducting from the keyboard, the way it used to be done in the days of Handel, Mozart, and Rossini. Although some have been successful with this method, on the whole it is better (in my view) to have a baton-waving conductor even for music of the eighteenth and nineteenth centuries.

The dramaturge and the casting of an opera

There is in most companies nowadays a dramaturge who helps both the producer and the conductor in various aspects of the opera. (In England, the term "producer" equates with the North American "stage director.") It is an extremely useful job. A lot of the preparation work that is done, particularly by producers, can be clarified by the dramaturge before and during the rehearsals.

Casting is a very thorny subject and often the cause of great friction among producer, casting manager, and conductor. Because singing is such a personal thing (the timbre of the voice, the matter of vibrato, and even of intonation), there are often very divergent views concerning the talent of certain singers. These days there are many good singers, but only a few who achieve real stardom. The fees that various singers charge can also be a knotty problem. When some singers start to get very high fees, others of similar standard and reputation will then ask for more money, and so the whole fee structure spirals. It is in the interest of opera managements to keep fees down so that the continual problems of financing the opera will be alleviated.

Removing a singer

This is more common these days, as singers are sometimes engaged several years in advance. I can think of some quite young singers who have grown to stardom very quickly, but were so overworked and in demand they did not have time to learn their new roles properly.

It frequently happens that, having engaged a singer three years earlier, he or she has developed differently from what one expected and their present style of singing is not what is required. Singers are dismissed for various reasons. It happened to me recently that a singer was completely unable to learn the English translation provided and therefore, despite the fact that he was world-famous, had to be dismissed.

Coaching and accompanying

Many conductors started out as pianists. Some are excellent accompanists. It is only necessary to name James Levine, who is not only a superb conductor of opera and symphony, but frequently gives recitals with singers he admires. Some conductors play the piano at their own rehearsals. However, in a musical ensemble rehearsal it is much better for the conductor to conduct and to have an accompanist who plays. It is preferable for the conductor to indicate his tempos and to beat time as he will with the orchestra. This way, the singers learn what to expect.

The coaching strategy depends a great deal on the talent of the singer. Fine singers are not necessarily very good musicians. They may have wonderful voices but are often not very schooled in the theory of music. A lot of them sing more by instinct than by note, and they have to be coached in a special way. There are quite a number of famous singers who don't read music all that fluently. More recently, however, young singers (even Italians!) have become highly educated and sensitive musicians, and risen above the Rossinian concept of "voce, voce, e più voce."

Rehearsal requirements

Rehearsal requirements depend to a large extent on whether the production is new (when a lot of staging rehearsals will be required), or old (and being revived with new singers and a new conductor and perhaps even a new orchestra). Such a revival will require fewer rehearsals than the first run of a new production.

Depending on the difficulty and length of a piece, there will be from two to five orchestra-alone rehearsals, one or two *Sitzproben* (a "sitting rehearsal" with singers and orchestra but no staging), then normally two to four stage and orchestra rehearsals, depending on the length of the work. *Die Meistersinger* requires many more stage and orchestra rehearsals than

La bohème, for example. There is often a pre-dress rehearsal in which the whole work is performed in one rehearsal, or if very long in two rehearsals. The dress rehearsal itself is like a performance, frequently with audience.

One of the difficulties in assessing how many orchestra rehearsals are required is the fact that in many houses the musicians change from one rehearsal to another, so that you do not always have the same orchestra playing in any given performance. This can be a terrible problem. Indeed, conductors such as Simon Rattle have famously refused to conduct operas if the musicians are going to change.

For me, it has become such a fact of life that I no longer worry too much about it, although I try to have as much rehearsal as possible with the orchestra alone, and with the various *Besetzungen* (changes in personnel), so that before we get to the stage, or even the *Sitzproben*, every member of the orchestra has learned the work. When a guest conductor comes to a house for the first time, it is difficult for him or her to tell how many players have actually been to the rehearsals, and how many are extras (i.e., not permanent members). In many cases, in order to save money when extras have to be engaged, management does not give them *any* rehearsal!

Acoustical balance in the house

One of the great difficulties in the opera house is balancing the orchestra with the singers. Many composers have a tendency to over-orchestrate and to write very rich and full-sounding orchestration against one voice. Therefore, it is essential that people should be round about the house during rehearsals, listening. I have always been very pleased to have as many "spies" as possible checking the balance.

The type of voice that might sing any given role will vary from theatre to theatre and performance to performance. The problem in some old opera houses, and even in certain new ones, is that the acoustics are favorable neither to the voices nor the orchestra. The hall is either too dead or too resonant, for instance, or the orchestra is too far underneath the stage to be heard properly. The acoustical design of an opera house is of *extreme* importance.

Language and supertitles

It is very good if the conductor knows the language in which the opera is being sung. Most conductors have a basic knowledge of Italian, German or French. It becomes a little more questionable when the language is Russian,

Czech or Hungarian. The recent interest in Russian operas and additional interest in the operas of Janáček, Dvořák and Smetana has meant that many musicians have tried to learn the Slavonic languages, in order to be able to cope with their difficulties. Most opera houses nowadays have coaches who teach not only the role, but also correct pronunciation and dialect.

Supertitles have pros and cons. In favour of singing in the local language is the argument that one is *supposed* to be able to understand the words, in order that one can really follow the intricacies of the plot and the meaning of the libretto. On the other hand many singers, especially sopranos on high notes, find it almost impossible to make their diction as clear as it should be, and many English-speaking singers tend to sing in English less well than they do in Italian, German, or Russian. Whether this is their fault (because they haven't learned to sing properly in English), or whether it is a fact that in no language can the words be *really* 100 percent clear, is uncertain.

Supertitles are *extremely* useful to the audience in order that they understand everything that is being sung. The titles which are used at the Metropolitan and now in Vienna (electronic screens on the back of the chair in front of you) are the best type, because they do not actually disturb anybody. Many people, especially producers, object to supertitles because they say the audience is looking at them the whole time, instead of watching the opera. There is a certain amount of truth in that, but I find that I myself am not disturbed by supertitles, and still less by this new type which can be switched on or off at will. However, the conductor must ensure that the language is properly translated, and not unintentionally funny. When someone translated the phrase in *Tosca* about giving her *occhi neri*, which means "dark eyes" (the word *nero* means "dark" as well as "black"), the translator put "give her black eyes." This is the kind of mistake which raises titters in the audience at the most serious moments in the opera.

Conflict between stage and music directors

This is a perennial problem. In certain cases the director is more illustrious than the conductor or the singers. In some cases they are equally famous and well regarded. In every case, it is necessary that the stage and music directors work together harmoniously. Riccardo Muti was once doing a production of *La clemenza di Tito* at Salzburg. The producers had started the rehearsals without him, as he was unavailable for the first two weeks. Upon arriving he was told that he would have to adopt the tempos of the *recording* that the two producers had used. The two producers thus insisted that Riccardo Muti use Colin Davis's tempos! Naturally Muti was not going to accept that, even though Colin Davis is a very well-known Mozartian. He walked out. I can't remember whether the conductor who replaced him was docile enough to accept the vinyl tempo, but it gives you a little idea as to what the friction can be like between stage and music directors.

There are also *Konzept* productions of operas, in which the stage directions of the author or composer are given little importance. The producers attempt to present what they consider lies *behind* the actual notes and *behind* the stage directions of the authors. I am rather suspicious of nebulous "concepts," and infinitely prefer the type of production where the spirit, if not the letter, of the stage directions and the actual course of the story is preciselly followed. Many producers, however, consider it their duty *not* to do that, but to produce their own concept of the outer and inner meaning of the work. Their scenery, costumes, ideas, and even the *plot* can be quite different from what the composer intended.

One trend taken to ridiculous lengths is that of changing the milieu and period of an opera. Producers use the specious argument that modern audiences need to be able to empathize with the characters on stage, and can only do this when they see modern rather than period costumes. This very often means that the opera is set in a period when the story could not possibly have happened. This obfuscates the story to the point where no first-time visitor to the opera could possibly understand what is supposed to be going on.

I have seen *Jenufa* updated to a time when communism was in force in Moravia, and so there could be neither a *Kostelnička* (sextoness) nor a mill owner! To update *Kát'a Kabanová*, or place it in Brno in Janáček's time, as some producers have done, is to make a mockery of this particularly Russian setting and its nineteenth-century social and sexual mores. Sillier still is updating Verdi's *Otello* to modern Cyprus, again because none of the incidents in the opera could possibly take place in a twentieth-century milieu. I have seen the chorus cut from *Eugene Onegin* because its director imagined the opera as a Chekhov play. The same director arranged that "The Dance of the Comedians," one of the most brilliant pieces in Smetana's *Bartered Bride*, be played on a honky-tonk piano because he had decreed that the Comedians were performing in a local village hall and therefore a full symphony orchestra would be inappropriate! On that occasion the conductor meekly agreed to the mutilation of this great orchestral showpiece. I would have walked out.

Scandalous productions of operas in which the original meaning is either distorted or completely altered are often considered very successful. For me the ideal production is one which obeys the wishes of the author and the composer. One must respect them, whatever changes in taste or fashion may suggest.

As regards the relative importance of conductor and producer, it has become a question of "pecking order." In the early twentieth century, the conductor was the boss and he dictated how the producer should stage an opera. He even chose the scenery. In recent years, however, the situation has reversed. The producer now has complete control over the design, the staging, and even the music. To an older conductor like myself, the complete ascendancy of the producer over the musician has largely ruined the pleasure of working in opera.

Looking back over fifty years

The business has changed unrecognizably, chiefly because there are some countries and some governments that regard opera as being a hobby for the rich, and who think all classical music is elitist. This is particularly unfortunate when the people in charge of doling out the cash for artistic enterprises are themselves so philistine as to believe the only true barometer of popularity is the number of records sold. In Vienna, the opera performances are frequently discussed in Parliament, but in England and America, politicians nowadays are largely interested in pop music.

I have a very wide repertoire, from Purcell to Shostakovich, Mozart to Britten. I know that these composers are no longer contemporary, but I have generally looked to music of the past for inspiration and like to leave the music of the future to the younger generation. It is impossible for me to describe the Mackerras signature in the pit, but I hope it means, above all, setting the right tempo, and balance among the various parts in the orchestra and between stage and orchestra in order that the singers can be clearly heard, with the different strands in the orchestra distinctly brought out. In the end, it all comes down to experience of what *works* in the theatre.

7 The orchestra speaks

ROBERT L. RIPLEY

The day has finally come. You are about to have your first encounter with a "major orchestra." The first rehearsal is at ten a.m. You arrive at the hall in good time. The orchestra manager greets you cordially and says he will introduce you to the orchestra. It is 9.59. You stand in the wings. The orchestra is tuning. Now all is quiet. The manager escorts you on to the stage, and gives you a nice introduction. There is a smattering of polite applause. You mount the podium, and say how happy and honored you are to be there. You are ready to begin. The first work to be rehearsed is the Beethoven *Consecration of the House* Overture, and the players have been apprised of this. (You like those nice big opening chords!) You give a good hefty downbeat and . . . nothing happens! In a split second, you say to yourself, "What's wrong?!" Then you hear it; the chord is late. But why? You start the next chord and the same thing happens. So it goes, through the next three chords. Almost inadvertently, the orchestra is sending you two messages: (1) We want to be led. (2) Not one of us will play until we are sure that everybody else is playing. An orchestra – especially a major orchestra, with a large budget – develops an instinct as to when to play. They know that their jobs are on the line with every note. It is uncanny, but it works. They all play exactly together. To you, the young conductor, they are late. To them, they are right on time.

I learned the lesson of the delayed response when I joined the Cleveland Orchestra after World War Two, in the first season of George Szell's tenure. He opened his first rehearsal with the Beethoven "Eroica." I was eager to do everything just right, and was nervous. I had heard of Szell's reputation as a taskmaster, so when the downbeat came, I played exactly with it – all by myself. I thought I had lost my job, but Szell never batted an eye, though he surely heard it, along with the whole orchestra. Needless to say, I never made that mistake again.

To a conductor, a major orchestra is like a freight train. It has to be cajoled and pulled along. Once it gets going, things go more easily; but there is always this bit of lag, especially on chords. So *The Consecration of the House* was a poor choice for an opening salvo. Besides the slow introduction, it is all pretty academic and stilted. You would do better with a Berlioz overture (NOT *Le corsaire*!), or perhaps Dvořák's *Carnival* Overture, or one of many others. You, the orchestra, and the audience, would be happier and the rest of your concert will be better received if you start with something familiar.

The rehearsal

Orchestras want to be led and conductors want to lead them. A young conductor is often concerned to demonstrate a point of view and show initiative, but a major orchestra will immediately recognize a new point of view. They will size up a new conductor immediately; from the moment you walk in. Did you notice that they looked sort of blank when you got up on to the podium? They are saying "Show us!"

As a guest conductor, you will probably find that you have only four rehearsals. The Music Director gets five. The management may even say "no overtime." It is not the most cordial way to treat a guest, but that is the way it is. You must use your time to the best advantage: *plan carefully*.

The most productive approach from the players' standpoint is the formula: "play through, work out (and then later), play through again." Do not, under any circumstances, start working on things right away in your first runthrough. It will all be a total waste of time, and will alienate you from the orchestra immediately. You might as well go home. No matter what happens, just play the thing through – overture, symphony movement, whatever. Of course if there is a total breakdown, you have to start again where you left off, but that should never happen, because the first piece you rehearse should be something familiar. So play it through, but do not try to do everything in this first playthrough. Give the orchestra a general sense of your conception of the piece with good hand signals. Leave balance, intonation, ensemble, etc., for your working out; but remember what you want to correct, or change. This is important. You must be able to remember what you want to do. (You could even mark the score as you go along, to remind you.)

When you have played the piece through once, go back to the beginning and set to work adjusting things. All this may take quite a bit of time, so never go back to the beginning again after working through the piece. (It is bad psychology and the orchestra will think you are treating them like children.) If you have more time, take up something else. Go back to the first piece the next day, or that afternoon. A good orchestra will not forget what you want, especially if you indicate it with your conducting technique.

There can be some variation of this formula; in the event that you are doing Mahler, Bruckner, or something where the movements are very long, it only makes sense to do the movements in sections. Use your own best judgment, but when you play through the movement again, remember that your motions should be designed to remind the players of what you have already told them. Pierre Monteux was a man of few words and economical gestures. He conducted quietly but absolutely clearly. If he wanted to emphasize a great, quick crescendo, he simply raised his baton about six inches and said, quietly, "And here." The whole roof would blow off!

There are, of course, many examples of how not to start a rehearsal. Leonard Bernstein occasionally came to conduct the Boston Symphony. He always came on stage ten minutes late and then spent ten minutes more greeting old buddies. We lost twenty minutes already. Bernstein conducted with much fervor and sometimes outlandish gestures, but the orchestra sounded marvellous. About ten minutes before the end of the rehearsal, he would yell out, "I *must* have overtime!" There is nothing more infuriating for an orchestra than to have overtime suddenly thrust upon them, especially if they have already lost twenty minutes. It upsets afternoon obligations, such as teaching schedules, and many contracts now provide that all overtime must be pre-announced. Be aware that this announcement today might cost you a hefty fee or players simply walking off. The management won't be happy paying for it either and will remember this when time comes to ask you back. What Lennie wanted, however, Lennie got. He was "L.B." and "Big Box Office." Bernstein was, after all, a genius, a great conductor, and very likeable. Someone asked his father what he thought about his son's great success, and he said, "How did I know he would turn out to be Leonard Bernstein?"

The first time Ormandy conducted the Boston Symphony, he came on stage and said how wonderful it was to be there with us. He said, "It has been a lifelong dream of mine to conduct the Boston Symphony – and now, finally, I am doing it. Now I have lived – now I can die!" Then he said, "What would you like to start with?" Without waiting for an answer, which of course he would not get anyway, he said, "I think we should start with the Hindemith, don't you? Yes, let's start with Hindemith." Orchestras do not like rhetorical questions. He was a very good conductor, though, and you have to give him credit for being able to follow a huge presence like Stokowski, and last for over forty years! His best lines were "I guess you thought I was conducting, but I wasn't," and "I purposely didn't do anything, and you were all behind."

Power and respect

Creating a rapport with your orchestra is crucial. If you can develop respect between the orchestra and the conductor, you are on solid ground, and the orchestra will play its very best for you. If you are doing a new piece, the orchestra will want to show you how well they read. They will go all out just to hear you say, "Wonderful!" But be careful how much you say. Bernard Haitink has a beautiful rapport with the Boston Symphony. It was virtually "love at first note." Everything he says is succinct, businesslike, and eminently correct musically.

In the players' view, the less you talk the better. Arthur Rodzinski put it well: "Less talk, more sixteen [sic] notes." Still, it depends what you have to say. Erich Leinsdorf talked quite a bit, and he liked to tell the story of the piece, if there was one. He would say, "Of course you know the story of this?" and of course, the orchestra would reply, "No!" He would then tell us the story in some detail. That kind of talk is fine. The more he talks, the less we have to play.

The more you talk, however, the more careful you will need to be with what you say. Talking in rehearsal is a form of power and it can lead an orchestra to assert its own power, sometimes without a conductor realizing it. When Leinsdorf first came to the BSO, we soon discovered that he had a favorite word: "juxtaposition." He talked about "the juxtaposition of the thematic material between the strings and the winds." Soon it was "juxta-position this" and "juxtaposition that." Finally, I said to my stand-partner, "The next time he says that, let's give him some applause." (Since our hands are busy in an orchestra, we applaud by scraping our feet.) It was not long before he said it again, and we "applauded." Soon, the whole cello section picked it up, and then the whole orchestra. This went on for a few days, and he seemed not to notice. Then one day, he suddenly caught on. He said, "The juxta . . ." – noticed the "applause" – and that was it. He never used that word again. Talk if you like, but except for stories or jokes, your talking had better have something really good to contribute to the performance. And remember, do not talk at all until you have done one playthrough.

Another ingredient in creating rapport is the physical set-up. The players sit in a semicircle around the podium. Remember that this set-up feels like school if you are sitting in the orchestra; there is the teacher with the nondescript pupils sitting around. You are bound to feel a sense of power when you mount the podium – not to mention having that stick in your hand! Be careful how you use this power. You are nothing without the orchestra, but the orchestra could play without you, as has been done many times.

Gennadi Rozhdestvensky, one of our great contemporary Russian con-ductors, does not use a podium. He is a short man, but he likes to walk around while he is conducting, sometimes into the orchestra, even in con-cert. He has quirky, funny little conducting patterns, alternating between stick and left hand. He is loads of fun and keeps rehearsals short. He is also an exceptionally fine conductor. *The Rite of Spring* with him was the best

I ever played. I happened to run across him in Japan a few years ago in a record store. I introduced myself, and asked him if he was looking for his records. He said, "Noooo. Too boring!" Not taking yourself too seriously as a conductor might seem impossible, but it is essential to win the orchestra's best playing.

Ultimately, though, an orchestra is most interested in the quality of the music making. Not using a podium and saying "we" instead of "you" will help, but it won't paste over musical weakness. John Barbirolli came to Boston as guest conductor in January 1959, having succeeded Toscanini at the New York Philharmonic in 1936. He was young then (thirty-seven) and bore the burden of comparison with Toscanini. He was much maligned by the press, and it seemed not to be a happy experience for him in general. He stayed only seven years before returning to his native England. Over the years, the impression had lingered in America that Barbirolli was not much of a conductor – but here he was in Boston, many years later. What were we getting? He was a very slight man, modest in bearing and soft of speech. He started with Brahms's Symphony No. 2, a piece the BSO had played dozens of times, and he spent an hour and a half on it doing quite the opposite of what I have been advocating here. He picked and fussed about every detail, but it soon became apparent that this man was a fine musician, and that everything he said contributed to a better performance. His attitude was so loving and cherishing that we were only too happy to obey him. When he eventually finished, at intermission, the entire orchestra rose spontaneously in a standing ovation! Imagine! A major orchestra, applauding a conductor for a rehearsal of Brahms's Second! It was one of the most moving experiences of my musical life. Needless to say, it was a fine performance.

The great conductor (for an orchestra)

To articulate what makes a great conductor is nearly impossible, but they are all businesslike, know exactly what they want, have excellent musical taste, are not sarcastic, and treat the players with respect. They inspire the players to do their best in the sense that they make them *want* to do their best. A rapport develops as the work unfolds, and you find yourself giving a standing ovation, as in the case of Barbirolli, or at least, having conversation at intermission, such as, "Boy, this guy is really good!"

Haitink is typical; it is all business and one feels the player is being treated as an equal. He took the BSO on a European Festivals tour in 2001, and demanded extra rehearsals. Orchestras do not like to rehearse a lot on tour. It is fatiguing, and the repertoire should be well rehearsed before the trip.

Figure 7.1 Charles Munch conducting the Boston Symphony Orchestra in 1956 with Zino Francescatti as the violin soloist. The author is seated in the cello section, directly above the head of the soloist

He got his way but the orchestra didn't mind (really), because the concerts just got better and better! He knows exactly what the orchestra needs, but it is hard to say more . . . The better a conductor is, the less you know why. Rozhdestvensky humbles himself immediately by not using the podium, and then keeps the rehearsals short; he trusts the orchestra. This is all good psychology and makes an orchestra just want to play better. I played with de Burgos once thirty years ago, but other players tell me he is also excellent. He trusts the orchestra and does not repeat a lot. He seems to be satisfied that if it is good today, it will still be good tomorrow. Barbirolli was an exception. He was a nit-picker, as I said earlier, but he was so cherishing – so loving of every bit of the music – that you just got carried along with him. The BSO loved Charles Munch, partly because he followed Serge Koussevitzky. They couldn't believe a conductor could be so nice. It was too good to be true, but it was. Eventually the orchestra did suffer, and the critics were not kind. But the orchestra made some beautiful records, because he listened, and corrected things. I now prefer the more free-wheeling BSO "Eroica" with Munch to Szell's recording with the perfect Cleveland Orchestra.

Marek Janowski first came to the BSO about ten years ago as a last-minute substitute for Giuseppe Sinopoli, who was ill. We had never heard of him, but he took charge immediately, adjusting balance very much like Szell. The program began with the *Meistersinger* Overture, followed by one of the Schumann symphonies. The most extraordinary thing happened: the orchestra sounded entirely different from Wagner to Schumann! I never heard such a change in sound from one composer to another, not even with Szell. The whole orchestra was raving about him and people started talking about him as a successor to Ozawa.

Reminders from the players

Many of these will seem obvious to you, but you might be surprised to know how often they are overlooked.

1. *Know the score!*

   Not just the principal parts, but every last note of every instrument. Stravinsky said, "A good conductor is one who has the score in his head, and not his head in the score." Well, the two times I played with him, he had his head deep in the score (and he conducted only his own works). He was not a very good conductor, but what he said was right.

2. *Speak up!*

   The acoustics on the stage are usually not as good as in the hall, so be sure you are reaching everybody. The "back stands" of the string sections, starting with the third stand, are generally neglected. All too often, the back stands have no idea what is going on up front. Look at them when you have something to say to the strings and reach out to them as you conduct the sections; remember too that the basses are far away. You may think that they are not watching you, but they are. If they feel you are engaged with them, and with the music, it will make all the difference in the sound you get. Communicate with the entire orchestra! When a score would call for reduced strings, Stokowski would always have the very last stands play. It kept them on their toes, gave them a sense of belonging, and sounded wonderful.

3. *Keep your remarks positive.*

   Avoid saying "Don't." Instead of "Trumpet, don't play so loud, you're killing the oboe," say "Trumpet, a little less," or better, just indicate it with your hand; a little hand motion is fast, effective and unlikely to embarrass anyone.

4. *Never be sarcastic and don't lose your cool.*

   While it is hard to articulate what an orchestra likes, it is easy to say what we hate. When I was in Cleveland with Szell, we played the Brahms Violin Concerto in Akron on a Tuesday night. Szell was "milking" the oboist in his big solo at the beginning of the second movement for all he was worth. When he finished, the oboist made a "gimme a break" gesture (like brushing a fly from in front of you). The next day, there was a rehearsal with the chorus for the season finale of Beethoven's Ninth. Szell became more and more impatient and finally blew his top in the scherzo, banging his music stand in tempo, and yelling, "I'll teach you to play in rhythm****!" The committee chairman ran to the phone to call the union President and tell him that Szell was acting like a madman and swearing at the orchestra. (The union President was actually useless against a character like Szell!) When the timpanist came to the all-pervasive rhythmic figure in the scherzo, he played it right on the button. Szell yelled, "Good!" (although it must have made him furious to have to admit it.) Then, at some point he stopped, giving some very grumpy instructions, and he yelled in the same sentence to the oboist, "And when I want *espressivo*, I want *espressivo!*" It was all, of course, about the Brahms the previous night, but knowing that didn't make it all any more fun. After a couple of days, the oboist gave Szell a bottle of wine with a card saying "from a repentant sinner," and we concluded the season. The committee did talk with the manager, but the manager replied with the reports that this was our best ever performance. We did not forget this incident at contract time.

5. *Don't "conduct the mice."*
Keep your hands above your waist, so everybody can see them. This is often forgotten.

6. *Give clear cues.*
Cues are important for the confidence of the players, especially if they have had a long stretch of rests to count. Harpists, percussionists and the tuba will thank you.

7. *Conducting from memory is dangerous.*
Do not risk finding out your memory is faulty by painful experience. Use the score and *turn the pages.* Do not find yourself fumbling for your place; the orchestra is long gone ahead of you. Many conduct at least the standard repertoire from memory, but you must have every note mastered. Someone asked Steinberg how he memorized. He answered, in his gruff way, "I don't memorize! I know it!"

The only conductor, to my knowledge, who not only conducted without the score in concerts, but also in rehearsals, was Dimitri Mitropoulos. He was a wonderful conductor and a great man. He also evidently had a "photographic memory." He knew every rehearsal letter, or number, or the measure numbers in everything he conducted: *Wozzeck*, Schoenberg, Wagner, Strauss operas – everything. Even more incredibly, when he came as guest conductor to Cleveland, he had all the names of the orchestra members memorized. He told someone that he had done it on the way out on the train. I am sure he did that with all orchestras.

Seiji Ozawa comes a close second to Mitropoulos. He conducts all of his concerts from memory, except perhaps a new concerto accompaniment. Still, he always has the score in front of him, on the music stand, unopened. His memory is prodigious and he spends several hours a day memorizing scores. He knows all operas, as well as every orchestral work. It can be done, but do not take any risks.

8. *The baton is only a tool.*

The choice to use a baton is completely up to you. When Leinsdorf came to Boston he was not using a baton. His motions were sometimes difficult to follow, so the Artistic Committee, upon direction of the players, asked him to use a baton. He was surprisingly nice about it, but it did not help much. We asked him to go back to the hands. The point is, your beat must be clear, baton or not.

9. *Save your best for the concert.*

Koussevitzky always gave his all in rehearsal; whatever was being played at that moment was the most important thing in the world (in his world, anyway). Saving something for the concert, however, can spark the orchestra and make for a better concert.

Claudio Abbado was quite low-key in rehearsals. When he came to America, he knew almost no English, so did not talk much. He used a miniature score, and when he would stop the orchestra, he would hold the score right up to his face. After what seemed to be a long study he would take the score down and say, almost inaudibly, "Is *piano*? Is *pianissimo*?" It was not terribly inspiring. But in the concerts, suddenly he was on fire! It was a tremendous boost to the orchestra, so unexpected the first time, and of course, it made concerts really exciting.

While every conductor has to develop an individual style of rehearsing, if you perceive restlessness in the orchestra, you are doing something wrong. Is your tempo too slow? Are you following, instead of leading? Are you communicating? Are you talking too much? Pay attention to the faces of those around you and react accordingly.

10. *Mark your bowing in the parts and in your score.*

Working out bowings can be tedious in rehearsals. It takes time, and the rest of the orchestra has nothing to do, becomes bored, and you lose discipline. It is best to work on bowings separately with the principal string players. Once you have made decisions, and put the bowings into the parts, put them in your score, too. Many conductors will bring their own parts, with all their bowings, markings, dynamics, etc. in them. Of course, this is not to say that there can never be changes, but it does save a lot of time to have things already marked.

11. *Don't skip intonation.*

Working on intonation is a bit wearing, too, but must be done. For multiple voices, always build a chord from the bottom note up. Do not just have everybody simply play the chord. Sometimes it is clear that one or another instrument is out of tune, but if not, then build from the lowest note.

12. *Don't conduct* only *the melody.*

It has been said, "Don't conduct the melody." That is a bit of a misnomer; you are not going to conduct the bass line. What this really means is, don't conduct *only* the melody. While you must communicate with whoever is carrying the ball at any given point, there are also elements of balance to adjust along the way, with the left hand, and whatever may come up at any moment. Szell was a master at this. One felt that he was over the whole orchestra all the time. It was a marvel to watch him conduct the fugue in the Hindemith *Symphonic Metamorphosis on Themes by Weber*. Szell also had an apprentice program in Cleveland, and it was interesting to watch him work with the budding conductors. He was a born teacher. He never took a conducting lesson in his life; but he made a pest of himself around the opera houses asking questions of everybody, conductors, players, singers, and stagehands. He knew everything and was only too happy to let you know it. He said three things which have stuck in my mind: (1) Remember that the orchestra has played the piece many more times than you have conducted it (unless it is brand new), so do not waste their time with your needs. (2) Never stop the orchestra without telling them why. (3) Remember that you have a wrist. It can be very helpful.

13. *Learn about the players.*

You do not have to be a Mitropoulos, but do learn at least the names of the principal players. They will appreciate it. Ask if there are brief biographies; you will have a better appreciation of the depth of their abilities. Even more importantly, get and read a copy of their contract (most are available on the Internet). The personnel or orchestra manager will tell you what you need to know about rehearsal limits, but reading the actual contract will give you a better sense of how the whole organization functions.

14. *Use a metronome.*

A metronome is absolutely indispensable. You should not be a slave to it, but you need it for reference, and to set boundaries. Szell had a big fight with Nathan Milstein about rushing in the Tchaikovsky Violin Concerto. He told Milstein that he was rushing. Milstein denied it (all the while, chewing on a cigarette holder: no cigarette, just the holder). Szell said, "Look, I have a metronome in my arm (grabbing his right forearm), and you are rushing!" Well, it turned out to be a beautiful performance, somehow. A few years later, Szell decided he would play a Mozart piano concerto with us, conducting from the piano. (He was a wonderful pianist.) He was very nervous about it and had extra rehearsals. In the final rehearsal, he began rushing in the finale! He stopped and said, "Now if I go ahead here a little bit, you simply must come with me!"

When Stokowski came to Cleveland for two weeks, he tried to get us to loosen up, without much success, saying, "I'm sorry. Some morning, your wife is going to wake up and find a metronome in bed beside her!" When Szell returned, he cried, "What's the matter? What's the matter? Two weeks with Stokowski, and you can't play a straight 4/4?"

15. Don't use every last second.

Even though you are entitled to use every bit of your rehearsal time, try to avoid doing it. Don't make the personnel manager come on stage to be sure that you stop on time. Show your confidence in the players by trusting their professionalism to that extent. This is just a bit of psychology, but it may enhance your relationship between conductor and players. You won't lose a thing by doing this and it is a gracious gesture that will be much appreciated.

Our common objective

What is a symphony orchestra? We are about one hundred in number. We are a microcosm of society, in politics, religion, interests, income – everything. Yet we must unite in producing the one thing we have in common: music. Your task, as conductor, is to bring this unity to realization. You must inspire us to forget the differences among us. We need each other and our objective is clearly identical: producing the highest quality of performance. We have all devoted countless hours, days and years to perfecting our musical skills. To excel on a musical instrument requires more years of study than almost any other field of endeavor. Isaac Stern said, "It takes five years to learn how to play the violin badly." Maintaining musical skill is a never-ending process. There is no real vacation for an instrumental musician. (Paderewski is purported to have said, "If I don't practice for one day, I know it. If I don't practice for two days, the critics know it. If I don't practice for three days, the public knows it.")

The American Symphony Orchestra League reports that there are twenty-one major orchestras in the United States and three in Canada, determined by the size of the budget. Adding Europe, Japan, and South America there might be a total of forty great orchestras, each with about one hundred players – only four thousand people out of the world's billions. There are far fewer great conductors, but we are both becoming endangered species. With our similar backgrounds and similar objectives, it should be natural to maintain mutual respect as we go about our work. Recall, if you will, our remarks about the physical arrangement of the stage, and the feeling of power generated for the conductor by simply standing on a podium! Yes, you are in charge, but it is a privilege for all of us to be doing what we do. Will you join us in harmony and humility before our mutual objective of excellence of performance?

In the end, it is not about either of us. Let the music govern. If you are inspired, you will inspire the orchestra, and the right things will happen.

PART TWO

History

8 The rise of conducting

JOSÉ ANTONIO BOWEN

The history of conducting is hardly a linear progression of technical watersheds. The modern practice of conducting emerges slowly over several generations, but through a variety of different practices in different countries, genres and venues. During the first half of the nineteenth century, audible time-beating, different forms of divided leadership, and violin-bow direction all continue, with experiments in where to stand, which way to face, what to hold and generally what to do to bring order as larger ensembles struggle to play increasingly complex music.

To complicate things further, the rise of conducting happens while other aspects of European music-making are changing. The eighteenth-century musician may not have had a high place in society, but it was a clear place. The Kapellmeister was either a civil or high-level private servant charged with providing musical events from start to finish. This would generally include composing, copying, rehearsing, and performing the music. Musicians "wrote" music largely as notes for their own performances. Then technological changes made cheap music printing and mass-produced pianos possible. Political and economic changes ended the wealth of many royal patrons, who disbanded their orchestras and "freed" the musicians, creating a new middle-class market for their services. While musicians tried to piece together a living from teaching, composing, and performing (in both private and the new public concerts), music-making fragmented. The ability to purchase a piece of music on paper (instead of hiring musicians to perform) was a profound shift. The ability to compose for an unseen and unsophisticated public changed the nature of scores (which gradually incorporated details that would previously have been either assumed or given orally in rehearsal) and led to new ways of thinking about musical production. Composers now produced musical works (which had to be protected with new copyright laws) while others could learn simply to read notes and play an instrument. The very definition of a musician had changed.

Today, we routinely classify musicians as either composers or performers, but the early conductors were both. Conducting emerged simultaneously with the rise of an independent performer who was a "mere" interpreter of another's work. The role of these new musical interpreters in performing a canon of great musical works quickly became a topic of discussion in the (also new) musical press. At first, conductors were hardly capable of interpreting at all; conductors and music critics alike seemed content if orchestras played without major mishap. The gradual increase of power and ability into the conductor's baton, however, raised questions about how it should be used. Not everyone was pleased when Liszt tried to transfer his virtuoso style from the piano to the podium or Wagner learned to control the tempo of the music in midstream. Some pleaded that the conductor should serve the composer, but the power, prestige and money gradually shifted to conductors, who became the focus of modern music-making.

Early leadership

Musical leadership (if not also conducting) has existed since musicians began to gather together in groups. For small groups, eye contact or a head nod still works and is often unnoticed by all but the musicians. Larger groups require more formal leadership. Not surprisingly, one of the earliest reports of a huge ensemble (eight hundred performers in 709 BC) also comes with a report of "Pherekydes of Patrae, giver of Rhythm," who sat on a high seat, surrounded by the players waving his golden staff so that the "men began in one and the same time" and beating "with his stave up and down in equal movements so that all might keep together."[1]

While the baton has no musical properties, it has long been a symbol of power: the Pope has his staff and the Queen her sceptre. A mace too is a large club that symbolizes authority; it is still carried in university processions and set before the Speaker in the House of Commons. Military leaders also adopted this symbol of power, which may be how drum majors began to use a large mace (grasped in the middle) to lead marching bands in the seventeenth century. Even in the nineteenth century, Spontini still grasped a thick staff in the middle like an orchestral field-marshal and used it not to beat time, but to command. Jean-Baptiste Lully (1632–87), the Maître de musique for Louis XIV, also used *une canne*, a very large stick which he banged on the floor as required. In 1687, while conducting 150 musicians in a performance of his *Te Deum*, he beat perhaps too forcefully and stabbed his toe with the sharp point. He refused to allow his physician to remove the gangrenous toe and died two months later.[2] Audible time-keeping continued in French opera until the nineteenth century, although later conductors were more careful.

In vocal music, however, there is a long tradition of using the hands. Hands are capable of more varied signs and there are many ancient and modern systems for indicating pitch or melodic shape with the hands.[3] In some cases, the shape of hand signals used as a mnemonic aid for melodies became the basis for later notational systems.[4] Medieval choir directors held a staff in the left hand as a symbol of office, but led the choir with the right hand. In the eighteenth century, a rolled-up paper was used to beat time for large choral groups. This was replaced by the baton for the large choral festivals of the nineteenth century, but for small *a cappella* choirs, conducting with the hands remains traditional to this day.[5]

With the rise of rhythmically complicated polyphonic choral music, it became necessary to coordinate the different parts with a visible pulse, and many sixteenth-century treatises give instructions for how to mark the *tactus*. Some authors complain about audible time-beating and generally prescribe a simple up and down motion of the hand to control the music. Koch tells us that the strong beat is called a "down-beat" because the hand moves down on this beat and up on the weaker beats.[6] Rousseau tells us that the Italians also beat time up and down, but that the French additionally move the hand to the left and right.[7] In 1701, lexicographer Thomas Janowka describes *tactus* for an ordinary measure as a right-hand movement of down, left, right, up: the pattern that became the standard.[8] Until the early nineteenth century, either silent or audible time-beating (*tactieren*) with batons, rolled-up papers or the hands remained largely a church-choir activity (see Fig. 8.1),[9] while directing (*dirigieren*) with an instrument (i.e. leading by example with a keyboard or the violin) was the standard procedure for opera or instrumental music. This was a reflection of the differing musical styles and conventions, but also of practical logistics; the more scattered the forces for a large choral work, the more likely there was to be a time-beater.

Keyboard and violin leaders

As the *basso continuo* became the rhythmic engine of seventeenth-century music, it became easy for the keyboard player to lead. The keyboard player was often the Kapellmeister, who organized, rehearsed, and usually composed the music, and the keyboard was always part of the ensemble. While the right hand could add notes, it could also be raised to signal an entrance, while the left hand continued to play the bass line. If things began to fall apart, both hands could quickly pound out a rhythm, returning the conductor from the role of a signal-giver to that of an audible time-keeper. C. P. E. Bach advocated keyboard leadership on precisely these grounds:

> The keyboard, entrusted by our fathers with full command, is in the best position to assist not only with the other bass instruments, but the entire ensemble in maintaining a uniform pace . . . The tone of the keyboard,

Figure 8.1 Frontpiece of Johann Gottfried Walther, *Musiklexicon* (1732). Johann Kuhnau beats time with two rolls of paper in the Thomas-Kirche and has his back to the band. The organist pictured is thought to be J. S. Bach.

correctly placed, stands in the center of the ensemble and can be heard clearly by all . . . Should someone hasten or drag, he can be most readily corrected by the keyboardist, for the others will be too much concerned with their own figures and syncopations to be of any assistance.[10]

Playing the melody and standing in front, the violinist was also in a good position to lead by example. As musical style changed during the eighteenth century and the keyboard bass was gradually eliminated, the leader (in England), *Konzertmeister* (in Germany), *premier violin* (in France) or *capo d'orchestra* (in Italy) could lead the orchestra by beating the neck of the violin in the air, making other movements or simply playing louder (again leading by sound rather than by sight). Flautist Johann Joachim Quantz and violinist Leopold Mozart lobbied in favor of violin leadership, arguing that melodic nuances were more important than the rhythmic and harmonic control possible at the keyboard.[11]

As the keyboard disappeared from orchestral music at the close of the eighteenth century, it appeared that the violinists would triumph, as they did indeed in France.[12] In England, Italy, and Germany, however, opera and concert music in the eighteenth and early nineteenth century were most often led by some form of divided or alternating leadership, although these arrangements varied greatly. Composers like Bach, Haydn and Mozart could lead from either position depending on the situation. In German and Italian opera houses, the violinist was responsible for the orchestra and led the instrumental music, while the performer at the keyboard focused on the singers. Even the Gewandhaus Orchestra in Leipzig, the first orchestra devoted exclusively to symphonic music rather than opera, retained this model of alternating leadership.

Gewandhaus

From its founding in 1781 until Mendelssohn became its first baton conductor in 1835, the Gewandhaus had four keyboard conductors: Johann Adam Hiller (1728–1804), Johann Gottfried Schicht (1753–1823), Johann Philipp Christian Schultz (1773–1827), and Christian August Pohlenz (1790–1843). Initially they beat time from the keyboard; it is reported that Hiller planned to beat time for two measures before the beginning of Beethoven's Symphony No. 5, but not all of the players remembered the plan and the symphony had to be restarted.[13] While these men continued to sit at the keyboard, they eventually "conducted" only the numbers with singers, the arias and duets that separated the symphony movements, and the concluding piece of each half, which was usually a grand chorus from an opera or oratorio. The instrumental music, which was increasingly seen as the serious portion of the evening, was led by the concertmaster, who stood, as did all the musicians until 1905.[14]

Beethoven's Symphony No. 9 created unprecedented challenges. From 1817 until Mendelssohn's arrival, the first three movements were led by the concertmaster Heinrich August (Karl) Matthäi, but since the final movement involved the chorus, it was "conducted" from the keyboard. As Wagner witnessed in 1830, this arrangement was insufficient for the challenges of the new music.

> At that time, this institution was run in a very casual manner: instrumental works were not led by any conductor but rather by the first violinist (Mathäi [sic]) from his desk; but as soon as any singing began, the prototype of all fat and happy music directors, the highly popular Pohlenz, would appear at the conductor's stand with a very imposing blue baton. One of the strangest events was the annual performance [from 1828–30 and 1834–37] of Beethoven's Ninth Symphony in this manner: after the first three movements had been played through like a Haydn symphony by the orchestra on its own as best it could, Pohlenz would appear, not to direct an Italian aria, a vocal quartet, or a cantata, but to undertake this most difficult test of a conductor's skill . . . Pohlenz sweated blood but the recitative never came off, and I really began to wonder uneasily whether Beethoven had not written nonsense after all.[15]

Most music, of course, did not require this level of leadership. Once started, even most Beethoven symphonies could be played by following the concert-master, who was also allowed to lead concertos until 1843.[16] Similarly, a few notes from the keyboard were enough to keep choral music from crashing to a halt. As the complexity of music increased, however, both violin and keyboard conductors proved to be inadequate.

Divided leadership in England

From Handel to Mendelssohn, English musical life was dominated by all things German, but what in German practice was largely alternating leadership between the keyboard and the first violin became an established system of divided leadership in England. For the "Grand Commemoration of Handel" of 1784 at Westminster Abbey, the 525 performers were jointly led by Joah Bates (1741–99) who led the choirs from the organ, and England's leading violin-bow conductor, Wilhelm Cramer (1746–89), who directed the orchestra.[17] When Haydn came to London in 1791 and 1792, he sat at the keyboard while Johann Peter Salomon, the impresario who had arranged the concerts, led from the violin.[18] From the middle of the eighteenth until the middle of the nineteenth century, English concert notices were unique in listing two directors for most performances. At least some of this continued attachment to divided leadership was due to the cooperative nature of the Philharmonic Society.

The Philharmonic Society was established in 1813 with a fiercely democratic set of laws; women were offered full membership, program decisions were made by the directors, and both the violin "leader" and the member "at the pianoforte" rotated for each concert. Music critic George Hogarth described the division of conducting duties:

> The duty of the leader was not only to execute his own part with exemplary accuracy and firmness, but to attend to all the other performers, who were to look to him for the time of the movements, and to be governed by his beat. His coadjutor, at the pianoforte, and with the full score before him, was to watch the performance and to be ready to correct any mistake. This method, borrowed from the usages (far from uniform) of foreign theatrical and other orchestras, was liable to obvious objections. Neither of these functionaries could efficiently perform his duties separately, and they could not perform them jointly without interfering and clashing with each other. The leader could not execute his own part properly, and at the same time attend to, and beat time to, the whole band; while the person at the pianoforte could scarcely exercise any influence on the "going" of the performance without coming into collision with the leader.[19]

Over the next forty years, this increasingly out-of-date system, and the restriction of having only a single rehearsal, forced the Philharmonic to limit its repertoire to older and easier works.[20] The press began to complain about both standards of playing and the repetition of the same repertoire.[21] Critics like Henry Chorley, who had heard continental orchestras, were quick to point out the benefits of increased central control.

> No unfortunate flute there chirps half a note before its time, – no plethoric bassoon drops one of its thick Satyrlike tones in the midst of a pause, – no horn totters on the edge of coarse and mail-coach falseness when the tug of difficulty comes![22]

Given this history, London would seem an unlikely destination for conductors, but as the Society became wealthier it began to commission works and to hire famous guest conductors.

Spohr and the baton

According to legend, initiated by his own account, Louis Spohr (1784–1859) introduced the baton on April 10, 1820, while conducting his second symphony with the Philharmonic Society in London. Spohr's three descriptions of the event, however, do not correspond and suggest different dates and that he may only have used a baton in rehearsal.[23] While the word "conductor" now appeared on the program, there are no other reports of this event, and Spohr's claim that "the triumph of the baton as the time-giver was decisive, and no one was seen any more seated at the piano during the performance of symphonies and overtures" is certainly false.[24] All witnesses continue to complain that the conductor "sits there and turns over the leaves of the score, but after all he cannot, without his marshal's staff, the baton, lead on his musical army. The leader does this, and the conductor remains a nullity."[25]

On his first visit to London in 1829, Mendelssohn was led "to the pianoforte like a young lady" where he produced a baton and "some perhaps laughed a little."[26] This time, however, the event was confirmed in the press.

> Mr. Mendelssohn conducted his Sinfonia with a baton, as is customary in Germany, France etc., where the discipline of bands is considered of more importance than in England . . . We hope to see the baton ere long at the Italian Opera; it matters not whether it be a violin-bow or a roll of parchment.[27]

When Mendelssohn returned in 1832, the violin leaders objected to his baton and Mendelssohn could see no reason to appear as the conductor at all, but Michael Costa, John Ella and Giacomo Meyerbeer convinced him to go on with his baton.[28] By the following year, however, the baton was in regular use at the Philharmonic. Both a leader and a conductor continued to appear in the program until 1846, when Sir Michael Costa (1806–84) was appointed the first permanent conductor, on the condition that he would have full responsibility for the performance.[29]

The introduction of the baton, however, happened repeatedly. The reports of first use include Haydn, at the first performance of *The Creation* in 1798,[30] Ignaz Franz Mosel in Vienna from 1812,[31] and Johann Reichardt (1752–1814) who removed the piano from the court opera in Berlin in 1776 and directed from a separate desk.[32] Hallé reports that Daniel Türk (1750–1813) was using a baton in 1810, with motions so exuberant that he occasionally hit the chandelier over his head and showered himself with glass.[33] While Spohr, Spontini, Weber, and Mendelssohn all adopted the baton, Schumann disapproved:

> For my part, I was disturbed, both in the overture and in the symphony, by the conductor's baton, and I agreed with Florestan that in a symphony the orchestra must be like a republic, subordinate to no higher authority.[34]

In France, the baton was used to beat audible time, but the violin bow might wave silently. The earliest reference to baton conducting is of the nuns at

St. Vito in 1594. A contemporary composer reports that both instrumentalists and singers sat at a long table.

> Finally the Maestra of the concert sits down at one end of the table and with a long, slender and well-polished wand (which was placed there ready for her, because I saw it), and when all the other sisters clearly are ready, gives them without noise several signs to begin, and then continues by beating the measure of the time which they must obey in singing and playing.[35]

The next two hundred years saw this innovation repeated until baton conducting gradually found acceptance between 1820 and 1840.

It is not clear when Spohr first switched from using a roll of paper, but Sir George Smart reports that in 1825, he sometimes "beat time in front with a short stick."[36] As a virtuoso violinist, Spohr felt at a disadvantage to most Kapellmeisters, who were expected to sit at the keyboard. Spohr told Moritz Hauptmann "that he would give a hundred *Louis d'or* to be able to play the piano," and Hauptmann agreed: "Spohr's inability to play the piano is one of the main reasons why our new operas come to grief in nine cases out of ten."[37] While he could have led as he played, Spohr preferred to stand at a desk and use his hands. For rehearsals, he used a string quartet.

After jobs in Gotha and Frankfort, he settled in Kassel for a long residence (1822–59). He allowed no liberties from the players and was thought precise and plain. Liszt invited Spohr to do most of the conducting at the Bonn Beethoven Festival of 1845 (probably the most reported musical event before the opening of Bayreuth).[38] Spohr received almost universal praise for his "faultless style" in Beethoven's Ninth.[39] Despite a huge performing force (from five to seven hundred) that was generally not thought terribly good, Smart believed "the pianos and fortes were so well attended to that I never heard this Sinfonia so well performed before."[40] Chorley also praised the dynamics, and Morris Barnett pointed out that "it is the fashion with some to say that Spohr's baton is made of cotton – if so the other directors would exchange their iron for the softer material."[41] It is unclear how Spohr beat time, or if he did at all, but the virtue of the baton was established.

Weber

Already an established composer, Carl Maria von Weber (1786–1826) was appointed Kapellmeister in Breslau while only eighteen years old. From the start he conducted by beating a roll of paper silently, experimented with seating, and reorganized administration and rehearsals; his energetic efforts in all of these areas, and equally persistent resistance to them, would continue

Figure 8.2 Weber conducting at Covent Garden in 1826. The baton is probably a roll of paper.

throughout his life. He resigned after two years in Breslau and toured as a virtuoso pianist. He conducted his *Silvana* in Berlin in 1812 and greatly impressed Brühl, the Intendant there, who thought Weber accomplished in three rehearsals what would have been difficult in six or seven. He continued with his roll of paper as a Berlin critic described his conducting as "quiet, judicious, firm and noiseless."[42] He was appointed to the Prague Opera in 1813 where his reforms again led to rebellion. He finally settled in Dresden in 1817 where he tried to introduce a baton.

Most reports, however, put a roll of paper in his hands. In concert he might be standing (see Fig. 8.2), but in the theatre he would sit, as was customary. Smart observes that in Dresden, Weber "beat time with a roll at a square pianoforte."[43] Some early reports complain of quick tempos, but there is general agreement that while Weber was uncompromising and energetic in rehearsal, moving from stage to orchestra to correct mistakes, he was dignified and restrained in performance. There are also reports that he did not beat time continuously. Berlioz assumed this was because "Weber trained it so well that . . . he would give the tempo of the Allegro, sometimes beat the first four bars, and then leave the orchestra to proceed on its own."[44]

Weber was also the first conductor to articulate for the conductor a role beyond keeping the band together. When asked about tempos in his opera *Euryanthe*, Weber outlined a relationship between tempo and inner feeling that would become the core of Wagner's theory a generation later. Weber saw the conductor initially as a referee between the singers who bring "a certain undulation to the meter" and the instrumentalists who divide time "into sharp grooves like the swing of a pendulum. Truthfulness of expression demands the fusing of these opposing characteristics."[45] Weber wanted to encourage individuality, which was required for the "emotional expression" of music, while "preventing the singer from letting himself go too much." While others were just beginning to think about how performers were also interpreters, Weber claimed that most of this expression came from gradual shifts in tempo.

> The beat, the tempo, must not be a controlling tyrant nor a mechanical driving hammer; it should be to a piece of music what the pulse beat is to the living man. There is no slow movement without pieces that demand a quicker motion in order to avoid a sense of dragging. In the same way, there is no Presto that does not require a contrasting, more tranquil, execution of many passages, for otherwise the expressiveness would be lost in excessive speed. But the foregoing should not, in heaven's name, be taken by any singer as justification for the type of eccentric interpretation which arbitrarily distorts certain bars, and arouses in the listener a painful reaction as unbearable, as watching a juggler deliberately put his limbs out of joint. The acceleration of tempo, as well as the retarding, must never give rise to a feeling of abruptness, jolting, or violence.[46]

As did Wagner, Weber insisted that interpretation and tempo shifts be subtle, and that the conductor, as time-keeper, had an even more important role to play; not only was the conductor to keep everyone playing together, but to make music express emotion by gently manipulating the tempo. Weber, however, was ahead of his time. With orchestras still barely paying attention to conductors, it would not be until late in Mendelssohn's career that the first successful orchestral ritardandos would be reported.

Spontini in Berlin

Gaspare Spontini (1774–1851) brought military discipline and all of its trappings to the Berlin Opera from 1820 to 1842. While probably not the first conductor to be despised in spite of his results, this Napoleon of the orchestra realized that obedience to a powerful conductor could raise standards. He was childish and vain, but had a dramatic flair which applied both to his own appearance and the proceedings on stage. Moritz Hanemann played under Spontini and writes:

> Like a king, Spontini strode into the orchestra, and taking up his field-marshal's position, he looked all round with his piercing eyes, fixing them on the heavy artillery – that was what he called the cellos and basses – and then gave the signal to begin. Like a bronze statue he stood at the desk, moving only the lower part of his arm. He was the perfect model of a conductor. The orchestra players sat in wholesome fear of their master, but nevertheless played with undiminished enthusiasm from the beginning down to the last note.[47]

When Spontini came to Dresden in 1844, Wagner was required to have a baton made: a thick ebony staff with ivory knobs at either end. Wagner reports that Spontini held it in the middle "with his whole fist, and manipulated it in a way to show one plainly that he looked on the baton as a marshal's staff, and used it not for beating time with, but commanding."[48] Hanemann's description of Spontini standing "like a bronze statue" would seem to confirm this, as would Spontini's own emphasis on the eye: "my left eye is for the first violins, and my right for the second violins; wherefore, to work by a glance, one must not wear spectacles as bad conductors do."[49] Other witnesses suggest he did beat time.

> These two masses [of orchestra and chorus] are under the sole guidance of the conductor, seated close to the stage with his back to the audience; and as he only follows the score and marks time.[50]

This same English visitor recognized the superiority of this mode of direction to the English one of "two distinct beats," but still did not "entirely approve of the position in which the conductor is placed, being too conspicuous to the whole house, and thus apt to distract its attention by the incessant waving of his wand."[51] Like other aspects of conducting, the placement of the conductor remained highly variable through the early nineteenth century.

Eighteenth-century manners dictated that all performers face the audience. Adding the musical requirement that the keyboard be centralized, Quantz proposed an arrangement with the tip of the harpsichord facing the audience, "so that none of the musicians turns his back to the listeners."[52] Both Haydn and Salomon faced the audience in 1791–3 and this practice was still common when the first conductors appeared. In 1826, Weber "took his place on stage facing the audience."[53] It is reported that both Clementi and Mendelssohn faced the Philharmonic, but they were almost certainly only partially turned to the players, as Wagner caused a stir in 1855 by wanting to be fully in the center and not diagonal to the players or audience. Further, Mendelssohn conducted the *St. Matthew Passion* in 1829 with his right side to the orchestra as "it was not yet customary for the conductor to turn his back to the audience, except at the opera."[54] Mendelssohn's sideways position seems to have been the preferred compromise. Generally this meant facing the first violins, with the left shoulder to the audience. At the Bonn Festival, Smart complained that this was a bad plan as both Liszt and Spohr "had to turn round to them [the singers] and to the secondo side when necessary."[55] While conductors did sometimes face the stage in the theatre, it was often at the prompter's box, so they had to wheel around to face the orchestra. While Spontini's position facing both orchestra and stage was imitated, sideways conducting persisted in the concert hall until the end of the century.[56]

Facing the orchestra allowed for greater discipline, and Spontini became conducting's first drill sergeant. His performances were renowned for their precision and dynamic extremes.

> Spontini's *piano*, played by the whole mass, sounded like the *pianissimo* of a string quartet, and his *forte* surpassed the loudest thunder. Between these extremes were his inimitable crescendo and decrescendo. He bestowed the greatest care on the light and shade. By means of numerous rehearsals, sometimes as many as eighty, everyone who took part in them became completely familiar with the operas. As a result of constant rehearsal the ensemble was impeccable.[57]

With the support of Frederick William III, Spontini could call both sectional and tutti rehearsals as he pleased and only go forward with the performance when it did not require much conducting. He also limited his conducting to his own and a select few other works. This probably explains the contradictory reports about his awkward motions and whether he moved much at all: by the time of the performance the production ran itself.

When Wagner heard Spontini conduct his opera *Fernand Cortez* in 1836, he was overwhelmed by the dynamic contrasts and a level of rhythmic precision beyond anything he had yet encountered:

> The spirit of his conducting astonished me in a way virtually unknown to me before . . . the exceptionally precise, fiery and superbly organized way the whole work was brought off was entirely new to me.[58]

But Spontini pursued accuracy and precision as ends in themselves, and Wagner found the performance cold. Wagner would eventually try to turn conducting away from the pursuit of precision toward the realization of internal truth, but for the moment, conducting still needed discipline.

Mendelssohn and the consolidation of power

Like the opera conductors Weber and Spontini, Felix Mendelssohn Bartholdy (1809–47) was primarily interested in raising standards. He also used a baton, largely faced the band while conducting, and had to reform the organizations he conducted. While Spontini succeeded in Berlin and at the opera, where he had the resources for unlimited rehearsals, his methods did not transfer to other venues. It was Mendelssohn who consolidated power on the podium for choral and concert conductors and established modern methods of rehearsal.

The first battle in raising standards was to get performers to notice the conductor. While Spontini used intimidation and Costa tried to fine his orchestra into submission, Mendelssohn seems to have always remained the calm gentleman. Virtually everyone who recalled Mendelssohn on the podium had a story about his kindness. Devrient, for example, wrote that "he knew how first to commend every point that was at all commendable, and then with the greatest delicacy and firmness point out the defects."[59] Berlioz added that "his criticisms are invariably good-humoured and polite. The choir would be more grateful for their good fortune if they knew how rare these qualities are among chorus-masters."[60] Both Mendelssohn's music and his manners were the perfect match for English society; with his father's wealth, Mendelssohn was technically an amateur. But his concern for the working conditions of musicians also earned him deep respect.

When Mendelssohn arrived at the Gewandhaus he increased the strength of the orchestra from forty to fifty, weeded out some of the bad players and hired Ferdinand David (one of the best violinists in Europe) as the new concertmaster. All of this greatly improved the quality of the orchestra, but Mendelssohn also "never rested till he succeeded in effecting a real improvement in the position of the members of the orchestra."[61] He managed to increase wages and secured pensions. In exchange, Mendelssohn increased the number of rehearsals and the Gewandhaus became perhaps the best orchestra in Europe.

Rehearsals, however, were also becoming more sophisticated. The London Philharmonic, for example, had a single open rehearsal every Saturday before its Monday evening concerts, but with an audience, complete performances and applause, these "rehearsals" were hardly different from the concerts. Under Mendelssohn, however,

> The orchestra was compelled to "buckle to" its duty with a new and strange closeness to attention. The trial of Mozart's familiar symphony in E flat, must have been amazing to some, interesting to others – humiliating perhaps to a few, who remember Philharmonic rehearsals of entire

symphonies infinitely more difficult at which the band has never once been stopped, and of solos where neglect sufficient to destroy the chance of a singer or instrumentalist has been overlooked.[62]

Mendelssohn's interruptions led to the suggestion that Saturdays become more of a "private rehearsal" as "it is clear the audience is not qualified to judge of the nature of the many interruptions."[63] Even more astonishing to contemporaries was Mendelssohn's ability to hear and correct wrong notes.

> He not only heard it but knew whence it came. Once during a grand performance, when there were about three hundred singers and over two hundred instruments, all in chorus, in midst of the music he addressed a young lady who stood not far from him, and said to her in a kindly way, "F, not F sharp."[64]

During the 1830s and 1840s, other composer-conductors were also inventing new rehearsal techniques. Spohr, who wrote long operas, added reference numbers (which became modern rehearsal letters) to scores and parts to facilitate working on shorter sections. Berlioz wrote music that was so different and new, he was often able to bring it to performance only through the use of sectional or "partial rehearsals."

Toward the end of his career in the 1840s, critics began to notice that the sum of Mendelssohn's innovations placed more responsibility for the performance on the podium.

> A man who has as it were lived in an orchestra – whose habitual duties as director have enabled him to detect individual errors amidst the densest mass of performers – to guide them when hesitating at new rhythm or unaccustomed effects, and to infuse one spirit into them – above all who occupies the post as a distinguished composer – stands altogether in a different light from those who have hitherto filled it as a temporary distinction.[65]

Musicians and critics began to realize that this new form of leadership involved many non-musical skills; Weber, Spontini, and Mendelssohn were all highly successful administrators and their musical success was due as much to their ability to reorganize and persuade as it was to increased technique. So at the same time that higher levels of precision began to be desired, it was recognized that conductors needed new skills.

Berlioz also had these administrative and musical skills, and most of his treatise is devoted to these. While the conductor has to "criticize the errors and defects," "economy of time should be reckoned among the most imperative requisites of the orchestral conductor."[66] But Berlioz also thought a conductor needed

other almost indefinable gifts, without which an invisible link cannot
establish itself between him and those he directs; the faculty of
transmitting to them his feeling is denied him, and thence power, empire,
and guiding influence completely fail him. He is then no longer a
conductor, a director, but a simple beater of the time, – supposing he
knows how to beat it, divide it, regularly.[67]

Critic James Davison thought Berlioz had this ability and made explicit
the connection between "enchanting their attention" and the "marvelous
precision."[68] Mendelssohn's improvements were also connected to a magical
ability to engage with the orchestra.

The magnificent band followed him as if under a spell, which his genius
alone kept unbroken . . . The eyes of the musicians were all, as it were,
focused within his own; he communicated with them as if by electricity.[69]

The possibilities for abuse also quickly became apparent. "I am struck
with what you say about conductors; a first-rate leader ought to be a really clever man, though, alas! we know from experience that, given a man
with a certain amount of stupid audacity and unselfconsciousness, he often
achieves more than a skilful [sic], intelligent musician!"[70]

Liszt and the new vocabulary of gesture

The influence of Franz Liszt (1811–86) on conducting remains grossly underestimated. At age thirty-five, he accepted his last fee for playing the piano
and devoted the rest of his life to conducting, composing and teaching. He
spent ten years (1848–58) as a resident conductor, leading the most difficult modern repertoire, and continued to conduct into the 1880s. Many
of the conductors in the next chapter (including Bülow, Damrosch, Mottl,
Nikisch, and Weingartner) spent time as Liszt piano students or were deeply
influenced by Liszt's playing. Wagner's protégé Bülow, who married Liszt's
daughter Cosima and then lost her to Wagner, first studied interpretation,
instrumentation, and Beethoven with Liszt.

Liszt read widely and his copious letters and essays outline a sophisticated
German idealist theory of art. He thought sculpture was the most accessible
art because of its basis in the human body.

All the arts are based on two principles: reality and ideality. Ideality is
perceptible only to cultivated minds but the reality of the sculptor can be
perceived by everyone because its prototype is the human form, familiar to
all . . . This, however, is not the case with music: it has not reality, so to
speak; it does not imitate, it expresses. Music is at once both a science like
algebra and a psychological language that is intelligible only to the poetic
consciousness.[71]

As in Schopenhauer, Hegel, and later Wagner, music expresses ideal "passions and feelings." The performing artist attempts to connect this ideality with the reality of the work in performance, although as for Wagner, the inner content of the music is more important then surface features. For Liszt this meant that technique and virtuosity were empty without "the true expression of the character of the piece."[72]

While Liszt is remembered as perhaps the greatest piano virtuoso of the nineteenth century, his early reviews hardly mention the mechanical or technical; instead critics focus on his poetic and musical taste: "To do justice to the performance of Master Liszt is totally out of our power; his execution, taste, expression, genius, and wonderful extemporary playing, defy any written description."[73] Liszt, today, is too often compared to Paganini. For Liszt, virtuosity was a means to an end. What Liszt heard in Paganini was not technique, but soul.

> René, what a man, what a violin, what an artist! Heavens! what sufferings, what misery, what tortures in those four strings! . . . As to his expression, his manner of phrasing, his very soul in fact![74]

For contemporary audiences, Liszt had a "divine energy"[75] and brought out the "spirit" of the music in a new way. "Liszt does not just play the piano; he tells at the piano."[76] It was Liszt, more than any other nineteenth-century performer, who transformed the performer from a machine (who merely recreated pitch sequences) into a poet.

When he moved to conducting, Liszt attempted to recreate this relationship, but whereas Liszt had complete control of the technical requirements of the piano, his conducting was usually shackled by limited rehearsals and his attempt to abandon traditional technique. Liszt thought time-beating was "a senseless, brutal habit which he would like to forbid in all his works. Music is a sequence of notes which demand to enfold one another, not something to be chained together by thrashing the beat." He asked conductors to "scarcely mark the beat," and complained of "mechanical, measured, chopped up beating up and down which is customary in many quarters."[77] It is no wonder his results were mixed.

> Liszt does not beat time, he only marks the accents. An orchestra, that is not absolutely intimate with him and his musical intentions, would hardly be able to manage under Liszt's conducting.[78]

In the age where Mendelssohn and Berlioz had only just established standard practice, it is no wonder orchestras were mystified, when Liszt tried to reinvent conducting technique as he had on the piano.

In his short conducting "manifesto" Liszt connects his earlier theory with his practice. Beethoven's work uses a higher level of rhythmic phrasing which requires a bond

> between the musicians at their desks and the musicians placed in charge of them, but a bond unlike that which is struck by imperturbable time-beaters. For there are certain passages where simply to maintain the beat and each individual part of the beat | 1, 2, 3, 4 | 1, 2, 3, 4 | very much runs counter to a meaningful and intelligible form of expression. Here, as elsewhere, the letter kills the spirit – a death sentence which I would never sign.[79]

While he could deliver both as a pianist, Liszt emphasized the poetic over the mechanical, summarizing his thesis as "We are pilots not oarsmen."[80] As a conductor, this meant Liszt had to invent new movements.

The descriptions of Liszt on the podium present a catalogue of modern conducting gestures.

> For motives with a singing character, he waves his white hand in long slow curves in the air, then suddenly clenches his fist when a firm chord occurs. During agitated rhythms, the baton often moves with each sixteenth-note, if he has not already taken it out of his hand as he often does. As the ending comes with loud, broad chords, he lifts up both arms and spreads his hands out wide; at a *piano* entrance, his whole body suddenly seems to sink down, only to grow massively as the crescendo comes. Liszt often goes right up on his toes as high as he can and reaches his arms above his head. He does not need the score. He scarcely looks at it, just glancing if at all for a moment, which he makes himself, as for example for a long flowing theme in a slow tempo and simple time, when he casts his eyes down, with his arms folded and not moving a muscle. Then he is all ears, responding totally to the majestic stream of melody, until he suddenly rises to life to engage his daring and energy.[81]

Liszt's contemporaries found these gestures original and strange, but they have become recognizable as the physical vocabulary of modern conducting. This new body language was (and often still is) a distraction, but it was Liszt's way of trying to communicate the inner nuance to the orchestra.

Wagner

Initially, charisma was thought necessary only to command the attention of the orchestra. Gradually, however, the "master-spirit to command" was connected not to increased precision but to an "imaginative glow."[82] While the word *interprétation* is largely absent from Berlioz's treatise and other

Figure 8.3 "Forte and Piano," anonymous caricature of Liszt conducting (*c.* 1851)

mid-century writing, it is at the heart of *Über das Dirigieren*, the treatise by Richard Wagner (1813–83). Berlioz writes about rehearsals and beating time, but for Wagner these are only the means to an end.

For Wagner, as for Liszt, Beethoven demonstrates that music can be about something; it has an emotional or intellectual content. Interpretation is the art of discovering this "poetic object" and then transmitting "to the layman an understanding of these same works."[83] In the same way as Liszt worked from inside out, the answers to all questions about the nuances of performance are found in the inner content of the work; Wagner was deeply influenced by the dramatic performances of Wilhelmine Schröder-Devrient who was acclaimed for her powerful acting, even though, as Wagner admitted, she "had no voice at all."[84] But vocal beauty is only skin-deep and Wagner uses the metaphor of a speaker reciting a poem in an unknown language:

> only the most superficial aspects of the work can be taken into account: the speaker can never articulate and emphasize the words according to his own conviction, but must stick strictly and slavishly to the most random superficiality of sound as represented by the phrase he has learned by heart.[85]

Wagner insists that performers must understand the content to make sense of the surface details. In this way, Wagner elevates and ties performance to the creation of true art, and thus to German idealism. Performing artists now join other Romantic artists as priests of truth.

The most important nuance for revealing musical truth turns out to be tempo – precisely what the conductor controls. The correct tempo leads almost automatically to correct phrasing. In *Über das Dirigieren*, however, Wagner complicates things by writing that tempo is determined, not by the poetic content of the music, but by something called *melos* and described as sung melody in all its aspects. Wagner argues that all music is dramatic; how it is sung determines what it says. The proof for Wagner is that earlier composers used only the general Italian tempo indications.

> Bach hardly ever gave any tempo indication at all, and in a purely musical sense this is the ideal course. It is as though he were asking "how else can one who does not understand my themes and figures and feel their character and expression be helped by an Italian tempo indication?"[86]

Not surprisingly, Wagner thought he understood Mozart and Beethoven better than anyone else and by all reports took new tempos: his slow tempos were extra-slow while he took some Allegros more quickly and some more slowly.[87]

For Wagner, however, the character (or *melos*) changes through the course of a movement and the tempo must respond to these changes. And thus the most contentious debate in conducting begins:

> When I now turn to consider more closely this principle, summed up in the phrase, modification of tempo – a thing our conductors are so ignorant of that they stupidly denounce it as a heresy – the reader who has followed me thus far will realize that what we are dealing with is the principle conditioning the very life of music.[88]

Like Weber, Wagner proposes that tempo should be flexible and that the conductor should subtly increase and decrease the speed of a piece in response to changes in character. Liszt's piano performances were also known for these tempo modulations, but where he was largely unsuccessful in transferring this technique to the podium, Wagner succeeded.

While Liszt tried to move the orchestra with new gestures, Wagner talked to the orchestra and explained what he wanted to do. (This may have added to his difficulties in England.) While many criticized his baton movements, the loudest complaints were about the results. Wagner was repeatedly criticized for "frequently hurrying or slackening the time,"[89] and "so many quickenings and slackenings of tempo, we never heard in a Haydn-symphony before."[90] Wagner advocated a "continuous modification" of the time, and was, it seems, successful in practice.

While Wagner stressed that these tempo modifications should be "imperceptible" or "unnoticeable,"[91] opinions about their magnitude were divided. In Vienna one critic recalled "the surpassing delicacy of all effects;

modifications of force and tempo were almost incessant, but were for the most part modifications by a hair's breadth only."[92] Smart, however, reported: "he reduces the speed of an allegro – say in an overture or the first movement – fully one third on the entrance of its cantabile phrases."[93] Davison saw it as a general principle for Wagner to "slacken the speed in cantabile passages" and this Wagnerian tradition continues to this day.[94]

Conducting would, in fact, remain largely Wagnerian, in both theory and practice, until the beginning of the twentieth century. Even today, loyalty to the emotional content of music, as theorized by Wagner and Liszt, remains a common principle. The danger to the surface of the music, however, was recognized almost immediately. Many were critical of Wagner's modifications to Beethoven's scores, both tempo adjustments and re-orchestrations, even though they were always made in the hope of clarifying the inner meaning. Tempo modulation reached a peak in the beginning of the twentieth century, but was soon losing the battle to a new breed of conductors who rejected both the practice of tempo modification and the philosophical idealism upon which it was based.

9 The Central European tradition

JOSÉ ANTONIO BOWEN AND RAYMOND HOLDEN

In the second half of the nineteenth century, the conductor developed into an independent musical being, who took sole charge of the performance and was devoted generally to the execution of scores by others. With the deaths of Wagner and Brahms, the public's admiration and loyalty shifted from the composer to the virtuoso conductor. On posters, programs, and record jackets, the names of conductors grew larger as they gradually began to dominate the publicity that accompanied orchestral and operatic performances. By the middle of the twentieth century, conductors had become central to the marketing of music by record companies, opera houses, and concert organizations and were powerful figures in the music business.

With the increasing dominance of the conductor in the nineteenth century, two types of conducting emerged: Mendelssohn's more mechanical model of a "transparent" conductor, as preserved at the Leipzig Conservatory, and the more "subjective" approach of Liszt and Wagner, where the execution of the "external" musical details was dependent upon finding the true "internal" meaning of the work. The latter idealist view became dominant and helped to establish both a core repertory of Austro-German musical works and the German Romantic ideology that sustained them. As the visibility of composers diminished, their scores gradually acquired an iconic status and later conductors challenged this model of performance, proposing a reversal of interpretative loyalty from the interior to the surface of the score. By the middle of the twentieth century, the printed material was paramount and the modifications that a conductor could make to the text were severely limited.

The twentieth century also saw the dominance of German conductors wane. During the late nineteenth century, there was little foreign competition to challenge Hans von Bülow (1830–94) and the other Wagnerians, but, in the early part of the twentieth, the "*come scritto*" approach of Arturo Toscanini (1867–1957) competed with the aura of Wilhelm Furtwängler (1886–1954). While Furtwängler, Bruno Walter (1876–1962), and Otto Klemperer (1885–1973) deviated little from Wagnerian principles, Herbert von Karajan (1908–89) took his place in the middle of the century with a unique mixture of modern precision and traditional German mystique. The absence of a dominant Central European conductor in the years immediately

Meiningen.

Herzogliches Hoftheater.

Sonntag, 14. December 1884:

Zweites Abonnements-Concert

der

Herzogl. Hofkapelle

unter Leitung des **Herrn von Bülow.**

PROGRAMM:

1) **Hector Berlioz:** Ouverture zur komischen Oper „Beatrice und Benedict."
2) **Hector Berlioz:** „Rêverie et Caprice", Romanze für Violine mit Orchester, Op. 7.
   (Herr Concertmeister **Fleischhauer.**)
3) **Camille Saint-Saëns:** Tarantelle für Flöte und Clarinette mit Orchester, Op. 6.
   (Herren Hofmusiker **Genennichen** und Kammervirtuos **Mühlfeld.**)
4) **Edouard Lalo:** Suite espagnole für Violine mit Orchester.
   a) Allegro non troppo, b) Scherzando, c) Intermezzo, d) Andante, e) Finale.
   (Herr Concertmeister **Fleischhauer.**)

Zehn Minuten Pause.

5) **Camille Saint-Saëns:** Zweite Sinfonie, A-moll, Op. 55.
   a) Allegro moderato, b) Adagio, c) Scherzo presto, d) Finale. Prestissimo.
6) a) **Berlioz:** Sicilienne (Beatrice und Benedict.)
   b) **Bizet:** Danse bohèmienne (La jolie fille de Perth.)
7) **D. F. E. Auber:** Ouverture „Fra Diavolo."

Preise der Plätze:

Fremdenloge 3 M. Erster Rang 3 M. Sperrsitz 3 M. Parquetplatz 2 M.
Zweiter Rang 2 M. Sitzparterre 1 M. 20 Pf. Orchester 2 M. Stehparquet 1 M. Amphitheater 80 Pf.
Stehparterre 80 Pf. Gallerie 50 Pf.

Während der Dauer eines Musikstücks bleiben die Thüren geschlossen.

Anfang: 4¼ Uhr.   Ende: 6¼ Uhr.
Kasseneröffnung: 3½ Uhr.

Der Billetverkauf findet bei Herrn Hoftheaterkassier **Helbig** (Marienstrasse 1) und an der
Herzoglichen Hoftheaterkasse statt.

Sonntag, den 21. December: **Drittes Abonnements-Concert.** Programm: **Russische Meister:**
Borodin, Glinka, Rimski-Korsakoff, Rubinstein, Tschaikowsky.

Druck von H. Marbach in Meiningen.

Figure 9.1 Poster for a concert by Bülow and the Meininger Hofkapelle

following his death indicates clearly the change that has occurred in musical culture in general and the core values of conducting in particular.

Bülow

Of the conductors who came into regular contact with Wagner, Hans von Bülow was the most influential. After studies in Dresden and Leipzig, Bülow attended a performance conducted by Wagner at Dresden in 1849 and, the following year, heard the première of Wagner's *Lohengrin* at Weimar under Liszt. These performances were a watershed for the young Bülow, who abandoned his law studies in favour of music. After periods of consultation with both Liszt and Wagner, he worked as a conductor at the Zürich Stadttheater in 1850. He conducted at least eight productions there before his tempestuous personality led to his dismissal. He moved to the theatre at St. Gallen, but in 1851, Bülow stopped conducting to become a piano pupil of Liszt, who considered him his rightful successor. Liszt encouraged his protégé to expand his musical horizons through composition and musical journalism, and examples of his writing were published in the *Neue Zeitschrift für Musik*.

After a period in Berlin (1855–64), where he worked as pianist and pedagogue, Bülow was appointed Hofkapellmeister at the Munich Hofoper in 1865. There, he expanded his conducting repertoire, developed his mature performance aesthetic, and conducted Wagner's operas for the first time. Along with readings of *Lohengrin, Tannhäuser,* and *Der fliegende Holländer*, he famously directed the world premières of Wagner's *Tristan und Isolde* and *Die Meistersinger von Nürnberg* in 1865 and 1868 respectively. But, from the repertoire that Bülow performed at Munich, it is clear that he had to balance his passion for Wagner's music with his wider responsibilities as Hofkapellmeister, which included a performance of *Catharina Cornaro*, an opera by Franz Lachner, a musician vilified by Wagner.

An important innovation that Bülow instigated at the Hofoper was his reform of the rehearsal process. A perfectionist by nature, he began preparing the artists by instructing the répétiteurs musically, who then worked individually with the singers. After this initial phase, the singers were then involved in stage and ensemble rehearsals accompanied by the piano. Bülow also reformed the way in which the orchestra rehearsed, and insisted that each of the sections be prepared separately before full rehearsals could begin. When he was satisfied with the progress of the orchestra and the singers, he brought both groups together for *Sitzproben* – rehearsals where singers and orchestra rehearsed the music seated and without stage action – followed by stage and, finally, dress rehearsals.[1] The broad tenets of this scheme are still used in opera houses today.

Figure 9.2 Photo of Bülow and the Hofkapelle in Berlin

Bülow left Munich in 1869 and pursued a career as a pianist. In 1877, he returned to the podium as Hofkapellmeister at Hanover, where he first performed Beethoven's *Fidelio*, continued to explore the early Romantic operas of Marschner, conducted works by Meyerbeer, Glinka, Boieldieu, Spontini, and Auber, and expanded his Mozart repertoire. The operas that Bülow performed would have been heard in German, a practice that continued in all major German-speaking opera houses until the middle of the twentieth century.

In 1880, Bülow was appointed Intendant of the Meininger Hofkapelle. With the help of his patron, Duke Georg II, he exploited the expanding railway network and telegraph system, and transformed the Hofkapelle into the first modern touring orchestra. With the exception of 1883, Bülow toured annually with the ensemble, conducting 162 concerts throughout northern and central Europe. At the Grand Duchy, his duties also included an annual series of subscription concerts at which he explored, amongst others, the music of Beethoven and Brahms. At the 1880 subscription concerts, for example, he devoted a whole series to the music of Beethoven, culminating in two performances of that composer's Symphony No. 9 on the same evening. Bülow was also keen to reform orchestral practice at Meiningen and introduced the pedal timpani, the five-string bass and the Ritter alto viola into the orchestra. He also had the orchestra stand during performances, tried to make them play from memory – an experiment that had little chance of success – and altered the orchestration of some of the scores that he conducted.

Bülow left Meiningen in 1885 and was appointed conductor of the Berlin Philharmonic's subscription concerts in 1887. As conductor of that series, he became increasingly notorious for his speeches from the podium, the most controversial of which was given on March 28, 1892, when he unleashed a diatribe in favour of Bismarck. Along with his duties in Berlin, he conducted at the Hamburg Stadttheater, where his reading of Bizet's *Carmen* was criticized heavily by Felix von Weingartner (1863–1942), who recalled that

> the first performance of *Carmen* under Bülow induced in me a feeling of acute discomfort, almost of horror . . . Why these incongruities in such a natural piece of work? Why these tricks, these pauses, these discriminations for which there is no warrant either in the instructions given by the composer or in the music itself? Why that positively ridiculous procrastination over the opening and many other parts of this sparkling opera?[2]

In contrast, Richard Strauss (1864–1949) argued that "to anyone who ever heard [Bülow] play Beethoven or conduct Wagner, or who attended his music lessons or listened to him during orchestral rehearsals, he was bound to be the example of all the shining virtues of the reproductive artist."[3] Whether this opinion is correct or not, few would dispute the influence that Bülow had on subsequent generations of conductors.[4]

Levi, Richter, and Mottl

With the establishment of the Bayreuth Festival in 1876, Wagner attracted leading conductors to perform there. Of particular importance was the so-called "Nibelungen Chancellery," which included Hermann Levi (1839–1900), Hans Richter (1843–1916), and Felix Mottl (1856–1911). Each was a devoted Wagnerian who championed that composer's works with a missionary's zeal. Although their religious and cultural backgrounds differed sharply, their career paths had much in common. Levi, for example, studied at the Leipzig Conservatory, and, like most conductors from the Central European tradition, rose through the ranks of the opera-house system. After being appointed Hofkapellmeister at the Munich Hofoper in 1872, and later Generalmusikdirektor, he pursued his interest in the music of Wagner and Mozart and was able to encourage the young Weingartner and Strauss.

Figure 9.3 Three Bayreuth conductors: Hermann Levi, Hans Richter, and Felix Mottl

Weingartner was particularly impressed by Levi's abilities and recalled that he reduced his stick technique to a minimum, using only "slight, pregnant and most characteristic gestures."[5] He also recalled that Levi had catholic taste, and was able to perform a variety of musical styles with equal ability, a "capacity which allowed him to master the style of *La Muette de Portici* with the same elegance as the *Nibelungen* or *Don Giovanni*, and the spiritual nature of his interpretations."[6] But Levi is probably remembered best for leading the world premiere of Wagner's *Parsifal* at the Bayreuth Festival in 1882, and the consequent polemic concerning the relationship between that composer's anti-Semitic stance and the Jewish artists that he engaged to further his artistic goals.

Hans Richter worked as Wagner's assistant at Tribschen and was later given the task of auditioning singers and assembling the orchestra for the first Bayreuth Festival. He was also a conductor at that festival and made return visits to Bayreuth throughout his career. Although born in Hungary, Richter studied at the Vienna Conservatory, where his abilities as a versatile musician were soon apparent. In later years, his diverse skills ensured that the musicians he directed held him in high esteem. He was especially influential in Vienna from 1875, where he was the conductor of the Philharmonic's subscription concerts and the Hofoper. His reputation soon spread and he was particularly popular in Britain. There, he led the annual series of "Richter Concerts" at the Queen's Hall from 1879, was engaged regularly at Covent Garden, was appointed Music Director of the Hallé Orchestra in 1899, and directed the first concert of the newly formed London Symphony Orchestra in 1904. While he was considered a leading conductor of Beethoven's works, he also championed the music of contemporary composers. Along with performances of compositions by Strauss, Stanford, Cyril Scott, Sibelius, Franck, and Bartók, Richter led the first performances of Brahms's Symphonies Nos. 2 and 3, and Elgar's *Enigma Variations* and *The Dream of Gerontius*.

Like Richter, Felix Mottl was an alumnus of the Vienna Conservatory, where he studied composition with Bruckner, who encouraged him to explore the music of Wagner. After working as a musical assistant at the Bayreuth Festival in 1876, Mottl accepted a post at the Ring-Theater in Vienna in 1878 and then moved to the Leipzig Stadttheater in 1880, where he worked under Arthur Nikisch (1855–1922). Between 1881 and 1903, he took charge of the Hofoper at Karlsruhe, where his readings of Wagner raised the status of the local theatre to that of an important artistic centre. His interest in Wagner's music also resulted in a string of historic performances at the Bayreuth Festival after the composer's death. Mottl's fame soon spread and, during his tenure at Karlsruhe, he was invited to conduct at Covent Garden and at the Metropolitan Opera. The music of Wagner continued to dominate his activities and it was fitting that the last work he performed was *Tristan und Isolde*. Of that reading, Bruno Walter, Mottl's successor at Munich, later recalled that "although I had met him but casually, the manner of his death affected me deeply. He had been conducting *Tristan* and had collapsed while Isolde was pronouncing the words: 'Death-doomed head, death-doomed heart[.]' He died a few days later."[7]

Damrosch, Seidl, and Muck

Leopold Damrosch (1832–85), Anton Seidl (1850–98) and Karl Muck (1859–1940) helped establish a German legacy in America. Each had a broad repertoire, gave a number of American premières, had a gift for organization, were devoted to the music of Wagner, applied strict discipline, and had a conducting style that was influenced by Richter's controlled gestures. Damrosch's interest in *Zukunftsmusik* was encouraged by Liszt, who appointed him concertmaster at Weimar. In 1858, Damrosch left the orchestra to concentrate on conducting and was appointed Kapellmeister with the Breslau Philharmonic Society. With that organization, he explored the works of Liszt, Wagner, and Berlioz and became a champion of new music. In 1871, he moved to New York, where he conducted the Männergesangverein Arion, founded the Oratorio and Symphony Societies, conducted the New York Philharmonic, and established German opera at the Metropolitan Opera. His sons, Franz (1859–1937), later known as Frank, and Walter (1862–1950), became musicians and continued his legacy.[8]

Although born in Hungary, Anton Seidl studied at the university and conservatory in Leipzig. After Richter introduced him to Wagner in 1872, Seidl joined the "Nibelungen Chancellery" at Bayreuth and was involved in the preparation of the first complete performance of *Der Ring des Nibelungen*. Richter and Wagner were seminal to Seidl's development as a musician and he referred to the former as his Jesus Christ and the latter as his law-giving God.[9] Seidl's enthusiasm for Wagner was rewarded when the composer recommended him as conductor to the management of the Leipzig Stadtheater. Consequently, the impresario Angelo Neumann (1838–1910) engaged him to conduct his touring opera company, a troupe that specialized in the performance of Wagner's operas and music dramas. Seidl's readings of those works soon attracted international attention and, after a brief time as conductor in Bremen, he succeeded Damrosch at the Metropolitan Opera, where he conducted the American premieres of *Die Meistersinger von Nürnberg* and *Tristan und Isolde* in 1886 and *Der Ring des Nibelungen* in 1889. In 1891, Seidl was appointed Music Director of the New York Philharmonic Orchestra.

After completing his Ph.D. in classical philology in 1880, Muck studied piano at the Leipzig Conservatory. His progress was quick and he soon made a successful debut as a piano soloist with the Gewandhaus Orchestra. But he rejected the possibility of an academic or a solo career and accepted the post of chorus master at Zurich in 1884. He then held conducting jobs at a succession of theatres, including Salzburg, Brünn (Brno), and Graz. After being appointed conductor at the Deutsches Landestheater in Prague in 1886 by Angelo Neumann, Muck was engaged to perform with that impresario's touring Wagner troupe, with which he directed the local premieres of *Der Ring des Nibelungen* at St. Petersburg and Moscow in 1889 and 1891 respectively. Muck then joined the staff of the Berlin Hofoper in 1892, rendered Wagner's works at Covent Garden from 1899, performed *Parsifal* at the Bayreuth Festival between 1901 and 1930, conducted the Vienna Philharmonic between 1904 and 1906, and was music director of the Boston

Symphony Orchestra between 1906 and 1908 and, again, between 1912 and 1918. At Boston, Muck pursued his interest in new music, but after the United States entered World War I, Muck was arrested and interned. When the hostilities ended, he returned to Germany, where he conducted the Hamburg Philharmonic between 1922 and 1933. Although Muck's readings were rooted firmly in the traditions of the nineteenth century, he was one of the first conductors to record for Victor in 1917.[10] More important, he, like Damrosch and Seidl, was concerned that standards of performance should take precedence over transcendent meaning, thus laying the foundation for Toscanini's further move away from German idealism in America.[11]

Mahler, Weingartner, and Strauss

Gustav Mahler (1860–1911), Felix von Weingartner, and Richard Strauss had careers that followed similar paths: they were influenced by Hans von Bülow, they rose through the ranks of the Central European opera-house system, they were leading composer-conductors, and they were directors of the Vienna Opera.

As distinguished Wagnerians, Mahler, Weingartner, and Strauss applied and modified that composer's thoughts on re-orchestration. But sharp differences soon emerged, particularly in the performance of Mozart's operas by Mahler and Strauss. It has been stated often that Mahler led a Mozart renaissance at the Vienna Hofoper during the first decade of the twentieth century. But Strauss had already begun to revivify and to reassess Mozart's operas during the late 1890s at the Munich Hofoper. With the Intendant Ernst von Possart, Strauss established a string of theatrical and musical innovations that were seminal to the performance of those works by subsequent generations of conductors and producers. The innovations of Strauss and Possart involved moving their productions of Mozart from the large Nationaltheater to the small, ornate, rococo theatre at the Residenz; reducing the orchestra to twenty-six players; using sets and costumes characteristic of the eighteenth century; revising the translations with the help of Hermann Levi; editing the orchestral and vocal material so that, where possible, it corresponded with Mozart's autographs; staging the Prague version of *Don Giovanni* and, therefore, reinstating the epilogue, which had fallen from favor during the nineteenth century; and using a fortepiano for the recitatives, played by Strauss, who acted as both conductor and continuo player.[12] Moreover, Strauss refused to retouch the music of Mozart, preferring, instead, to present the works in their original form. In contrast, Mahler, when performing *Le nozze di Figaro* in Vienna, inserted into Act 3 a whole scene of Beaumarchais, which he set to music; added new recitatives to supplement the originals; altered the orchestration and dynamics;

inserted and omitted passages; and used parts of the overture and other works as *intermezzi*. Similarly, when performing *Così fan tutte*, he cut and altered the articulation and dynamics of the overture, arias and ensembles, retouched the orchestration throughout the opera, and inserted music, both from Mozart's other works and from material within the opera.[13]

But to suggest that Strauss did not retouch the music he performed would be false. While he did not adjust the scores of Mozart, he did alter the text of some Beethoven symphonies. This was also true of Weingartner, whose modifications to that composer's scores are set out clearly in his treatise, *On the Performance of Beethoven's Symphonies*. For him

> One of the essential conditions of the style of an execution must be *clearness* . . . even a perfectly correct rendering does not always make the intentions of the master as clear as they become by reading the score . . . Indeed it must be confessed that many passages awaken a feeling of confusion rather than of pleasure . . . Passages do occur . . . where notation alone would not suffice, and in such cases I was obliged to have recourse to instrumental interference . . . Real innovations, with the assistance, of course, of the instruments prescribed, I have undertaken partly in accordance with the proposals made by Wagner, and partly on my own responsibility; they only occur in the very rare cases in which there was absolutely no other means of obtaining the effect which Beethoven wished to produce.[14]

Mahler, Weingartner, and Strauss were at the height of their powers when the recording industry began to emerge. While Mahler made no gramophone recordings, he did make a number of piano rolls. Mahler was apparently "filled with wonder and admiration for the process,"[15] but the rolls he recorded allow only an intriguing and partial glimpse into some of his methods as a performer.

Strauss also recorded on piano rolls, but lived long enough to make a substantial number of gramophone and radio recordings that leave a clearer impression of his practices and principles as a performer. For example, in his 1926 recording of Mozart's Symphony No. 39, he pursues a policy of tempo integration that takes into account the work's internal and external structures; a highly organized approach that was typical of his readings of Mozart's works in general.[16] Similarly, in his recordings of his own music, he also adjusted his tempi in an organized manner, and the speeds that he used in his 1922, 1929, and 1944 recordings of *Don Juan* indicate clearly his methods as a conductor and the tempi that he considered appropriate for the work (see Table 9.1).[17]

Weingartner, too, recorded piano rolls and made acoustic recordings of works from the Austro-German canon, and then re-recorded complete symphonies by Beethoven and Brahms after the introduction of electrical

Table 9.1 *Richard Strauss's speeds in his 1922, 1929 and 1944 recordings of* Don Juan

Bar/Section	Printed metr. mark	Superscription and printed instructions	1922	1929	1944
1 [first subject]	𝅗𝅥=84	Allegro molto con brio	𝅗𝅥=84	𝅗𝅥=84+	𝅗𝅥=84
71 [transition passage]		tranquillo/dolce [winds and brass]	𝅗𝅥=76	𝅗𝅥=63	𝅗𝅥=63
90 [second subject I]		tranquillo/molto espress. [clarinet I and horn I]	𝅗𝅥=72	𝅗𝅥=63	𝅗𝅥=63
149 [second subject I]	𝅗𝅥=60	un poco più lento	𝅗𝅥=60	𝅗𝅥=60	𝅗𝅥=60
153 [second subject I]	𝅗𝅥=76	a tempo, vivo	𝅗𝅥=76	𝅗𝅥=76	𝅗𝅥=76
156 [second subject I]	𝅗𝅥=72	poco sostenuto	𝅗𝅥=66	𝅗𝅥=63	𝅗𝅥=63
166 [transition passage]	𝅗𝅥=84	a tempo, molto vivace	𝅗𝅥=84+	𝅗𝅥=84+	𝅗𝅥=84
197 [transition passage]	𝅗𝅥=92	a tempo/molto appass. [violas and celli]	𝅗𝅥=92	𝅗𝅥=92	𝅗𝅥=92(−)
232 [second subject IIa]	𝅗𝅥=76	a tempo ma tranquillo/*sehr getragen und ausdrucksvoll* [oboe I from bar 235 second half]	𝅗𝅥=60	𝅗𝅥=60−	𝅗𝅥=60
305 [transition passage]	𝅗𝅥=69		𝅗𝅥=56 [bar 306]	𝅗𝅥=56 [bar 306]	𝅗𝅥=56 [bar 306]
313 [second subject IIb]	𝅗𝅥=84	a tempo/molto espr. [horns from bar 314 second half]	𝅗𝅥=84	𝅗𝅥=84	𝅗𝅥=84
351 [development]	𝅗𝅥=92	a tempo, giocoso	𝅗𝅥=92	𝅗𝅥=92	𝅗𝅥=92
421 second half [development]	𝅝=63	sempre molto agitato	𝅝=60–3	𝅝=60–3	𝅝=60
447 [development]	𝅗𝅥=72	molto tranquillo	𝅗𝅥=63	𝅗𝅥=63	𝅗𝅥=60
457 [transition passage]		a tempo primo	𝅗𝅥=84+	𝅗𝅥=84	𝅗𝅥=84
474 [recap. first subject]			𝅗𝅥=84+	𝅗𝅥=84+	𝅗𝅥=84+
510 [recap. second subject IIb]		molto espr. [horns and celli bar 510 second half]	𝅗𝅥=84	𝅗𝅥=84+	𝅗𝅥=84
569 [transition passage]	𝅗𝅥=100	stringendo [from bar 570]	𝅗𝅥=100 [from bar 564]	𝅗𝅥=100 [from bar 564]	𝅗𝅥=96
586 [coda]	𝅗𝅥=72	tempo primo, poco a poco più lento (ma sempre alla breve)	𝅗𝅥=76	𝅗𝅥=63	𝅗𝅥=58

recording in 1926. While the record companies and Weingartner benefited by marketing him as a leading conductor of the music of Beethoven and Brahms, a close study of his programmes shows a tendency to balance new music with unfamiliar works.

Nikisch

Like Richter, Arthur Nikisch was a Hungarian and an alumnus of the Vienna Conservatory. As a student in Vienna, he won prizes for composition, piano and violin and developed a passion for Wagner's music. He encountered the composer personally on May 12, 1872 when Wagner conducted the Vienna Philharmonic in a programme that included Beethoven's Symphony No. 3. Nikisch was a member of the violin section for that performance and was struck immediately by the character of the reading. Ten days later, he again played under the composer's direction for a performance of Beethoven's Symphony No. 9 at Bayreuth. These concerts were seminal to Nikisch's development as a conductor and he later stated that his experiences under Wagner affected his understanding of Beethoven in particular and his performance style in general.

After appointments with the Leipzig Stadttheater, the Boston Symphony Orchestra and the Budapest Opera, Nikisch replaced Carl Reinecke as Gewandhauskapellmeister at Leipzig in 1895. That year, he also accepted the post of conductor of the Berlin Philharmonic's subscription concerts. The character and content of the Leipzig and Berlin series differed sharply. In Leipzig, where the subscription concert's role was artistic, social, and educational, Nikisch's programmes often balanced symphonic music with Lieder and/or chamber music, whereas in Berlin, where the subscription concerts occupied only a small part of the Philharmonic's concert diary, he rarely included music from other genres. Moreover, as the Gewandhaus Orchestra was also involved in opera performances at the Stadttheater, Nikisch's national and international tours were given largely with the Berlin Philharmonic.

As a devoted Brucknerian, Nikisch regularly performed that composer's symphonies, and he directed a complete cycle of the works in numerical order, during the Gewandhaus Orchestra's 1919–20 season. He was also a champion of new music and, at his concerts in Berlin and Leipzig, he regularly performed compositions by Franck, d'Indy, Sibelius, Elgar, Rakhmaninov, Strauss, and Mahler. He never allowed the music of one composer to dominate his seasons and, unlike Bülow, was circumspect when programming Beethoven. Nikisch encouraged female artists and, at Leipzig, women soloists performed at more than two thirds of his concerts. He was also keen to encourage new talent and often engaged young musicians. Arthur Schnabel benefited from this policy and recalled that

> my performance [of Brahms's Piano Concerto No. 2] was very well received too – thanks to Nikisch. I believe he told the Press beforehand to be friendly towards me. I did not fare so well, however, when a little later I played the first Brahms concerto in Berlin, also with Nikisch. The leading newspaper attacked him for allowing me to play the slow movement too slow (as the paper thought). They did not understand how a man like him could participate in such a distortion of a grand work. Years later I was told that Nikisch had written a letter to the offended journalist, telling him that a young artist is entitled to do things wrong and so he did not stop me.[18]

The practices and principles that Nikisch established in Berlin and Leipzig formed the basis for his work abroad. Of particular importance were the concerts that he gave in London, where he made his debut at the Queen's Hall on June 15, 1895. He then returned to the British capital regularly and performed at Covent Garden, where his readings of Wagner were critically acclaimed, and with the fledgling London Symphony Orchestra, with which he pursued his interest in new music, toured, and made commercial recordings. Nikisch's legacy was secured only partially by a handful of recordings that he made for Deutsche Grammophon and HMV, including his historic recording of Beethoven's Symphony No. 5, the first of a complete symphony.

Mengelberg

Willem Mengelberg (1871–1951) studied at the Cologne Conservatory with Franz Wüllner and Adolf Jensen, and graduated with prizes in conducting, piano, and composition. In 1892, he became music director in Lucerne, and in 1895, he was appointed conductor of Amsterdam's Concertgebouw Orchestra, where he remained for fifty years. His intense working practices ensured that the orchestra soon reached an international standard. As his fame spread, he made a series of high-profile guest appearances throughout eastern and western Europe and the United States and was engaged as principal conductor of the New York Philharmonic Orchestra between 1922 and 1930.

With the Concertgebouw Orchestra, Mengelberg championed the cause of new music, often inviting composers to conduct their works. To ensure the best possible results, he regularly prepared the orchestra in advance of their visits. Of particular importance were his relationships with Mahler and Strauss. Mengelberg's marked scores of Mahler's music contain retouches and suggestions by the composer, along with comments by the conductor.[19] His interest in Mahler's music reached a climax in 1920, when a festival of that composer's music was staged in Amsterdam to mark the twenty-fifth anniversary of Mengelberg's tenure with the Concertgebouw Orchestra. Strauss also had an extended relationship with Mengelberg, with whom he shared the direction of a festival of his music in London in 1903. The composer-conductor enjoyed working with the Concertgebouw Orchestra, which he conducted on nineteen occasions, and he dedicated his tone poem, *Ein Heldenleben*, to Mengelberg and the orchestra.

One of Mengelberg's creeds was "*jede Note deutlich*" (every note clear), but his acute attention to detail sometimes resulted in startling tempo fluctuations. His desire to illuminate nuance often led to lengthy, heated, and voluble rehearsals at which he sometimes talked for over half the allocated time. In an effort to achieve musical detail and to enhance the poetic content, he used string portamento and rubato extensively. He had no hesitation about making what he called "changements" to scores, arguing that his wide experience as a conductor and the knowledge that he gleaned from his teachers meant that the modifications that he made were in sympathy with the composer's wishes. Seemingly oblivious to shifting trends in performance style, he continued to practice techniques popular during the early decades of the twentieth century until the 1940s, when his readings were criticized by some for being fussy and old-fashioned. From extant film footage of Mengelberg, it is obvious that he conducted with tremendous radiant energy and that he used a clear and demonstrative baton technique.

Walter, Klemperer, and Furtwängler

Between the wars, Bruno Walter, Otto Klemperer, and Wilhelm Furtwängler dominated German conducting. While they rarely employed the extravagances and alterations of Mengelberg and Mahler, they remained committed to a Romantic and subjective approach and rejected the more objective methods that were emerging in America and Britain. Walter, for example, claimed that a faithful reproduction of a work must also reproduce the feelings and mental associations that had inspired the composer. He argued that "to do justice to the *Leonora* overture, the conductor must be inspired during his performance by thoughts of dark dungeons and hopelessness."[20] In realizing their intentions, Furtwängler, Walter, and Klemperer continued to manipulate tempo in the manner of Strauss. This meant that the tempi of large sections or movements were rendered in direct proportion to other speeds in the performance. Furtwängler was particularly skillful when applying this technique and the composer Paul Hindemith recalled that "Furtwängler possessed the great secret of proportion . . . he understood how to interpret phrases, themes, sections, movements, entire symphonies and programs as artistic unities."[21]

Walter and Klemperer were devoted acolytes of Gustav Mahler, but their thoughts on re-orchestration differed sharply. Walter argued that "whatever can be adduced against [retouching] on the grounds of *literary fidelity*, I must declare myself against the radical rejection of retouching . . . [but Wagner's] suggestions about the performing of Beethoven's Ninth . . . seem to go too far."[22] Nevertheless, when performing symphonies by Schumann, "instrumental retouching becomes an unavoidable duty . . . [because] the original orchestration is unable to do justice either to the spiritual content of the work or to its thematic clarity, either to the spirit or to the letter."[23] In contrast, Klemperer stated that

> the retouching of Beethoven, Schumann and others was an essential feature of Mahler's interpretation of their works. [But] I cannot go all the way with him on this point. He retouched in the spirit of his age. I believe it was unnecessary, and that one can bring out the full content of such music without retouching.[24]

Furtwängler's approach to reorchestration was similar to that of Walter. The concept of textual fidelity was an issue to which Furtwängler returned often in his writings, and his notebook entry from 1930 is typical of his attitude in general. He argues that

> literal rendering plays a major role in the practice and reception of music today . . . and [p]lacing the creator above the private person is naturally quite self-evident, . . . [but it is mistaken] to propagate literal rendering as such as an "ideal." If it is an ideal, it is at best a pedantic one.[25]

A tangible example of Furtwängler's methods can be heard in his readings of Beethoven's Symphony No. 9, where he regularly adjusted the orchestration in the spirit of Wagner. Curiously, not all of Furtwängler's amendments are annotated in his marked score and the exact nature of his retouchings can be only determined by comparing marked score with recorded sound. For Furtwängler, therefore, the essence of the music was not found simply in the text. The printed score was merely the basis for a more complex reading that required external intervention to unlock its true content.

Unlike the previous generation of conductors, Walter, Klemperer, and Furtwängler left a substantial number of gramophone recordings. But their individual and collective discographies are deceptive and are not representative of their activities as a whole. Furtwängler, for example, began his career as a recording artist in 1926, with readings of Beethoven's Symphony No. 5 and Weber's overture to *Der Freischütz*. Of the other commercial recordings that he made between the wars, only five were of major compositions;[26] the rest were short works, arrangements or extracts from operas and incidental music composed in the eighteenth and nineteenth centuries. This stands in sharp contrast to the works that he performed at the subscription concerts he led with the Berlin and Vienna Philharmonics and in Leipzig during the inter-war period, where two thirds of the concerts contained music by a living composer. Walter and Klemperer also championed the cause of new music though their early activities in the concert hall have not been represented fully in recorded sound. While it was to the advantage of the record companies to market Walter, Klemperer, and Furtwängler as curators of the great Austro-German canon, the virtual absence of music composed after the first decade of the twentieth century from their discographies has led to serious misunderstanding of their performance aesthetics as a simple extension of nineteenth-century practices, rather than as an evolving philosophy that embraced the principles of the past within a modern context.

Others of this generation, like Carl Schuricht (1880–1967), Hans Knappertsbusch (1888–1965), and Karl Böhm (1894–1981), also worked in this evolving German Romantic tradition of conducting. Schuricht, who took the Vienna Philharmonic (with André Cluytens) on its first tour of the United States in 1956, was committed to the traditions of the nineteenth century and used expressive phrasing and rubato. Böhm, who studied Wagner's operas and music dramas with Muck at Bayreuth, later accepted appointments at Munich, Darmstadt, Hamburg, and Dresden, where he conducted the premieres of Strauss's operas, *Die schweigsame Frau* and *Daphne*. His tempi were often slower than many of his contemporaries, but his dramatic energy and his classical approach complemented the music of Strauss and Mozart. Knappertsbusch studied at the Cologne Conservatory, rose through the ranks of the Central European opera-house system, succeeded Walter at the Munich Staatsoper and worked at the Bayreuth Festival. Like Klemperer, Knappertsbusch favoured magisterial tempi, and although he continued to apply the principles of the nineteenth century, his performances did not contain the excesses of Mengelberg. While his readings of Wagner and Bruckner were respected widely, he was indifferent to an international career, an attitude that was not shared by Karajan.

Karajan

Herbert von Karajan was a pivotal figure. Some commentators have argued that he was the culmination of the Central European tradition, while others considered him the beginning of a new era in conducting. After studying at the Salzburg Mozarteum and the Vienna Academy, he made his conducting debut at a privately organized concert with the Mozarteum Orchestra at Salzburg in 1929. That year, he was appointed first Kapellmeister at the Stadttheater in Ulm, where his potential was recognised quickly. In 1934, he moved to Aachen, where he was given the post of Generalmusikdirektor, which he retained until 1941. In 1937, he conducted for the first time at the Vienna Staatsoper with a performance of Wagner's *Tristan und Isolde*; the following year, he made his debuts with the Berlin Philharmonic and at the Berlin Staatsoper. There, his reading of *Tristan und Isolde* was praised highly, resulting in the epithet, "das Wunder Karajan." From 1939, Karajan began to spend more time in Berlin and his popularity soon began to rival that of Furtwängler. Karajan conducted occasionally in the occupied territories during the war and questions about his political affiliations dogged him after the hostilities, although he remained adamant that his membership of the Nazi party was for professional rather than political reasons.[27] He completed denazification in 1947, but had already begun to perform regularly in Vienna, London, Milan, and Salzburg. In 1951, he conducted Wagner's *Der Ring des Nibelungen* at the Bayreuth Festival and, in 1955, he signed a lifetime contract with the Berlin Philharmonic Orchestra. The following year, he succeeded Karl Böhm as artistic director of the Vienna Staatsoper, and, in 1969, he was appointed artistic advisor to L'Orchestre de Paris. As a shrewd businessman who sought out the most advanced audio and video technologies to make over eight hundred recordings and films, some proclaimed him "Generalmusikdirektor of Europe."

Karajan often dedicated much rehearsal time to perfecting sonic detail while his performances focused on a sweeping legato that earned the moniker, the "Karajan line." He claimed to admire Toscanini for his precision and clarity, and Furtwängler for his elasticity and expression. He attempted to combine these elements in his readings by extracting precision through rigorous and detailed rehearsal, and elasticity through closing his eyes and allowing his players the freedom to realize his inner sound-image in performance. He argued that

> If I exert control, it is in rehearsal. When I rehearse, I am like a man with a microscope. I hear everything, every sound. But in the performance, I let them be free . . . Young conductors often make the mistake of carrying details into the concert. I leave them at the rehearsal. At the concert I hear inside myself. I don't let errors of detail distract me.[28]

For many, Karajan was a paradox: he brought modern techniques into his rehearsals but embodied the old world with performances of inspired transcendence; he cultivated both the aura of a glamorous superstar and the image of a humble servant of the music; he moved sparingly on the podium but achieved a sweeping legato, and he proclaimed loyalty to the text but was criticized for betraying typical Austro-German practices.

Karajan's contemporaries and successors

A combination of factors meant that some of Karajan's contemporaries were unable to pursue their careers in Germany and Austria during the middle of the twentieth century. The rise of the Nazis in Germany during the 1930s, America's desire to import culture during the inter- and post-war periods, and the Soviet dominance of the German Democratic Republic contributed to the fragmentation and dispersal of the Central European tradition. Erich

Leinsdorf (1912–93), for example, fled to the United States in the 1930s and was engaged by the Metropolitan Opera, New York, the Cleveland Orchestra, the Rochester Philharmonic Orchestra (1947–56) and the Boston Symphony Orchestra (1962–69). In his book, *The Composer's Advocate: A Radical Orthodoxy for Musicians* (1981), he challenged the established values of the Central European conducting tradition and focused on the performer's obligation to "authentic reproduction of the composer's work."[29] While Leinsdorf rejected some of the practices of his predecessors, he returned briefly to Europe after World War II and conducted the Berlin Radio Symphony Orchestra between 1977 and 1980. But many émigré conductors continued to live abroad, including Fritz Reiner (1888–1963), George Szell (1897–1970), Jascha Horenstein (1899–1973), Eugene Ormandy (1899–1985), and Georg Solti (1912–97). Although they began their careers in Central Europe, their adopted homelands benefited most from the traditions that they retained and later modified.[30]

Karajan's abilities as a conductor and as a self-publicist frequently overshadowed the activities of his contemporaries who remained in Europe, resulting in the public often undervaluing their achievements. Günter Wand (1912–2002), for example, was a renowned interpreter of works from the Austro-German canon, whose readings of Bruckner's symphonies were of particular importance. Although he held posts with major orchestras throughout much of his career, he only became known internationally during the 1980s. With the death of Karajan, Wand's standing rose still further, and his performances of Bruckner's works were received reverentially.

The next generation of artists, including Wolfgang Sawallisch (b. 1923), Klaus Tennstedt (1926–98), Kurt Masur (b. 1927), Michael Gielen (b. 1927), Nikolaus Harnoncourt (b. 1929), Christoph von Dohnányi (b. 1929), and Carlos Kleiber (b. 1930), matured during Karajan's years of dominance. Most rose through the ranks of the opera-house system and have held important positions with leading orchestras in the United States and Great Britain. Unlike many of their predecessors, Sawallisch, Gielen, and Dohnányi tend to be circumspect when altering tempi and adjusting the orchestration of the works that they are performing. Harnoncourt, who worked as an orchestral musician under Karajan, became a leading figure in the early-music movement and later worked successfully as a guest conductor with orchestras like the Concertgebouw Orchestra of Amsterdam and the Berlin Philharmonic, takes a slightly different stance. His creative use of string technique, his pragmatic approach to the juxtaposition of modern and period instruments, and his integration and manipulation of tempo has created a sound world that is both individual and, for some, controversial.

Carlos Kleiber was born in Berlin and spent his childhood in South America with his father, the Austrian conductor, Erich Kleiber (1890–1956).

After studying chemistry, he worked as a répétiteur at the Gärtner-platztheater in Munich in 1952. Thereafter, he was engaged as a conductor at opera houses in Vienna, Düsseldorf, Zurich, Stuttgart, and Munich. In 1978, he resigned as a tenured conductor and has since refused to accept a permanent engagement. Today, Kleiber is active only as a guest conductor, performing a very restricted repertoire that includes Wagner's *Tristan und Isolde* and Strauss's *Der Rosenkavalier*. He travels alone, values his privacy, has no agent, gives no interviews, and negotiates his own contracts. Musicians enjoy his rehearsals, which draw heavily upon his sense of humour, vivid imagery, and his little memos to players, called "Kleibergrams." Although he works infrequently, he remains a highly respected and sought-after conductor.

Klaus Tennstedt's international career began late in life. After studying violin with his father and at the Leipzig Conservatory, he was appointed concertmaster of the Halle Municipal Theatre Orchestra. But he abandoned the violin after a growth between two fingers of his left hand was discovered and he turned, instead, to the piano and conducting. As a Kapellmeister, he held posts at Chemnitz, Dresden, and Schwerin before defecting to Sweden in 1971. In 1974, his performances in Toronto and Boston were acclaimed critically and he was invited to conduct important orchestras in both North American and Europe. In 1978, he had the distinction of being the first German to conduct the Israel Philharmonic and, the following year, began a string of appointments that culminated in him being made music director of the London Philharmonic Orchestra in 1980. But fame was accompanied by physical and emotional failure, and he had to abandon his post in London for medical reasons. While Tennstedt's readings of music from the eighteenth and nineteenth centuries differed sharply from those of Kleiber, both used tempo fluctuations that reflected past practices rather than current trends.

Like Tennstedt, Kurt Masur spent his early and middle careers in the German Democratic Republic. After a series of minor posts, he was appointed Music Director of the Leipzig Gewandhaus Orchestra, a job that he retained for twenty-six years. Subsequently, he has held the post of music director with both the London and New York Philharmonic Orchestras. His New York tenure was particularly uneasy, and although he was respected for his discipline and skill, he lacked the public appeal of some of his predecessors. The reason for this was due, at least in part, to his chosen repertoire, which continued to center on the Austro-German canon. While British and American orchestras and audiences have become more interested in hearing indigenous conductors who allow the music to "speak for itself," they continue to long for the charisma and dynamism of an iconoclastic leader who can unlock music's mysterious truth. While Bernstein was both, Masur was neither modern enough nor charismatic enough for New York.

Pundits have criticized conductors from the next generation for either failing to reach the standards set by their older colleagues or, worse, for trying to emulate them. The Bayreuth Festival performances of Daniel Barenboim (b. 1942), for example, have been both praised and criticized for their similarity to those of Furtwängler. Although some of the Beethoven readings of Christian Thielemann (b. 1959) reflect Klemperer's approach to tempo, both he and Franz Welser-Möst (b. 1960) have won respect while distancing themselves from the practices of the late nineteenth and early twentieth centuries. Despite the efforts of major record companies, none of the younger generation of Central European conductors has achieved the status of past generations, but this may have nothing to do with their skill or ability. Without the ideology of German Romanticism to support the mysterious discovery of internal meaning in each performance, the myth of the maestro might finally be dead.

10 The French tradition

DAVID CAIRNS

To trace anything as definite as a tradition, even in one country, with an activity as egoistic as conducting, is a delicate and hazardous task. Realistically considered, perhaps, the French tradition boils down to a list of conductors, from Jean-Baptiste Lully (1632–87) to Pierre Boulez (b. 1925) – the former keeping time by thumping the ground with the long stick which was to cause his death from gangrene when he inadvertently jammed the point into his toe, the latter shaping complex meters with batonless hands, and still, happily, very much with us.

True, conductors tend in practice to be conservative people (though the opposite is the case with two of the greatest, Berlioz and Boulez). They can often be shown to have reproduced quite closely what they grew up learning to do: making the same cuts and the same ritardandos and accelerandos as their mentors did, omitting the same exposition repeats, and so on. Even then, however, the reproduction, colored by the mind and temperament of the individual concerned, is likely to take on a new character and become something different. Tradition, as Stravinsky's dictum has it, is made, not inherited.

It is also difficult to identify a tradition over a period as long as several centuries. To take the single example of France's most prestigious and long-lasting musical body, the Société des Concerts du Conservatoire, what continuity can be traced between the orchestra which Wagner praised for what he regarded as the best-prepared and executed performances of Beethoven's symphonies that he had ever heard, and the coarse, lackluster band that recorded Berlioz's *L'enfance du Christ* in 1951 under André Cluytens (1905–67) – a version which, though complacently awarded the Académie Charles Cros Grand Prix du Disque, has tired routine written all over it. Yet the same orchestra, recording the work fifteen years later (again under Cluytens), sounds like a different group of players.

Tradition, said Mahler, is slovenliness. Plenty of examples of tradition in that sense can be selected from the history of Parisian music-making, let alone from what went on in the provinces (and if I concentrate on Paris, that is because it dominated the musical life of the nation to an extent not found in any one city in the other main western European countries). Choosing at random, one could cite Spohr's criticism of the Théâtre-Italien orchestra under Jean-Jacques Grasset (c. 1769–1839): "to mark the time by continual movements of the body and the violin, as M. Grasset does, is absolutely useless,"[1] or Berlioz's anatomy of the same orchestra, section by section, in the *Berliner allgemeine musikalische Zeitung*: the violins only saved from total incompetence by four Conservatoire students with a working knowledge of the instrument (the opening of the Act 1 trio in *Fidelio* was so badly played that the pit broke into loud laughter), one adequate viola, one good cello out of a total of three (the other two being given more to nodding off than to playing), and so on.[2] Or from modern times, one could cite the propensity of French orchestral musicians for carrying on conversations during rehearsals. In this connection, I still remember vividly a rehearsal of Spontini's *La vestale* given by one of the Paris radio orchestras which I attended in the 1970s. On entering the hall I was struck by a kind of continuous humming noise clearly audible behind the music, which I took at first to be due to an over-energetic heating system, before I realized that it was the players talking.

Going back to the eighteenth century, one could quote Mozart, writing from Paris in 1778 at the time of the premiere of his Symphony No. 31:

> I was very nervous at the rehearsal, for never in my life have I heard a worse performance. You have no idea how they twice scraped and scrambled through it. I . . . would gladly have had it rehearsed again, but as there was so much else to rehearse, there was no time left.

Having at first decided to skip the concert, he changed his mind and went, but not before he had resolved that

> if my symphony went as badly as it did at the rehearsal, I would certainly make my way into the orchestra, snatch the fiddle out of the hands of Lahoussaye, the first violin, and conduct myself![3]

In the event, the symphony seems to have gone well enough, so there was no need to. But the incident will sound a chord of recognition in those who have experienced the perfunctoriness and spirit of routine of the bad side of French tradition – what I once called "mayhem in the great French tradition of vandalism against their own masterpieces."[4] A century earlier the same tradition drew a stinging rebuke from the French composer Ernest Reyer when, writing in 1864, he stigmatized

> the systematic and senseless cutting which destroys [an opera's] shape and its very character. And look how we treat the dead, who have no way of protesting or defending themselves. There is not a work of the old German school – not one – and scarcely any of the French that is not hacked about and changed at the whim of the director or the irrepressible creative urge of some artist or other.[5]

A similar negligent spirit reigns in Georges Prêtre's recording of the (admittedly complete) *Damnation de Faust* made four years after the shredded *Troyens*, in 1969. Yet Prêtre is a conductor who, in a more serious environment, with sufficient rehearsal, is capable of good work, as he showed when he conducted *Samson et Dalila* at Covent Garden in the 1980s.

It is not my intention to disparage French musical life, however. Against the examples just quoted could be set the passionate dedication, the exceptional training, discipline and esprit de corps of the Conservatoire orchestra in its early days, in the 1820s and 1830s, about which all contemporary testimony agrees, and which gives the lie resoundingly to the often-stated generalization that the French are too sceptical and individualistic to combine effectively in large-scale musical ensembles. Like any other such organization, the Conservatoire orchestra has experienced ups and downs, splendours as well as miseries, in its long history. Equally, French musical life, alongside its mediocrities, has generated and nurtured many fine conductors, from Habeneck and Berlioz to Boulez, via Colonne, Monteux, Munch, and Désormière, to single out only the most obvious names.

How good the conductors who antedated recording really were we have, of course, no direct means of knowing, though Berlioz's prowess is widely attested, and we may be pretty sure that Edouard Colonne (1838–1910) was a more faithful performer of Berlioz's music than either Jules Pasdeloup (1819–87) or Charles Lamoureux (1834–99): Pasdeloup whom Berlioz called "that blockhead" and whose performance of the "Fête" from *Roméo et Juliette* he avoided by staying in bed;[6] and Lamoureux, whom George Bernard Shaw contrasted unfavourably with Charles Hallé – Hallé's conducting of the *Marche hongroise*, wrote Shaw, created a sensation at St James's Hall in 1892, "taken at about half the speed at which Lamoureux vainly tries to make it 'go'."[7]

Early practice

The quality of their seventeenth- and eigtheenth-century predecessors is virtually impossible to assess, if only because what they did as conductors left no distinct impression: conducting in the sense that we understand the activity – its role, its enormous prestige – did not then exist. Mozart's threatened intervention, in the incident quoted above, or even Berlioz's actual intervention, sixty years later, springing forward to give the beat when Habeneck lowered his baton to take a pinch of snuff at a crucial point in the composer's *Grande messe des morts*,[8] would be almost unimaginable today; an equivalent modern scenario would be Michael Tippett seizing the baton from Sir Adrian Boult at the premiere of his second symphony in

1958, when – as happened – the orchestra broke down and had to start again.

Nor does the technique of conducting, in those far-off days, admit of generalization: the methods used varied too widely. Articles on early music are often written as though practice was uniform, when in fact – as one would expect – there were differences not only between but within countries. The premiere of Mozart's "Paris" Symphony was led by Pierre-Nicolas Lahoussaye (1735–1818) from the violin – the method preferred by Quantz. Yet even in the Baroque and early classical periods, as illustrations show, some conducted neither with the violin nor at the harpsichord or forte-piano, but with a baton or a roll of paper. This was especially so in church performances. (Or they might use the hands alone, particularly if conducting smaller vocal groups.) A handheld stick or small staff of some kind was obviously a more practical way of keeping a large ensemble of musicians together than direction (seated) at the keyboard or (standing) with a violin.

A conductor might vary the method according to the circumstances. François-Antoine Habeneck (1781–1849) directed the three-hundred-plus performers of Berlioz's *Grande messe des morts* (1837) with a baton, but when he conducted the eighty-strong Conservatoire orchestra he indicated the beat with the bow of his violin, as he did when conducting opera. The problem of securing good ensemble in a pit as wide as that of the Paris Opéra, and of ensuring that the singers and choristers on stage, in what were often elaborate productions, kept time among themselves and with the orchestra, was acute. Time-beating by banging on the floor, such as was responsible for Lully's demise, went on at the Opéra throughout the eighteenth century. It was frequently deplored but accepted as unavoidable, and it survived into the nineteenth century. Habeneck's use of a bow instead of the long pole was actually a step forward,[9] but he was in the habit of rapping with it on the prompt box, and was still doing so in the 1850s, according to a satirical feuilleton of 1852 written by Berlioz and entitled *Une victime du tack* (the tale of an inoffensive prompter driven into terminal decline by the noise of the conductor's bow on the roof of his retreat).[10] Berlioz's condemnation of audible time-beating of any kind, in his *Traité*,[11] shows that it was still in use in France in that period. The anecdote confirms, incidentally, that the modern placement of the opera conductor, with the orchestra spread out in front of him, was established only gradually.

As orchestral music shed the continuo and became more complex and technically exacting, and later, as concert halls increased in size to accommodate it and to meet the demands of a growing public, directing from the keyboard naturally disappeared. In most countries, too, the violinist-conductor had been replaced by the baton-wielding maestro by the mid-nineteenth century. Not in France, however. There the violinist-conductor continued to be, for a long time, the norm. As late as 1878 Edouard Deldevez (1817–92), in his influential *L'art du chef d'orchestre*, was still arguing that the violin was the conductor's natural instrument and that only a violin could do the job properly.[12] Georges Kastner in his *Cours d'instrumentation* – officially recognized by the Institut and adopted at the Conservatoire, as was his *Treatise* – was another authority who championed the violinist-conductor.[13] This was French practice as well as theory. All the chief conductors of the Conservatoire orchestra up to and including Deldevez (who held the post from 1873 to 1885) were violinists, except François-Georges Hainl (1807–73), who was a cellist.

It followed logically that they conducted not from the full score but from a violin part with instrumental cues written in. Deldevez said that the ideal was a specially prepared five-line score, comprising violin part, vocal line, two lines for cues, and bass.[14]

Here, in however odd a form (as it must strike us today), is something that can be called a French tradition. It could have surprisingly good results. Mendelssohn said that Habeneck, marking time with his bow, produced a performance "more precise than one would ever expect," when he heard him in Paris in 1832.[15]

Habeneck

Habeneck, the founder and first conductor of the Conservatoire orchestra, was probably the best of the string players who directed that famous band (though Holoman also thinks highly of Deldevez[16]). He was certainly superior to Narcisse Girard (1797–1860), who succeeded him at both the Société des Concerts and the Opéra, and to Hainl, and probably, too, to Théophile Tilmant *aîné* (1799–1878). At least in the case of the Beethoven performances that were such a feature of his programs, by frequent and painstaking rehearsal he came to know the music so well that the lack of a full score must have ceased to be the disadvantage it naturally seems to us. At the Opéra too, though we may wonder how a violin part with cues could possibly suffice for directing works as complex and demanding as *Guillaume Tell* or *Les Huguenots*, there again the long rehearsal period would to some extent have enabled him to overcome that obstacle. But the Opéra was never so close to Habeneck's heart as his beloved Société des Concerts. Routine and slackness in the run-of-the-mill repertoire were frequently encountered at the Opéra even during Habeneck's years at the helm (1824–46) – it could take an important premiere to make the old place rouse itself and pull out the stops – but that was rarely so at the Conservatoire, at least in the early years. Though the Beethoven symphonies came round again repeatedly, the sense of adventure and excitement, the conviction of conductor and orchestra that they were engaged in a heroic enterprise, a historic mission, persisted for some time. The musicians were conscious of belonging to an elite, selected from the best pupils of the Conservatoire and the best members of the three main Paris theatre orchestras (most of them ex-Conservatoire students themselves) – the Opéra (the majority), the Opéra-Comique and the Théâtre-Italien – but emancipated from the routine of the opera pit and its mediocre standards and ephemeral repertoire.

Habeneck had long dreamed of popularizing Beethoven's music in Paris. As a young man, in the 1800s, he had led student performances of one or two of the symphonies; later, at the Concerts Spirituels, he had introduced individual movements, and in the late 1820s his great plan came to fruition. By that time he was a prominent and powerful figure in Paris musical life and a senior professor of violin at the Conservatoire. He had to proceed with caution: Beethoven had the reputation, among French orchestral players, of being obscure and horribly difficult to play. In November 1826, thirty or so of the best musicians were invited to dine at his apartment in the Rue de la Tour d'Auvergne, bringing with them their instruments so as to celebrate St. Cecilia's Day with a little music. On arriving they found music stands set out, with the parts of an unknown piece on them. They worked on it till dark. At dinner – announced by Madame Habeneck with the words, "In the name of Beethoven, *à table*"[17] – it was revealed to have been the "Eroica." It was the "Eroica" that, sixteen months later, after many more sessions with an orchestra augmented to eighty-six players, inaugurated the opening season of the Société des Concerts. The Conservatoire Hall, resonant ("the Stradivarius of concert halls"[18]), compact, seating about a thousand people crammed close together, has lost its warm acoustic thanks to modern reconstruction of the stage area in concrete and steel and the installing of plush seats; but in March 1828 – as for more than a century subsequently – the impact of Beethoven's revolutionary work played by more than eighty well-trained musicians fired with missionary fervour must have been prodigious. The concert stands as one of the great events in the history of music in France. No wonder Habeneck boasted that he had "discovered" Beethoven. That Sunday afternoon, the other five concerts of the opening season, and those that followed, galvanised Parisian musical life, especially among the younger element.

It had been done, more than anything, by long, patient rehearsal. The ninth symphony, which was finally performed in 1831, was prepared movement by movement over three seasons. Habeneck does not seem to have been a conductor of any obvious flair; but he believed in the music and inspired his players with the same belief, and achieved by hard work the exceptional accuracy of ensemble and fidelity of expression which so impressed the serious music-lovers and musicians who attended the Conservatoire concerts in those first years. More than a decade later, Wagner found the same discipline and spirit still active when he heard the ninth symphony rehearsed and performed in November 1839.[19]

In the 1840s, as Habeneck's health declined, the orchestra's standards slipped and its élan faltered. Glinka, who heard it during his stay in Paris in 1845, was disappointed with it (and also noted the musicians' penchant for taking snuff during rehearsals, especially in difficult passages[20]). It is doubtful if the orchestra ever equalled the achievements of the best of the Habeneck years under any of his three immediate successors, Girard, Tilmant, or Hainl. All three were lesser men. The leading French conductor, after Habeneck, was Berlioz.

Berlioz

There is no doubt that Hector Berlioz (1803–69) surpassed Habeneck, not simply as conductor of his own music (in which Habeneck, though game, could only approximate to what the composer wanted) but in Beethoven as well. Berlioz was one of the first of a new type of conductor – the complete, all-seeing, all-hearing maestro of the kind that we recognize. He used a baton and the full score, and orchestral parts with rehearsal letters added, he introduced sectional rehearsals (for the percussion as well as for strings, woodwind and brass), had an ear so acute that he could detect the minutest fluctuations of pitch,[21] conducted with both thoroughness and flair, and in his handling of his players combined authority with what the London critic Edward Holmes called "the art of conciliating them [and of] engaging their best efforts in his behalf . . . his demeanour being perfectly simple, free from airs of superiority, or any assumption of the great man."[22]

Berlioz's tours of Germany and Austro-Hungary in the 1840s, 1850s and early 1860s, and his visits to St. Petersburg and London, had a far-reaching effect on the development of orchestral playing and the conductor's craft. Hallé thought him "the most perfect conductor that I ever set eyes upon, one who held absolute sway over his troops, and played upon them as a pianist upon the keyboard," and praised his "decisive" beat and his meticulously clear "indication of all the nuances."[23] César Cui, writing in the winter of 1867–8, said that "of all the conductors we have heard in Petersburg Berlioz is unquestionably the greatest," with an unequalled grasp of Beethoven (Berlioz conducted five of the symphonies – Nos. 3–7), and also remarked on his neat, exact beat.[24] (Evidently his style had changed, becoming more economical. In 1843 Spontini criticized him for his over-expansive gestures.[25] This is a salutary reminder that eyewitness observations, upon which music historians are so dependent, are valid only for the time when they were made.) The young Hans von Bülow, who heard Berlioz conduct *La damnation de Faust* and other works of his in Dresden in 1854, called him "incomparable," and related how the Kapellmeister, Krebs, actually rebuked the orchestra for having "played so magnificently under the baton of a 'foreigner'! What a public humiliation for the local conductors, under whose direction the orchestra had never managed to show such zeal and ardour."[26]

At the announcement, in 1850, that Berlioz was forming a new orchestra, the Société Philharmonique de Paris, everybody wanted to play in it, so great was his prestige as a conductor.[27] It was his *Traité* and his *L'art du chef d'orchestre*, not Kastner's or Deldevez's, that were read and studied worldwide. He was the first to attempt a systematic analysis of the technique of conducting. If, unlike Wagner, he did not philosophize about interpretation and the "soul" of a piece of music, that does not mean that they were not as important to him as to Wagner, merely that he was French, not German (though claimed as spiritually a German by admirers like Cornelius and Griepenkerl and the ladies of the Leipzig Singakademie).[28] His two performances of Beethoven's Symphony No. 9 in 1852 revealed what had been till then to Londoners a sealed book; in the words of one reviewer, it was "the greatest victory ever yet attained in the development of Beethoven's intentions."[29] In the same season the critic J. W. Davison, a passionate admirer of Mendelssohn, hailed Berlioz's conducting of the "Italian" Symphony and the Violin Concerto as the most faithful he had ever heard.[30]

All this entitles Berlioz to be considered one of the pioneers of modern conducting. But if the future belonged to him, the present, in his own country at least, emphatically did not. It was probably the combination of not being a violinist-conductor and being a composer-conductor that prevented him from achieving an official position. Composer-conductors were regarded as suspect: they were too interested in programming their own works. The violinist-conductor, the conductor who had, as it were, come up through the ranks, was still the norm, the baton-conductor the exception, the outsider, as Berlioz was fated, in Paris, to remain. (His instrument was not the violin but the flute.) His fame as a conductor was won in Germany, Russia, and London.

In this he was again a precursor, the first French conductor to be acclaimed and actively sought-after abroad. Berlioz came near to being offered, or accepting, appointments in Vienna, Dresden, London, and New York. Later French conductors would occupy important positions outside France: Pierre Monteux (New York, Boston, San Francisco, London), Charles Munch (Boston), Pierre Boulez (London, New York). In Paris, Berlioz generally had to assemble his own orchestra from scratch each time and gamble on the receipts covering the outlay on musicians' fees, copying of parts, hire and heating of the hall, and the other expenses incurred by a freelance concert-promoter. *La damnation de Faust*, in 1846, lost him so much money that he gave no further concerts in Paris till 1850, when he founded the Société Philharmonique, a co-operative body organized on the lines of the Société des Concerts. Despite a promising start, it lasted only two seasons.

Pasdeloup, Lamoureux, and Colonne

By this time there were several such competing organizations in Paris. The Société Philharmonique's main rival, the more successful (partly because more strongly backed) Société Sainte Cécile, founded by another violinist-conductor, François Seghers (1801–81) lasted till 1854. In the event, both were surpassed by the success of Pasdeloup's Concerts Populaires de Musique Classique. Pasdeloup, who had been timpanist in the Société Philharmonique, began by founding the Société des Jeunes Artistes du Conservatoire, in 1853, then in 1861, with backing from a rich financier, hired the five-thousand-seat Cirque Napoléon and engaged an orchestra of 110 players. Tickets were cheap, and the growing public for serious music, debarred from the exclusive Conservatoire concerts, flocked to his. Berlioz was not alone in having a low opinion of Pasdeloup's skills – Saint-Saëns said he was "d'une incapacité immense" – but he was an enthusiast and did much to popularize not only the classics (the German classics especially) but also new music.

From the 1870s onwards, Pasdeloup increasingly lost ground to his rivals: Lamoureux's Nouveaux Concerts, then the Société Nationale de Musique (which championed the new generation – Saint-Saëns, Lalo, César Franck, d'Indy, and others), and above all Colonne's Concert National founded in 1873, which a year later became the Association Artistique. By 1903 the Association had given more than eight hundred concerts, featuring particularly the music of Berlioz, Beethoven, Wagner, and Saint-Saëns, but also offering a wide repertoire of French and foreign works, and setting new standards for the performance of symphonic music. Colonne had a huge impact on French musical taste. In the words of Romain Rolland:

> No one did more to break down the barriers separating the French public from foreign art. At the same time he was actively influential in spreading a knowledge of French art abroad. And while he was conducting concerts in Europe and America, he invited the great German Kapellmeisters and

foreign composers to direct the Châtelet orchestra: Richard Strauss, Grieg, Tchaikovsky, Hans Richter, Hermann Levi, Mottl, Nikisch, Mengelberg, Siegfried Wagner, and many others.[31]

Monteux and Munch

With Colonne begins a new era in French musical life. The Théâtre du Châtelet, home of the Concerts Colonne, is still today a center of operatic and symphonic activity in Paris. More immediately, one of France's greatest conductors was nurtured there. In 1890, while still a student, the fifteen-year-old Pierre Monteux joined the viola section. Four years later he became Colonne's assistant conductor and choir master. From then on his rise was assured. In 1911 he was appointed chief conductor of Diaghilev's Ballets Russes and directed the premieres of, among other works, *Petrushka, Le sacre du printemps, Le rossignol, Daphnis et Chloé,* and *Jeux* (many years earlier he had led the violas in *Pelléas et Mélisande* at the Opéra-Comique).

Monteux excelled not only in French music but also in Beethoven and Brahms (as a youthful member of the Geloso Quartet he played a Brahms quartet in the composer's presence). His younger contemporary Charles Munch (1891–1968) carried on the Franco-German tradition of Berlioz, Colonne, and Monteux: from 1926 to 1933 Munch, who had trained as a violinist, was Furtwängler's concertmaster at the Leipzig Gewandhaus. In the latter year he made his conducting debut. He was over forty, but his progress was rapid, and in 1938 he was appointed chief conductor of the Conservatoire orchestra, where he remained till 1946, when he went to the Boston Symphony. Munch was a more mercurial conductor than Monteux. He prepared his players thoroughly, but believed in the impulse of the moment; successive readings of a work could differ widely. His Berlioz was admired in France for its verve but had a less sure sense of tempo and structure than Monteux's.[32]

Monteux and Munch were by no means the only highly successful French conductors of the twentieth century. Philippe Gaubert (1879–1941) – like Berlioz, a flautist – led the Société des Concerts from 1919 to 1938. Holoman considers him one of the best in the society's long history.[33] Roger Désormière (1898–1963), who worked with the Ballets Russes and at the Opéra-Comique, was widely admired for his Debussy performances, and also promoted both Baroque (Rameau, Lalande) and contemporary music (Messiaen, Boulez). André Cluytens was Munch's successor at the Conservatoire, but made his greatest name in opera (a leading French Wagnerian, he conducted several times at Bayreuth). The inter-war period, with Stravinsky, Ravel and Les Six all producing new works, was a boom time in orchestral activity in Paris; there was a huge increase in the number of concerts. Quantity, though, did not always mean quality. Désormière complained that the Conservatoire orchestra's Tuesday rehearsal was treated "as a meeting where you recount the interesting things you did on Monday (fishing, pinocle or other amusements); the rehearsal should start at 9.30, but I've never been able to begin before 10, and at 11 these gentlemen leave."[34]

Boulez

The supreme French conductor of recent times is Pierre Boulez. As a composer-conductor he is in the tradition of Berlioz and, though very different in nature and personality, shares some of his predecessor's characteristics as a performing musician: rhythmic precision, clarity of beat, sense of the practical, passionate attention to detail. But whereas Berlioz remained outside the establishment and despite many attempts succeeded only sporadically in getting the powers that be to espouse his cause and override bureaucratic opposition, Boulez outmaneuvered the establishment by joining it: his pioneering Institute for Research and Acoustic-Musical Co-ordination (IRCAM) was set up at the behest of the President of the Republic, Georges Pompidou. (It is perhaps not entirely unsymbolic, however, that Boulez's home for many years was in Germany.) Some find him a rather cold conductor; but of his mastery of the craft of conducting there can be no doubt. He is the most generally admired and respected French musician of recent times. More than any other conductor, by his advocacy and his lucid, scrupulous, and powerful performances he has brought the music of the first half of the twentieth century – that of Debussy, Bartók, Stravinsky, Varèse, Schoenberg, Berg, and Webern, at least – to a wider public than ever before; and, within the limits of a very decided taste, he continues to champion new music.[35]

But the last word should go to the Société des Concerts. After nearly a hundred and forty years of fluctuating though sometimes splendid achievement, the Conservatoire orchestra was reconstituted, on November 14, 1967, as the Orchestre de Paris, with a program consisting of *La mer*, Stravinsky's *Canticum sacrum*, and the *Symphonie fantastique*, under Munch, who became its first conductor. The refounded orchestra was the linchpin of the grand plan of the Director of Music at the Ministry of Culture, Marcel Landowski, for the reconstruction of music in France – a plan which included new orchestras in Lyon, Angers and Nantes and new regional conservatoires. Nine years later the Choeurs de l'Orchestre de Paris was founded under Arthur Oldham, and France at last had a first-rate large-scale choir, traditionally the weakest link of the Société des Concerts.[36]

Thirty-five years on, after vicissitudes from which no orchestra, least of all in France, is immune, the Orchestre de Paris appears in lively health under its present conductor, the German Christoph Eschenbach. Eschenbach is a pianist – something of a new departure in the orchestra's history. But the high morale and conspicuous esprit de corps which now animate it may be seen as a link with the early days of its famous predecessor – perhaps, after all, a tradition, reborn.

11 The Italian tradition

MICHAEL ROSE

The conductor, in any form recognizable today, emerged later in Italy than in other European countries. Italy had no Habeneck or Berlioz, no Spohr or Mendelssohn – and later, as the role of the professional conductor developed, no Bülow or Richter or Nikisch. It was not until the first years of the twentieth century that a real Italian star exploded on the international scene, and if the blaze of Toscanini's fame has tended to obscure the activities of his predecessors, that is chiefly because they had been obliged to struggle for so long with the last vestiges of a ubiquitous native tradition that would not easily relax its grip.

The dominating feature of that tradition was opera. The Italians invented opera, and they remained faithful to it as their main form of musical expression and social enjoyment for the best part of three centuries; in spite of the jigsaw of political frontiers it spread remorselessly over the whole peninsula, and was accompanied by a parallel decline in other forms of music. Church music (much of it on operatic lines) remained in constant production, but the history of Italian instrumental music, after the great days of the Baroque concerto, is one of gradual attenuation; the few interested Italians tended to go abroad – Boccherini to Spain, Clementi to England, Cherubini and Spontini to Paris. Italy was "the land of song," and symphonic developments in other parts of Europe were regarded at best as irrelevant to the melodic invention that was the real purpose of music, at worst as a serious threat to it; orchestral complication was viewed with mistrust. Small wonder, then, that Rossini, Donizetti and Bellini followed their predecessors to Paris where new possibilities were opening up in both orchestral and operatic fields, leaving behind them a pack of lesser figures to feed the home market with renewed helpings of the operatic formula that had served Italian audiences for so long.

By the 1860s, however, the tide was turning: the Parisian operas of Meyerbeer (who, having craftily adopted the first name of Giacomo, could be accepted as a sort of honorary Italian) were already introducing Italy to a more adventurous use of the orchestra, and the works of Verdi's middle period were creating a new and more complex format for dramatic expression. As the last chamber activities of the old ducal courts disappeared in the newly united kingdom, philharmonic societies with middle-class patrons took their place. There was a new cultural seriousness in the air; Beethoven was gaining ground, the name of Wagner could be timidly mentioned, and there were signs of a revival of instrumental composition. But it was still opera, in its evolving form, that was to be the main beneficiary of this long overdue recognition of the possibilities of the orchestra.

The role of the conductor to the end of the eighteenth century

As elsewhere, the first Italian conductors were simply time-beaters: generally a performer who kept his colleagues together while singing or playing from his own part-book, using either the staff, which traditionally marked his office, or a rolled-up scroll of music, but often relying on simple movements of the hand. Up to the sixteenth century the singers had only their own parts, with no barlines. It was the coming of opera and the growth of instrumental music that made a score and barlines essential. But though instrumental groups in the Baroque period were directed by the principal violinist with his bow, we know very little about how the earliest operas were conducted. The first Florentine examples, where the accompaniment was confined to a small ensemble, could be treated with the intimacy of chamber music, but as opera developed and dramatic action became less static, a range of instruments had to be balanced with the needs of singers moving about the stage. Theatre records show that the composer was often present at the harpsichord, where he no doubt set the tempo and gave cues while filling out the continuo bass, but as late as 1739 Charles de Brosses observed: "They beat time in church for Latin music but never at the opera, no matter how large the orchestra or how complicated the piece being played." And he noted the problems this caused in the accompanied recitatives which were then beginning to find their way into *opera seria*: "the execution of these . . . is very difficult, especially for the instrumentalists, because of the capricious changes of pace, which are not indicated by any conductor's beat."[1]

Eventually the increasing size of opera orchestras (the San Carlo in Naples around fifty players by the middle of the eighteenth century, the Scala, Milan, sixty-seven by 1778) and the growing complexity of relations between orchestra and stage brought about the system of dual responsibility that became standard over the whole of Europe: the *maestro al cembalo*, at the keyboard, continued the role of filling out the harmonies and accompanying the recitatives – he taught the singers their notes, rehearsed them, and in performance marked the tempo for them with his hands or by stamping his feet; the principal violinist, or *capo d'orchestra*, reading from a violin part, directed the orchestra by playing confidently (and generally loudly) with bold gestures of his bowing arm.

Figure 11.1 Caricature of the Neapolitan composer Nicola Logroscino banging on the side of his harpsichord (Pierluigi Ghezzi, *c.* 1740/50)

Any system of divided authority risks confusion, not to mention disagreement and rivalry, and there is evidence of stamping, tapping, and banging on the side of the harpsichord as methods of keeping performers together. (See Fig. 11.1.) Banging was anyhow an established practice in choral performances, as Goethe found at Venice in 1786:

> The performance would have been even more enjoyable if the damned conductor had not beaten time against the [choir] screen with a rolled sheet of music as insolently as if he were teaching schoolboys. The girls had so often rehearsed the piece that his vehement slapping was as unnecessary as if, in order to make us appreciate a beautiful statue, someone were to stick little patches of red cloth on the joints . . . I know this thumping out the beat is customary with the French; but I had not expected it from the Italians. The public, though, seemed to be used to it.[2]

And apparently remained so. Seventy years later the English baritone, Charles Santley, was at High Mass in Milan Cathedral. "The conductor was a great nuisance," he wrote. "For *bâton* he used a piece of music twice doubled and folded flat, with which he beat the first two beats of every bar on the book in front of him. In a quick three-four movement the constant flip-flap engrossed the attention . . ."[3]

Audience and orchestra in the early nineteenth century

Since the opening of the first public opera house in Venice in 1637, local Italian audiences had come to regard opera more and more as a social occasion where they could indulge their passion for theatre – much as the Spanish do with bullfights or the English with football – rather than as a musical or dramatic experience. The conventions of Metastasian opera were rigid and predictable, the mainly classical plots pretty well known, and in any case most Italians would go to see the same opera night after night; what they really wanted was a chance to cheer the star castrato in a favorite aria, or boo some unhappy lesser mortal who had not the luck to please them. The emphasis on enjoyment never failed to provoke comment from foreign visitors. "Chess is a marvelous invention for filling the gap of those long recitatives, and music perfect for interrupting too great concentration on chess,"[4] wrote de Brosses (an admirer of Italian opera for all that), and even when the long recitatives gave way to more varied dramatic treatment the situation showed no signs of changing. At La Scala in 1816, "during the . . . overture, several very expressive accompanied recitatives, and all the *pièces d'ensemble*," wrote Spohr, "the audience made so much noise that one could scarcely hear the music . . . All over the house, people conversed aloud. Nothing more insufferable can be imagined for a stranger who is desirous to listen with attention, than this vile noise."[5]

Nevertheless the playing at La Scala "very much surpassed" Spohr's expectation. At the San Carlo too the execution was precise: "under the correct and spirited but somewhat too loud direction of Signor Festa, [the orchestra] had studied it well, though they were somewhat wanting in *nuances* of *piano* and *forte* . . ."[6] In 1831 Berlioz (who it must be said had not yet been to Milan) found the Neapolitan orchestra excellent "compared with those I had encountered till then," though he rather spoils it by adding "it was quite safe to listen to the wind instruments," and he still notes "the highly disagreeable noise made by the conductor tapping with his bow on the desk."[7] Mendelssohn remembered that it was "a tin candlestick" on which the four quarters of each bar were beaten, "which is often more distinctly heard than the voices (it sounds somewhat like *obbligati* castanets, only louder)."[8] So did this mean that Festa, who was sixty by 1831 with other duties to attend to in Naples, had taken a night off? Or was the tapping so universal that Spohr thought it not worth mentioning? Berlioz was told that "without it the musicians would sometimes have been hard put to it to play in time" – which, as he adds, "was unanswerable." And old habits die hard: in 1892 in London, when the seventy-year-old Arditi shared the conducting of *Eugene Onegin* with the young Henry Wood, "he still continued to tap every first beat of the bar on the top of a Bechstein conductor's piano whenever the music was at all complicated."[9]

If the orchestras at La Scala and the San Carlo generally commanded qualified respect, in the smaller provincial theatres even Stendhal, that passionate apologist for the Italian operatic scene, was forced to admit that "there are certain notes which their fingers just do not possess the necessary dexterity to strike correctly."[10] And in Rome, where the orchestra at the Teatro Valle was "permitted to chatter in a loud voice, to applaud the singers when the audience disapproves of them, to leave and resume their seats, and from time to time straddle across the partition which separates the orchestra from the pit,"[11] Spohr found that the Italian obsession with melody at all costs put yet another obstacle in the way of orchestral discipline:

> The ignorance, want of taste, and stupid arrogance of [the Roman orchestral players] beggars all description . . . Each individual makes just what ornamentation comes into his head and double strokes with almost every tone, so that the *ensemble* resembles more the noise of an orchestra tuning up than harmonious music. I certainly forbade several times every note which did not stand in the score; but ornamentation has become so much a second nature to them, that they cannot desist from it.[12]

The baton

Although the official titles of *maestro al cembalo* and *primo violino capo* were retained long into the nineteenth century (at La Scala until 1853), the disappearance of *secco* recitative in all but *opera buffa* was rapidly making the role of the keyboard in operatic performances irrelevant. The composer of a new opera was still expected to "accompany" the first three performances at the piano, and while he did so his was clearly the authoritative voice: Donizetti wrote of the importance of seating the composer in such a way "that he can indicate to the principal violinist, by word and gesture, the various *tempi* that he desires."[13] But after the first three nights this authority passed solely to the *primo violino*. "Signor Rolla . . . directed as first violin," wrote Spohr in 1816. "There is no other directing whether at the piano, or from the desk with the baton, than his, but merely a prompter with the score before him, who gives the text to the singers, and if necessary, the time to the choruses."[14] Twenty years later, when the authority of the conductor had been well established elsewhere in Europe, the Scala orchestra was still led by Cavallini (Rolla's successor) "for they have no conductors in Italy,"[15] and even the great Paganini, fresh from Paris, found his proposal for a conductor of the modern type at Parma rejected as newfangled and unacceptable.[16]

Under the circumstances it is perhaps not surprising that the first Italians to establish a conducting career in anything like the modern sense did so outside Italy. Gaspare Spontini (1774–1851), who moved to Paris in 1803 and leapt into fame with *La vestale* four years later, entered conducting history in 1820 with his appointment as Generalmusikdirektor in Berlin, where he became probably the first Italian to conduct an orchestra with a baton. Spontini's Berlin activities belong essentially to the story of German conducting,[17] though the fanatical pursuit of precision and tyrannical control for which he was famous recall Toscanini as much as any German successor. And Toscanini springs to mind again in the case of Michele Costa (1808–84), another disciplinarian with an iron grip on his players. Costa, who later anglicized his name to "Michael", settled in London in 1830 as *maestro al piano* at the King's Theatre, where within two years he had abolished the existing system of dual leadership and, following the example of Spohr, Weber, and Mendelssohn, taken up the baton as sole director. His immediate success and lasting influence on London's musical institutions are an English story,[18] but Moscheles noted in 1849 that "[he] wields his baton more in Italian than German style,"[19] and his tempos in symphonic works were criticized for a tendency that has often been seen as characteristic of Italian conducting. Verdi knew this, yet considered Costa "one of the greatest conductors in Europe;"[20] on the other hand Sterndale Bennett, hearing that Costa was to conduct the Philharmonic concerts, wrote to J. W. Davison: "I hope not: the only advantage would be that we might hear the whole of Beethoven's symphonies in one night and still have time to spare for supper."[21] There were similar feelings about another Italian who ended up in England: Luigi Arditi (1822–1903), famous in the drawing rooms of Europe as the composer of *Il bacio*. Arditi's long career took him to New York, St. Petersburg, and Vienna, but seldom to Italy: "He can conduct anything," observed Shaw, "and come off without defeat, thanks to his address, his experience, and his musical instinct. But symphony is not his department."[22]

By far the most important of the Italian conductors of this generation, however, was Angelo Mariani (1821–73; see Fig. 11.2), whose career, apart from two brief interludes, took place entirely in his own country. Mariani is normally credited with being the first conductor to use the baton in Italy, although exactly when he did so is not easy to establish. At Messina, where

MDCCCLVII.

AD ANGELO MARIANI CAVALIERE

*Interprete supremo, ed tutore
delle più riposte bellezze musicali*

L'Orchestra

per l'apertura del nuovo Teatro Remeneo

Figure 11.2 Angelo Mariani at the time of the premiere of *Aroldo* in 1857

he became *maestro concertatore* and *direttore d'orchestra* in 1844, he was unable "to give proof of what [he] could do" because of protests by the Sicilian musicians at having to play "under a *foreign boy*,"[23] which suggests that he was already trying out some stronger form of central control. Two years later he made his Milanese debut at the Teatro Re with Verdi's *I due Foscari*, and followed it at the Carcano with a *Nabucco* that nearly landed him in prison for "having given Verdi's music an expression too evidently rebellious and hostile to the Imperial government."[24] But it was in 1852, when he began a lifelong association with the Teatro Carlo Felice in Genoa, that he showed his true mettle, enlarging and improving the orchestra until it became the best in Italy, conducting it (certainly with a baton by now) with skill and authority, and making himself responsible for every detail of the performances in a way that had never been seen in Italy before.

His taste was adventurous: his virtuosity found an ideal vehicle in the operas of Meyerbeer, and when he doubled his position in Genoa with a similar post at the Teatro Comunale in Bologna he opened with Verdi's latest opera, *Un ballo in maschera*. His arrival on the scene came at a fortunate time for Verdi, whose development as a composer was reaching a point that demanded the services of a real conductor. At the rehearsals for the premiere of *Aroldo* at Rimini in 1857 his expertise was crucial to Verdi in the new and complex orchestral writing of the final act; when a performance of *Aroldo* was mooted in Paris, Verdi advised against it, saying "without Mariani the opera is impossible." The warm personal relationship which grew up between the two men in the years following *Aroldo* was not to have a happy ending, but Mariani's passionate advocacy of Verdi's music never diminished, and reached its crowning point in Bologna in 1867 with the Italian premiere of *Don Carlo*. Mariani surpassed himself, and the Milanese critic Filippo Filippi wrote:

> The first and greatest credit for this marvellous achievement is due to the
> conductor, Angelo Mariani, for whom no praise, no epithets, can
> suffice . . . Not only did he rehearse and conduct the score, but he thought
> of everything, down to the smallest detail of the staging. From the
> orchestra his genius (it really is genius) sparkles; one would say that by
> richness of colour, by fire, by the magic of sonority, he creates another *Don
> Carlos* within the *Don Carlos* of Verdi.[25]

Four years later he made operatic history with the first performance of a Wagner opera in Italy. *Lohengrin*, at Bologna on November 1, 1871, was a sensation, and Bülow, who came from Germany and attended several performances, added the enthusiastic praises of the Wagner camp. *Tannhäuser* in the following year, though no failure, made less impact, and seven months later Mariani was dead.

Clearly Mariani had the kind of personal magnetism that we associate with star conductors today. A good-looking man of great charm (which he used ruthlessly to attain his ends), he was severe and sometimes irritable in rehearsal, but in the theatre, "from the eminence of his conductor's rostrum, he dominated the orchestra, the stage and the adoring crowd of spectators."[26] Verdi, in whose eyes Mariani in his later years could do nothing right, was nevertheless clear about the importance of the new development. "Always remember", he wrote to Ricordi, "that the success of our operas lies most of

Figure 11.3 Verdi in 1879, a cartoon in *Vanity Fair* published when he visited London to conduct the *Requiem*. "The fire, which burns in . . . his dramatic music, is revealed undiminished . . . as soon as he holds the baton in his hand . . . [He] does not merely beat time, he conducts in the fullest sense of the word, he mirrors the musical ideas in his expression, his stance and the movement of his baton." (August Guckeisen, cited in Marcello Conati, *Interviews and Encounters with Verdi* [London: Gollancz, 1984], p. 125.)

the time in the hands of the conductor. This person is as necessary as a tenor or prima donna."[27] And to Escudier: "See how right I am to say that one single hand, if secure and powerful, can work miracles. You have seen it with Costa in London; you see it even more with Mariani at Bologna."[28] When reported as having described Mariani as "a fine conductor who overdoes all his *tempi*" he explained: "he has this tendency, to give more *brio* to the pieces . . . Besides, I should have the same tendency, if I were a conductor."[29] But he also saw the dangers of the new role, and wrote to Ricordi:

> I want only one creator . . . We all agree on [Mariani's] worth, but here we are not talking about an individual, however great, but about art. I cannot concede the right to "create" to singers or conductors . . . Once you praised an effect that Mariani got out of the overture to *La forza del destino* by having the brass in G enter *fortissimo*. Well, I disapprove of this effect. These brass instruments, *a mezza voce* as I conceived them, could not express anything but the religious chant of the Father Superior. Mariani's *fortissimo* completely alters its character, and the passage becomes a warlike fanfare that has nothing to do with the subject of the drama, where war is purely episodic.[30]

The succession to Mariani

Mariani's example had a profound, if gradual, effect on the Italian musical world. At the San Carlo, the old ways continued until the 1870s (Verdi refused to allow performances of *Forza* and *Don Carlo* there because of the lack of an authoritative conductor), and at La Scala in 1865 Santley witnessed the survival of the old methods under Alberto Mazzucato (1813–77), *maestro concertatore* since 1854, whose *primo violino*, Eugenio Cavallini, had been director of the orchestra for seventeen years before that.

> Cavallini [directed] the orchestra with his fiddlestick . . . taking the time from Mazzucato, who, seated in front of the stage, beat the time with his hand, whilst the chorus-master stood in front of his regiment also beating time. Altercations between [Cavallini] and the principal instruments were not uncommon. I remember one . . . [which ended] in the double-bass requesting the conductor to "shut up," as he did not know what he was talking about.[31]

Nevertheless, the growing importance of the orchestra was changing traditional attitudes, and after Mariani's death three contenders were waiting in the wings for the position of Italy's leading conductor: Franco Faccio (1840–91), Emilio Usiglio (1841–1910), and Luigi Mancinelli (1848–1921). Usiglio, a brilliant young promise, seemed at first destined to step into Mariani's shoes, but his dissolute lifestyle compromised his career and after he had been too drunk to conduct *Aida* at Perugia in 1874 his reputation for reliability suffered. Usiglio's deputy, who saved the day on that occasion, was the young Mancinelli, a budding composer who was already considered brilliant enough to accompany the Scala orchestra to the Universal Exhibition in Paris in 1878, and to conduct the inaugural season of the new *società orchestrale* at La Scala in the following year; he was later to build an international career as an authoritative and skillful director in London, Madrid, New York, and Buenos Aires, but he never achieved the preeminent position in Italy that Mariani had left vacant.

Faccio, on the other hand, unquestionably did. Like Mancinelli he began as a composer, but at the age of twenty-six turned exclusively to conducting, and only five years later succeeded Eugenio Terziani, Mazzucato's successor, as *maestro concertatore e direttore per le opere* at La Scala. After a bad period, the Scala orchestra was in need of strong direction, and in spite of his gentle manner Faccio provided it with panache for the next eighteen years. "He maintains the most perfect discipline," wrote Giulio Ricordi to Verdi; "he is very severe and reserved with the members of the orchestra who esteem and obey him without a whimper . . . [and has] a secure, calm and effective beat which brings about a truly commendable performance."[32] By the time of the Paris visit, the Scala orchestra was once again the best in Italy; the programmes were varied, and the French press praised "the precision of attack, the clarity of sound and the scrupulous care for nuance" of the visitors, who played "with incomparable assurance. The indications given by the conductor are rigorously obeyed, without the smallest deviation – a spirit of ensemble perfect in the tiniest details."[33]

The Paris visit was a remarkable tribute to the new interest in symphonic music that was by now spreading across Italy. In Turin, which provided the only other Italian orchestra at the exhibition, an early symphonic culture had been nurtured by a pioneering series of weekly *concerti popolari* set up in 1872 under the conductorship of Carlo Pedrotti (1817–93). Until his appointment as director of the Teatro Regio at the age of fifty-one, Pedrotti had been known mainly as a composer, but during the next fourteen years he transformed the musical life of Turin until it rivalled that of Milan and Bologna, and laid the foundations of the orchestra that Toscanini was to direct twenty years later. Even greater persistence in the symphonic repertory came from the composer Giuseppe Martucci (1856–1909), whose very first concerts in Naples included Berlioz, Schumann, Wagner, and the first performance of Brahms's second symphony in Italy, and who later, in Bologna, conducted the Italian premiere of that most symphonic of operas, *Tristan und Isolde*. At his concerts at the Turin Exhibition in 1884, Martucci's Neapolitan orchestra distinguished itself from its colleagues from Turin, Milan, Bologna, Rome, and Parma by giving complete symphonies (instead of the single movements then favored) and actually including no operatic music at all, apart from overtures.

Martucci's conducting in Turin was seen to be markedly different from the more "extrovert" manner of Mancinelli and Faccio, but then Faccio, in spite of his wide range of taste (his last triumph at La Scala was the first Italian *Meistersinger*), remained essentially an opera man. Early in his career, rehearsals for the revised version of *Forza* initiated a close friendship with Verdi which lasted all his life. He was responsible for the Italian premiere of *Aida*, the revised version of *Simon Boccanegra* and in 1887 the *prima assoluta* of *Otello* – all of them under the grilling eye of the composer himself (and, in the last case, with the nineteen-year-old Arturo Toscanini playing as second cello). Faccio, in fact, is often seen as the link between Mariani and Toscanini, and in point of quality he certainly was. When Faccio took *Otello* to London in 1889, Shaw wrote: "The interpretation of Verdi's score, the artistic homogeneity of performance, the wonderful balance of orchestra, chorus, and principals, stamp Faccio as a masterly conductor. The work of the orchestra and chorus far surpasses anything yet achieved under Signor Mancinelli at Covent Garden."[34]

Toscanini

Arturo Toscanini (1867–1957) marks a watershed in Italian conducting. He brought to their logical conclusion the reforms begun by Mariani, and summed up the opposition of Italian conducting to the more romantic, "interpretative" approach that had originated with Wagner and Liszt. But his international career also marked the end of an era, and his long life carried him over into an altogether new musical world of recordings, publicity, and media adulation. Though he began his career in opera, and directed at La Scala what is still regarded as one of the greatest regimes in operatic history, after 1929 he conducted no opera in Italy at all, and outside it only a handful of seasons at Bayreuth and Salzburg before he broke with both on political grounds. He was the first Italian conductor to make an international name in the concert hall, where his repertoire, though perhaps cautious by the standards of his contemporaries, included Berlioz, Brahms, Tchaikovsky, Debussy, Richard Strauss, and above all Beethoven, whom he regarded as the greatest of all. His passionate commitment to Verdi, who praised him warmly as a young man, and to Puccini, with whom he had a cordial but stormy working relationship, was perhaps to be expected given his background and temperament. But his championship of Wagner was also lifelong: he opened his first season in Turin with *Götterdämmerung* when he was twenty-eight, his first season at La Scala with *Meistersinger* three years later, and made his farewell there with an all-Wagner concert at the age of eighty-five.

It was respect for Wagner that occasioned the first of those clashes with the entrenched habits of Italian audiences for which Toscanini was to become famous. At a performance of *Tristan* at Turin in 1897 he demanded the lowering of the house lights, an unheard-of procedure in a country where (despite Mariani and Faccio) opera was still a social occasion. When the audience reacted angrily he stopped conducting and, the lights being turned up, furiously smashed the lamp on the conductor's desk; the rest of the performance took place in half-light, Toscanini sitting, hardly moving his baton. The incident illustrates two things: the devastating nervous tension which could explode at a moment's notice into an outburst of totally ungovernable rage, and the uncompromising determination to obtain, in the orchestra, on the stage, and in the auditorium, the most perfect possible conditions for the presentation of a work of art. As director at La Scala he returned to the attack, lowering the house lights, getting the ladies of the audience to remove their hats, and refusing to allow encores. This last was hard: even Mariani, during the original *Don Carlo*, had found nothing odd in telling Verdi, "we had to repeat *four times* the famous eight bars for orchestra that conclude the trio in the third act,"[35] and audiences were not going to give in easily. Nor was Toscanini. On the last night of the 1903 season, unable to get his way, he walked out at the end of the second act of *Ballo in maschera* and did not come back to the Scala for three years.

Though his seven years as artistic director at the Metropolitan added American glamour to his reputation, the summit of Toscanini's operatic career was achieved in Milan between 1920 and 1929. As absolute master of a reorganized opera house he came as near as he ever did to realizing his vision of the ideal operatic performance; he exercised dictatorial control over every aspect of the production, coached the singers personally, inspired and terrorized the orchestra in equal degree, and finally banned encores. But his fanatical perfectionism, combined with growing opposition to the Fascist regime, eventually brought an end to his Scala career, and for the last twenty-five years of his life he lived in New York where he worked entirely with the Philharmonic Symphony Orchestra and orchestra of the NBC.[36]

It is from this period that his many recordings date. Toscanini is the first conductor in Italian history whose actual performances can be heard today, and the first thing that strikes one about them is intensity, and intensity at a level that can hardly be found in any other conductor. Even in old age, videos show a facial expression of fierce inner concentration that easily explains the famous outbursts of temper (which can also be sampled on recordings made live at rehearsals). Thanks to his notoriously accurate memory, he used no score, leaving him free for constant, piercing eye contact with his players;

there is a classical immobility of stance, and a wide, majestic beat. But there is no caressing movement to suggest the sense of intimate communication of, say, Bruno Walter, and still less is there the unpredictable flexibility of Furtwängler, whose strictures on his great rival were harsh:

> He has no innate manual talent, and what he does have has been fought for and worked upon. But certain striking shortcomings have remained; above all the enormous waste of space in the *forte*. The size of his beat in the *f* is such that it makes any differentiation impossible. As a result, these *tuttis* are all the same . . . and the conductor's ability to bring out differences within the *forte* . . . is quite minimal.[37]

But Furtwängler was of all conductors the furthest in spirit from the Italian instinct for directness, clarity, and precision that Toscanini epitomized; one can almost believe the story of the leader of the Scala orchestra who, watching Furtwängler's famously wobbly upbeat at his first rehearsal, leaned forward and whispered "Coraggio, maestro!" Equally one can understand (though not necessarily condone) Alma Mahler's plaintive sigh when Toscanini took over *Tristan* from Mahler at the Metropolitan in 1909: "the nuances in his Wagner were distressing."[38] The incandescent sense of original creation which characterized Toscanini's finest performances was the product of two deeply held convictions: first, an overriding insistence on the primacy of the composer's intention and the unique authority of the printed score; and second, an unshakeable belief in the power of the singing line to sustain and bind the elements of musical structure. "The motif of every rehearsal," wrote the BBC violist, Bernard Shore, "is '*Cantando, sempre cantando!*' 'You must sing every note you play, sing even through your rests!' '*Ah cantare, cantare!*' 'Music, unless you sing, is nothing!'"[39] But the deliberately uncluttered directness of this approach and the continual search for melodic intensity could produce inflexibility and, in later years particularly, a relentlessness of tempo and attack that left little room for the subjective "nuances" of his German contemporaries.

For his many admirers, Toscanini was quite simply the greatest conductor in the world, and though this view might perhaps be contested today, he was certainly the greatest Italian conductor. "Maestro" in professional circles never meant anyone else. But in the end his Italian-ness was a matter of nationality and temperament, not of tradition. His insistence on fidelity to the composer's score, though it had a profound influence on his successors, was certainly no part of any normal Italian practice; his reforms deliberately attacked established attitudes, and the world recognition of his mastery in symphonic music was something entirely new in the history of Italian conducting. And in any case, by the end of his long life the values and priorities of the musical world were changing; internationalism was beginning to blur the edges of traditional habit, and temperament, rather than tradition, was becoming the index of national style.

After Toscanini

For any Italian conductor whose life coincided with Toscanini's, comparison was inevitable, and it is ironic that the one man who looked like surviving it should have died tragically at the age of only thirty-six. But the meteoric career of Toscanini's special protégé, Guido Cantelli (1920–56), took up the American and symphonic aspects of the Toscanini legacy, and though the temperament was Italo-American any specifically Italian tradition is hard to identify. Much closer to the true lineage were three senior figures whose international fame did perhaps suffer from the Toscanini effect.

The eldest, Tullio Serafin (1878–1968), devoted his long career entirely to opera and was in many ways the traditional conductor Toscanini never was. A very different character, he achieved his ends by sensitive coaching and quiet insistence, and though he was responsible for the first *Rosenkavalier*, *Wozzeck*, and *Peter Grimes* in Italy his greatest contribution was in the field of traditional Italian singing. He worked with Callas, coached Sutherland, and was the father figure behind the post-war revival of Italian *bel canto* opera; he left in his recordings a model of perfectly balanced operatic conducting in a sphere that Toscanini hardly touched, and that has never received more unfailingly natural and idiomatic treatment.

Nearer to Toscanini in style and dynamism was Victor De Sabata (1892–1967), whose early successes as conductor of the Monte Carlo Opera included the premiere of Ravel's *L'enfant et les sortilèges* and the French premiere of Puccini's *La rondine*. When Toscanini finally left the Scala in 1929 De Sabata moved back to Milan for an association with Italy's first opera house that was to last fitfully until the end of his life, and would include visits to Munich and Berlin with the Scala company and a triumphant *Otello* in London in 1950. Though he was widely admired for his Beethoven, Debussy, and Wagner (*Tristan* in particular), his home was always Italy, and his musical sympathies were grounded in the world of late Verdi, Puccini, the *verismo* composers, and the new symphonism of Respighi. To this repertory he brought an aristocratic brilliance and fiery intensity that can often recall Toscanini, though there is greater spontaneity, and an acute ear for the subtleties of orchestral color. His few recordings include a *Tosca* that ranks with Toscanini's *Falstaff* and *Otello* as one of the classics of recorded Italian opera.

And finally there is Vittorio Gui (1885–1975), a more modest figure whose distinguished career was almost entirely confined to Europe. As a result he has tended to be taken for granted, but this is to underrate a highly intelligent and accomplished conductor. Perhaps significantly, he was the only one of the three to be invited to conduct at the Scala during Toscanini's directorship (opening the 1924 season with *Salome*), and in 1933 he beat Toscanini by three weeks as the first Italian to conduct at Salzburg. He championed Brahms in Italy, conducted more contemporary music than most of his colleagues (he was personally congratulated by Debussy), but ranged back to Mozart, Gluck, and Purcell and made a speciality of rare and neglected operas. The vital buoyancy of his style made him an irresistible conductor of *opera buffa*, and he was a leading spirit in the Rossini revival of the mid-twentieth century; his recordings with the Glyndebourne company in this repertory remain models of elegance, humanity, and wit.

In a short survey that concentrates on representative figures it is inevitable that many names fail to get the attention they deserve: Verdi's faithful pupil Emanuele Muzio (1821–90), for example; or Giovanni Bottesini (1821–89), the double-bass player turned conductor whom Verdi chose to direct the premiere of *Aida* in Cairo (though only, it must be admitted, after Mariani and Muzio had turned it down); or Beecham's favourite Verdi conductor, Leopoldo Mugnone (1858–1941), who gave the first performances of *Cavalleria rusticana* and *Tosca*; or Cleofonte Campanini (1860–1919), who put on the first *Otello* in New York, conducted all over the world, and ended up in Chicago. And that is not to mention the dozens of worthy practitioners across the country propping up what was left of the local operatic tradition. But by the time the careers of Serafin, De Sabata, and Gui drew to a close, air travel and ease of communications, the growing power of the media, the development of radio and television, and above all the establishment of the recording industry as a dominant factor in musical life, were all creating a vast musical supermarket, in which personality was everything and tradition had little place.

A conductor like Carlo Maria Giulini (b. 1914), who came to maturity in this world, was exposed as a student to a range of music that would simply not have been available to an earlier generation of Italians. The orchestra of the Accademia di S. Cecilia in Rome, a late product of Italy's growing interest in symphonic music, had been inaugurated by Martucci in 1908 and by the 1930s, in Giulini's own words, "was one of the greatest"; as a member of the viola section he found himself playing under the batons of Furtwängler, Klemperer, and Walter, and later making his own debut conducting Brahms on the same podium. By the early 1950s, he was a conductor at the Scala (where a recording of *L'italiana in Algeri* provides evidence of the dynamic brilliance of his earlier style), but his vision of the integrity of opera drove him to a perfectionism that rivalled even Toscanini's, and to an increasing disillusionment with the working conditions of opera. From 1967 he turned to symphonic conducting, with deeply considered, spacious performances of the German repertory whose warmth and flexibility recalled his early admiration for Walter – and in later years, it must be added, the more eccentric tempos of late Klemperer as well. But his taste remained catholic, and in 1990 he completely rethought and recorded a blazingly convincing interpretation of that oldest of warhorses, *Il trovatore*, which shocked traditionalists – and magnificently illustrated the change in attitudes that was still possible at the heart of the Italian musical heritage.

Of Giulini's successors in the next generation Claudio Abbado (b. 1933) has most obviously followed the Giulini model, combining some fifteen years as director at the Scala with orchestral appointments in Vienna, London, and Chicago, before leaving Milan for the Vienna State Opera and finally, in succession to Karajan, the Berlin Philharmonic. His rival, Riccardo Muti (b. 1941), has also done the international rounds: the New Philharmonia in London in succession to Klemperer, the Philadelphia Orchestra following Ormandy, and the Scala the minute Abbado left it vacant. Of the two, Abbado has absorbed more of the central European ethos, with a persuasive rather than a dictatorial manner at rehearsal and a fine ear for integrated detail and balanced orchestral sound; Muti, a firm disciplinarian with a sharp wit, produces high-voltage performances that are perhaps closer to the Toscanini inheritance, and therefore more overtly Italianate. But both men still share with Giulini three characteristics that are widely seen as Italian: a vital feeling for rhythm, a powerful sense of melody, and a passionate directness of musical approach. Muti, in an interview in 1990, attempted to define what it was about Toscanini that was typically Italian.

> I mean, to go direct to the music, to the essence of the phrase, just straight to the point. I think that has influenced many generations of conductors that may sound completely different from Toscanini, but still are under his influence in this strict approach to the music . . . I don't think that Giulini, or myself, or other Italian conductors, think in vocal terms when we conduct. But, of course, we . . . ask players to sing; *cantare* – that means to be extremely *espressivo* . . . I don't think that it is a limitation . . . I would not say that Italians are special [in this] . . . It is just that our temperament is different.[40]

So is it tradition, then, that has survived – or simply temperament? As Giulini said: "If you ask me what makes an Italian conductor I have not the answer."[41]

12 The American tradition

JOSÉ ANTONIO BOWEN AND DAVID MERMELSTEIN

The history of conducting in America is at once bound to the profession's European fortunes and characterized by various attempts to break free from those bonds. And if the separation of New World from Old World may never be complete, that is no argument against that struggle's centrality in American musical life. Set against the privileged role of the symphony orchestra in America, the relationship to commercial enterprise, transformations in technology, and the continually growing power of celebrity, is the tale of a young nation both drawn to the artistic traditions of the cultures that spawned it and increasingly determined to forge its own path.

The religious traditions on which American society was largely formed did not encourage the growth of a new musical culture. In addition to the practical problems, Puritan Boston and Quaker Philadelphia had religious objections that contributed to the slow start of concert life. But with growing urbanization, a burgeoning sense of nationhood, and the discovery that music could be morally edifying, the seeds of formal concert life took root. Founded in 1815, Boston's Handel and Haydn Society was primarily devoted to the performance of sacred choral works, while a Philharmonic Orchestra founded by Gottlieb Graupner in 1810 lasted for fifteen years, performing the first complete American *Messiah* in 1818. The multipurpose band, however, remained the most common musical ensemble in nineteenth-century America, and like the rest of American musical concert life at mid-century, variety was its hallmark. Arrangements of Wagner (whom Sousa admired as "the Shakespeare of Music") and the latest quickstep happily coexisted in both indoor and outdoor settings in an attempt to get many Americans to attend their first concert.[1] The European touring virtuosos soon employed the same strategy: Norwegian violinist Ole Bull played "Yankee Doodle" alongside Beethoven, and though Jenny Lind's audiences "would sit unmoved" during "Casta diva," she brought the house down with "Home Sweet Home" as she toured the country with impresario P. T. Barnum.[2]

Aghast at these "entertainments," German immigrants sought a separate forum for more "serious music." When founded in 1842, the New York Philharmonic Society was 42 percent German; by 1855, the figure was 79 percent.[3] Many, if not most American musical organizations at this time were controlled by Europeans or their American backers, who believed in the superiority of European musical culture and supported transplanted European musicians in America, a state of affairs that continued well into the twentieth century.

After the Civil War, the excess capital flowing from rapid industrialization allowed wealthy philanthropists to establish American orchestras in St. Louis (1890), Chicago (1891), Cincinnati (1894), Philadelphia (1900), and Minneapolis (1903). Largely filled with immigrant musicians, these orchestras occupied a special place in American musical life. Unlike their European counterparts, they were largely funded by small groups of "guarantors" who desired full-time ensembles dedicated only to symphonic music.

European orchestras were often stepchildren to the more important opera. The players of the self-governed Vienna Philharmonic still play primarily for the opera, as did the Philharmonic Society in England. In France, nothing could compete with the Paris Opéra, and while every Italian town of any stature supported an opera house, there were almost no independent orchestras.[4] Orchestras in America, however, were founded as independent bodies representing a higher form of art, which reflected the moral character of the city. For Theodore Thomas, "A symphony orchestra shows the culture of a community, not opera,"[5] which for Thomas was too much like "entertainment." As a result, these new orchestras purged the opera, band, and lighter music of typical programs and concentrated on complete presentations of European masterworks. The same moral impulse also led patrons to build new temples exclusively for this orchestral music, and New York's Carnegie Hall (1891), Boston's Symphony Hall (1900), Chicago's Orchestra Hall (1904), and Cleveland's Severance Hall (1932) are still in use today. The conductors of these sacred ensembles inherited enormous power.

"In Boston the leader of the orchestra is a good deal bigger than the mayor," wrote a Cleveland reporter, and Mahler urged a colleague to take a position because of the "unlimited sovereign power. A social standing such as the musician cannot obtain in Europe."[6] The European conductors like Seidl, Gericke, Muck, Reiner, Fritz Busch, and Walter, who migrated to America, all began as opera conductors. With the exception of Mengelberg's Concertgebouw, European orchestras did not generally enjoy the single-minded attention that Thomas, Stock, Stokowski, Ormandy, Koussevitzky, and others gave their American orchestras.[7] Though Damrosch, Seidl, Toscanini, Mahler, Leinsdorf, Monteux, and Szell all began their American careers at the Metropolitan, they soon became dedicated to independent symphony orchestras. So while the vast majority of conductors in American were born and trained in Europe, they were gradually shaped by the institutions and ideals of their adopted country, no one more so than Theodore Thomas (1835–1905).

New York from Thomas to Toscanini

The country's oldest orchestra, the New York Philharmonic Symphony Society, was founded as a musicians' co-operative offering three concerts a season (a very part-time concern for the musicians), and it might have fallen to the competition had it not been for the vision and popularity of Theodore Thomas. Thomas was an American paradox, combining American pragmatism with German ideals, and in many ways his career mirrors the creation of a distinctly American attitude toward symphonic music. After immigrating from Germany at age ten, he played in the touring orchestra for Jenny Lind under the jeweled baton of Louis Jullien (1812–60), whose combination of flamboyant showmanship and orchestral discipline impressed the young Thomas.[8] In 1864, he began a series of increasingly serious concerts in Irving Hall, but he wanted to play difficult music and that required more rehearsals and better players. Thomas financed this by starting an outdoor summer series in Central Park Garden, which featured lighter music and allowed the audience to eat, drink, and converse (see Fig. 12.1). A hundred and fifty concerts per summer brought him popularity and allowed him to keep his orchestra together. In 1869, he took this to the next logical step, and the Thomas Orchestra began to tour (sometimes for as much as half the year) from Maine to San Francisco and from Montreal to Georgia, on what became known as the "Thomas Highway."[9]

Thomas remained certain that "the best in art" would eventually prevail but thought the social and economic conditions were not yet right:

> The incessant pressure of work which every American feels, prevents the men from paying much attention to music, but as the country advances in age and begins to acquire some of the repose which age brings, there will come possibilities of development which cannot now be estimated.[10]

In the meantime, he attempted to raise public tastes by conducting potpourri concerts across America. His combination of high standards, moral certainty, and showmanship paid off. Nor was his demonstration that commerce could serve high art lost later on Toscanini and Stokowski. In 1873, he founded the Cincinnati May Festival, and he was hired as chief conductor of the New York Philharmonic Society in 1877.

The Philharmonic had turned to Thomas because of pressure from the New York Symphony, which Leopold Damrosch (1832–85) had founded in 1878. Leopold was succeeded by his Breslau-born son Walter (1862–1950) who, like his father, added Berlioz to the mostly German repertory. While the Philharmonic remained a co-operative, giving half a dozen concerts per year, the Symphony began to make the transition to patron support and brought Tchaikovsky to conduct the opening of Carnegie Hall in 1891, the

Figure 12.1 A cartoon of Theodore Thomas conducting one of his summer concerts in New York's Central Park

same year Thomas was enticed to Chicago and its promise of a full-time orchestra.

Anton Seidl (1850–98) took over the Philharmonic after Thomas. He, too, had toured the country, with his Seidl Society, and he led the premiere of Dvořák's "New World" Symphony in the presence of the composer at Carnegie Hall in 1893. His popularity and focus now matched Thomas's, and had it not been for his premature death, he might have continued Thomas's legacy in New York.

With two orchestras where other cities had one, New York was divided socially, financially, and musically. The Damrosch family had provided powerful competition to the Philharmonic, but with the younger Damrosch now prepared to retire, the Philharmonic and the New York Symphony finally merged in 1928. Now all that the new Philharmonic Symphony Society needed was a conductor who could combine American pragmatism and art in the manner of Thomas.

Boston

Though its roots were thoroughly German, and its Japanese music director lasted nearly three decades, the Boston Symphony Orchestra's image remains that of a "French" orchestra. The reason is simple: for the better part of the twentieth century (from 1919 until 1962), the orchestra was led by three conductors with decidedly Gallic leanings. Two of them, Pierre Monteux (1875–1964), and Charles Munch (1891–1968), were actually French; the other, Serge Koussevitzky (1874–1951), had sympathies and talents that placed him firmly in the same camp.

The father of the BSO, Henry Lee Higginson, was a Viennese-trained music-loving businessman who hired only German conductors, beginning with George Henschel (1850–1934) in 1881 and then Wilhelm Gericke (1845–1925). Higginson wanted to purify the orchestra for symphonic music and forced his players to sign contracts that they would never "play for dancing."[11] When Gericke suggested a little light music during the second half of concerts, Higginson directed him instead to imitate Thomas and create separate promenade concerts in 1885, precursors of the Boston Pops concerts so famously associated with Arthur Fiedler. At the "real Symphony Concerts," Higginson supported Gericke's programming of Brahms's symphonies, even when "the audience left the hall in hundreds."[12]

Gericke returned to Boston for a second tenure after Arthur Nikisch (1855–1922) and Emil Paur (1855–1932) had each led the orchestra. Gericke was succeded by Karl Muck (1859–1940), who also served as the BSO music director twice, leaving for 1908–12, when Max Fiedler held the job. Muck, who had directed the Vienna Philharmonic, brought iron discipline to the BSO.[13] He introduced over forty new works to Boston, including music by Mahler, Bruckner, Sibelius, Debussy, and the American premiere of Schoenberg's *Five Pieces for Orchestra*, and his legacy ran deep; it was thanks to him that conductors like Monteux and Koussevitzky inherited an ensemble that could fulfil their ambitious goals.

Henri Rabaud (1873–1949) was the orchestra's first French conductor. He lasted less than a year, but he reset the ensemble's compass, charting a course made real by Pierre Monteux, whose five-year reign (1919–24) would be marked by an almost total reorganization of the BSO, including changes to personnel, repertory, and performance style. Monteux had conducted French opera at the Metropolitan, and in Boston he introduced works by Debussy and Milhaud, but also new music by English, Spanish, and Polish

Figure 12.2 Pierre Monteux in rehearsal with the Boston Symphony Orchestra in the summer of 1958 at Tanglewood

composers. He left Boston to work with the Concertgebouw, under Mengelberg, but he returned to America to lead the San Francisco Symphony from 1936 to 1952.[14] In the 1950s, Monteux revived his association with the BSO, appearing frequently with the orchestra (see Fig. 12.2) and even sharing the podium with Munch during the orchestra's first and second European tours. In 1961, at age eighty-six, he signed a twenty-five-year contract, as principal conductor, with the London Symphony Orchestra. A noted champion of music education throughout his life, Monteux claimed Neville Marriner, André Previn, and David Zinman as students.

The Koussevitzky years (1924–49) represent the orchestra's golden age, a time when technical standards reached a peak and the repertory performed was of a scope unmatched in the annals of American music-making. Koussevitzky lived an extraordinary life; a double-bass virtuoso who married extremely well, he first appeared as a conductor with the Berlin Philharmonic in 1908 and then set himself up in Moscow with his own orchestra. The Russian Revolution brought him to Paris, where he gave the premieres of Ravel's orchestration of Musorgsky's *Pictures at an Exhibition* and Honegger's *Pacific 231*.

Once in Boston, Koussevitzky began to remake the orchestra. A Sibelius exponent on a par with Kajanus and Beecham, an unequaled Tchaikovskian, and a master of the French style, Koussevitzky was likewise a tireless champion of American music, giving premieres of works by Barber, Copland, David Diamond, Howard Hanson, Roy Harris, Walter Piston, and William Schuman, among others. It was also during his tenure that the BSO unionized, the last major American orchestra to do so. In the summer of 1935, Koussevitzky and the BSO first presented concerts at Tanglewood, in western Massachusetts, starting a tradition that endures to this day. In 1940, Koussevitzky created the Tanglewood Music Center, arguably the most prestigious summer music-training institute in America.

Charles Munch was Koussevitzky's able successor in Boston. He continued commissioning works from composers whose careers Koussevitzky had nurtured, but the emphasis in repertory shifted heavily toward the French. Like Monteux, Munch was a superb violinist, and under his baton, orchestral standards were further honed.

Between Münch and Ozawa came a decade-long return to the orchestra's roots, with Erich Leinsdorf (1962–9) and William Steinberg (1969–72), who simultaneously served as music director of the Pittsburgh Symphony. Both were distinguished exponents of the German school (though their repertory certainly expanded beyond such narrow limits), with important, but not seminal, American careers.

Despite being a protégé of Münch, the Japanese Seiji Ozawa (b. 1935) represented a break with the past. Appointed while he remained the music director of the San Francisco Symphony, he was Boston's youngest music director. A noted technician with a commitment to modern music, Ozawa was at first embraced in 1972 as one who would honor the BSO's vaunted traditions while offering a welcome freshness, but his lack of palpable charisma and his absence of a speciality eventually caused critics to suggest that the orchestra's celebrated personality was eroding. Few lamented his eventual departure for the Vienna State Opera.

James Levine, who takes over in Boston in 2004, is another excellent technician, with an instinctive sense of orchestral color. In the tradition of

Toscanini, Szell, and Solti, among others, Levine cut his teeth in the opera house, conducting at the Metropolitan Opera for more than a quarter of a century. His decision to continue at the Metropolitan – rather than devote himself exclusively to his new symphony – represents a departure from the established American standard.

Chicago and Cleveland

To an unparalleled degree, orchestral leadership in Chicago has been defined by a *type* of music director, the conductor-autocrat, for whom technical and expressive excellence are twin priorities. The pattern was set early on – indeed, at the beginning – in 1891, when Thomas was lured to the city to found the Chicago Symphony Orchestra.[15] In Chicago, Thomas finally had a permanent orchestra that could concentrate on the most difficult, modern, and serious repertoire; under his baton, the orchestra gave the American premieres of works by Bruckner, Dvořák, Elgar, Glazunov, Grieg, Massenet, Smetana, Richard Strauss, and Tchaikovsky.

Thomas was followed as music director by his assistant, Frederick Stock (1872–1942), also born in Germany, also the son of a bandmaster, and also a violinist. Together, Thomas and Stock built the orchestra into a professional ensemble, instilling in the Chicagoans the discipline and general excellence that Fritz Reiner (1888–1963) and Georg Solti (1912–97) would later refine. Stock's thirty-seven-year tenure remains the longest in the orchestra's history. During those years, Chicago programs featured much American music, and the orchestra began children's concerts and the summer tradition of concerts in Ravinia Park. In May 1916, while on tour, the CSO recorded the "Wedding March" from Mendelssohn's *Midsummer Night's Dream* at the Columbia Studios in New York City, becoming the first American orchestra to record commercially under its regular conductor.

The example set by Thomas and Stock was a pattern to be repeated by Reiner from 1953 to 1963 and Georg Solti from 1969 to 1991. But there would be interregnums as well. Between Stock and Reiner came the Belgian Désiré Defauw (1885–1960), the first of another Chicago type – conductors famed for their sensitivity and destined for cult status. Along with Defauw, this group includes Rafael Kubelík (1914–96), a Czech who preceded Reiner, and Jean Martinon (1910–76), a Frenchman who succeeded him. Both were hampered by a commitment to new music, which met with neither public nor critical acclaim. Under Daniel Barenboim (b. 1942), who followed Solti, the CSO retains its characteristic sound.

For many, the Reiner years (1953–63) represent the CSO's peak. After working throughout Europe, Reiner was engaged by the Cincinnati Symphony Orchestra in 1922. He became a professor of conducting at the

Curtis Institute in 1931, where his students included Leonard Bernstein and Lukas Foss, and he led the Pittsburgh Symphony Orchestra before coming to the CSO. His work with the Symphony, brilliantly and widely caught on a series of classic RCA Victor recordings, brought it to the front rank of American orchestras at a time when American ensembles in general were improving, thanks largely to the plethora of gifted conductors who had fled the Nazis.

Along with Bruno Walter (1876–1962) and George Szell (1897–1970), Reiner helped define an era of music-making in America, in which high standards were seldom compromised and the Germanic repertory from Mozart to Richard Strauss achieved an almost holy status in the concert hall. In 1957, Reiner invited Margaret Hillis to form the Chicago Symphony Chorus, which became the first permanent choral ensemble in the United States to be affiliated with a major symphony orchestra.[16]

Like Reiner and Solti, Szell was a Hungarian Jew with a perfection-ist's instincts. He began as an opera conductor in Europe, and conducted at the Metropolitan during his first years in America (1942–6). When he assumed the mantle of music director in Cleveland (1946–70), he inher-ited a provincial American ensemble. That he made the words Cleveland Orchestra synonymous with luminous, unblemished playing is a testament to his unshakeable will and ceaseless exhortations. Since his death, the or-chestra has remained among the top American ensembles.

With the exception of an abortive appointment as music director of the Los Angeles Philharmonic in the early 1960s, Georg Solti was primarily considered an opera conductor until his appointment in Chicago in 1969. Solti had been the first to record all of Wagner's *Ring* cycle and was the music director at Covent Garden from 1961 to 1971. Despite this, Solti was soon perceived as something of a Reiner *redux*. Like Reiner, Solti kept the players disciplined and further refined the so-called "Chicago Sound," a brassy muscularity of distinctly American appeal, but unlike Reiner, Solti sometimes sacrificed interpretative flexibility, and his readings have been criticized as hard, shrill, and resolutely loud.

Philadelphia

Public concerts began in Philadelphia in 1757, and opera, chamber music, and the co-operative Germania Orchestra (from 1856 to 1895) were annual features. The Music Fund Society founded in 1820 for "the relief of decayed musicians" gave chamber music and even orchestra concerts in its own two-thousand-seat hall. In 1855, it built the even larger three-thousand-seat Academy of Music, which would become home to the Philadelphia Orchestra. There was even a move to have Theodore Thomas found the

Philadelphia Orchestra.[17] But it was the German Fritz Scheel (1852–1907), a former assistant to Bülow, whose series of concerts in Woodside Park in 1899 finally galvanized the Music Fund Society to secure 120 guarantors, enough to announce the first six concerts of the Philadelphia Orchestra the following year. Scheel recruited players from Germany and created a widely praised orchestra. Karl Pohlig was hired from Stuttgart to take over, but he returned to Germany in 1912 to be replaced by Leopold Stokowski (1882–1977), who would make the orchestra famous.

Stokowski was an import of a different kind. British by birth, but of Polish and Irish descent, he worked as an organist and choirmaster before turning to conducting. With no experience, he needed the help of pianist Olga Samaroff, who became his first wife in 1911. Samaroff arranged for a 1909 debut in Paris with herself as soloist and secured him employment with the Cincinnati Symphony Orchestra, where he spelled his name "Stokovski" to prevent people from putting "a cow" in his name.[18]

In Philadelphia, Stokowski led the way in demonstrating how an orchestra conductor could transform a city. His innovations began with programming: in 1916 he grabbed headlines with the American premiere of Mahler's Symphony No. 8. Soon after arriving, he asked the sceptical board for $15,000 to do the piece nine times in Philadelphia and once in New York; ticket demand was so high that $10,000 worth of orders could not be filled.[19] The American musical elite descended upon the city, mostly to be impressed by what the young conductor had achieved. For some, the massive spectacle and the golden-haired conductor without a score were too flamboyant, but the city, orchestra, and conductor became forever linked.[20]

Stokowski remained committed to modern programming and gave hundreds of American premieres, including *Le sacre du printemps*, *Wozzeck*, *Pierrot lunaire*, and symphonies by Shostakovich, Sibelius, and Mahler. While his modernist ambitions nearly bankrupted the orchestra, he pushed on to Bartók, Schoenberg, and Varèse.

His innovations included moving all the violins to the left side, which continues to be almost universally imitated in America. This, along with his emphasis on color, increased dynamic range, and the use of "free bowing," helped him create the "Philadelphia Sound." Impressed by technology, he began recording with the Philadelphia Orchestra in 1917, and went on to make the first electrical recordings with a symphony orchestra in 1925 and carry out early experiments in stereo and television for Bell Labs.[21] He also appeared in several Hollywood films.

As controversial as he was popular, Stokowski hoped to create larger and more sophisticated audiences, and he used drama and his fame to popularize even the most difficult music. Lighting effects, new media, abandoning the baton (in 1929), conducting from memory, creating an orchestra for the Hollywood Bowl, collaborating on *Fantasia* (1940), chastising his audience, and reorchestrating Bach were all means toward the same end. Eventually, Stokowski grew too big even for Philadelphia, and he went on to form new orchestras, including the All-American Youth Orchestra, and guest-conduct throughout the world, before settling with the Houston Symphony Orchestra (1955–60).

Stokowski left Philadelphia in the hands of Eugene Ormandy (1899–1985), who had been appointed professor of violin in Budapest at the age of seventeen. He made his conducting debut, with the Capitol Theatre Orchestra, in New York in 1924, conducting Tchaikovsky's Symphony No. 4. A chance encounter with the impresario Arthur Judson led to two guest weeks in Philadelphia, which led to his immediate appointment with the Minneapolis Symphony Orchestra. He left to share the podium with Stokowski in Philadelphia in 1936, but soon (1938) had it to himself for a record forty years, becoming conductor laureate in 1980.

Usually conducting without baton or score, Ormandy continued to strengthen the orchestra until many heard it as the finest in the world. But despite (or perhaps because of) the orchestra's precision and the voluptuous "Philadelphia Sound," he was not always taken seriously as an interpreter. Ormandy contributed to this image by conducting much Tchaikovsky and Dvořák, timid Beethoven and Brahms, and plenty of Strauss, Bruckner, Kodály, Debussy, and Ravel, with some re-orchestrated Bach. Equally notable, if less remembered, he gave the premieres of works by Webern, Rakhmaninov, Bartók, Britten, Hindemith, Milhaud, and by the American composers Barber, Creston, Diamond, Hanson, Piston, Rorem, Schuman, and Sessions.

Philadelphia has yet to put a native-born American in charge of its esteemed orchestra. Ormandy spotted Neapolitan Riccardo Muti (b. 1941) conducting in Florence and invited him to guest-conduct in Philadelphia, where he made his US debut in 1972. He succeeded Klemperer as principal conductor and then music director of London's New Philharmonia before Philadelphia enticed him to succeed Ormandy (1980–1992). Amid concerns that the orchestra was losing its characteristic sound, Philadelphia next turned to Wolfgang Sawallisch, who is being succeeded by Christoph Eschenbach in 2003.

New York from Toscanini to Bernstein

The career of Arturo Toscanini (1867–1957) is too wide-ranging and important to be contained within the restrictive rubric of "American conductor."

Toscanini was one of the most recognized figures of the twentieth century, and among the most talented. Debate has swirled over whether he inflicted unintentional harm to music by his sheer dominance and his failure to promote new music in the later stages of his career, when his influence was at its height.[22] But there can be no denying that much of what modern audiences perceive as the role of the conductor was codified by Toscanini's approach to the job. Autocratic, opinionated, visionary, deft and, above all, talented, Toscanini used his fame to promote music that he believed in, while summarily ignoring scores that failed to provoke him. Among the greatest interpreters of Wagner, Verdi, and Beethoven, Toscanini cast himself as a leading "objective" conductor, though today his standards of absolute fidelity would not match his inheritors'. His performances were not always fast – as has been suggested – but they often were, and he was in many ways the musical opposite of the probing Wilhelm Furtwängler, frequently, if not always accurately, described as his great rival.[23] The ability to summon musical force in a way matched only by Solti years later was a characteristic of Toscanini's conducting style, in which solidity of ensemble and drama were hallmarks.

The great impresario Gatti-Casazza, who engaged Toscanini at La Scala, also brought him to the Metropolitan Opera, where the premiere of Puccini's *La fanciulla del West*, with Caruso and Destinn, was only one of numerous highlights.[24] Toscanini's relationship with the New York Philharmonic, which began in 1926 and reached its apex when he was its chief conductor from 1930 to 1936, was an artistically rewarding one. His stewardship ranks among the orchestra's most fecund periods, and his departure was widely lamented.[25]

Toscanini did not remain absent from America for long. The creation for him of the NBC Symphony lured him back. It was not the quality of the musicians nor the exorbitant fees he would be paid that caused Toscanini to return, but rather the notion that these concerts would reach millions of listeners through the radio.[26] And it is for this reason that Toscanini's seventeen years with the NBC Symphony are so important. They were classical music's high-water mark in America, a time when a great many "ordinary" Americans regarded European art music as a real part of their lives. Leonard Bernstein's attempts to cultivate a youth audience in later decades, via television, stem directly from Toscanini's evangelical efforts.

The reputation of the Greek-born Dimitri Mitropoulos (1896–1960) has gone into sharp decline since his untimely death. A musician of uncommon insight and sensitivity, Mitropoulos could whip orchestras like the recalcitrant New York Philharmonic into a fever pitch, all the while exploring scores in a way wholly his own. A highly skilled pianist, Mitropoulos had a prodigious musical mind and would conduct scores from memory when that approach was still a novelty. After Koussevitzky brought him to Boston in 1936, where he caused a sensation, he succeeded Ormandy as music director of the Minneapolis Symphony (1937–49), turning this unlikely heartland city into a center for modern music. While there, in 1940, he made his landmark recording of Mahler's Symphony No. 1, the first ever. His years with the New York Philharmonic, unquestionably the pinnacle of his fame, were fraught with tensions. His began his tenure with the orchestra in an extremely short-lived partnership with Stokowksi, but in 1950 was named sole music director. In 1956, Leonard Bernstein, a Mitropoulos protégé, was engaged as associate conductor, and by 1958, Bernstein had supplanted Mitropoulos. It has been suggested that the kind and unworldly Mitropoulos was done in by a cabal of Bernstein supporters and the press, but the quirks of Mitropoulos's temperament, musical and otherwise, and his uncompromising aesthetic render such pat explanations untenable.[27]

That Leonard Bernstein (1918–1990) should now emerge as the central figure in American music makes perfect sense. These were the years when the nation, now a dominant world power, had come fully into its own. Not only was he the first native-born American to serve as music director of the New York Philharmonic, the nation's oldest, and arguably most prominent, podium, but he was also a harbinger of trends that would persist to the present day. While Thomas, Stock, and many of the European conductors who dominated American music-making in the twentieth century (Walter, Szell, Reiner, Ormandy, et al.) were American citizens, Bernstein was a born-and-bred American. Harvard-educated and a composer of Broadway musicals, Bernstein was exuberant, uninhibited, and embracing of the media in a manner that would make even Stokowski and Toscanini blush. His success emboldened other Americans to follow his path, even if unconsciously. It was a trajectory very much the opposite of what had been the American story in classical music, with Bernstein succeeding first in America, then on the international stage, and finally emerging as a wizened figure revered in Europe.

His Harvard years were followed by studies at the Curtis Institute, where Reiner taught him conducting. In the summers, Koussevitzky schooled him at Tanglewood. By 1943, Bernstein was assistant conductor of the New York Philharmonic under Rodzinski. His now legendary debut, which brought instant fame, came in November of that year. In 1958, he succeeded Mitropoulos, another mentor. His prodigious series of recordings with New York (all on Columbia), frequent tours with the ensemble, and regular appearances on television earned both Bernstein and the Philharmonic a rare kind of exposure. Leader and band were celebrities, with Bernstein emerging not just as a mainstream cultural figure, but also, especially in the late 1960s and early 1970s, as a prominent embodiment of what the author Tom Wolfe dubbed "radical chic."[28]

The music-making itself drew mixed reviews. At his best, Bernstein, whose flamboyant podium manner often provoked ridicule, was a conductor who generated enormous excitement, infusing even familiar music with enviable vigor and freshness. Some early performances were criticized for a lack of musical weight, and the later ones for too much. Still, his range was vast, with Copland, Gershwin, Ives, Mahler, Haydn, and Beethoven specialities.[29]

A tireless apostle for introducing the young to music, Bernstein's celebrated Young People's Concerts, begun in 1958 and televised, have now achieved cult status in America. Bernstein was also a fine pianist, who often conducted from the keyboard, and, of course, a successful composer, though no doubt all the more so for his conducting fame.

Conducting after Bernstein

In Bernstein's wake have come a series of American-born conductors with notable careers. Lorin Maazel (b. 1930) now holds Bernstein's old job as music director of the New York Philharmonic, and he previously held similar posts in Cleveland and Pittsburgh. Leonard Slatkin (b. 1944), James Levine (b. 1943), and Robert Spano (b. 1961) have also been successful on the home front. Kent Nagano (b. 1951) and James Conlon (b. 1950) had to seek success in Europe, as did Michael Tilson Thomas (b. 1944), generally considered Bernstein's chief protégé. But all three now perform regularly in America. After a highly regarded tenure leading the London Symphony (1988–95), Thomas is now ensconced in San Francisco, where he has made serious American music a priority in a way unheard of since Bernstein and Koussevitzky.

The public perception of conductors in America has increasingly been shaped by technology and the media. With the move from sound reproduction to sound-and-picture reproduction, it is worth speculating that some of the fame achieved by conductors after Bernstein is due to their "telegenic" looks. The question certainly hovers over several recent high-profile appointments. Though the musical credentials of Esa-Pekka Salonen (b. 1958) at the Los Angeles Philharmonic, Thomas at the San Francisco Symphony, and Franz Welser-Möst (b. 1960) at the Cleveland Orchestra make them worthy candidates for their positions, all three have had their images reproduced in publicity campaigns that make them especially visible on program brochures, banners, and even billboards.

Yet the increasing importance of the mass media in American conducting does not necessarily suggest a fundamental break with tradition. Though the autocratic approach favored by Toscanini, Reiner, Szell, and Solti seems consigned to history's ash heap, the idea of an individual shaping musical life in a major American urban centre seems very much alive. Ozawa's long tenure in Boston is only just ended. Salonen's stay in Los Angeles has exceeded a decade. Thomas, beloved in San Francisco, seems likely to remain. In Cleveland, a city where music directors tend to last a decade or more, Welser-Möst, in his early forties, has a contract through 2012. And Levine may enjoy a long tenure with Boston, as he already has with the Metropolitan. Only Philadelphia and New York, both of which appointed older men, seem destined to seek new talent relatively quickly. Thus, the American tradition connecting cities to their conductors survives.

13 The English tradition

STEPHEN JOHNSON

If there is a clear turning point in the history of British conducting – a point at which the modern era may be said to begin – it is marked by the arrival in England of the Italian conductor Michele Costa (1808–84). In 1829, Costa was sent by the composer Niccolò Zingarelli to direct a Birmingham performance of the latter's *Cantata on the Book of Isaiah, Chapter XII*, though in the event he only sang in it. The following year Costa settled in London, where he became *maestro al piano* at the King's Theatre and adopted the anglicized Christian name Michael. He made his mark quickly and indelibly. In less than two years he had abolished the prevailing system of dual leadership (see chapter 8) at the King's Theatre, and established himself as sole director, with the baton as his tool and symbol of authority.

London audiences had seen visiting conductors use the baton before, notably Spohr, Weber, and Mendelssohn; but as a resident Costa was able to carry on a sustained campaign. Nearly four decades after Costa's appointment at the King's Theatre, George Bernard Shaw wrote that

> by dint of constantly beating time, Sir Michael has secured the foremost place in the very thin ranks of our conductors. His place is undisputed. With the exception of Mr. August Manns, whose labors are confined to the nobler field of abstract music, he is the only chief under whose *bâton* orchestras display good training. The merits which he successfully cultivates are precision and refinement, and both go so far in music that their attainment alone would entitle him to his high position.[1]

Nevertheless Shaw saw significant limits to Costa's achievement:

> That highest faculty of a conductor, which consists in the establishment of a magnetic influence under which an orchestra becomes as amenable to the *bâton* as a pianoforte to the fingers, we do not give Sir Michael Costa credit for. Instead he has the common power of making himself obeyed, and is rather the autocrat than the artist.[2]

Writing for the 1906 edition of Grove's *Dictionary of Music and Musicians*, Ralph Vaughan Williams was inclined to underline Shaw's autocrat/artist distinction: "Perhaps the exaggerated respect paid to Costa during his lifetime has caused too violent a reaction since his death. There can be no

Figure 13.1 "I Spy" caricature of Michael Costa in *Vanity Fair* (July 1872)

doubt that that he was a very fine band-master, whatever may have been his shortcomings as an interpreter."[3]

Apart from his use of the baton, Costa also emerges as a modern figure in the history of conducting in the stories of his autocratic behavior: contemporary accounts that describe his drilling of orchestras focus on his personality as well as his methods. The composer Charles Stanford, for instance, made a party piece out of one Costa anecdote. Rehearsing for a performance of Beethoven's *Fidelio*, Costa apparently discovered that the librarian had lent his orchestral parts to the conductor August Manns, who had removed Costa's pasted-over alterations.[4] Stanford's version apparently went like this:

> COSTA Send for the librarian.
> *(Enter that official trembling)*
> What have you done with my parts?
> LIBRARIAN "They were lent to the Crystal Palace and Mr Manns must have restored them."
> COSTA You are dismissed![5]

Another potent early influence was the French conductor Louis Jullien (1812–60), who arrived in England from Paris in 1838, and who is reckoned to have directed at least twenty-four promenade concert seasons in London over the next two decades. Jullien had a Berliozian sense of scale and theatre. For a concert at the Exeter Hall in 1849 he used an orchestra of around four hundred players. Like Costa, Jullien frequently rewrote the scores he conducted, and he made a point of incorporating spectacular instruments such as extra-large bass drum, double-bass saxophone and a fifteen-foot high octobass (contra-double-bass). Jullien cast himself in the role of educator and entertainer. In doing so he brought a certain amount of serious repertoire (Mozart, Mendelssohn, a movement or two from a Beethoven symphony) to a wide audience, though his methods eclipse anything contrived by Stokowski at his most colorfully populist. In 1842, Charlotte Moscheles, wife of the composer and pianist Ignaz Moscheles, reported that

> we have a novelty more interesting . . . than Christmas trees – I mean Jullien's new Promenade Concerts. Drury Lane Theatre is converted into a large room, in which the "one shilling" public freely circulates, regardless of the music; the boxes are filled by the "haute volée." Jullien directs a good orchestra, sometimes with a *bâton*, sometimes playing a "flauto piccolo," which with its shrill tone marks the rhythm. After each piece he throws himself back as if he were exhausted, on a red velvet arm chair; his dress-coat discovers half a mile of white waistcoat; his dance tunes, strongly spiced with drum, bassoon, and trumpet, are attractive to all, but specially to the schoolboy, who would not think it Christmas if he did not go to Jullien's concerts.[6]

Mrs Edmond Wodehouse describes similar scenes when Jullien conducted his "Monster Quadrilles," scored for huge forces and usually inspired by some topical event or theme of the day. It seems however that Jullien was keen to make some distinction between these sensational extravaganzas and what he considered higher art: "All pieces of Beethoven's were conducted with a jewelled baton, and in a pair of clean kid gloves, handed to him at the moment on a silver salver."[7]

The Germans: Manns, Hallé, and Richter

Jullien may have brought Beethoven to a wider public, but there were those who felt that a more serious kind of evangelical work was needed. In 1855, George Grove, recently appointed secretary of musical events at the Crystal Palace, invited the German conductor August Manns (1825–1907) to conduct the resident wind band. Manns quickly set about reorganizing the band as a symphony orchestra, and instituted the Saturday Concerts, offered – like Jullien's Promenade Concerts – at popular prices, but concentrating on the kind of repertoire Jullien had either ignored or felt necessary to offer in diluted, easily palatable forms: complete symphonies by Beethoven, cycles of symphonies by Schubert and Schumann, works by Berlioz and Wagner, and new works by British composers, who were sorely in need of such championship. In marked contrast to Costa and Jullien, Manns approached the scores of these composers with reverence for the letter, normally refusing to alter them in any way. Grove himself provided "analytical and historical" program notes for Manns's programs – an innovation later imitated by Henry Wood, for whom Manns's Saturday Concerts were a musical lifeline. It was in the Crystal Palace, rather than at Jullien's spectaculars, that Wood found the inspiration for his own Promenade Concerts.

Manns was responsible for giving Britain its first permanent symphony orchestra – but only by a historical whisker. In 1857, the city of Manchester organized a huge, six-month-long art exhibition, for which another German-born conductor, Charles Hallé (1819–95), was engaged to conduct a series of concerts. Hallé, who had come to Manchester from Paris after the Revolution of 1848, had been directing the city's Gentlemen's Concerts and, like Manns and Grove, he had felt great potential for musical education in the region. Rather than allow the festival orchestra to be disbanded, Hallé engaged it for a new series of concerts in 1858, and thus the Hallé Orchestra was born. The survival of the orchestra owed a great deal not only to Hallé's personal energy and determination, but also to his technical skill: "As a conductor, Hallé was in the front rank; his beat was decisive, and although his manner was free from exaggeration, he imposed his own readings on his players with an amount of will-force that was unsuspected by the London public at large."[8]

Important as these early figures are, none of them was an "interpreter," according to Vaughan Williams, for whom the key figure was another German: Hans Richter (1843–1916), Hallé's successor in Manchester (1897–1911), who first appeared in Britain in 1877 as co-conductor with Richard Wagner in the Albert Hall. For Vaughan Williams, "Richter revolutionised English ideas as to how classical music should be rendered, and made Wagner intelligible to English audiences for the first time." It was the advent of Richter, he continues, which "may be said to have killed off the 'Mendelssohn tradition' in England."[9]

When Wagner first came to London to conduct the Philharmonic Society in 1855, he found his efforts to impose a freer, more expressive performing style on the players thwarted at virtually every turn. Mendelssohn had been dead for eight years, and Costa had held the reins at the Philharmonic for nearly ten, but Wagner had no doubt who was to blame. For Wagner the playing of the Philharmonic reflected Mendelssohn's insistence "that a slow tempo was the devil."[10] Wagner found the experience of conducting British orchestral musicians in 1877 just as frustrating. According to Shaw, who attended some of the rehearsals, "When he laid down the *bâton* it was with the air of a man who hoped he might never be condemned to listen to such a performance."[11]

Then it was Richter's turn. The composer Hubert Parry described how Richter "conducted wonderfully and drilled the incompetents with vigour."[12] For Shaw, Richter's achievement went much further:

> Then Herr Richter stepped into the conductor's desk; and the orchestra, tapping their desks noisily with their bows, revenged themselves by an ebullition of delight and deep relief, which scandalised Wagner's personal admirers, but which set the fashion of applauding the new conductor, whose broad, calm style was doubly reassuring after that of Wagner . . . A point missed would bring him quickly to earth, alert, yet still gracious; but a point overdone – nothing short of monumental stolidity could endure his eye then. For the rest, he could indicate the subdivisions of a bar when it was helpful to do so.[13]

But Richter's modesty and musicianly practicality were only one side of his persona as conductor. After attending one of the "Richter Concerts" the conductor had begun in London in 1879, Arnold Bennett sensed something knowing in Richter's performance: a conductor very much aware of the impression he was creating.

> Richter has all the air of a great man. He seems to exist in an inner world of his own, from which, however, he can recall himself instantly at will. He shows perfect confidence in his orchestra, and guides them by little intimate signs, hints suggestions . . . Having started his men, he allowed them to go through the second movement of Tchaikovsky's *Pathétique* Symphony without conducting it at all (I understood this is his custom with this movement). They played it superbly. At the end he clapped delightedly, and then turned to the audience with a large gesture of the arms to indicate that really he had nothing to do with that affair.[14]

Richter's "air of a great man" also attracted the wry attention of Debussy's Monsieur Croche: "If Richter seems like a prophet when he conducts the orchestra, it is because he *is* Almighty God! (And you can be sure that God would not attempt to conduct an orchestra without first having consulted Richter!)"[15]

In the story of the development of the image of the conductor as a quasi-religious figure in Britain, Richter is a crucial influence. But there was more to this than the exercise of power to theatrical or even mystical ends. The effect of Richter's conducting, along with that of his countrymen Felix Mottl

(1856–1911) and Hermann Levi (1839–1900), who both visited London in 1893, was described by Vaughan Williams: "The musical public awoke to the fact that a conductor can play on his orchestra just as a pianist can play on his instrument. The cult of the 'virtuoso' conductor became as fashionable as that of the Prima Donna."[16] When Elgar dedicated his First Symphony "To Hans Richter, Mus. Doc., true artist and true friend," the use of the phrase "true artist" reflects how distinctive Richter's achievement in this respect still seemed when the symphony first appeared in 1908.

Wood, Beecham, and Boult

The first British-born conductor to achieve status in his own country comparable to that of Richter, Hallé, Manns, Jullien, and Costa was Henry Wood (1869–1944). In 1895, Robert Newman, manager of London's recently opened Queen's Hall, invited him to conduct the newly formed eighty-strong orchestra for a series of Promenade Concerts. He was to continue conducting the concerts there until the Hall was destroyed during a German air raid in 1941 (see Fig. 15.1 on page 206), after which Wood and his "Henry Wood Proms," as they were now known, moved to the Albert Hall. Wood started his concerts with relatively popular repertoire, but he gradually introduced more challenging large-scale works by Beethoven, Brahms, Wagner, and Tchaikovsky, and then, more daringly, Strauss, Debussy, Elgar, Sibelius, Rakhmaninov, and Skryabin. In doing so he established a tradition for range of repertoire and championship of the new, which remains at the heart of Proms programming to this day. Wood approached the performance of new music with a missionary zeal, devoting seventeen rehearsals to Strauss's *Ein Heldenleben* in 1903, and exhorting his orchestra like a general on the eve of a fearsome campaign before introducing Schoenberg's *Five Pieces for Orchestra* to a largely hostile London audience in 1912: "Stick to it gentlemen! This is nothing to what you'll have to play in twenty-five years' time."[17] Thirty-three years later, Schoenberg remembered Wood's efforts on his behalf with warmth: Wood, wrote Schoenberg, was "a perfect musician, a great educator, a great benefactor of music and a most charming gentleman."[18]

It was the need to transform the Queen's Hall Orchestra into a band capable of taking on a wide and growing repertoire of new and unusual music that forced Wood into becoming, in the eyes of Adrian Boult,

> one of the greatest masters of the craft of conducting. For many years the Proms had only three rehearsals for the six concerts each week, and in order that the programme should be adequately rehearsed, every detail was

thought out beforehand, and not only the scores, but every orchestral part, was marked by him, even to the point of showing where the beat would be split in a *rallentando*, so there could be no mistake whether there had been time to rehearse the passage or not. Later he was given one rehearsal for each concert, but he never knew the present luxury of two rehearsals for each concert and two orchestras in each week. His use of the stick, too, was masterly. It was unusually long and provided with a large cork handle, which enabled him to get a balanced swing by holding this stick at the end close to the handle at the point of balance, so that the fingers could direct the movement with practically no effort, as the stick and handle balanced each other. He was thus able to conduct three-hour rehearsals with a minimum of fatigue.[19]

The viola player Bernard Shore recalls Wood taking pains to ensure that the members of the orchestra were focused on his baton. "Why don't you look at my stick? It's clear enough! Every morning I practise my baton for half an hour in front of the glass!"[20]

Frustrating conditions may have been the spur to greater personal and technical development, but Wood also began to push for change. He managed to get better rehearsal time for his Queen's Hall Concerts, and was even able to start sectional rehearsals. He introduced women to his orchestra in 1913, experimented with a variety of seating plans, and cracked the long-established system of "deputies," which Costa had wrestled with half a century earlier. According to this surreal system, players at Wood's Promenade Concerts could send substitutes to attend rehearsals, attending themselves only for the concert performance. When Wood insisted that players attend both rehearsal and performance, some left the Queen's Hall Orchestra, forming the London Symphony Orchestra as a self-governing body in 1904. But Wood's will prevailed, and the practice ceased.

Wood's achievements were important and lasting, but in all the praise lavished on him, there was relatively little for him as an "interpreter," much more – in Boult's above-quoted phrase – for his mastery of "the craft of conducting." His great antithesis in this respect was Thomas Beecham (1879–1961). This was certainly Boult's verdict: "The fundamental difference between Wood and Thomas Beecham, was that Beecham would improvise a performance, and bring off that performance; with Wood it was all carefully and accurately prepared."[21]

Beecham's love of improvisation was evident in more than the quality of his performances. He had an almost promiscuous flair for setting up orchestras, opera companies, and concert seasons. Amongst his creations were the New Symphony Orchestra (1905), the Beecham Symphony Orchestra (1909), the Beecham Opera Company (1915), the London Philharmonic Orchestra (1932), and Royal Philharmonic Orchestra (1946). Of course the list would not have been quite so impressive if Beecham had not had considerable family capital at his disposal. It was the backing of his father, Sir Joseph Beecham, mayor of the Lancashire town of St. Helens and a wealthy manufacturing chemist, that enabled him to put on his first opera season at Covent Garden in 1910, which included the British premiere of Strauss's *Elektra*, Delius's *A Village Romeo and Juliet*, Humperdinck's *Hänsel und Gretel*, Smyth's *The Wreckers*, Debussy's cantata *L'enfant prodigue*, Wagner's *Tristan und Isolde*, Bizet's *Carmen*, and Sullivan's *Ivanhoe*. With the possible exception of the Bizet, it was hardly a recipe for commercial success.

The advantages of being born with a rich, music-loving father were clear from the start. In 1899, Sir Joseph engaged Richter and the Hallé Orchestra for the inaugural concert of St Helens' new town hall. At the last minute Richter was unable to appear, so the twenty-year-old, self-taught Beecham took his place conducting Beethoven's Fifth Symphony, Tchaikovsky's Sixth, and the preludes to Wagner's *Tannhäuser* and *Meistersinger* without rehearsal and from memory. The repertoire was fairly typical for an English orchestral concert at the end of the nineteenth century, but it was far from prophetic of Beecham's later course as a conductor. Like the composer Vaughan Williams, the young Beecham soon felt a need for an antidote to the Germanic saturation of his country's musical life. Vaughan Williams found it in his own country's folksong and in the teaching of Ravel. Beecham found it in French music and culture in general, and later in the early masterpieces of Stravinsky, particularly *Firebird* and *Petrushka*: "I was attracted to his music because it corrected Teutonic tendencies towards adiposity and flatulence."[22]

Beecham's reaction against German dominance was theatrical but in essence sincere. Once this is understood, his rejection of much of the core German symphonic repertoire (Mozart very much excepted), and of its most noted exponents, begins to make sense. This distaste for "adiposity and flatulence" was the reason why, as the critic Neville Cardus put it, "he tended to reduce the stature, the form and the spaciousness of music of intellectual substance."[23] It also helps explain (along with a generous pinch of old-fashioned Anglo-Saxon xenophobia) such oft-quoted, cultivatedly scandalous remarks as "I would give the whole of Bach's Brandenburg Concertos for Massenet's *Manon* and would think I had vastly profited by the exchange,"[24] or his reported verdict on Richter, "All those damned foreign importations! Take Richter. He could conduct five works, no more."[25] Other influential foreign figures were dismissed in similar cavalier terms. Mengelberg and Toscanini were "old humbugs"[26] and he flatly rejected an opportunity to hear Mahler conduct on the grounds that "Obviously Mahler conducted egoistically."[27]

Parochial and possibly defensive though such remarks may be, they can also be seen as perversely symptomatic of the independence of mind and spirit that made audiences and orchestras treasure Beecham's performances. His lack of German thoroughness, combined with unique personal charisma, would certainly not have been disadvantages in a culture which has tended to make heroes of inspired amateurs. "He obtains his results from sheer magnetism, and not from the accredited art of the conductor – stick-technique,"[28] was Bernard Shore's diagnosis.

> It was confidence in himself . . . which was perhaps the secret of his influence over orchestras – plus, of course, knowledge of the score. An amateur, maybe – but an amateur of genius! As far as baton technique goes, it might almost be said that he had little of it. Many orchestra players have told me he had none. I have seen him get his baton entangled in his coat tails. Famous opera singers have assured me that they received scant help from him on the stage; he concentrated on the orchestra.[29]

Beecham conducted from memory until late in his career. There was an element of the cavalier in this too.

> Outside Mozart and other preferred composers, his memory occasionally failed him. With no score on the desk to set him right, he usually resorted when in a musical fog to vague circling motions with both arms, like a swimmer doggedly doing the breast stroke. Virtually conducted by the first violin and other section leaders, the performance would either limp untidily along to a full-close or, in extreme cases, peter out miserably.[30]

But there were huge compensations. Thomas Russell, a viola player under Beecham, praised his "exquisite phrasing and emotional depth."[31] Boult compared Beecham to Furtwängler, another far from technically perfect conductor, and one for whom Beecham maintained a kind of puckish regard. Charles Reid makes another, possibly more spiritually pertinent comparison: "When in full cry he spouted molten rock. He was the first volcano English music has ever known and may well be the last. For a parallel one must cite another age and country. In more than one aspect, Beecham was Hector Berlioz reincarnated and transplanted."[32]

Surprisingly, the cavalier, volcanically spontaneous Beecham took well to the recording studio. His recordings are still widely available, and many of them continue to hold up well in the critical comparisons of the musical press – by no means only in Britain. The success of Adrian Boult (1889–1983) in the studio is easier to explain. His first national triumph was in 1930 when he conducted the first concert by the BBC Symphony Orchestra. The BBC had taken a gamble in appointing a relatively little-known forty-one-year-old to train its new orchestra, but the risk was rewarded.

The critic of the *Morning Post* was impressed before the program proper began:

> In the very sonority of *God Save the King*, which opened the first BBC
> Symphony Concert in the Queen's Hall last night, we felt that London now
> possessed the material of a first-class orchestra . . . we had from the
> technical point of view, the best English orchestral playing since the
> war . . . not to mention the admirable conducting of Adrian Boult, to
> whom . . . must go a very considerable share of credit for the triumphant
> success of the evening.[33]

For Boult, like Wood, the baton was central to his art, but the key influence for
him was not Wood but the German conductor Arthur Niksch, whom Boult
had observed in rehearsal during his studies at the Leipzig Conservatory
(1912–13).

> That long stick held in a tiny white hand, seemed to say so much, and
> express so completely the music as felt by Nikisch, that a great deal of
> verbal explanation at rehearsal was unnecessary, and so the tension and
> friction of many rehearsals were avoided; and even his wonderful left hand
> had less to do than most, because his stick said so much.[34]

Boult emulated Nikisch's use of the "long stick" throughout his career.
But his baton technique was only one aspect of the wide executive ability
that left such a mark on the BBC Symphony Orchestra.[35] Bernard Shore,
who was principal viola under Boult, praised his

> quick assimilation of scores in every kind of idiom. He finds his way about
> quickly, and is able to take the orchestra with him straight to the root of
> the matter. He organizes both other people and himself, smoothly and
> without fuss or agitation; and although his repertory covers the whole
> realm of orchestral music, he conducts most of the well-known works
> from memory. It is significant that when Toscanini conducted the BBC
> Orchestra in 1935, in his rehearsals he scarcely touched Brahms's Fourth
> Symphony or the "Enigma" variations – two of Boult's greatest
> interpretations. He was indeed able to cut down the allowance of rehearsal
> time – a tribute to Boult's orchestra training.[36]

Boult's old-world sangfroid on the platform did not impress everyone and he
was almost certainly the model for Glenn Gould's caricature, Sir Nigel Twitt-
Thornwaite, "dean of British conductors." But his achievement in forming
the BBC Symphony Orchestra, and with it bringing a huge range of new
and unusual repertoire to British audiences, was lasting. That the orchestra
has subsequently proved so adaptable, responding more than effectively to
such strikingly different conductors as Pierre Boulez (chief conductor from

1971–5) and Günter Wand (a frequent guest in the 1980s and 1990s) is an indication of the strength of the tradition Boult established.

Barbirolli and Klemperer

As a young rising star, John Barbirolli (1899–1970) succeeded Toscanini at the New York Philharmonic in 1937. The verdict of the *New York Times* critic, Harold C. Schonberg – "though clearly talented, [he] was not ready for so demanding a position"[37] – was widely shared, though not always so charitably expressed. But his achievement in rebuilding the war-devastated Hallé Orchestra, and transforming it into what Beecham is said to have called "the finest chamber orchestra in the country,"[38] remains one of the great inspirational stories in the history of British conducting.

Then there is Otto Klemperer (1885–1973), principal conductor of the Philharmonia Orchestra from 1959, and the orchestra's saviour when founder Walter Legge attempted to disband it in 1964.[39] Klemperer was responsible, along with the Ukrainian-born Jascha Horenstein (1898–1973), for spearheading the Mahler revival in Britain in the early 1960s, and for bringing what some saw as a valuable re-injection of solid German values into British conducting. The rhythmic energy of his Beethoven – despite his often slow tempos – stemmed, Klemperer felt, from his stress on the importance of the upbeat: "it's the upbeat and not the downbeat that makes an orchestra attentive. Then the first beat always has a certain weight . . ."[40]

But the "weightiness" of Klemperer's performances, especially in his last years, also provoked antagonism, and gave added impetus to a revolution that had been fermenting for some time. Although Klemperer took a limited notice of modern scholarship when it came to orchestral forces in Bach, his performing style came in for growing criticism. For the critic of the *Times*, his 1960 cycle of the Brandenburg Concertos was "a curious mixture of modern loyalty to history and traditional suet pudding . . . Much of the music sounded humdrum, or uncharacteristic of Bach's thought as our age conceives it."[41] Klemperer's typically ferocious disapproval of the attempts of the harpsichordist George Malcolm to decorate the continuo parts certainly did nothing to dissuade Malcolm from his efforts to find a more historically aware performing style in the music of Bach and his contemporaries.

Gardiner, Norrington, and Rattle

An element of reaction against Klemperer's monumental approach to Bach and Beethoven can be felt in the musical direction of two key British figures in the British "period performance" movement: John Eliot Gardiner (b. 1943) and Roger Norrington (b. 1934); in fact Gardiner's much-acclaimed recording of Bach's *St. Matthew Passion* (1989) seems at times like a deliberate counterblast to Klemperer's 1967 version – especially in its light, dancing rhythms, and the absence of what Klemperer called a "certain weight" on the first beat of the bar. Gardiner and Norrington have made a point of rejecting German traditions: the arch-Wagnerian Furtwängler has been something of a bugbear for both. Gardiner has turned partly to Toscanini as a corrective, for example praising the way (in conversation with this writer) in which Toscanini articulated the string sextuplets at the beginning of Beethoven's Symphony No. 9 precisely as sextuplets, rather than rendering them as a Furtwänglerian misty tremolo. In Norrington, however, something of Beecham's legacy can be felt in his flair for "improvising" in performance, and in his love of provocative statements:

> What are modern instruments? The instruments we call modern often haven't changed in essence for as much as a century. We've got this strange museum culture – and it's up to us to change it. We're the revolutionaries, the iconoclasts. We're the ones who are making things new.[42]

This swinging backwards and forwards, one minute embracing Central European thinking and practice, reacting against it the next, has long been characteristic of British intellectual and artistic life. It is perhaps inevitable, in view of the United Kingdom's unique and complicated position vis-à-vis continental Europe: sometimes keen to enter into relationship with the mainland, at other times defensively insular – insistent that it belongs, as General de Gaulle put it, to "le grand large" (the open sea) rather than to Europe.[43] But it is also possible that a figure has recently arisen who holds out the hope of uniting the two tendencies, or at least of bringing them into a creative dialectical relationship. The appointment of Simon Rattle (b. 1955) as the music director of the Berlin Philharmonic Orchestra in 2002 is a rare honor from a major German cultural institution to a British artist. Critical reactions to such risky ventures as the performing of Deryck Cooke's "performing version" of Mahler's incomplete Symphony No. 10 (for a long time regarded with anything from suspicion to outright hostility by the German musical press) shows, amongst other things, that German critics are increasingly taking Rattle seriously as the leader and standard-bearer of one of its most famous cultural exhibits. Rattle has long been receptive to German influences: witness his growing recent admiration for Günter Wand. But at the same time he offers something else. Elmar Weingarten, Intendant of the Berlin Philharmonic until 2000, greeted the news of Rattle's appointment with these words:

I don't know if it's a big risk, because Simon is a really British conductor and the orchestra is really very, very German. I want to stress I value both things highly, but seeing them come together will be fascinating. German musicians generally tend to be ploughing deep into whatever they play, very seriously, and the thing I find about British conductors, whether it's Colin Davis or Roger Norrington, is that they enjoy themselves much more when they make music, and Simon has a wonderful ironic distance in some things he does – when he does Haydn or Rameau the music sparkles with wit. I don't mean he distances himself, but he lets the music dance and enjoys listening to it.[44]

14 The Russian tradition

DAVID NICE

It was not until the mid-1930s that a Russian school of conducting began to reap what had been so carefully sown at the beginning of the century. In the constant swinging back and forth of the pendulum whereby Western conductors were welcome (in the late 1920s), then avoided (up to the dissolution of the Association of Proletarian Musicians in 1932), then welcome again, and finally shunned when Stalin turned his country upside down in 1937, there turned out to be more virtue than necessity in relying on homegrown talent. Since then, the line has been unbroken, and even at a time when the ranks of the old guard are rapidly diminishing, the tradition seems to have passed effortlessly to a whole new generation of younger conductors taking up positions with orchestras in the West.

Illustrious visitors: the nineteenth century

Russia in the nineteenth century was far too busy establishing and consolidating its musical institutions to breed that luxury, the great interpreter. In any case, the rival factions who so blurred the lines of real distinction in the 1860s, combined with the lack of any recorded evidence, make it difficult for us to establish any kind of objective truth. Was that leader of a truly national aesthetic, Mily Balakirev (1837–1910), a fine or a mediocre conductor when he took charge of the Russian Musical Society concerts? The composer and critic Alexander Serov was "convinced that the very least musician of a vaudeville orchestra would have conducted both the *Eroica* and [Mozart's] Requiem better than Balakirev had" in the 1868–9 season; but then Serov was allied to the reactionary forces antipathetic to Balakirev and his "mighty little handful" (*moguchaya kuchka*) of composers.[1] Those on Balakirev's side, chiefly Vladimir Stasov, the mouthpiece of *kuchkist* art, and César Cui, one of the inner group of five, inevitably dismissed the competition – Anton Rubinstein and Konstantin Lyadov, conductor of the Imperial Opera and father of the more famous composer – while placing Balakirev in the pantheon of composer-conductors Wagner and Berlioz.

One truth was indisputable, however: the visits to Russia of Berlioz, in 1847 and the winter of 1867–8, and of Wagner in 1863, had shown Russian musicians what great conducting could truly be. When Berlioz first arrived in St. Petersburg, Russian concert life was squeezed into the Lent weeks when the Imperial Theatres were closed and an ad hoc orchestra consisting mainly of Germans was hastily assembled with the help of a conductor from the Italian opera. Stasov, despite his conflicting impressions of Berlioz's music, was in no doubt of the French visitor's talents as a conductor, nor of the temporary influence of his genius:

> Berlioz arrives in a city. He gathers together musicians of all kinds and calibres. He seldom has more than two or three rehearsals . . . Then suddenly this group is transformed in to an orchestra; it becomes one man, one instrument, and plays as though all of its members were finished artists. Berlioz's concerts end. He leaves. And everything is as it was before – each man for himself. The mighty spirit that had inspired everyone for a moment is gone.[2]

In Moscow the standards were too low to transcend, and when Berlioz visited the Bolshoi to hear a performance of Glinka's *A Life for the Tsar*, he found the music unrecognizable.

When he returned as a very sick man in 1867, it was a different story. Whatever he may have thought of the composers who had sprung up in the *kuchkist* movement – and according to Rimsky-Korsakov's autobiography, he thought very little of them – Berlioz was delighted to conduct the orchestra of the Russian Musical Society, which, he told a friend, "understands so quickly and so well."[3] Cui praised his Beethoven interpretations as exact and thoughtful, contrasting them to Wagner's more affected readings nearly four years earlier. Again, this may have been a barb from a *kuchkist* aimed at the establishment, because the forces Wagner conducted in February 1864 had been those of the Imperial Orchestra, and Serov had been his chief guide. "The orchestra is very good, very strong (24 first violins), intelligent and competent," Wagner wrote to his friend Josef Standhartner, "and they are thrilled to play at last under a decent conductor."[4] That he was more than simply decent was recorded by Tchaikovsky, who echoed Stasov's comments on Berlioz by according to Wagner alone as Beethoven interpreter "the authority or power that transforms the orchestra until all the players become as if one soul, one great instrument."[5]

Composer-conductors: bridging the gap

Tchaikovsky's seal of approval was given, in a letter to his patroness Nadezhda von Meck, some fifteen years after the event. By the late 1880s, having progressed himself as a conductor from uncertain beginnings, Tchaikovsky had two other masters to place alongside Wagner for an inspiration he could never achieve – Hans von Bülow and Arthur Nikisch, whose "mysterious sorcery" he witnessed for himself for the first time on a visit to Leipzig.[6] He had much for which to be thankful on home territory from the thoroughgoing professional who had replaced Konstantin Lyadov at the Mariinsky Theatre in 1869. Eduard Napravnik (1839–1916), who held on to the reins at the Mariinsky until his death, became the figurehead of Russian operatic conducting, although in fact he had been born in Bohemia. The premieres he gave in the Imperial Theatre included several of his own operas and such cornerstones of the Russian repertoire as Dargomïzhsky's *The Stone Guest* (1872), Musorgsky's *Boris Godunov* (1874), Rimsky-Korsakov's *The Snow Maiden* (1882), and Tchaikovsky's *Mazeppa* (1884) and *The Queen of Spades* (1890). It was an honor for a composer to be in such reliable hands. Yet when interpretation rather than mere diligent execution might be required, Tchaikovsky was the first to note Napravnik's shortcomings. In writing to Karl Albrecht in 1878 of the special circumstances under which *Eugene Onegin* might flourish, he declared that "the conductor must not be a machine, nor even a musician *à la* Napravnik: he cares only about getting a C sharp and not a C but I want someone who will be a true guide to the orchestra."[7]

Nikisch, in Tchaikovsky's eyes, fitted that bill exactly. Moscow and St. Petersburg were to agree when Nikisch became the best loved of all visitors there; the eleven-year old Prokofiev gave us a vivid description in a letter to his father of a Nikisch concert he attended with his mother in December 1902. Excitedly recapturing the adulation surrounding Moscow's idol before and after his interpretations of Glinka's Overture to *Ruslan and Lyudmila*, Tchaikovsky's First Piano Concerto (with Nikolai Medtner as soloist), and Grieg's *Peer Gynt* Suite No. 1, two movements of which were encored, Prokofiev briefly ventures his first piece of criticism: "I felt that the overture came out generally smoother and better than with Safonov," who had directed the Moscow branch of the Russian Musical Society from 1899 to 1905.[8] Prokofiev would also complain, with a more mature judgment, that he "dragged out the tempi" of Wagner's "Liebestod."[9] For all Nikisch's long-term service to Tchaikovsky's music after the composer's death in 1893, Tchaikovsky would have been partly delighted to see his spiritual son and heir Sergey Rakhmaninov (1873–1943) favorably compared to the German conductor.

Rakhmaninov had returned to conducting, determined to play his part in improving standards at the Bolshoi Theatre by signing a five-month contract as conductor in the spring of 1904. Working with Chaliapin on Glinka's *A Life for the Tsar* and Dargomïzhsky's *Rusalka*, Rakhmaninov also conducted several symphonic concerts that year, and it was one of these that his fellow pianist and composer Nikolai Medtner singled out for a special place in his memory. "I shall never forget Rakhmaninov's interpretation of Tchaikovsky's Fifth Symphony," Medtner wrote in 1933:

Before he conducted it, we heard it only in the version of Nikisch and his imitators. True, Nikisch had saved this symphony from a complete fiasco (as conducted by its composer), but then his pathetic slowing of the tempi became the law for performing Tchaikovsky, enforced by conductors who followed him blindly. Suddenly, under Rakhmaninov, all this imitative tradition fell away from the composition, and we heard it as if for the first time; especially astonishing was the cataclysmic impetuosity of the finale, an antithesis to the pathos of Nikisch that had always harmed this movement.[10]

To hear a performance corresponding to this description captured on a recording, we have to turn to Mravinsky's Tchaikovsky. Rakhmaninov's recorded legacy as a conductor, on the other hand, is pitifully slight, for the obvious reason that listeners in the America he later made his home always wanted to hear Rakhmaninov the pianist. Even his own interpretation of his Symphony No. 3, which exists alongside the orchestral version of the *Vocalise* and the tone poem *The Isle of the Dead*, was only captured for posterity on the strength of a promise that he would return to the studio as soloist in the First Piano Concerto. He should have followed it up with his haunting swansong, the *Symphonic Dances*, but the project was jettisoned when a record-company executive labelled the work "insignificant." Never mind: what holds in Medtner's commentary on the 1904 performance can also be applied to the 1939 recording of the Symphony No. 3, which has similarly foundered in more indulgent hands. The technique is formidable; rarely a bar passes without magisterial command of every dynamic nuance and of the Romantic rubato built in to the score. As a composer-conductor with effortless control, Rakhmaninov is the equal of Mahler and Strauss. His only rival in this respect on the Russian scene in the early 1900s, Alexander Glazunov (1865–1936), has been famously mocked for incompetence and inebriation, not least at the disastrous premiere of Rakhmaninov's Symphony No. 1, and his approach remained that of an amateur. Yet Nikolai Malko (1883–1961), a true professional, observed that "performing his own compositions he [Glazunov] could impart to the orchestra precisely that which was characteristic of the work, and it would reach the musicians and through them the listener."[11] That certainly pertains to the 1928 recording of his ballet *The Seasons*, all airy grace and needlepoint precision.

Beginnings of the Russian school: Tcherepnin and Malko

The gratitude with which Rakhmaninov's contemporaries received him as an alternative to the ubiquitous Glazunov gives us a good idea of the conducting vacuum in turn-of-the-century Russia. Musical institutions flourished, but the priority remained the promotion of new or recent music, with the conductor as the humble servant of a living tradition. Such, it seems, were the talents of Vasily Safonov (1852–1918) and of another Tchaikovsky pupil, the brilliant pianist Alexander Ziloti (1863–1945), who from 1901 to 1903 took charge of the Moscow Philharmonic Society before running an enterprising concert series of his own until 1917. His example was soon to be followed by a virtuoso double-bass player from the Bolshoi, Serge Koussevitzky (1874–1951) who turned conductor and began his own series with financial help from his wealthy bride in 1909. Koussevitzky's technique was less than graceful at the start of his conducting career, if distinguished contemporaries are to be believed; the kind of new music he featured in his programmes, including suites from the Stravinsky ballets hot on the heels of their Ballets Russes premieres, was later to be given a more masterful treatment in his Paris and Boston spectaculars.[12] Another, less glamorous alternative to Koussevitzky was Konstantin Saradzhev (1877–1954), co-instigator with Vladimir Derzhanovsky of the challenging concert season which took place every summer in Moscow's Sokolniki Park. He would continue his duties in Moscow dependably during the early Soviet period. Meanwhile, the interpreters who would secure Russia's musical future were at last being created, rather than merely born, in the newly instigated conducting classes at the St. Petersburg Conservatory.

The course that changed Russia's conducting history came about as part of Rimsky-Korsakov's reforms when he returned to the Conservatory, no longer its director, after the revolutionary upheavals of 1905. He divided the Department of Theory between composition and conducting, appointing Nikolai Tcherepnin (1873–1945) as professor of the conducting course. Tcherepnin, according to Prokofiev's detailed and amusing autobiography of his student years, was an excellent talker, instilling in his pupils the importance among other things of painstaking score preparation and a strong preparatory upbeat; but he was incapable of showing how to conduct complicated meters and "whenever he stepped up to the podium, the orchestra fell to pieces under his baton."[13] He nevertheless nurtured the two most important conductor-teachers of the next generation. One was Alexander Gauk (1893–1963), whose clear-headed professionalism maintained an enterprising repertoire and reasonably high standards with the Leningrad Philharmonic, the former court orchestra, in the early 1930s, and the USSR State Symphony Orchestra from 1936 to 1941. The other was Nikolai Malko. Although he may have learnt more during his year in Berlin with Felix Mottl than he had in the Conservatory conducting classes, Malko understood the value of the great personalities there, Rimsky-Korsakov, Lyadov, and Glazunov as well as Tcherepnin, and carried the tradition through the years of revolution on to the first, vibrant decade of Soviet musical life before emigrating in 1929. A born pedagogue, Malko left behind a clear analysis and definition of manual technique in his *The Conductor and His Baton*.[14]

One of Malko's star pupils, Boris Khaikin (1904–78), reflected his professor's pioneering work with Fokine at the Mariinsky Theatre, where the status of the ballet and opera conductor improved dramatically alongside a new plasticity of choreography from 1909 onwards. In 1918 the studios of Stanislavsky and Nemirovich-Danchenko began to develop a new concept of the "actor-singer," fusing the tradition of the Bolshoi with the detailed realism of the Moscow Arts Theatre. The conductor's role was to reflect, as faithfully as possible, the dynamics of the soul reflected in the stage drama, and Stanislavsky's teachings had a profound effect on Khaikin's interpretation, which sometimes liberated itself from strict tempo demands to mirror more accurately the staging in question. The intimacy of the Stanislavsky-Nemirovich-Danchenko Theatre's production of Tchaikovsky's *Eugene Onegin*, still in the repertoire after over two thousand performances, is reflected in Khaikin's 1955 Bolshoi recording. It is a flexible far cry from the more grandiose interpretations of the 1970s and 1980s. Similarly many of the Bolshoi performances conducted by Alexander Melik-Pashayev justify seemingly erratic tempo changes through an idiosyncratic view of what the drama demands. Sometimes, as in the case of the Soviet approach to the role of the people in Musorgsky's *Boris Godunov*, the ideological message dictated the conductor's decisions, not always in the best interests of the music.

Soviet developments

Among the most surprising, yet logical developments of the Soviet arts in their infancy was the foundation of the orchestra Persimfans, in 1922, which prided itself on perfect communism. Spearheaded by the intellectually dazzling cultural commissar Anatol Lunacharsky, the title was an acronym of "Pervyi Symphonicheskiy Ansamble bez dirizhor" (first symphonic ensemble without conductor). Under the guidance of Lev Tseitlin, a violin professor who had once been the leader of Koussevitzky's orchestra in Russia, the players of Persimfans had an equal say in the shaping of an interpretation, sending a representative out in to the hall to check ensemble balance and passing discreet glances during performance as they sat in a widely described semicircle. In the course of its first year, Persimfans gave 210 concerts not only in the Great Hall of the Moscow Conservatory but also in workers' clubs and factories. Soon it was performing works as complex as Prokofiev's *Scythian Suite*, and the composer gave one of the clearest impressions of this "institution so essentially communistic in spirit" in the diary covering his 1927 return visit to the Soviet Union:

> Without a conductor the orchestra took much more trouble and worked harder than it would have with one; a conductor would have to battle with passages of technical difficulty and ask for important voices to be brought out. Here the players are very conscientious, play by nature musically and with great concentration; all dynamics and nuances are precisely observed. No question of learning their parts at rehearsal; they prepare the most difficult passages at home beforehand. On the other hand, problems arise: a ritardando, for example, which with a conductor will come about quite unproblematically, may take them a good twenty minutes to straighten out, because every player slows down in his own way.[15]

Like many of the admirable experiments conducted throughout the 1920s, Persimfans did not survive the upheavals of the early 1930s. Although Stalin's purges were still in the future, the unstable conditions of artistic life fractured the development of orchestral institutions and their conductors. In the mid- to late 1920s, visiting great names dominated the scene (among them Otto Klemperer, who was one of the few conductors to be granted an audience with the Persimfans), only to stay away during the rise of the aggressive and inward-looking Proletarian Musicians' Associations. Their dissolution in 1932 seemed to signal a new dawn, but in fact it was only the signal for the state screw to turn on all the arts; nonetheless, back came the foreign conductors for a while. Several, including Austrian-born Fritz Stiedry and the Frenchman Georges Sebastian, already held permanent positions with leading orchestras. The native tradition seemed to have lost its way, even though Khaikin, Alexander Gauk and the fascinating, wilful and unpredictable former precentor Nikolai Golovanov (1891–1958), were doing what they could with orchestras badly in need of new instruments and supplies from the West.

Mravinsky in Leningrad

Then, in the unpromising year of 1938, the greatest success story in Russian orchestral history began when the thirty-five-year-old Yevgeny Mravinsky (1903–88) succeeded Stiedry as principal conductor of the Leningrad Philharmonic Orchestra. Having graduated from the Leningrad Conservatory classes of Malko and Gauk to work in the two great opera houses of Leningrad and Moscow, Mravinsky proved with customary single-mindedness that he was a symphonic conductor first and foremost by preserving his relationship with the Leningrad Philharmonic for half a century, and maintaining his tenure there for forty-four years. When the orchestra was finally allowed to tour outside the Soviet Union in the post-Stalin years, the West discovered the full force of a Tchaikovsky symphony shorn of false pathos – exactly, in fact, as Medtner had earlier described Rakhmaninov's interpretation. There are times when Mravinsky's approach to Tchaikovsky can seem over-drilled: in his 1960 studio recording of the Fifth, the hectic onslaught of the finale almost misses the sense of conflict in its processed articulation. At its most successful, though, his approach still manages to convey a sense of what lies behind the notes even at its most controlled. In the first movement of the "Pathétique" Symphony and the scintillating later stages of the Fourth, the mixture of passion and precision is unsurpassable.

With the full dynamic range meticulously realized, including some of the most atmospheric pianissimos a conductor has ever achieved, and a forward-looking sense of structure that still allowed expressive phrasing a chance to breathe, Mravinsky's style became the epitome of an approach holding the Romantic and the classical in perfect equilibrium. Austere and hard-working rather than tyrannical, Mravinsky always insisted on a minimum of eight rehearsals no matter how many times he had conducted the work in question, an option which the state's attitude towards its musical figureheads encouraged. No outspoken freedom fighter, he nevertheless assisted in the unfolding chronicle of the Shostakovich symphonies from the Fifth through to the Twelfth, matching the uncompromising intensity of the Eighth symphony with an interpretation of severe truthfulness. Equally at home in the wide open spaces of Bruckner's Symphony No. 9 and Strauss's *Alpine Symphony*, which his love of nature led him to realize in unusual depth and grandeur, his wide repertoire also brought to Russian audiences contemporary scores by Stravinsky (a superbly taut reading of *Agon*), Honegger, and Bartók.

The next generation: Svetlanov, Rozhdestvensky, and Temirkanov

With the Leningrad Philharmonic's reputation as the supremely flexible instrument among orchestras, its sonorous cellos and basses offsetting the severity of its brass and the necessarily acerbic tone of the woodwind department, Mravinsky's apparent stranglehold over the position of number-one conductor in the Soviet Union might have stifled new talent in a nation less dedicated to the flourishing diversity of its musical institutions. The Moscow Philharmonic Orchestra enjoyed a renaissance for fifteen years between 1960 and 1975 under the precise but colorful guidance of Kirill Kondrashin (1914–81). An altogether more hard-hitting alternative arose in 1965 when Yevgeny Svetlanov (1928–2002), a pianist and composer first and foremost, who had also studied conducting with Gauk at the Moscow Conservatory, took charge of the USSR State Symphony Orchestra. He had already earned a reputation with expansive weighty interpretations of the major Russian operas at the Bolshoi Theatre; now he proceeded to make his new charge, in the words of Valery Gergiev, "an orchestra with a voice,"[16] a very loud and powerful one, with famously sandblasting trumpets and dark, weighty strings. He also had the benefit of the state recording company, Melodiya, in committing to disc what he subsequently claimed as the entire breadth of Russian symphonic music; it was through these recordings that Western record collectors truly came to know the wider Russian repertoire.

In the 1960s, too, another altogether more maverick figure rose to prominence. Gennady Rozhdestvensky (b. 1931) had been immersed in the world of the musical theatre from an early age, and in ballet rather than opera, fighting for the rights of a Bolshoi staff conductor in a tradition which since Fokine's joint revolution with Malko had become moribund and dependent on the dancers' whims. It has been largely thanks to his vivid sense of characterization and symphonic sweep that the ballet scores of Tchaikovsky and Prokofiev stand on their own feet without the choreography for which they were devised. Rozhdestvensky's love of the outlandish is testified to by his choice of favourite scores, Shostakovich's Gogol opera *The Nose* and the steel thrash of Prokofiev's Symphony No. 2, as well as by his interpretations and a batch of riotous orchestrations. His astonishing balancing act between a clownish geniality, which verges on the anarchic, and a rigorous grasp of form, between a laid-back, sometimes non-existent rehearsal process and a mastery of white-heat recreation in performance, point to an incarnation of a special Russian type. More obviously in control, though sometimes prone to the capricious gesture, is Yuri Temirkanov (b. 1938), who like Svetlanov and Rozhdestvensky, has maintained an equally vivid profile in opera house and concert hall. His attempts to balance the roles of conductor and producer at the helm of the Kirov Opera yielded traditionally handsome results in the 1980s, but his authoritative command of the St. Petersburg Philharmonic in performances of Shostakovich and Tchaikovsky, altogether more libertarian and extreme in tempo fluctuation than those of Mravinsky, will perhaps have the more lasting impact.

After glasnost: success, disarray and regeneration

Temirkanov's legacy at the Kirov, now Mariinsky once more, can only be eclipsed by the powerhouse phenomenon of Valery Gergiev (b. 1953). Working sixteen-hour days in an environment of seeming chaos and improvisation, Gergiev has baffled all the prophets of burn-out in the astonishingly productive years since he took over the reins in 1978. Rehabilitated Rimsky-Korsakov and Prokofiev operas, lavish new productions and a fluctuating but ever-luminous ensemble of singers, point to the artistic healthiness of the institution. More impressive still is the number of times Gergiev seems capable of shaping a truly great performance. A typical week at the Mariinsky in 2000 culminated in a marathon evening of Mahler's Sixth Symphony sandwiched between two major viola concertos by Gubaidulina and Kancheli. The results should have been ragged; yet the orchestral playing and all the dangerous corners were turned with dazzling assurance. Sometimes the Gergiev magic fails, especially on flying visits when rehearsals fail to materialize or when the repertoire lacks preparation, as in an ill-conceived Verdi festival exhaustively toured in 2001. Yet his support of new music, and the uncompromising approach he brings to such contemporary masterpieces as Gubaidulina's *St. John Passion*, shows a powerful figurehead still prepared to be very much of his time. At his best, the inner life Gergiev finds in every phrase and his natural, charismatic communication place him among the handful of true originals among conductors today.

Not all musical institutions found their way as brilliantly as Gergiev's Mariinsky in the post-glasnost era. Several old-guard orchestras lost their players to the new Russian National Orchestra, a still unfocused super-band underpinned by Western sponsorship and conducted with fitful intensity by Mikhail Pletnev (b. 1957). Among the casualties were Svetlanov's orchestra, its "USSR" now replaced by plain "Russian," sounding distinctly ragged in a recorded Mahler cycle. Though the conductor's drive and commitment towards completing a cycle of Myaskovsky's twenty-seven symphonies are admirable, an earlier, 1965 recording of the Fifth, when compared to later Olympia issues, shows us how far the super-band had declined by the late 1980s and early 1990s. In 2000 Svetlanov was dismissed from his post when Russia's cultural minister suggested he was spending too much time abroad. Knowing he had little time to live, he went out with a flourish two weeks before his death in May 2002, conducting the BBC Symphony Orchestra in Rakhmaninov's *The Bells*, a work whose terraced climaxes he drew out and sustained like no other conductor. Meanwhile, Rozhdestvensky re-entered and quickly exited the troubled Bolshoi scene with a typically daring attempt to give the world premiere of Prokofiev's *The Gambler* in its original version.

Yet the legacy continues in the new diaspora of brilliant young Russian conductors. In Britain alone there are three figures in prominent positions. Glyndebourne Festival Opera has appointed as its Music Director Moscow-born Vladimir Jurowski (b. 1972), a broad and weighty exponent of the great Russian symphonies in the Temirkanov tradition as well as a chameleonic interpreter of a surprisingly eclectic operatic repertoire. Vassily Sinaisky

(b. 1947) continues sterling work, and a fascinating repertoire, in Manchester with the BBC Philharmonic where he is Principal Guest Conductor, and twenty-four-year-old Tugan Sokhiev (b. 1977) is poised to take up the directorship of Welsh National Opera. Sokhiev's case points up the survival of a tradition which links the youngest with the oldest. He studied at the St. Petersburg State Conservatory with a figure who achieved belated worldwide fame after nearly seven decades of selfless service. Professor Ilya Musin (1904–99), who shortly before his death at the age of ninety-five, was still inspiring a whole new generation of conductors from all over the world, could easily have pipped Mravinsky to the Leningrad Philharmonic post in the 1930s. It has been suggested that anti-Semitism and Mravinsky's status as a card-carrying Communist played their part; but whatever the case Musin was both an inspirational teacher and a conductor of genius who shaped the music with the fine tapering of his expressive, baton-free hands, as his London debut at the age of ninety-two revealed. It is curiously representative of Russia's unshakeable musical continuity that Musin's most valuable gift, refined from his own teacher Malko's example, now rests in the hands of conductors at the beginning of their careers.

PART THREE

Issues

15 The conductor as artistic director

BRAMWELL TOVEY

In a famous 1941 wartime photograph (Fig. 15.1) Sir Henry Wood stands amid the ruins of London's Queen's Hall, atop the rubble and chaos of what had once been his artistic domain. The image is of desolation, but also defiance in the face of a Luftwaffe raid. Wood's biographer, Arthur Jacobs, has pointed out that two similarly earnest BBC officials were airbrushed out of the original.[1] Propaganda required the symbolism of the artist's civilizing vision amidst its destruction by the nefarious Nazis. Wood's hegemony over the Proms was drawing to a close. Although he was never officially artistic director, his association dated back to their inception in 1895. He died three years later, having seen his famous music festival transferred to the Royal Albert Hall where it prospers beyond his wildest dreams.

By way of contrast, in 1983 Simon Rattle was captured on film inspecting the building site of Symphony Hall, in Birmingham, with tousled hair barely suppressed beneath the regulation hard hat. Rattle was in the middle of an astonishingly successful period as Principal Conductor and Music Director of the City of Birmingham Symphony Orchestra (his title changed during his tenure).[2] Not entirely coincidentally, the last two decades of the twentieth century saw the rebirth of Birmingham as an international city. 1960s urban planners had wreaked almost as much havoc as the Luftwaffe did in wartime. Concrete was universally employed as the material of the moment as the city was rebuilt. Paradoxically, *musique concrète* was successfully featured amongst Rattle's programming as he took the CBSO around the world for over two decades, winning renown for Birmingham and personally embodying the renaissance of its reputation.

Both Wood and Rattle presided over musical empires that were inextricably linked to their own prestige. Their longevity was exceptional: in Rattle's case a mere twenty years, while Wood was on the podium of the Proms for a few weeks shy of half a century. Despite the disparity in their tasks and titles, each was de facto the director of his institution's artistic activities and widely recognized as such.

Figure 15.1 Sir Henry Wood among the ruins of London's Queen's Hall in 1941

Conductors and directors

The music director of a modern, professional symphony orchestra is both the artistic director and an administrator, and is typically contracted to conduct between nine and fifteen weeks of concerts each season.[3] If a conductor holds the position of principal conductor or artistic advisor the responsibilities are unlikely to be as comprehensive. Further, the programming issues for a conductor of a broadcasting orchestra, as well as personnel issues, funding, and administration, are likely to be quite different from those of an independent orchestra. In broadcasting orchestras, direction is more likely to be in the hands of producers or station directors with individual or corporate agendas. Self-governing orchestras also require a different emphasis in musical leadership. Sir Colin Davis (b. 1927) enjoys the position of Principal Conductor of the London Symphony (as opposed to music director) precisely because he does not have many of the administrative responsibilities outlined below, these being assumed by the orchestra members themselves.

The position of music director evolved from composers who were responsible for the musical affairs of religious or aristocratic patrons. Johann Sebastian Bach's association with the music of Leipzig (1723–50) and Joseph Haydn's period as Kapellmeister to the Esterházy family (1761–90) are the most familiar landmarks in the early history of musical direction. Both gestured from the keyboard and did little conducting, but their musical authority was founded upon their status as composers. François-Antoine Habeneck, who was associated with the Société des Concerts du Conservatoire in Paris (1826–49), and Theodore Eisfeld, the first named director of the New York Philharmonic (1852–65), were among the earliest musical leaders of permanent ensembles who were not major composers and whose function was to choose and perform the works of recently established masters.

The first recognizably modern artistic director of an orchestra was Felix Mendelssohn, who presided over the Gewandhaus Orchestra from 1835–47. His contract with the Leipzig town council (negotiated on his behalf by a lawyer) represented a radical change from the traditional patronage enjoyed by Bach and Haydn. While Bach and Haydn composed most of the music for their own performances, Mendelssohn became a musical patron himself, introducing works by Robert Schumann and Hector Berlioz and reviving the then neglected music of J. S. Bach, and he vigorously supported his musicians.[4]

After the peripatetic life of a piano virtuoso, Franz Liszt consolidated his musical activities in the city of Weimar (1848–61) under the patronage of the Grand Duke Carl Alexander. While this move was motivated by a desire to transform himself into an orchestral composer, Liszt also used his role as Hofkapellmeister (and the isolation of Weimar) to champion the music of the so-called "New German School." Twenty-five of the forty-four operas he conducted in Weimar were contemporary, and he was especially generous in tackling the difficult works of Berlioz and Wagner. The latter was particularly commendable as Wagner was *persona non grata* in Weimar after his role in the 1849 Dresden uprising.[5] The problems and challenges facing modern music directors would have been familiar to Liszt. Local politics, interference from officials who oversaw the funding of his activities, social climbers, hostile critics, the jealous intrigues of composers ignored by him (and in the case of Schumann, supported by him), and endless innuendo about his private life all sound depressingly familiar to anyone in charge of a musical enterprise in the twenty-first century.

By the end of the nineteenth century, musicians like Hans von Bülow at the Meiningen Court Orchestra (1880–5) and Felix Weingartner at the Royal Concerts in Berlin (1898–1907) helped establish the importance of a musical figurehead for the many permanent orchestras that were evolving all over Europe and America. The concept of the conductor (as opposed to the composer) as artistic authority of an orchestra was firmly entrenched by the beginning of the twentieth century. On the occasions when a composer was the artistic leader, such as Gustav Mahler at the Vienna Opera (1898–1908) or Edward Elgar at the London Symphony (1911–12), composing was regarded by their employers as more of a distraction than a complementary activity. During the second half of the twentieth century music directors of major orchestras were rarely conductor-composers.[6]

The modern music director

It is an axiom of orchestral life that it is impossible to make a financial profit from the establishment of a full-time orchestra. Independent orchestras can only be guaranteed in perpetuity by the establishment of large endowment funds, the interest from which is used to fund operations (as in the United States), or by considerable public funding based on national cultural aspirations (as in some European countries). Both means of funding require additional corporate and individual support. From the outset it appears necessary to establish a working formula between financial requirements and artistic aspirations; the successful music director must navigate both areas and will aim for *artistic excellence with fiscal responsibility.*

Music directors are usually appointed by representatives of the board, musicians, and the senior administration of an orchestra. External input is sometimes sought from recording contacts, soloists, music educators, or other experts who live within the community, but further external consultation with public funders such as arts councils, sponsors, or major individual donors is unnecessary. Occasionally board members (customarily business-oriented individuals) appoint music directors without wider consultation, particularly ignoring the opinions of their most valuable resource – the musicians. Such actions are irresponsible and contrary to the duties and obligations of governance to conduct all business in the best interests of the institution. A music director cannot expect to succeed without the support and respect of the musicians of an orchestra. Similarly, the quality of the partnership between the music director and the chief executive of an orchestra is extremely important. The best partnerships enjoy mutual support and a clear understanding of each other's roles and responsibilities.

Robert Sunter, formerly Head of Music at the Canadian Broadcasting Corporation, recently chaired an orchestra's search committee for a new music director and set out the following criteria for the hiring of a music director:

We agreed we were looking for someone with artistic and leadership qualities who would also understand corporate and individual fundraising, public and government relations, marketing imperatives and compromises and who would know how to continue to develop our audience base. Not only would the ideal candidate have to be ready to engage in these extra-musical activities, but he or she would have to be keen to do so.

We developed a matrix to evaluate candidates. Under artistic leadership, it asked if the conductor under consideration was currently a music director or had been one. Did he or she have any strong connections in the music industry? Did he or she have knowledge of and a commitment to (or a readiness to commit to) Canadian music and soloists? Was she or he a "team player"? Under musical leadership, we listed wide-ranging repertoire and experience outside the symphonic milieu – opera, ballet, chamber music, choral, children's concerts, and pops [a very important part of most North American orchestral activities, but virtually unknown in Europe]. The key questions concerned technique and musicianship, rehearsal style and efficiency, organizational skills, rapport with our orchestra, rapport with other orchestras, stage presence, and audience communication skills. Last and paramount, was that difficult question of whether the conductor had: "The ability to raise the level of our orchestra."[7]

Advocacy of the institution has been a prerequisite since the advent of public as opposed to private concerts in the early nineteenth century. More recently, since the decline of music as a school subject and the availability of music of all types on radio and recordings, live music itself has needed serious philosophical advocacy. This has been the largest social change in orchestral life since the Second World War and has led to orchestras developing "outreach" activities. In particular, politicians have realized there are few votes to be had in funding what is perceived to be (quite unjustifiably) an "elite art form," unless popular initiatives are attached.

All music directors of independent orchestras are required to be part of their orchestra's fundraising campaigns. Such activity is rarely vocational. In the present writer's experience, potential sponsors and donors welcome the opportunity to hear the artistic vision of an orchestra articulated by its musical head. Special projects, such as new music, or rare events like Berlioz's *Grande messe des morts* or Schoenberg's *Gurrelieder*, usually require leadership gifts. Business people are often entranced by the magic of the footlights. Visionary philanthropy within the community enables the sponsor to stand avuncularly in the wings, yet visible for all to see, thus satisfying their paradoxical requirements of due modesty and wide publicity. Few conductors have the courage or knowledge to talk financial figures with sponsors. Boards should realize this and ensure that specific requests for money come from the chief executive, an appointed board member, or the appropriate staff. An orchestra's music director is more valuable unsullied by the risk of rebuff. However, exceptional situations, such as impending bankruptcy or capital fundraising, perhaps for a new hall or renovations to existing facilities, will require the music director to be more closely involved. Similarly, when musicians' contracts are being negotiated, the music director's sympathies will lie naturally with the musicians. For this reason it is best to remain aloof from negotiations. Intervention in this process should be timely, appropriate, and above rancor. Politically, it is wise to ensure in advance that such intervention will be respected by both parties.

The administrative functions of the music director vary in direct proportion to the effectiveness of the chief executive. Once again, in marketing strategies the music director's vision should be central to the orchestra's self-awareness. In an ideal situation orchestra stakeholders (musicians, board members, senior staff, major supporters) will have collectively expressed their mission statement in both strategic and long-term planning documents. In reality, such documents are usually composed in response to the bureaucratic requirements of public funders. The music director will be the public voice of the ambitions of the institution. Where funding bodies require a music director's report as part of the grant application it is important to be pragmatic and sensible. This is no place for the hyperbole of agents or publicists.

It is unlikely that an orchestra will have sufficient local profile unless the music director is closely involved in the community. Visits to schools and civic organizations will help an orchestra maintain a healthy public persona. A clear personal understanding of the role of music and musicians in our society is essential. Most modern audiences lack a philosophical perspective of the part music plays in their lives. Similarly, close involvement with music teachers will bring a practical understanding that each generation needs to renew our understanding of music as an art form.

Although essential, advocacy is principally a political function and like other peripheral tasks (such as marketing and public relations) can only be an adjunct to the main role of providing artistic leadership to the musical institution.

Conducting the ensemble: musical leadership

First and foremost, the music director must be a conductor and musician of technical and artistic excellence who enjoys the respect and support of the musicians of the orchestra as *primus inter pares* (first among equals). It is the music director's responsibility to establish a working atmosphere where every musician can fulfill his or her individual potential. The establishment of mutual trust between music director and musicians is of paramount importance, yet the psychology of this relationship remains disarmingly elusive to theory.

While the concert experience will always remain the supreme test of a music director's relationship with an orchestra, the rehearsal process provides the principal opportunity for a music director to achieve higher standards. Careful organization of rehearsal time and prior notification of how time is to be used ensures that musicians can be properly prepared. Undoubtedly, idiosyncratic behavior, poor rehearsal technique and lack of collegial respect will gradually undermine any orchestra's confidence in its musical leader.

Creating the ensemble: personnel

The music director has traditionally been responsible for auditioning and recruiting musicians. This essential function has been appropriately tempered in modern times by other musicians shouldering some of the responsibilities. The individual excesses of music directors have been curbed and the casting couch consigned to oblivion.

Most orchestras now require auditionees to perform anonymously behind a screen. This protects everyone concerned from accusations of bias or prejudice. The majority of applicants for positions in professional orchestras are below the age of thirty-five. Orchestras rarely appoint older players via the audition process. One victim of this process has been the experienced musician who no longer wishes to be musically naked in front of his or her peers. Violinist Sol Turner was a member of the Chicago Symphony under Frederick Stock but resigned to become a full-time member of the NBC Radio Orchestra. In 1962 while playing with the CSO as an extra musician under music director Fritz Reiner, he was distracted during his warm-up on stage.

> I turned round and saw it was Dr. Reiner. My immediate thought was to apologize. "That's okay," said Reiner. "You know, your hair is grey, but your heart is still warm."[8]

The next day the personnel manager casually mentioned "the old man would like you to come back and join the symphony." Turner worked for Reiner, Giulini and Solti before retiring due to ill health in 1977. Such positive discrimination on the grounds of experience is beyond the scope of the modern music director.

By way of contrast Sir Adrian Boult describes an audition for the BBC Symphony Orchestra in 1931, where he heard

> a middle-aged and respected first violin member of London orchestras
> [London players still famously "moonlight" for other orchestras] who was
> a familiar figure for years . . . His audition included the last few pages of
> [the] *Götterdämmerung* first violin part and I sat back, prepared to fill in
> the glorious brass chording in my mind . . . Alas, I had no fun; the
> arpeggios were unrecognisable.[9]

Such situations underline the importance of job security to the professional musician and emphasize the role and responsibility of the music director in granting tenure.

Once the successful auditionee has passed into the ranks of the orchestra, the music director customarily has the power to confirm or deny tenure. There is often a great deal of peer pressure to continue the employment of individuals who after a trial period (one or two years) have become part of the orchestra community. The music director need only be concerned with the best long-term interests of the institution. Does this player deserve to be a tenured member for life? Short-term difficulties are of no consequence if the answer is negative, although the need to dismiss players can sometimes cause problems for the music director. In 2001, Charles Dutoit resigned his music directorship of the Montreal Symphony on the eve of his twenty-fifth anniversary season after the American Federation of Musicians publicly challenged his alleged decision to commence dismissal proceedings against several players.

Uniquely, in Great Britain musicians are invited to perform with the orchestra for any number of trial periods. These can be as short as one concert or as long as a year. Conversely, dismissal from Britain's self-governing orchestras is far more ruthless and immediate than anything tolerated from a music director.

In most countries, however, contracts between managements and musicians have clauses enabling the music director to address a musician's deficiencies. Such responsibilities need to be exercised with dignity and integrity. Initially, the music director's authority should be used in a supportive fashion, in order that the musician can articulate any problems of a personal or technical nature that might be unknown. It is advisable to take soundings in confidence from the principal player of the section. Every orchestra is a community of artists and as such develops a strong identity. Nothing unites an orchestra more than maltreatment by a conductor. If a music director believes a musician is underachieving then the music director must expect every action to be closely monitored by the group at large. If the musician is not treated in a professional manner then the music director is likely to be isolated and without support, no matter how justified the concern.

The music director also oversees the use of substitute musicians. In the best situations, the principal of the section or the concertmaster will work with the personnel manager to achieve the highest quality available. A music director relies on principal players and mutual trust is essential.

Curating the ensemble: programming

The music director is also a curator: a programmer of music that needs to include traditional, neglected and contemporary repertoire. While unlikely to choose every single work and artist in the season, the music director is likely to be the focus of critical comment and the orchestra's marketing initiatives.

Eccentricity of taste can only be of temporary interest; an intelligent music director should have a broad range of repertoire. While the music director whose command of the classical repertoire is strong is traditionally perceived to be the best orchestra builder, a willingness to recognize personal weakness or lack of sympathy in certain areas of repertoire is also important.

As part of the curatorial function the music director's duties customarily include selecting or recommending guest conductors. Astonishingly, this is sometimes abused as music directors seek podium exchanges to enhance their freelance careers to personal financial advantage. Despite the clearly unethical nature of this practice it is still in widespread use. For orchestras it flouts a fundamental principle of custodianship, namely to serve the best interests of the institution at all times. It is fallacious to believe that a lesser conductor will place the music director in a better light. Professional orchestral musicians are artists, and while opinions about individuals will vary, they want high-quality leadership; it is unwise to issue invitations without consulting their expertise.

The selection of soloists, too, brings up the issue of personal empathy. Since almost every orchestral program requires at least one soloist, it is highly probable that unfamiliar soloists will be needed each season. Regular auditions of young artists bring their own rewards. Knowledge of established soloists is an essential requirement, either through live performance or accredited recommendation.

The music director relies on an artistic administrator to keep abreast of emerging soloists (this task is sometimes performed by the chief executive of the orchestra). For the most part it is not necessary or desirable for conductors to liaise directly with managers, agents, artists, and other music producers. Indeed, such contact can compromise an artistic administrator's ability to negotiate on behalf of the orchestra.

Superficially, it may appear that the personal interests of the music director can be in conflict with the best interests of the institution. This need not be so, provided the music director adheres to the principle outlined earlier of "artistic excellence with fiscal responsibility." This mantra provides the basis on which a music director can enjoy support throughout an organization and ultimately lead to significant achievement.

It should not be forgotten that a music director cannot be responsible for financial profligacy. Given the public nature of the role, the music director will be identified with the financial fortunes of the institution, but every orchestra has its own system of checks and balances to ensure money is spent wisely. The music director, in alliance with the artistic administrator and chief executive, will present a season that should be scrutinized in minute detail by a programming committee and approved at a board meeting. Many orchestras, anxious to take advantage of last-minute opportunities, or just plain slack in their budgeting arrangements, appear to accept and market programming before budgets have been properly established. This is inadvisable and does not fit the principle of "artistic excellence with fiscal responsibility." Ultimately, boards, not conductors, sanction budgets and bear responsibility for financial excesses.

Period performance

The growth of period performance practice in the last three decades of the twentieth century created a major change in programming choices. Modern music directors are faced with a myriad of new interpretative issues in the performance of Baroque and Classical music. Sir Henry Wood famously performed Bach's Third Brandenburg Concerto with a full-size string section. Such extravagance today would be risible.

There can be no comparison between historically informed and idiosyncratically malformed performance practice. The often omitted aria in Handel's *Messiah*, "If God be for us, who can be against us?" is exquisite when sung by a counter-tenor, but orchestras not directed in an historically informed manner will fail to provide satisfactory accompaniment for this timbre of voice. The chorus "Behold the Lamb of God" in Prout's edition, with five hundred singers, is bereft of rhythmic effect and fails to communicate the very tangible pathos achievable with a period interpretation. Of course, the obvious fun in Beecham's recording of the "Hallelujah Chorus" can be enjoyed at home without the embarrassment of having to witness cymbals, bass drum, trombones and clarinets floundering around in the rest of the work. Mozart's realization of *Messiah* and Stravinsky's *Pulcinella* "after Pergolesi" remain as reminders that genius creates its own rules. This is a battle already won and unlikely to trouble future generations.

Requesting wooden sticks from the timpanist or *senza vibrato* from string players would have been unthinkable in the middle years of the twentieth century. Baroque styles of bowing can be replicated sympathetically on the modern bow, though not as effectively as on a bow of Baroque design. On assuming the position of Principal Conductor of the Canadian Broadcasting Corporation Orchestra in Canada in 1981 John Eliot Gardiner requested that CBC purchase Baroque bows for each string player. Sadly, this innovation was not sustained by his successor, and corporate accountants sold off the bows after Gardiner resigned. Should a music director encounter intransigence for historically informed practices, the likelihood is that he or she has failed to create the necessary atmosphere of experimentation in rehearsal.

For financial as much as artistic reasons, orchestras need to perform the music of Bach, Handel, and Vivaldi. While high-quality period-performance ensembles will continue to provide Baroque and Classical aficionados with a very attractive alternative to the traditional symphony orchestra, we should not banish this repertoire from our larger symphony halls.

There should be no doubt about the stimulating effect of programming neglected or unfamiliar music. For most orchestral players, early music provides a welcome relief from the routine of Classical and Romantic repertoire. Programme committees and marketers faced with financial criteria prefer a more traditional approach, and a perfect balance between familiar and unfamiliar is probably unattainable. In this area the music director's powers of persuasion will be sorely tried.

Educational programming

Music directors should participate fully in concerts for children. School concerts are downgraded in importance when the artistic leader is absent. It makes no sense that the orchestra's most publicized individual should be absent from the podium when children are attending.

This is, however, a specialist area where most music directors lack experience and knowledge. The music director should take advice and support from leading music teachers in the community. For school concerts, the guiding principle is to ensure that the teacher's preparation in the classroom is directly connected to the positive experience of the concert, and that can only happen by working with the local music teachers.

British orchestras and composers have developed sophisticated education programs. Musicians visit schools within the community and work on creative ideas that see fruition in performances on stage with the full orchestra. Composers provide musical frameworks into which creative work done in the classroom is inserted. Such activity provides insight into the composition and performance of music and is of immense practical value to teacher and pupil. It is also challenging to musicians who must develop ancillary skills not normally utilized when playing within the greater collective.

Music education is under threat in many countries and needs visible support. It is worth remembering that in 1749 J. S. Bach was involved in a public debate over whether music was a subject worth cultivating in schools.

Contemporary music

The greatest of curatorial opportunities facing a music director are in the field of contemporary music. Many music directors eschew new music, preferring to leave it to guest conductors and assistants, but orchestras often have access to special funding for composer-in-residence positions. A composer-in-residence should not only write music for the orchestra, he or she should also be involved in the presentation and selection of new music and in educational and community activities.

Some composers have powers of verbal communication that overcome prejudice with a *bon mot* from the stage. Others antagonize listeners with autobiographical tales of woe, or perhaps are only able to communicate with a potted version of their doctoral thesis. Such alienation is avoidable and is a problem of presentation. Some funding agencies (the Canada Council, for example) insist that orchestras present new music alongside traditional works within major subscription series concerts. This line of thought contradicts all established common-sense practice for curating new work in other art forms. Who would think of exhibiting Damien Hirst alongside Michaelangelo?[10] The well-meaning logic behind such philosophy, though, is to develop the taste of current symphony subscribers.

The art of curating a concert is most exposed when programming new music. Murray Schafer's work *No Longer than Ten Minutes* grew from frustration at the Toronto Symphony Orchestra's commissioning policy in the early 1970s. Milton Babbitt, disillusioned by the recalcitrance of the New York Philharmonic under Leonard Bernstein, spoke publicly about his frustrations in reference to his NYPO commission *Relata II*:

> Who will hear this piece? No one is concerned about my interested musical colleagues. There will not be a broadcast, a tape, a recording. There won't even be a published score. My associates across the country will not have any opportunity to hear it unless they get to Philharmonic Hall next week . . . the regular Philharmonic audience does not want to hear this piece. And why should they have to? How can it be coherent for them? It's as though a colleague of mine in the field of philosophy were to read his

paper on the Johnny Carson show. The milieu is inappropriate for the event.[11]

Babbitt's comments focus on the key issue in the relationship of orchestras to composers: what is the appropriate milieu for the presentation of new music?

Traditional orchestral audiences are perceived to be naturally antipathetic to the creative edge in musical art. At least one North American orchestra accepts major gifts of $10,000 from donors towards a specific concert, provided that no contemporary music is performed. Nonetheless, there is a great deal of interest in new music from audiences that might be more familiar with modern jazz or some elements of popular music. Indeed, the BBC Promenade Concerts at the Royal Albert Hall in London regularly draw capacity crowds of over six thousand for new music events. Several orchestras have established major festivals of new music (San Francisco and Winnipeg). While much harder for independent ensembles, such events are regularly accomplished by subsidized broadcasting orchestras.

Orchestra schedules are established around an annual pattern of subscription concerts. The selling of individual subscriptions provides most orchestras with the necessary cash flow to operate. Breaking this flow of activity requires an orchestra to take a financial risk. If a free week emerges outside subscription and educational activities many orchestras seek to sell their services to other organizations, such as choirs or ballet and opera companies. These groups are unlikely to pay the full cost of the orchestra but will generally offset a large portion of the bill and not involve the orchestra in any promotional costs. The presentation of new music is easily sidelined for such activity, but board members are financial custodians of public grants and need constant reminding that new music provides a fascinating and absorbing philosophical commentary on our times. The tediously repetitive refrain of "wishing to be relevant" finds no greater satisfaction than in programming contemporary music. The seemingly complex vocabulary of new music is far less daunting than, for example, Shakespeare's *Hamlet*, performed in English in Paris in 1827, when Hector Berlioz fell in love with Harriet Smithson's Ophelia without understanding a single word.[12]

An orchestra without a strong creative component risks fossilization. A period of such activity, intelligently curated, provides orchestras with a valuable focus on the creative edge of music. Working with contemporary composers and turning musicians' attention to developments in musical language will enhance the group's accomplishments in other areas of repertoire. The marketing benefits are similarly profound, with new audience members often from those demographics allegedly difficult to reach.

Figure 15.2 Bramwell Tovey with Leonard Bernstein, conducting a festival of the composer's music with the London Symphony Orchestra in 1986

Commissioning new works

While musical history is littered with the withered reputations of conductors and orchestras who have disdained new techniques that have proved permanent, the relationship between a music director and the contemporary composer remains potentially fraught with difficulty. The music director must be the servant of a composer, be they dead or alive, and in the case of the latter, whether or not the composer's personality is as challenging as their music.

The commissioning of composers is customarily at the discretion of the music director whose choices should be made based on close acquaintance with the composer's oeuvre. Sadly, because of local politics those choices often fall on composers who are excellent promoters of their own work. There is no correlation between quality of work and self-promotion.

The music director must be prepared to support a composer's work through the entire process of commissioning, writing, rehearsing, and performing. This can only be achieved if the music director is confident of the composer's technical abilities and individual aesthetic. Sympathy with the composer's style or language is not always necessary. An open mind will reap the greatest rewards: "Fearless for unknown shores . . . Chanting our chant of pleasant exploration."[13]

For most composers at the outset of their careers the opportunity to hear their work performed by a professional orchestra is a great watershed in their lives. For a conductor or orchestra it may be simply a prelude to a more self-aggrandizing work on the same programme. Inevitably, a new work will take more rehearsal time than a traditional work of similar length.

Composers may not appreciate that professional players should not peak at rehearsal and that an element of trust is a necessary function of everyday business between conductors and orchestras.[14] Without that trust there is little likelihood of improvement in performance.

Musical integrity

All of the above provides a practical guide to the task of the conductor as artistic director. The most important attribute, however, is musical integrity. Many great conductors of the past were despotic music directors. In the twenty-first century such behaviour is socially as well as musically unacceptable. Nonetheless, inspiration, authority, and discipline are essential in the performance of symphonic music. The notion of *primus inter pares* remains. The music director is a visible leader on stage, in the rehearsal room, and in public. It can be a wearying responsibility. Covert leadership, that is to say decisive leadership that is organic, unostentatious, and unobtrusive in style, and founded upon musical integrity, is likely to prove the philosophical model in the new century.

16 Women on the podium

J. MICHELE EDWARDS

The orchestral conductor stands elevated on a podium commanding the most prestigious musical organization in Western culture. As Elias Canetti observed, "there is no more obvious expression of power than the performance of a conductor."[1] This display of power conflicts with traditional views of women and may explain why conducting remains "the last male bastion" in musical life.

Like the gendering of genius, the "maestro myth" is male.[2] Jorge Mester, a conducting teacher at Juilliard when JoAnn Falletta became the first woman to earn a doctorate in orchestral conducting there in 1989, identified "forceful personality and charisma" as key elements, in addition to skill, for a major career.[3] These traits are conventionally identified with men and put women conductors in a double bind. Andrea Quinn notes that women conductors "need to get results by persuasion. It's pointless trying to throw your weight around. Coming from a man, that can be seen as authoritative. From a woman, it's just considered bossy."[4] Despite a host of obstacles, however, women have long been conductors.

Early women conductors

The earliest description of a baton conductor (in 1594) is of a woman, though like many early-twentieth-century women conductors, "the Maestra" at the convent in San Vito in Ferrara leads an all-women ensemble.[5] Fanny Mendelssohn Hensel (1805–47) conducted a mixed ensemble of men and women, but only in a private setting. Hensel began conducting her own large choral-orchestral works at private salons (*Sonntagsmusik*) in the early 1830s while her brother Felix developed a public conducting career. In a letter of December 28, 1831, Felix commented on his sister's cautious conducting of her cantata *Lobgesang* (1831) and then chided her about details of the orchestration and text selection.[6] After attending a Mendelssohn *Sonntagsmusik* in the mid-1840s, Johanna Kinkel (1810–58), a composer, pianist, and conductor, wrote favorably about Fanny's conducting:

> Fanny Hensel's interpretive skills impressed me even more than the great voices I heard at her house. I was particularly impressed by her conducting. The spirit of a work was grasped in its most intimate texture, pouring forth

Figure 16.1 Josephine Weinlich conducts the professional Vienna Ladies' Orchestra at the old Steinway Hall, New York (1871)

to fill the souls of listeners and singers alike. A sforzando from her little finger would flash across our souls like an electric discharge, enrapturing us in quite a different way than a wooden baton tapping on a music stand.[7]

In 1847 Fanny Hensel died while conducting a rehearsal from the piano of her brother's cantata *Die erste Walpurgisnacht* for one of the Sunday *musicales*.[8]

Emma Roberto Steiner (?1852–1929) and Caroline B. Nichols (1864–1939) were the first women conductors in the US to establish and maintain full careers.[9] Nichols was conductor of the Boston Fadette Orchestra, which she founded in 1888; it primarily toured summer resorts and vaudeville theaters on the Keith circuit throughout the US and Canada. Unlike similar women's groups, the Fadettes and Nichols developed a national reputation and a broad repertoire of six hundred pieces, including symphony movements, opera overtures, popular songs, and dramatic music used for silent films. Nichols claimed the Fadettes, who grew from six to twenty performers during their first decade, gave over six thousand concerts between 1890 and 1920. During a similar period, Emma Steiner toured as a conductor of light opera companies in the US, performing over fifty different operas and operettas. Heinrich Conried, who managed one of the opera companies she conducted, is said to have wanted to hire her for the Metropolitan Opera when he became manager there in 1903, but did not dare because she was a woman.

"New women" and their orchestras

Although the late nineteenth century included other women conductors, conducting opportunities increased with the all-women orchestras of the 1920s and 1930s, which also brought a shift from lighter music to symphonic repertoire. All-women orchestras played an important role in the careers of Elisabeth Kuyper (1877–1953), Ethel Leginska (1886–1970), Antonia Brico (1902–89), and Frédérique Petrides (1903–83).

Elisabeth Kuyper, a Dutch conductor and composer, founded four women's symphonies, first in Europe and then in the United States. Each of her orchestras – in Berlin (1910), The Hague (1922), London (1922–3), and the American Women's Symphony Orchestra in New York (1924–5) – encountered financial problems and was short-lived. The Berliner Tonkünstlerinnen-Orchester, although billed as an all-women ensemble, actually engaged men for brass, basses, and even some woodwinds.

Ethel Leginska (née Liggins), a concert pianist with a well-established international career, began conducting studies to gain insights into orchestration for her compositional activity, but was soon drawn to orchestral conducting. She studied during 1923 with Eugene Goosens in London and Robert Heger in Munich. Using contacts from her concertizing, she arranged guest-conducting appearances in 1924 with major orchestras in Berlin, London, Munich, and Paris. She often included her own orchestral compositions and performed piano concertos while conducting from the keyboard. Her American debut with the New York Symphony at Carnegie Hall on January 9, 1925 was the first appearance of a women conductor with a major American symphony, and in the summer she appeared at the Hollywood Bowl. During the 1925–6 season, she moved to Boston where on at least five occasions she appeared as guest conductor with the People's Symphony, comprised of former Boston Symphony players. In 1926, Leginska completely abandoned her career as a pianist to pursue conducting. In announcing this shift, Leginska, who was notorious for problems with nerves as a pianist, offered a surprising commentary:

> No one knows how I have suffered for the past seventeen years every time I have been obliged to face an audience. I have no regrets. Concert playing may be spectacular, but the great art is in composing and conducting. I am never frightened when I conduct.[10]

Figure 16.2 Ethel Leginska dressed to conduct (unidentified newspaper clipping, New York Public Library, Leginska clipping file)

Leginska shared traits with others identified as "new women" during the 1910s and 1920s: bobbed hair, concert attire modeled on men's formal wear (see Fig. 16.2), outspokenness about feminist issues, and a serious focus on work and career. Reviews of her early concerts were quite favorable.

Unable to secure a position as permanent conductor, Leginska founded the Boston Philharmonic Orchestra of ninety men, which played to large, enthusiastic audiences and received good reviews, but survived financially for only one season (1926–7). By spring 1927, Leginska had accepted a position with the newly formed Boston Women's Symphony, which made tours of fifty to seventy-five concerts each fall in 1928–30. Beth Abelson Macleod noted that this orchestra was more uniformly praised and suggested that Leginska's increased success was in part due to frequent rehearsals, and the longevity of working with the same ensemble. She also hypothesized that "the women in the group accepted her as their conductor in a way that many men in other orchestras had not. It is also possible that reviewers felt more comfortable watching a woman conduct a group of women than a group of men."[11] Leginska also served as conductor of the Chicago Women's Symphony Orchestra (1927–9), and in 1932 formed the National Women's Symphony, which performed only one concert. During the late 1920s and early 1930s, she gave particular attention to opera and guest-conducted with London, Havana, and Dallas symphonies. As society became increasingly less tolerant of women in public positions and unconventional careers during the 1930s, Leginska's opportunities, especially with orchestras of men, faded. In 1940 she moved to Los Angeles to teach piano and did not conduct again during the last thirty years of her life.

Antonia Brico went to Bayreuth in the summer of 1927 to study with Karl Muck, and was then selected for the conducting program with him at the Berlin Hochschule für Musik, becoming the first woman and the first American admitted to this prestigious program. After graduating in 1929, she made her professional debut with the Berlin Philharmonic to positive reviews, followed by appearances with the Los Angeles Philharmonic and major European orchestras. With the rise of Nazism, she returned and founded the Women's Orchestra of New York (later called New York Women's Symphony) in 1934. Performing in Carnegie and Town Halls, this orchestra was a fiscal and critical success. Believing she had proven women were capable musicians, Brico transformed the Women's Symphony into the Brico Symphony Orchestra in 1939. One of the earliest mixed orchestras, the new ensemble also performed to critical acclaim; however, the board of directors withdrew financial support in opposition to the inclusion of men, and the orchestra disbanded after one season. Brico, who was the first woman to conduct the New York Philharmonic on July 25, 1938, now found even guest-conducting opportunities dwindling. She moved to Denver in the early 1940s thinking she would be appointed permanent conductor of the Denver Symphony but was rejected without audition because she was a woman. She took church jobs to support herself and developed a private studio of conducting, piano, and voice students. In 1947, she was hired to conduct the Denver Businessmen's Orchestra (later renamed the Brico Symphony) and continued with this amateur group of women and men until 1985. The film, *Antonia: A Portrait of the Woman*,[12] documented her professional disappointments and briefly revitalized her career after its premiere in 1973. Brico was engaged as a guest conductor at Lincoln Center and the Hollywood Bowl, and made her first international appearances in nearly two decades. In 1977 she conducted her final New York concert with the Brooklyn Philharmonic.

Unlike Leginska and Petrides, Brico repeatedly denied being a feminist although she was very aware of discrimination against women. Her conducting style was probably also more conservative than Leginska's, given the restraint of Brico's teacher, Karl Muck.[13] Olin Downes, reviewing for the *New York Times* in 1933, noted that Brico "proved her knowledge of her scores, her careful study of every detail and her good technical power over the orchestra."[14] Conductor Kate Tamarkin (b. 1955), who saw Brico conduct the Los Angeles Philharmonic in 1975, thought Brico "conducted harder than any man I have ever seen. She beat Beethoven dead."[15]

After conducting study at New York University with John Lawrence Erb, Frédérique Petrides failed to find professional conducting opportunities, which led her to found the Orchestrette Classique (later called the Orchestrette of New York), an all-women orchestra with a particularly long and distinguished history (1933–43). Petrides and this chamber orchestra of twenty to forty members became known for innovative programming of little-known repertoire by well-known composers, premieres and performances of American works, and occasional performances of compositions by women composers. Premieres and performances conducted by Petrides were important to such American composers as Paul Creston, Julia Smith, David Diamond, and Samuel Barber. Her concerts at Aeolian Hall and Carnegie Recital Hall were well attended, and reviewed in New York newspapers. By 1943, however, women were being hired in formerly all-male orchestras due to the war and most of the all-women ensembles disappeared.

Petrides then developed a series of popular free outdoor concerts. The inaugural concerts in 1956 were given at Washington Square Park with an orchestra of men from the New York Philharmonic,[16] followed by the Carl Schurz Park Concerts (1958–62) and the West Side Orchestral Concerts (1962–77). Petrides founded another orchestra, the Festival Symphony (1960–75), for this project and performed the final two summer seasons with members of the American Symphony.[17] Petrides's career was almost exclusively with orchestras she created and for which she did extensive administrative work; however, she was successful conducting women's, men's, and finally mixed orchestras. Her conducting was described as "clean-cut"[18] with a "brisk, businesslike beat,"[19] and she was praised as an "able conductor with a musicianly sense for the right tempo."[20]

Boulanger

Nadia Boulanger (1887–1979) had no connection with all-women orchestras. Despite having less training than Leginska, Brico, and Petrides, she became the most successful woman conductor to emerge during the 1930s. Within a few short years after conducting her first full program in 1933 at the salon of the Princesse de Polignac, she had become known as an important conductor, making dozens of appearances with Parisian orchestras and becoming the first woman to direct the Royal Philharmonic and the orchestras of Boston and Philadelphia, and one of the very few [women] to direct the New York Philharmonic and the National Symphony. Before the end of the decade she had conducted for radio in France, Belgium, England and the United States, and directed a highly influential recording of works by Monteverdi that is still in circulation.[21]

Jeanice Brooks attributes her remarkable success to "her undeniable musicianship and legendary charisma,"[22] along with the projection of an image that reconciled Boulanger's conducting career with conventional understandings of acceptable behavior for women. This image stemmed initially from an article by Simone Ratel published in 1928, in which Boulanger's sexuality and gender were erased by comparing her with a celibate male (a priest) and discussing her activities within a framework of service (an acceptable female behavior). Boulanger's conducting was also characterized as an extension of her teaching: a result of chance rather than of ambition. Accounts of her conducting consistently reference her age, simplicity of dress, her synthesis of male and female traits (androgyny), and her reserved stage demeanor. Her decision to conduct without the potentially phallic baton (originally used only as a symbol of authority, held in the left hand)[23] reinforced this image and helped her career.

Writers in almost every pre-war account of Boulanger's conducting "avoided the vocabulary of subjective power (choosing, controlling, directing, interpreting) in favor of a vocabulary that stressed self-effacement and restraint."[24] For some critics, of course, these were simply feminine weaknesses.

> I will say sincerely what impression I had of weakness and monotony, at the sight of a lady, thin and rigid, raising her arms symmetrically and sempiternally, in a gesture always the same, left and right together, in a very school-mistressy style . . . order, precision: but where were the breath, the enthusiasm, the fire, the power that transports and lifts up?[25]

The very traits criticized here, however, are the ones that allowed her success in the mainstream.

> By defining the role of the conductor as one which did not require traditionally male qualities of leadership, but rather traditionally female characteristics of self-sacrifice and modesty, Boulanger and her public were able to meet narrative expectations in some ways while stretching their boundaries in others. For the most part these are not conscious strategies, but rather gestures of diplomacy aimed at reconciling two apparently irreconcilable ideas: the female gender of Nadia Boulanger the conductor and the supposed inability of women to conduct.[26]

Boulanger's strategy preserved normative social structures and did little to open a door for subsequent generations of women conductors. On the contrary, Boulanger reinforced a gender ideology that continues to limit opportunities and success for women conductors today.

United States

The presence of women conductors with US orchestras began with Europeans; Frenchwoman Catherine Comet (b. 1944) became the first woman in the principal conducting position of a fully professional orchestra with her appointment in 1986 as music director of the Grand Rapids Symphony. Comet, who at age twelve announced her intention to be a conductor to Nadia Boulanger and then studied privately with her for several years, was also Principal Conductor of the American Symphony Orchestra (1990–2). Iona Brown (b. 1941), born in Britain and trained in Europe, was hired as Music Director of the Los Angeles Chamber Orchestra, in 1987. Brown, who often led the orchestra with her bow from the principal violin seat, had already served as director of Britain's highly acclaimed Academy of St. Martin-in-the-Fields (1974–80) as well as Artistic Director of the Norwegian Chamber Orchestra in Oslo and Principal Guest Director of the City of Birmingham Symphony Orchestra. Not until 1989 was an American woman engaged to lead a regional orchestra: JoAnn Falletta (b. 1954) became music director for the Long Beach Symphony and two years later also music director with the Virginia Symphony.

The situation is clearly improving for women, but participation of women conductors and orchestral musicians is in inverse proportion to orchestra budgets: the bigger the budget, the fewer women are engaged. By 1988, only two women had even been associate conductors with major symphonies; "major" is a category reserved by the American Federation of Musicians for the approximately fifty orchestras with the largest budgets. Comet was again the first, serving with the Baltimore Symphony from 1984 to 1986. In 1985, Falletta became the second, when she was appointed Associate Conductor of the Milwaukee Symphony. Women finally broke into the second tier of the majors as music directors with the appointment in 1993 of Marin Alsop (b. 1956) to the Colorado Symphony.[27] In the fall of 1999, two more women embarked on appointments as music directors for second-tier ensembles: Falletta with the Buffalo (New York) Philharmonic Orchestra[28] and Anne Manson (b. 1961) with the Kansas City Symphony. No woman has yet held a conducting position with an American "Big Five" orchestra (Boston, Chicago, Cleveland, New York, and Philadelphia).

The chief increase in women conductors of professional US orchestras came during the decade between 1988 and 1998 when the number of

Table 16.1 *Top conducting positions with professional orchestras held by women. Compiled from information provided by ASOL*

Old categories	Majors		Regionals		Metropolitans		Totals
Current categories	I	II	III	IV	V	VI	
1988							
No. held by women	0		2		2		4
1990							
No. of orchestras	22	24	25	28			
No. held by women	0	0	2	2			
Percent held by women	0	0	8.0	7.1			
1998							
No. of orchestras	25	23	28	36	44	96	252
No. held by women	0	2	2	1	2	7	14
Percent held by women	4.2		4.7		6.4		5.6
2002							
No. of orchestras	25	31	27	40	53	111	287
No. held by women	0	3	0	3	3	8	17
Percent held by women	5.4		4.5		6.7		5.9

music director or principal conductor posts occupied by women increased from seven to twenty-eight. Among members of the American Symphony Orchestra League (ASOL),[29] the percentage of women remained virtually unchanged between 1998 and 2002. Table 16.1 provides data about the employment pattern for women conductors in the US.

The two most developed American careers belong to Falletta and Alsop, who were each told they could not become conductors. Falletta was told no woman had ever worked as a conductor, and a teacher at Juilliard's Preparatory Department told the young Alsop that "girls can't be conductors." Both, however, had families who supported their musical development. Falletta began musical training at age seven with guitar lessons because her family's New York City apartment was not large enough for a piano. Trips to concerts with her immigrant parents and sister sparked her interest in conducting. Alsop's parents are both string players with the New York City Ballet Orchestra. When her father learned of Marin's interest in conducting, he bought her a box of conducting batons. Both received conducting prizes early in their careers. In 1982 Falletta won the Toscanini and Bruno Walter awards and in 1985 the Stokowski Competition. In 1989 Alsop also won the Stokowski Competition and was the first woman awarded the coveted Koussevitzky Conducting Prize at Tanglewood, where she was a pupil of Bernstein, Ozawa, and Gustav Meier. Under Falletta, the Buffalo Philharmonic has returned to national prominence.[30] Alsop is founding conductor of Concordia, a New York chamber orchestra emphasizing jazz and "crossover" repertoire, and has held music director appointments with the Long Island Philharmonic

Figure 16.3 Marin Alsop in action with the Colorado Symphony

(1990–6) and Eugene (Oregon) Symphony (1990–6), as well as the director-ship of the Cabrillo Festival and an appointment as the Creative Conductor Chair with the St. Louis Symphony. In 1999 she accepted appointments as Principal Guest Conductor of the Royal Scottish National Orchestra and the City of London Sinfonia, and in 2002 she was engaged as Principal Conduc-tor of the Bournemouth Symphony Orchestra. Alsop's extensive experience as a violinist has helped create successful interactions with players, and her on-stage concert commentaries are well received by audiences. Both con-ductors have sizable discographies, broad repertoires that include American composers, and outstanding reviews from major journalists.[31]

Two additional conductors currently based in the United States are Gisèle Ben-Dor (b. 1955) and Keri-Lynn Wilson (b. 1967). Ben-Dor was born in Uruguay of Polish parents; she later immigrated to Israel (1973) and studied at the Tel Aviv Academy of Music and at Yale. She served as assistant conduc-tor of the Louisville Orchestra (1987–8) and the resident conductor of the Houston Symphony (1988–91) before becoming music director of the An-napolis Symphony (1991–7), Boston Pro Arte Chamber Orchestra (1991–2000), and the Santa Barbara Symphony from 1994. Ben-Dor's professional conducting debut with the Israel Philharmonic in Stravinsky's *Le sacre du printemps*, when she was nine months pregnant, led to a reinvitation. Twice she has stepped in at the last moment with the New York Philharmonic (in 1993 and 1999), conducting without rehearsal or scores; each time she has received complimentary reviews.[32] Winnipeg native Keri-Lynn Wilson earned bachelors and masters degrees in flute at Juilliard and then completed a masters degree in conducting at Juilliard with Otto-Werner Mueller. She was a conducting fellow at Tanglewood, worked as Claudio Abbado's assistant with the Vienna Philharmonic at the Salzburg Festival in 1992, and was the Associate Conductor of the Dallas Symphony (1994–8). Since then she has made guest-conducting appearances with the Berlin Philharmonic, Los Angeles Philharmonic, and Vienna State Opera.[33]

England

Before Alsop's appointment in Bournemouth, Iona Brown, Sian Edwards (b. 1959), Jane Glover (b. 1949), and Odaline de la Martinez (b. 1949) had already broken the barriers with many of England's leading musical institutions. After winning the first Leeds Conductors' Competition in 1984, Sian Edwards made her London debut with the Royal Philharmonic Orchestra a year later, then assisted at the Glyndebourne Festival, and made her American debut with the St. Paul Chamber Orchestra in 1988. After declining twice, she accepted an appointment as music director of the English National Opera in 1993, but left rather abruptly after two successful seasons – this was widely attributed in the press to the fact she is a woman. She has been particularly noted for her conducting of Russian music, a specialty gained during her conducting study in Leningrad with Ilya Musin.

Jane Glover, whose debut came a decade earlier, appears regularly at the Glyndebourne Festival, English National Opera, the Proms, and Britain's leading orchestras. Glover served as Artistic Director of the London Mozart Players (1984–91); she has an even longer association conducting the London Choral Society and continues her work with the Huddersfield Choral Society as Principal Guest Conductor. She made her debut in the United States in 1994, leading the Orchestra of St. Luke's with soprano Jessye Norman at Lincoln Center, and returns regularly to Glimmerglass and the New York City Opera. She wrote a doctoral thesis on Cavalli and early Venetian opera at Oxford, but she conducts Baroque to contemporary repertoire. Mozart remains a strength with "rigorous attack, beautifully nuanced and artfully shaped phrasing and attention to the inner workings of the score."[34]

Cuban-born Odaline de la Martinez became the first woman to conduct a BBC Prom Concert in 1984. She has since worked with major orchestras in Britain and abroad and is conductor of the European Women's Orchestra and her own Lontano chamber ensemble. Based in London, she has conducted in Columbia, New Zealand, and Canada, and served as director of the Cardiff Music Festival in 1994.

In a younger generation of British conductors are Wasfi Kani (b. 1956), Julia Jones (b. 1961), and Andrea Quinn (b. 1964). After a decade of designing computer systems, Kani took up professional conducting in 1986 and later founded Pimlico Opera, a small company which performs in unusual locations, including prisons. Jones has largely advanced through various posts in Germany from répétiteur to Principal Conductor of the Staatstheater Darmstadt (1995–7). After her highly praised 1996 interpretation of Verdi's *Un ballo in maschera* was compared favorably with that of Arturo Toscanini, she was engaged as Chefdirigentin with Oper Basel in the 1998–9 season.[35] Quinn, who became music director of New York City Ballet in 2001, worked previously at the Royal Ballet (1998–2001) and the Birmingham Royal Ballet. Her rather short tenure with the Royal Ballet at Covent Garden stemmed from criticism by orchestral players that she was not fully prepared. She apologized and then led well-regarded performances. According to Norman Lebrecht, "that would have been the end of the matter had she been a man. There is no shortage of male conductors who turn up with a half-read score and get away with a self-deprecating grin and a round of drinks. But with a female conductor, orchestras are less tolerant."[36] Quinn tendered her resignation in February 2000 and has stayed silent about the matter.

Europe

JoAnn Falletta has been the first woman on several European podiums, including that of Belgium's Royal Philharmonic Orchestra in 1992, but confirms the prevailing notion that European orchestras are eager to have women as guest conductors, although they are still reluctant to consider them for music director positions.[37] In 1997, Germany reported only six women conductors for its 163 symphonies.[38] Sian Edwards sees the shift towards a more co-operative relationship between conductor and orchestras as an opportunity for women conductors; however, these new women conductors "are misunderstood and mocked or ridiculed either as a goddess or a hysterical teenager."[39]

Swiss conductor Sylvia Caduff (b. 1937) became the first woman to hold a principal conductor position in Germany with her appointment in the late 1970s as Chefdirigentin with the orchestra in Solingen.[40] Not until two decades later did a native German woman hold a similar post; Romely Pfund (b. 1955) became Chefdirigentin for the Neubrandenburger Philharmonic in 1987. A resident of Dresden, Pfund's achievements may be partially due to the woman-friendly educational system of the former GDR. After guest appearances in the US, Russia, Europe, and Japan, Pfund became music director of the Bergische Symphoniker in 1998, which serves the cities of Remscheid and Solingen. Another Swiss conductor, Marie-Jeanne Dufour (b. 1955) became the first woman General Music Director of a German state theatre with her appointment in Meiningen after working with the Zürich and Hamburg opera houses as well as in Wiesbaden.

Frenchwoman Claire Gibault (b. 1945), particularly noted for her performances of French music as well as opera, was conductor of the Lyon Opera Orchestra and director of the opera workshop at the Opéra de Lyon (1990–8). At seventeen years of age, she was the first woman to win first prize for orchestral conducting at the Paris Conservatory, and by the late 1980s had conducted most of the major French orchestras. Her appearance with L'Orchestra del Teatro dell'Opera di Roma in 1986 made her the first woman conductor to appear in Italy in a professional orchestral concert. This was in a series of concerts called *Podio Donna* (literally "Woman and the Conductor's Podium") sponsored by the Commission for Equality. Gibault, who was also the first woman to conduct members of the Berlin Philharmonic (1997), makes regular guest appearances at La Scala, Covent Garden, Glyndebourne Festival, Edinburgh Festival, and both the Opéra-Comique and Opéra-Bastille in Paris. While in Lyon, Gibault has commissioned several contemporary works, including two operas, which have both toured extensively under her direction. In 2000 she returned to Italy as music director of Musica per Roma, leading opera performances there as well as making subsequent appearances at the Teatro Comunale in Bologna and at Rome's Teatro Nazionale during the following two years.

In 1997, Anu Tali (b. 1972) co-founded the multinational Estonia–Finnish Symphony Orchestra with her twin sister, Kadri, who handles the business aspects of the orchestra. Her debut recording with the orchestra paired Estonian composer Veljo Tormis with Sibelius and Debussy to very positive reviews.[41] She trained with Ilya Musin in St. Petersburg and has conducted the Estonian National Symphony, Moscow Symphony Orchestra, and Finland's Vaasa City Orchestra. Russian Veronika Dudarova (b. 1916) was Chief Conductor of the Moscow State Symphony Orchestra from 1960 to 1989 and founded the State Symphony Orchestra of Russia, where she continues as its Chief Conductor. Agnieszka Duczmal from Poland was the first woman to conduct at La Scala and conducts the Amadeus Chamber Orchestra in Warsaw.

Australia, Asia

Australian Simone Young (b. 1961) made her debut with Australian Opera in 1985 and later became the first woman to lead at the Vienna Volksoper, the Vienna Staatsoper, the Bayerische Staatsoper in Munich, and the Paris Opéra-Bastille. Young has conducted at Covent Garden and the Metropolitan Opera. Anthony Tommasini noted that "even the crusty, all-male Vienna Philharmonic has taken to her balletic conducting style and alert musical intelligence."[42] Seeking to elevate their prestige and improve their performance standards, Opera Australia engaged Young as music director for three years beginning in 2001. In a surprise move that was unpopular with the public, they announced in late 2002 that her contract would not be renewed because they could not afford her artistic vision.[43] Nicolette Fraillon (b. 1960), who was the first woman to conduct the Australian Ballet has now been appointed music director and chief conductor of the ballet company for 2003.

As in the US, Asian pioneers have often worked with all-women ensembles. Since winning first prize in the Concours International de Jeunes Chefs d'Orchestre in Besançon, France in 1982, Matsuo Yōko[44] (b. 1953) has developed a substantial conducting career, primarily in her native Japan. She has conducted the well-respected Ladies Orchestra Japan and Nagoya's Central Aichi Symphony Orchestra (since 1998) as well as making guest appearances with most of Japan's major symphonies.[45] China's first woman conductor, Zheng Xiaoying (b. 1932), was educated in China and at the Moscow Conservatory of Music. In 1989 she founded the Ai Yue Nu Philharmonic Society, an all-women orchestra playing both Western and Chinese music. Later she was Chief Conductor of China's Central Opera Theatre, and in 1998 Zheng was invited to form the Xiamen Philharmonic Orchestra.[46]

Barriers

The obstacles for women conductors are often concrete – symphony management, boards, donors, artist agents, critics, and teachers – but the reasons are often cultural or ideological. Orchestra boards, for example, often question a woman's ability to maintain discipline. Tim Page, of the *Washington Post*, admits that "It's silly to say that a woman cannot conduct an orchestra, but orchestras are [or] can be notoriously temperamental places; and if you have a few sort of entrenched sexists, who aren't going to play for a woman, that's going to be a problem."[47] By 2001 the three largest agencies in North America represented seventy-seven conductors, but still only four women.[48] The reason given, that it is hard to market women conductors, is another self-perpetuating myth.

The language of music reviews also tends to reinforce the common myths. Praise of women conductors often uses patronizing vocabulary. Rave reviews and articles about men frequently use terms such as "virile" and "muscular" – words that tend to exclude women – while women are described as "enthusiastic"– not a comparable term. Even the frequent use of "rare" or "unususal," even in women's own publications, reinforces the notion that women conductors are outside the mainstream.

A mentor is an essential ingredient for a conductor's success and while some women (Comet, Young, Alsop, and Manson, for example) have had male mentors (Slatkin, Barenboim, Bernstein, and Abbado respectively), the lack of active women role models has been a liability. The enrollment of women in a dozen of the top conservatories and conducting programs in universities shows about the same number of women today as ten or twenty years ago, and none of these institutions has a woman teaching orchestral conducting.[49]

Few women conductors want to discuss gender in the press, but women have of necessity had to adjust to what remains a male environment. When Nadia Boulanger faced a Boston Symphony Orchestra which was "disruptive, inconsiderate, [and] inattentive,"[50] her strategy for reestablishing order was to appeal to the men for the sake of the music, rather than complaining about their behavior. Falletta credits Jorge Mester at Juilliard with helping her learn to avoid apologizing for making appropriate demands on musicians. "The more I got into conducting the more I had to come to terms with how I was raised as a young Catholic girl. We were taught to be supportive, nurturing, gentle, kind."[51] As long as orchestras and management remain dominated by men, cultural conditioning about leadership will pose liabilities for women on the podium. Just before her Carnegie Hall debut with the New York Philharmonic in 1939, Boulanger told a journalist, "A priori, a man has more authority over a body of men . . . If men were perfectly frank I believe they should say they prefer to be led by men."[52] Symphony decision-makers need to move beyond their conventional comfort zone to create space for talented women.

Women have achieved greater success in choral music and opera. American conductors noted for their choral work include Gena Branscombe (1881–1977), Eva Jessye (1885–1992), Margaret Hillis (1921–98), Elaine Browne (1910–97), and Amy Kaiser (b. 1945). Canadian women Morna Edmundson and Diane Loomer are codirectors of Elektra Women's Choir. In opera, the conductor works in the pit rather than in the spotlight and this may have been more acceptable to audiences, orchestras, and even conductors. Jane Glover admits, "Maybe that's why I like it because I'm out of sight."[53] Further, the route to opera conductor often begins with rehearsal pianist and coach, a position frequently held by women at least in the US, and one more consistent with conventional roles for women: nurturing backstage. Many women have worked predominantly in opera: Sarah Caldwell (b. 1924), founder of the Opera Company of Boston in 1957 and first woman to conduct an opera performance at the Metropolitan Opera in 1976; Judith Somogi (1937–88), whose career was centered in Europe with the Frankfurt Opera (1981–7) after early success at the New York City Opera; and Eve Queler (b. 1936), who has received international acclaim for her concert versions of rarely performed operas presented by her own Opera Orchestra of New York.

Future

Is it really just a matter of time until women conductors are more visible and are hired as music directors for top orchestras? Even with the large number of music director vacancies in major American orchestras during 2000–2, Gwendolyn Freed reported that "knowledgeable sources say that no woman made the secret shortlists of candidates" for Philadelphia, New York, Cleveland, and St. Paul, nor subsequently at the Boston Symphony or Minnesota Orchestra.[54] In 1936, Petrides wrote "that the day is not far distant when the sight of women conductors will no longer evoke feelings of curiosity and surprise."[55] While the novelty of all-women ensembles did soon evaporate, so did the women conductors. Women orchestral players gained opportunities in mixed orchestras during World War II, and orchestras in the United States finally began to hire American music directors during the 1940s and 1950s, but only men. The situation has improved slightly since the 1930s, but conducting remains more resistant to women than almost any other field.[56]

Tim Page suggests that:

> What needs to happen for women conductors in general is one person must come along who has the amazing charisma and star quality and, of course talent – but talent is assumed – to break down the barriers once and for all. With all due respect to some wonderful musicians out there, I don't think that yet we have had that sort of a figure come along who just galvanizes everything she touches. I'm sure it will happen, and I'm looking forward to that day.[57]

To move toward that day more quickly, we need to increase public awareness of women conductors, and promote broad social and cultural changes to help dismantle the bogus rationalizations for not hiring women conductors. Women also need to support other women; for Opera Australia's 2002 season Simone Young hired women for three out of five guest spots. In

1999 Young engaged Karen Kamensek (b. 1970), an American, to assist her at the Bergen Philharmonic, and this helped pave the way for Kamensek's debut with the Vienna Volksoper, where she has now conducted more than sixty performances, and her appointment as General Music Director of the Städtischen Bühnen Freiburg beginning in 2003. Although Young resists identifying herself as a role model, she is helping talented women conductors build careers with her direct actions, as well as through her own pioneering career on many podiums.

17 Conducting early music

BERNARD D. SHERMAN

In Leipzig, Bach's predecessor Johann Kuhnau beat time with a rolled-up sheet of music paper, a common practice in church music (see Fig. 8.1). In Esterháza, Haydn led his symphonies from the first violin, a typical practice in the symphonic music of his time and region. But in London, when Haydn directed his last symphonies, he sat at the keyboard and shared leadership with the first violinist.[1] Shared leadership was common in opera: overall responsibility belonged to the *maestro di capella* at the keyboard while the instrumentalists were led by the first violinist. When Mozart directed his operas from the keyboard, he concentrated on the singers but also oversaw the entire performance.

These were the most common leadership practices of the eighteenth century. But today's historically informed performers almost never revive the rolled-up sheet of paper, and they lead from instruments only when the ensembles are relatively small – not, generally, in operas or large symphonies. Modern French Baroque specialists perform the ballet music of Jean-Baptiste Lully with careful consideration of the tension in the bow hairs, but rarely replicate his practice of beating time audibly with a stick. And in large late-eighteenth-century choral works, modern historical performers rarely revive "dual" direction, split between a time-beater for the chorus and an instrumentalist for the rest.[2] Instead, performers typically use today's highly refined conducting technique.

Of course, musical anachronism doesn't stop at the podium. Period-instrument orchestra players, for example, typically mark parts during rehearsal, adding dynamics, tempo changes, ornaments, fingerings, and bowings, even though part-marking by players became a standard practice only in the twentieth century.[3] Its prevalence today may reflect any number of developments, from modern concepts of the nature of musical works to the easy availability of pencils.[4] Still, what keeps it going in period-instrument circles is its usefulness to orchestras striving to meet modern standards of ensemble and interpretative detail. Indeed, for musicians, considerations of historical performance lead inevitably to practical questions. In our era of recordings and perfectionism, playing a period instrument is not considered an excuse for cracked or out-of-tune notes. To avoid such pitfalls, compromise with historical instrumental technique is common.[5] The same compromise applies in conducting.

Other questions about period-instrument conducting are not practical so much as philosophical: many assumptions about "historically informed performance" have come under attack in recent decades.[6] Nobody denies that there are limits to the historical verisimilitude possible – or desirable – for modern performers. And no area demonstrates these limits like conducting practice. Still, since the early 1990s, many practices that began in the "early music" movement (from increased tempos to reduced string sections) have become accepted by major symphony orchestras. Even if we acknowledge the inevitability of anachronism and compromise, we can still recognise how conductors can enrich their art by thinking about history.

Control

While modern mainstream conducting practice is highly standardized, the practices of the eighteenth century varied considerably, with several types of conducting often coexisting in one place. For example, seventeenth-century German music's most conservative conducting practice was the "even beating of metre" with the traditional "strict down–up beat" inherited from Renaissance choral practice.[7] It coexisted, however, with conducting practices that allowed more detailed central control, as when Wolfgang Caspar Printz wrote in 1678 that singers should watch the director when he "directs the measure faster or slower," on account of improvised ornamentation, "such as is made by an artistic musician, which lengthens the time of a beat."[8]

Different types of music were associated with these different conducting methods, and the properties of the music may have been part of the reason. The traditional down–up beat was associated with the conservative motet repertory with its steady *tactus*, while the direction Printz alludes to was associated with the modern, rhetorical "concerted" style, whose tempo inflections seem to demand more coordination.

Chapter 8 demonstrates that there was no consistent trend toward increased central control before the nineteenth century. Some (if not all) of J. S. Bach's music seems to demand a good deal of centralized leadership and he seems to have sought it. But a few decades after Bach, the keyboard direction preferred by Johann Samuel Petri involved less central authority. Petri wrote in 1767 that "formerly one took more trouble to see [the director] than nowadays, when one wishes that he were no longer necessary, or that he might beat only the first three bars or so of a piece."[9] John Butt suggests that "the 'absolute monarchy' of the director seems to have been eroded somewhat [in these decades], and the performers presumably took more of a role in dictating tempo and its fluctuation."[10] He speculates that the musical attributes of the *galant* style were a factor, since it was simpler in texture, essentially melodic, and more evenly paced than the styles that preceded it. More precise notation also appears to have reduced the need for directorial control.

Central control was, in any case, more important when dealing with larger ensembles and productions. The extravagant productions of the Paris Opéra required multiple conductors who sometimes beat time audibly. Later conductors at the Opéra used purely visual signaling; and by the turn of the century, the Opéra's director, Jean-Baptiste Rey, "exercised, with lasting success, many musical functions of what we now call a 'conductor'," although he did not necessarily beat time throughout a section.[11]

Neil Zaslaw points out that Mozart's letters consistently distinguish between the "time-beating" (*tactieren*) that he and others did when conducting large and often far-flung groups in church music, and the "directing" (*dirigieren*) done by leadership from instruments in the opera house and concert hall.[12] This distinction reflected, in part, the weight of tradition. But, along with the example of opera, it also conforms to a principle: when music or production required more control to be held together, such authority developed. Speaking generally, while specific practices varied, larger ensembles or productions were more likely to be controlled by a central leader.

Authority

Musical authority does not, of course, require modern conducting technique. J. S. Bach, for example, appears to have used a variety of leadership methods, none of them modern. He obtained excellent results by leading from the violin, according to his son C. P. E. (who preferred keyboard leadership).[13] On the other hand, a 1727 report describes Bach's leading a performance of his Cantata 198, the *Mourning Ode*, from the harpsichord.[14] And while Bach would not have led his sacred works from the organ in Leipzig, he might have done so in Weimar.[15] Furthermore, Bach might well have beat time in sacred music with the traditional (in Germany) rolled-up sheet of music paper.[16]

But regardless of the technique he used, Bach made a clear attempt to lead; he did more than just set a musical example from his instrument. Consider a 1738 description of Bach in Leipzig, which has him

> singing with one voice and playing his own parts, but watching over
> everything and bringing back to the rhythm and the beat, out of thirty or
> even forty musicians, the one with a nod, another by tapping with his foot,

the third with a warning finger, giving the right note to one from the top of
his voice, to another from the bottom, and to a third from the middle of it –
all alone, in the midst of the greatest din made by all the participants, and,
although he is executing the most difficult parts by himself, noticing at
once whenever and wherever a mistake occurs, holding everyone together,
taking precautions everywhere, and repairing any unsteadiness, full of
rhythm in every part of his body.[17]

This description shows Bach ensuring ensemble, communicating tempo,
and correcting intonation and other errors. (Bach's son wrote that his "hearing was so fine that he was able to detect the slightest error even in the largest
ensemble."[18]) He occasionally uses a nod or warning finger, as we might
still see from conductors today.

All of this may remind us of modern conducting. But should it? To Laurence Dreyfus, Bach's hyperactivity suggests the "pandemonium" that likely
resulted from his being stuck with amateur performers (some of whom were
inadequate) and limited rehearsal time for his "uncommonly demanding
music."[19] The physical set-up of his Leipzig church, where the continuo
organist faced away from the ensemble, did not help. Dreyfus concludes
"it would be surprising if Bach had *not* intervened with constant cues and
verbal directions." Other eighteenth-century condemnations of hyperactive
conducting may suggest that Bach was not alone in his conducting style,
and that such conducting technique often had limitations.[20]

On the other hand, the period-instrument conductor Andrew Parrott
argues that powerful musical personalities could always have communicated subtle performance intentions about their music to players, regardless
of the conducting technique they had available.[21] Bach worked regularly
with a small group of musicians who came to know his musical style and
preferences well, and he led ensembles regularly for many years. (Such experience is often the key to gaining skill as a conductor.) Thus he might have
developed effective conducting methods, however idiosyncratic or unlike
modern techniques they were, and however inadequate the musicians and
circumstances.

Others, however, say that the details of conducting technique always
make a musical difference. For example, Elliot Galkin asserts (on what
appears to be limited evidence) that using a violin bow to beat time – a
practice maintained by François-Antoine Habeneck in Paris in the 1830s
and Viennese waltz conductors in the twentieth century – made it difficult
to beat extremely fast tempos, because of the weight and unwieldiness of
the bow.[22] Leon Botstein argues that the conductor's baton has become
shorter today than it was even a century ago because of the need for greater
rhythmic accuracy in complex modern music.[23] Clive Brown argues that

the sharing of leadership by two instrumentalists in eighteenth-century orchestral music "militated against controlled manipulation of the beat for interpretive purposes," leading to relatively little use of unwritten rallentando or accelerando.[24] Of course, these inflections may have been possible with other techniques, such as leadership of a small group from one instrument. A report from the eighteenth century says, "If [Pisendel, leading with the violin] wanted to slow the orchestra down in the middle of the piece, he played only the first note of each measure, in order to give them more strength and expression, thus he held [the orchestra] back."[25]

It is impossible to know the degree to which Bach's conducting had technical limitations, or how he would have used modern conducting technique if it had been available. But Bach's cantata performances were clearly less polished than modern audiences would find acceptable. Still, since the cantatas were (to Bach) occasional works written to be a part of church services, the modern aesthetics of concert presentation might be irrelevant.[26]

Changing priorities

If so, the case illustrates a more general point: that while the increased precision of modern conducting arose partly in response to the metrical challenges of twentieth-century music,[27] it also reflected social, technological, and aesthetic changes.

We've seen already that larger production sizes tend to demand more conducting skill. What made production sizes grow in the nineteenth century was, in part, socio-economic developments. With the decline of aristocratic patronage, musicians needed to make a profit from paying customers at concerts. Profitability depended on volume in two senses of the word: having enough customers, which meant having ever-larger concert halls; and producing enough loudness so that ensembles didn't sound weak in these spaces. It is no accident that this trend coincided with the rise of modern conducting.

The rise of recordings had an enormous impact on aesthetics, which also affected conducting. Robert Philip demonstrated through early recordings that musicians of the late nineteenth century accepted wrong notes, imprecise ensemble, and sloppy rhythms far more readily than we do today. These musicians had grown up without ever hearing themselves or other musicians except during the moment of performance. As musicians increasingly realized that a recorded performance was to be preserved forever (and as they could listen repeatedly to their own performances), they focused on flawlessness as an overriding goal.[28] The development of advanced tape-editing techniques (and today, of digital editing) made it possible to attain even higher standards of surface perfection. Audiences and critics, now used to recordings, demanded flawless live performance.

As a result, the technical skills of an ordinary orchestral musician today outstrip those typical of the eighteenth or nineteenth century. And there can be little doubt that twentieth-century conducting technique became increasingly precise partly to make studio-quality perfection dependable in concert performance. Nor is there much doubt that, aesthetically and socially, even the most historically minded performers cannot go all the way back. We might recreate period conducting practices, but it would be nearly impossible for modern orchestras to allow themselves to play as loosely or informally as earlier musicians did, or for modern audiences to learn to accept them if they did.

Conducting as progress

Performers on old instruments typically deny that changes in pianos, violins, and brass and wind instruments since the eighteenth century should be considered progressive. Rather, they say, old instruments have properties that suit the needs of a specific period of music well. But the same arguments have not generally been advanced for conducting.

Why not? As noted above, some of the reasons are practical. Sigiswald Kuijken recorded Haydn's Esterháza symphonies from the violin, but recorded the London symphonies from the podium rather than with the "dual leadership" that Haydn used. The choice is far from uncommon, and it suggests a practical compromise between history and today's recording-based aesthetic. Limits in rehearsal time can lead to the same choice.[29] Philippe Herreweghe believes that modern conducting technique allows him to accomplish more in less rehearsal time, and Nikolaus Harnoncourt took up podium conducting – which he once described as an "anti-profession" – partly for the same reason.[30] (Although eighteenth-century performances had even less rehearsal time than modern ones, performance standards were not as high as ours. Modern technique lets us attain our standards quickly.) Finally, some practical reasons for using modern conducting practices are more crass. Well-known conductors are sometimes booked to record pre-conducting-era music because their names increase sales, not because the musicians need their guidance.

But other arguments for using modern practice are conceptual. Charles Rosen argues that period conducting practices were sometimes inadequate to what composers of then-new music sought, and that later practices eventually arose in order to meet the needs of this music. The orchestras of

Vienna and London, for example, failed to get through the premieres of Beethoven's "Eroica" and the Ninth Symphony without disaster; having a Carlos Kleiber on the podium might have helped.[31] And Anton Schindler reported that the composer sought a degree of tempo modification that went beyond his written orchestral scores – and beyond what was actually attainable in performance.[32] While Schindler's testimony on some points is famously mendacious, here he is at least plausible.[33] Significantly for our discussion, while Schindler claims that Beethoven wanted specific tempo inflections in Symphonies Nos. 2 and 3, he does not claim to have heard Beethoven conduct them. Schindler says that Beethoven would have needed far more rehearsal than was available to achieve his desired flexibility,[34] and that most orchestral performances of the time were less nuanced because of inadequate conducting and lack of rehearsal.

In any event, in the decades after its premiere Beethoven's Ninth received increasingly adequate performances. Nicholas Cook speculates that they contributed to the rising critical esteem of the symphony.[35] Performance standards improved not merely through increasing familiarity or longer rehearsals (Habeneck took a full year to prepare the Ninth for its premiere in Paris in 1831), but also through advances in conducting practice – some of which developed in response to the demands of Beethoven's music.

The principle may extend to other masterpieces as well. Sir Charles Mackerras has argued that the failure of contemporaries to appreciate Mozart's operas – many thought the wind parts were too complex and dominating – may in part reflect the shortcomings of contemporary rehearsal and conducting practice. Modern practices may convey the qualities of the music better, he implies.[36]

Conducting as tyranny

Many period-instrument performers, however, argue in favor of at least some period conducting practices. Leadership from an instrument is the only period practice that has become fairly common in the period-instruments movement (at least with smaller ensembles), and it has proponents. They claim that it fosters a degree of subtle interaction among ensemble members that modern conducting tends to squelch. The pianist Robert Levin, who has performed Mozart concertos with and without a conductor, says:

> As soon as you have a conductor you surrender the responsibility for performance into the hands of that conductor. When you play without a conductor and you have a concertmaster and a fortepiano (or Steinway)

player, they all listen because they have to make their ensemble by themselves. The result is a performance that is likely to be much tighter, much more active, and much more engaged than one with a conductor, because there's collective responsibility. The pianist behaves like the timpanist, keeping the orchestra rhythmically together in certain key sections, and the violinist leads in the melodic sphere – though sometimes there can be an overlap of these functions.[37]

André-Ernest-Modeste Grétry makes a similar argument in his 1789 memoirs: "The players become cold and indifferent when they do not follow the soloist directly; the stick that directs them humiliates them, takes away their natural wish to excel."[38]

Modern musicians who are in the habit of playing under a conductor may come to depend on podium leadership, where earlier musicians might have been more skilled at detecting subtle hints from soloists and other ensemble players. Playing without a conductor might, in this case, force modern players to reclaim some "responsibility" for performance and thus play in a more engaged way. (This of course does not necessarily lead to playing more historically.)

Some early-music groups take the ideal of individual responsibility further and work without any leader. John Butt describes musicians who see historically informed performance "as specifically the venue for democratised music-making, liberated from the hierarchical factory conditions of modern orchestral culture."[39] Some early-music maestros also speak of this sort of ideal. Herreweghe says, "In Bach, if something is not possible without a conductor, it's a sign that it's not a good interpretation." He adds:

> I think a lot of conductors of Romantic music face a danger in Bach and other Baroque music, because it's essential that this music come from the musicians themselves. It's essential in the architecture of the music that each musician has to be creative, and make music himself. If you conduct "too well" in a certain way, you kill that.[40]

But the historical claims are dubious. Even if period performances did not use a conductor in the modern sense, Butt notes, they typically

> had a director (often the composer) who clearly had a status and will that dominated the other performers. Moreover, while performers were extremely versatile, they were often far more rigidly ranked than even a modern orchestra would require. Such ranking usually mirrored a broader social ranking and much of the music was written to confirm or exploit the hierarchical nature of society in general.[41]

Thus, moving away from podium autocracy towards democratized ensembles may not revive the ethos of eighteenth-century ensemble performances, but instead might lead in the opposite direction. Trying to do away with hierarchy may be a projection of our priorities and our prelapsarian fantasies on to the past, rather than a revival of period ethos. After all, period orchestras aren't the only modern performers to try leading from an instrument or working democratically. A recent example is the Orpheus Chamber Orchestra, a group in which "the principal players (who revolve from work to work) settle on the details of an interpretation and convey them to their sections."[42]

We might add that leadership by instrumentalists can meet modern aesthetic priorities more easily with relatively small ensembles than with large groups. This may be why period performers have not adopted wholesale the practice of dual direction in choral works, symphonies, and operas even when it is known to have been used historically. A few have experimented: Nikolaus Harnoncourt pioneered the revival of "dual direction" in his recordings of Bach choral works from the 1960s and 1970s, and Christopher Hogwood made an early attempt at it in the Mozart symphonies. (There is no evidence that Bach directed from the cello or that he used a separate conductor for the choir, as Harnoncourt did.) But both Hogwood and Harnoncourt now routinely lead Bach and Mozart from the podium using modern techniques, and that is the general practice among their colleagues.[43]

Nor are the musical advantages of egalitarianism even with smaller groups beyond question. Butt, an experienced continuo player, thinks claims of this sort are naive. Some self-governing ensembles are indeed more engaged than those led by conductors, he says, but many others are less so. At least some musicians pursue orchestral over chamber and solo careers because they lack creativity or originality. Further, says Butt, with most ensembles "we're usually talking about an extremely complex dynamic in which *some* sort of focus [provided by a conductor] is better than none at all."[44]

In any event, doing without a conductor inescapably involves modern compromise. Without the rise in orchestral virtuosity that has taken place in the twentieth century, leaderless performances would not be able to meet the standards of modern recording-centered audiences.

We can, then, question the historical element of some motives and justifications for modern attempts at instrumental leadership. But we might still recognize that when Levin leads Mozart concertos from the keyboard, he is coming closer to Mozart's actual practice than when a modern conductor leads the orchestra – and that Levin and his colleagues have produced exciting results (even if some other performers trying it have not). Such results are the final justification most musicians would give for investigating performance practices.

Interpretation and history

Unsuccessful attempts at self-governing ensembles suggest a principle: an individual or noticeable interpretation typically requires a dominating personality, whether at the podium or on an instrument.[45] When might we want such an interpretation (as opposed to such ideals as letting the music speak for itself)? Some critics have indicated that they would like it in any performance.[46] Others argue that early performances of many works had little interpretive individuality. Ensembles often played a new work with one or even no rehearsal (a common situation historically). They would not have achieved "profound insight born out of years of reflection," even if their playing was stylistically apt.[47] In practice, early-music performers have run the gamut, from the deliberately under-interpreted[48] Mozart and Beethoven symphonies of Hogwood to the highly nuanced Bach Passions of Gardiner or Harnoncourt – both of whose Bach conducting is far more shaped and inflected than has been the norm in mainstream performance.[49] Both approaches have been given historical justifications.[50]

Even those who doubt that period premieres had much individuality have sometimes noted that concert life before the mid-nineteenth century focused primarily on new works, while the modern concert world centres on a small, often-repeated repertory of historic masterworks. The revisiting of a limited number of works may by itself cause audiences and musicians to demand more individualized interpretation than was needed in the work's own era.[51] This may be a justification for even the historically obsessed performer to seek highly individual interpretive nuance. (Might such individuality be less critical for light Baroque or classical works used by modern listeners for background music, or for revivals of music that modern audiences have not heard before?)

Why conductors might benefit from performance-practice studies

Dispensing with a modern conductor may lead to more engagement among musicians, or to under-interpreted runthroughs. The conducting technique of a period may reveal something valuable, or it might simply remind us of the challenges that eventually led musicians to develop more suitable methods. Differing conducting methods may have always affected musical outcomes, or powerful musicians might have found ways to communicate what they wanted, thus making the means employed not so crucial an issue. Yet even if such questions remain open, few historicists would argue for the abolition of modern conducting technique in period works, and few mainstream performers would deny that conductors can benefit from thinking about historical performance practice.

For example, the timpani and brass Beethoven knew had different properties from modern ones; it has been argued that Beethoven wrote so specifically for these properties that his orchestration loses some of its point when modern timpani or brass play in modern styles.[52] Conductors with the luxury of using some of these period instruments might consider it. Others might want to become familiar with the properties of these instruments before performing with modern ones.

Conductors can also profit from thinking about period idioms. In chapter 2, Charles Barber suggests learning period dances before conducting music that refers to them. Many other unwritten idioms played an important part in the performance of earlier repertory, such as alterations of rhythms from the written note. These were understood in an intuitive way that modern musicians cannot easily recreate. Musicians of, say, the French Baroque grew up "speaking" its idioms (Eric Van Tassel compares them to jazz musicians who knew swing-rhythm idiom without having it notated in front of them[53]), and, most importantly, didn't need to know any others. By contrast, modern musicians are stylistically polylingual and not one of the early styles is their mother tongue. They may therefore need leadership (and carefully notated parts) to come to a unified style in playing French Baroque or other period styles, as the original players did not – another justification for the anachronistic use of modern conducting practices. Sir Charles Mackerras adds one more: "There is such a wide divergence of opinion among the experts, that a conductor is required to tell the performers what type of interpretation is being adopted."[54]

Also important in some period music was the addition of ornamentation and embellishment, something that informed conductors can foster, as Sir Charles has shown since the 1950s. Further, the implications of notation (such as slur marks) varied over time and went through constant change. Brahms and Joachim argued over how to notate *portato*, with Brahms favouring what to Joachim was a dated indication that had come to mean something else.[55] To master the details in these and other areas can take a good deal of research, but it can be worth it, especially if you want to understand why the composer notated the music as he or she did.

Conducting as an information technology

We might think of modern conducting technique as an information technology. Technology can arise to facilitate what was already being done less effectively (for example, travelling by train or horse instead of by foot), but in the process it comes to allow new possibilities. While people communicated through words before writing, printing, telegraphing, and email, these new technologies did not merely allow conversation to be carried out over ranges of time and distance never imagined before; they also changed the way people used words. Orally transmitted epics, for example, use often-repeated formulae for verse-line endings because they are easy to memorize and extemporize with; the advent of the written word rendered these unnecessary. If modern virtuoso conducting is an information technology it similarly might transform *what* is communicated as well as how the communication is done. It makes us prone, for example, to more centrally controlled interpretative individuality and to cleaner execution than was historically imagined.

But this coin has another side: that studying historical performance can give insight into the specifics of a piece – why it was written and notated as it was – and perhaps reveal more as well. According to Lydia Goehr, it can challenge our attitude towards the nature of musical works, and, according to Butt, it can lead to a rethinking of the boundaries between work and performance; it even "grounds us in the present through renewed engagement in the past" in ways never possible before.[56] Even if such conclusions go beyond what most musicians aim for, they are still part of the reason that historical performance is likely to be an important part of future conductors' education, whether or not they have any interest in using period instruments and methods.

18 Training Conductors

HAROLD FARBERMAN

Much present-day conductor training is moribund, weighted down by highly questionable tradition and surrounded by self-serving myths and misconceptions. The training of conductors remains virtually unchanged from the early days of the composer-conductor timekeepers who stood before their bands of players with a complete knowledge of the creative fabric of their own compositions, but without a stitch of conducting technique. Conductor training still concentrates on learning and understanding the music, at the expense of the technical expertise needed to convey this knowledge to the orchestra. No other component of the symphonic world has remained so resistant to change, so we continue to graduate nineteenth-century conductors in the twenty-first century. The entire subject of conductor training needs fresh ideas, open minds, and a willingness to create a rapport with a new technical proficiency based on the demands of the music.

Four factors have kept contemporary conductor training from embracing new techniques. (1) The separation of pulse and music, which first emerged in the divided leadership of the eighteenth century, has fostered the notion that the two are indeed separable. (2) Traditional beat patterns have been accepted as the sum of conducting technique. (3) The myth of the "born conductor" continues to subvert the new models of training; why bother with classes if charisma is the central ingredient? (4) The increasing virtuosity of the orchestra has made the job of the modern conductor easier; modern professionals are capable of playing much standard repertoire without any leadership at all.

Pulse and music

Until the early nineteenth century (and later in England) the responsibility for keeping a body of musicians together was often divided between the conductor or Kapellmeister at the keyboard and the leader or *Konzertmeister* playing the violin. The exact delegation of duties varied widely in different countries and venues, but in general the keyboard "conductor" (often the composer) was the chief architect of the performance, while the subordinate concertmaster was charged with all of the details of execution including keeping time. This separation of pulse from music became accepted procedure.

Both parties experimented with signals, some audible, but mostly unmusical.[1] Audible time-keeping lasted well into the nineteenth century. Berlioz witnessed a performance at the San Carlo Opera in 1831: "The noise made by the conductor tapping his desk bothered me greatly. I was gravely assured, however, that without this support the musicians could not possibly keep in time."[2] Silent signals were also used and the modern beat pattern (down, left, right, up) was first described by Thomas Janowka in 1701.[3] Spohr and Berlioz used similar patterns and codified them into the diagrams used to teach conducting to this day.[4] These patterns and signals were used for a single purpose: beating or dividing the time for music ensembles. Spohr's musical instructions were delivered verbally, but his non-musical beat patterns (pulse) are still widely regarded as conducting technique. So while conducting technique has evolved to deal only with pulse, the training concentrates on the music, but without any technique for communicating the bulk of newly acquired musical knowledge.

Early training

Since there was no conducting as we understand it, there was no conductor training in the eighteenth century. At the beginning of the nineteenth century, Heinrich Christoph Koch (1749–1816) was one of the first to recognize the need for unique training for the composer chosen to hold together all aspects of performances at court. That this Kapellmeister should be a composer was axiomatic as he needed to have mastery of all aspects of composition, but Koch also demanded a knowledge of declamation, good singing, the languages of the text, and a knowledge of the passions.[5] Koch recognized that conductors needed a broad education, but technique and beat patterns did not figure as part of his educational program.

The nineteenth century brought real baton-wielding conductors to the podium and even different schools of interpretation, but little change to the way they were trained; learn the music and deal with the orchestra via beat patterns. While improved instruments, fine teachers, new musical methods, and improved techniques proliferated for the rest of the musical world, conducting remained in the grip of the separation of pulse from music and the acceptance of beat patterns as conducting technique.

The first treatise on conducting did not appear until 1855 when Berlioz dedicated twelve pages to the subject.[6] Berlioz looked at how the baton and new techniques could be used to create his performances; in addition to diagrams of beat patterns, he examined the use of the arm, the swing of the beat, syncopation, eccentric meters, the use of the then new Verbruggen electric metronome (invented in 1848), tuning the orchestra, and the proper use of rehearsal time.

Berlioz's treatise, however, did not lead to a new interest in conductor training. Between 1795 and 1846 music conservatories opened in Paris, Milan, Naples, Prague, Vienna, London, Brussels, and Leipzig. (In the United States, Peabody was the first conservatory in 1857, followed by Oberlin in 1865, the New England Conservatory in 1867, and Juilliard in 1924.) None offered courses in conducting. Despite Mendelssohn's success as a conductor, he offered no conducting classes when the Leipzig Conservatory opened in 1843. Even Wagner, author of his own treatise on conducting and mentor of so many great conductors (including Bülow, Seidl, Richter, and Mottl), did not include conducting in his proposed music school.[7] Conducting remained an on-the-job learning opportunity.[8]

In the last quarter of the century, the non-composing professional conductor became the rule rather than the exception and instructors were finally added to conservatory and music-school rosters. In Paris, Vincent d'Indy began teaching an orchestral and conducting class in 1905 at the Conservatoire de Musique. At the Vienna Hochschule, Franz Schalk became the head of the conducting class from 1909 to 1919, and Sir Adrian Boult was invited to establish what appears to be the first conducting class at the Royal College in 1919. Their students were well served musically, but these professors did nothing to create a new pedagogy; repetitive beat patterns continued to serve as technique and it was the music in the abstract, rather than the articulation of that music, that mattered.

Twentieth-century methods

Midway through the twentieth century, two ground-breaking books emerged to address the technical needs of the conductor. The first was *Lehrbuch des Dirigierens* by Herman Scherchen (1891–1966), published in 1929 and translated into English in 1933.[9] It is an important text because Scherchen argued that conducting technique exists and was a strong advocate for teaching it in classrooms, even though he was self-trained. His basic guide for conductors is hardly revelatory now: indicate the metrical course and expressive features of the music, and guide the players by correcting faulty playing. Scherchen needed only forty pages to cover the subject, but both he and Max Rudolf (1902–95) depend completely on basic beat patterns and pattern drawings as the cornerstones of conducting technique. Their diagrams are not very different from those proposed by Berlioz.

The first edition of Max Rudolf's *The Grammar of Conducting* appeared in 1950.[10] The book is musically knowledgeable and Rudolf attempted to move conducting technique away from "pedantic time-beating." He argued that the "beat must express the music with its great variety of feelings"[11] and he attempted to add expression to conducting; he drew his beat diagrams much larger so that they could express the subtlety of life-size gestures. The diagrams, however, remained variations of the basic beat patterns. In his chapter headed "Free Style" at the very end of the technical section, Rudolf spends less than one page indicating that "the direction of any beat may be changed to secure a particular result."[12] What Maestro Rudolf considered the end of technique, I believe to be the very beginning of a new kind of conducting technique, which eliminates non-musical pattern repetitions.

The "born conductor" and the apprentice

At the same time that conservatories were starting to teach conducting, a new impediment to conductor training formed. The most brilliant of the day's conductors – Bülow, Nikisch, and soon Toscanini and Stokowski – were morphed into *Übermenschen*, or supermen. With this celebrity came the notion that conducting was a magical gift: a mind-set that is damaging to all conductors and has severely hampered conductor training. But while the star conductor usually commanded center stage in symphony halls, another species of conductor was already in the pit, serving the opera and ballet.

The training for an apprentice opera conductor grew out of necessity. Piano-playing assistants already familiar with the languages in neighbouring countries were expected to play and conduct piano rehearsals, work with the chorus and soloists (including how to deal with intransigent artists), help on-stage singers by covering their weaknesses, act as prompter, and assist backstage, providing cues and creating sound effects. Most importantly apprentices were to observe how to accompany, deal with the difficulties of recitative, and learn to accommodate "tradition" (i.e. unmarked additions to the score accepted by singers as enhancing the music) without losing control of the performance. When apprentices were given the chance to conduct a performance, they were well versed in all aspects of the production.

This apprentice system produces roughly two types of conductors. The first worships the voice and follows the singers wherever they go musically; the contours of the opera are left to the artists on stage. The second type leads the production, especially the singers, and assumes responsibility for the overall shape of the drama. Conductors of the first type have had little success moving to the concert podium, but many of the second type (Mahler,

Strauss, Busch, Erich and Carlos Kleiber, Walter, Toscanini, Karajan, and most recently James Levine) have easily moved from the pit to the podium.

As a result of the "born conductor" myth, the opera apprentice system was the only real model of conductor training at the end of the nineteenth century and it continues even today. While the apprentice system is an informal training program, it remains because it provides a place for conductors to practice. It also, however, reinforces the myth of the "born conductor"; if a conductor succeeds in the opera house, then we assume that magical gift will transfer to the concert hall.

Skill sets

Harold Schonberg, the highly respected former music critic for the *New York Times*, tried to summarize the skills a conductor needed to be successful.

> The conductor must play several instruments well and have a working knowledge of every instrument in the orchestra; must be able to read the entries in a full score as easily as an accountant reads the entries in a ledger; must, while reading a score, assimilate its structure and meaning, decide what the composer wanted and then stimulate his men into achieving the vision; must have stocked in his mind, ready for instant use, all the standard works in the repertoire and a good deal of non-standard besides; must have the technique and memory that can break down and assimilate a contemporary new work; must have the kind of ear that can spot one wrong note in a welter of orchestral noise; must have absolute pitch (most great conductors have had this ability to hear a note or combination of notes and instantly rattle them off); must be able to compose, orchestrate and analyze, keep track of musicological research, especially that pertaining to performance practice; must have the knack of assembling programs that will advance the cause of art without permanently alienating the public; and above all must have – in addition to an elephant-like constitution – the mysterious thing known as projection; the ability to beam his physical and musical personality forward into the orchestra and directly backward into the lap of every listener in the audience. All great conductors have a remarkable power of projection. Without it, a conductor's music making tends to be negative. The audience must be enveloped in white-hot belief, and a conductor is great in direct ratio to his powers of communication.[13]

It is a daunting list of about nine items, but nine most musicians would accept. With the exception of the last item, it is the curriculum at most conservatories and, as such, requires further scrutiny.

(1) Play several instruments: a student should excel on one instrument and have at least a performer's knowledge of the piano and one string instrument. More than that isn't necessary.

(2) Working knowledge of every instrument: it would be a significant achievement to know the individual fingerings of all the instruments on the stage, but it seems unnecessary (beyond the middle school conductor, at least). The orchestra player knows the qualities, possibilities, and quirks of his or her instrument better than the conductor, unless the conductor happens to be a virtuoso on the same instrument. Still, a student must learn the ranges and differing colors of the string, wind, brass, and percussion groups, the qualities of sonority they produce, both individually and, more importantly, collectively in various combinations.

(3) Easily read a full score: knowledge of clefs, instrument keys, transpositions, speed of metronome markings, time signatures, and the meaning of musical terms in various languages remains an absolute necessity.

(4) Understand the structure and meaning of a score: harmonic, melodic, rhythmic and phrase analysis are relatively simple, but the "meaning" of music is inherently ambiguous and should not be fixed. (See below.)

(5) Decide what the composer wants and achieve the vision: a flood of scholarship and opinion on this subject has washed over the musical world in the last decades. What is clear (and fortunate) is that performance decisions change over time, if not from concert to concert. Compositions are live entities and should be subject to constant review. "Achieving the vision," whether vast or limited, inevitably becomes a series of compromises because of the inadequate manner in which baton technique is understood and taught.

(6) Technique and memory to assimilate a new work: does this mean the ability to memorize a new work? Toscanini's weak eyes forced him to memorize, but an open score on a stand during a concert is perfectly normal and acceptable. It is interesting to note that the writer links technique to "new work." The truth is that every single piece of music, regardless of style and period demands new and differing technical solutions.

(7) Absolute pitch and an ear for wrong notes: orchestra players are always impressed by conductors who possess perfect pitch, but it is useful only in rehearsals. Players generally know when they play wrong notes and will eliminate them. If they do not, the conductor must make the pitch corrections during rehearsals. Good players will also adjust intonation automatically, but conductors with excellent relative pitch can achieve the same intonation and balancing results in rehearsals as conductors with absolute pitch. Pitch recognition is a single element in a complex hearing process. How one listens is the important factor. In my view, a highly developed sense of perfect rhythmic articulation is far more important than perfect pitch in individual phrase construction and overall structure.

(8) Ability to compose and orchestrate: conductors must learn the mechanics of composition and orchestration. It is not necessary to become a composer, but it is necessary to learn basic musical procedures: creating melodic lines and shapes, accompaniments, writing counterpoints, combining instrumental colors and organizing new sonorities. These are the daily vocabulary of every conductor.

Any young musician with conducting aspirations and talent can learn most of these with patience and hard work. There is absolutely no mystery involved. Like any other musician, a conductor should be talented, musically and physically literate, inquisitive and intelligent. One could say the same for a violinist, a bassoonist, trumpet player or timpanist. Advancement toward becoming a professional in any arena is marked by hard work and a journey toward realization. Conducting is no exception.

Charisma

Violinist Carl Flesch wrote: "When all is said and done, conducting is the only musical activity in which a dash of charlatanism is not only harmless but absolutely necessary."[14] Harold Schonberg calls it "projection" and we have called it charisma, but it is essentially the myth of the "born conductor" again in disguise. The divinely delivered conductor has become a persistent and annoying yardstick for measuring the quality of conductors and it undermines the need for technique and training.

My conviction that "born conductors" do not exist may be hard to comprehend when we have an aggressive recording industry and an active music press that tell us differently. Young naturals, audacious talents who seemingly get it right without instruction, are constantly touted, but history reveals that the prodigies who continue to grow and fulfill musical expectations are likely to be instrumentalists or composers such as Mozart and Mendelssohn, but not conductors. There are virtually no prodigal conductors, and for good reason. Until recently conductors were valued for their maturity, not their precociousness. With the rarest of exceptions – Lorin Maazel comes to mind – musically gifted children do not begin their performing lives as conductors.

The path to the podium is not a direct one. Gifted adult musicians change career direction because their visions propel them beyond a single instrument to the challenge of music's most complex instrument, the symphony orchestra. While it is extremely helpful to have been a virtuoso musician, its effect while facing an orchestra is limited. Good conductors quickly discover the complex nature of the job and learn they will require significant social skills for dealing with a living instrument.

Conducting is a profession that lends itself to misunderstanding and overheated hyperbole as Mr. Schonberg's purple prose suggests. Conducting is often seen and not heard. Very early in his conducting career, Leonard Bernstein's podium style was correctly described as "flamboyant" and "showy." "Lenny" had charisma and audiences reacted. His teacher,

Fritz Reiner, was widely regarded as a master conductor yet his podium manner was quiet and reserved and he lacked visible charisma. Comparing the abilities of the mature Reiner to his gifted young student was grossly unfair, yet even at the outset of his career, Bernstein held his own with the concertgoing public – because they were swayed by what they saw.

Bernstein, an extraordinary musician and human being, went on to become one of his generation's greatest conductors, but it is important to understand that he was not born a great conductor nor was he a great conductor for much of his conducting career. Despite his larger-than-life personality and overtly visceral podium manner, he became a master conductor only in the last decade and a half of his life when his conducting style changed and he found a technical physicality that matched his intense musical vision. Simply put, he relied on his baton and hands instead of using his entire body as a beating tool. He focused his music-making. Even Leonard Bernstein, charisma notwithstanding, had to learn the physical art of conducting.

The virtuoso orchestra

A wealthy businessman and ardent music-lover developed a passion for a particular Mahler symphony and desired to "conduct" this massive work. He was not a musician, let alone a conductor, so he hired a private tutor to teach him the physical movements a conductor would make as the music unfolds, not unlike a silent actor lip-syncing a sung aria. After some rote physical training the businessman felt he was ready. He hired an orchestra, invited a private audience, and "conducted" the Mahler symphony. The event seemed a harmless eccentricity.

The businessman then hired a number of orchestras and venues to "conduct" publicly this same work and finally made a recording with a London orchestra. The bizarre series of events should have been dismissed as a non-musical hoax. Instead the recording received favorable critical notices inviting the notion that he must have been a "born conductor." In fact, this incident reveals just how far the improvements to the orchestra have outpaced the progress of conductors.

Orchestras can and will help technically deficient conductors create acceptable performances. Excellent orchestras will not allow performances to fall below their own artistic standards; the better the orchestra, the more careful they are of their reputation. This recording is the clearest possible document that the separation of music and mindless pulse is alive and well. The facts are sobering. The businessman imagined he was musically involved in motivating the performance of a Mahler symphony. Despite his active physical presence, nothing could be further from the truth. The orchestra took full control and fashioned an acceptable performance modeled on their past experience with the work. Careful listening reveals the downside to the orchestra's musical domination; without coherent direction the music loses a distinctive articulation. Many orchestras are forced to create performances because conductors forfeit their leadership rights due to technical deficiencies. As a result, many performances and orchestras worldwide sound alike. The orchestra has grown to its present astounding technical level, while conductors are content to beat endless repetitions of eighteenth-century patterns: movements so simple they can be learned by an untrained novice in a matter of days. Unwittingly, the excellence of orchestras has been a major culprit in derailing the need for technical training of conductors.

Contemporary training

For over two centuries then, advances in conductor training have been held back by this combination of (1) an initial separation in the leading of pulse and music, (2) the acceptance of beat patterns as technique, (3) the mythology of the "born conductor," and (4) the astonishing expertise and virtuosity of modern symphony musicians who provide excellence for all conductors, including incompetent pretenders. Conductor training programs have proliferated, but the curricula remain fixated on general musicianship. What actual conducting instruction there is generally happens as private tuition from the resident conductor, who conducts the school orchestra and uses the students as assistants. These programs are often judged by the quality of the teacher and the availability of podium time for the students.

Based on my experience with conducting students from a variety of countries and teaching styles, beat patterns remain the only conducting technique taught. The confirmation comes from watching the technical limitations of students as they face the orchestra. There are teachers who have moved beyond patterns, but they impart instinctive solutions to students without the technical knowledge that is essential to translate instinct into workable physical motion.[15]

Podium time for students varies greatly. In the Moscow Conservatory a student will have conducted all nine Beethoven symphonies before graduation (if their brochure is to be believed). No other program in Europe makes such a claim, although all schools will furnish a graduating student an orchestra, even if, as in some German conservatories, they have to hire a professional one in the absence of an acceptable school orchestra. All schools profess that opportunities exist for enterprising students to gain podium time while still in school: chamber ensembles, contemporary-music workshops, musicals, church choruses, etc. In the United States, podium time is rather limited, unless the resident conductor is away a lot, or a special laboratory orchestra is created for the conductor, as was the case at the Juilliard School of Music. Music schools that cannot furnish ample orchestral podium time for their conducting students should reconsider their programs.

An alternative conductor training program

With the help of Leon Botstein, I have developed a new conducting program for Bard College. It features (1) a conducting class of six to eight students in a non-competitive forum where students learn from watching each other as much as from the teacher. There are no private lessons. (2) All students must take a composition course and compose a six- to eight-minute piece for full orchestra, which will be performed as part of their graduation program. (3) All students must study either a string instrument or the piano throughout the academic year – unless they already play both instruments. (4) A string quintet is used instead of a piano for practice conducting. A single pianist's attacks, ritards, and tempo changes are always together, but flaws in the baton will be more clearly heard in the reaction of the individual string players. Further, a hands-on working knowledge of string articulations is gained over time. During the summer, students are members of the four-week Conductors' Institute and conduct a full orchestra every day. It is a conducting program heavily weighted toward podium time and new ideas about technique.

Sensitive student conductors quickly realize they cannot make orchestras respond to their wishes. When the usual physical gestures fail they usually fall back on verbal explanations. These frustrations have led me to explore a new visual and physical approach, which, tied to the premise that *music makes technique,* has led to new possibilities for creative baton movement.[16]

Students should retain whatever works, but acknowledge that the first step in recreating any score is to reject the non-musical repetitive beat patterns. Constant time-beating is physical illiteracy. In its place the conductor must create new baton movements to match the shape and flow of the music. Once the necessary traditional musical homework has been done (melodic, harmonic, and structural analysis, tempo and thematic relationships, etc.) the conductor must physically present this concept of the composer's text in a musically intelligent manner to the orchestra.

After a detailed "visual score study" of every mark in every measure, the conductor attempts to identify specific baton movements and placement of the baton as dictated by the look of the music. The very topography of a page of music, divorced from pitch and harmonic values, can inform a conductor of the character, weight and sonority of the music. The visual imprint of the music immediately impacts on the placement of the baton and the strokes that will follow. Baton strokes should indicate music and not just pulse; long, short, or curved strokes, different speeds and rebounds can be used to indicate different types of legato and staccato, weight and character. The wrist is capable of every articulation at any speed and with as much or as little weight as is necessary to illuminate the music. The wrist is the conductor's greatest asset. Technical clarity saves rehearsal time and eliminates verbal explanation.

The placement of the baton in the "conductor's space" will define the clarity, density, and character of the orchestral sounds. If the conductor's space is centered and focused the orchestra will reflect that solidity. If on the other hand the conductor moves from place to place on the podium and jumps, bends, or otherwise contorts his body, the sonic fabric of the orchestra will often fracture and suffer. Dynamic levels can be tied to different horizontal zones; the softest zone is the closest to the body with the arm in a V-shape, which restricts movement and dynamic possibilities to the wrist. Loudest is the furthest from the body with the arm at full extension. The traditional assignment of right hand for pulse and left hand for expression continues to divorce music from pulse, even if leadership is assigned to one person rather than two or three people. Either hand can and should show both pulse and musical intent, and work independently of one another. Classical composers, especially Beethoven, used section seating as a compositional tool and intentionally wrote for instruments in different stage areas. Depending on the imagination of the conductor, each arm could be assigned an instrumental group, a recurring rhythmic device or harmonic sonority in a specific conductor's space. In effect the conductor has the option of orchestrating gestures just as the composer orchestrates materials. The effect on the orchestra is instantaneous. They quickly grasp the musical intent of the technical gesture and the difference in weight, attack and articulation of the events are immediate.

I also advocate using the vertical dimension to trace the pitch contours of moving lines ("Registration") with the tip of the baton. Practice scales with the baton. Imagine a keyboard on its side with the high notes higher than the low ones. Set the metronome and for each click, touch a note on the imaginary keyboard in a major scale with the tip of the baton. Sing the pitches. Try other speeds, keys, and arpeggios. As you do more exercises you will begin to feel the difference in the baton between a half step, a whole step, thirds, fifths, etc. Your baton will become accustomed to space with pitch entities and your conducting technique will take on a new dimension.

Example 18.1 Beethoven, Symphony No. 1, second movement, with new beating patterns

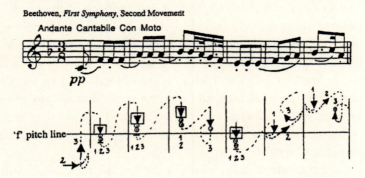

In Ex. 18.1, Beethoven gives us three measures (1, 2 and 4) of repeated pitches. Since there is no linear movement within the measures, the traditional pattern motions should be eliminated. The first two strokes (beats) must be exactly the same and the third stroke (beat) must begin exactly where the first two began, but with an upward curved legato stroke. The new baton movement is the direct result of the shape and character of the music: music makes technique. It allows the conductor the physical freedom that traditional patterns cannot match because formula patterns were not created for musical purposes.

Erich Leinsdorf wrote: "The simple fact that sound is a part of personality has . . . made me dubious about so-called baton technique. I have always refused to teach conducting, supporting my refusal with the argument that the motions are of no consequence."[17] Leinsdorf failed to understand the value of the baton and the function of the arms in creating sonorities. Of course baton technique exists, but it cannot be disengaged from the music. Changing the point of origin of the motion of the baton (in the conductor's space) as well as the weight (from the wrist, arm, or even the shoulder) and delivery of the stroke (from any of the zones) will change the sound of the orchestra. I have heard student conductors do it countless times. A conductor need only be aware that a technical option exists to change an orchestra's sound.

Conductor variety

Toscanini is reported to have said "Conductors are born. Conducting cannot be taught." But the physical art of conducting can and is being taught to young conductors. Talent cannot be taught, but talent alone is not enough to move a musician from the commonplace to brilliance.

If a "born conductor" template exists, then there should be some commonalities among any list of distinguished conductors, say Koussevitzky, Mahler, Strauss, Kleiber, Klemperer, Solti, Monteux, Leinsdorf, Reiner, Boult, Beecham, Mitropoulos, Barbirolli, Furtwängler, Bernstein, Karajan, Toscanini, Walter, Stokowski, and Szell. While all enjoyed international success, a surprising number of them lost the respect of their orchestras, audiences and critics and had to change posts. But other than the culturally imposed barriers of sex and race, they share no magical conductor DNA. Musical tastes, formative years, conducting styles, and performance results varied greatly. They were short, tall, thin, fat, bald, hairy, handsome, and plain. They ranged from tough (Reiner) to kind (Walter), and even saintly (Mitropoulos). Many said little while Bernstein talked endlessly. Most were dour, while Beecham enjoyed using his wit. Some had technical skills, while others needed and received help from their players. Surprisingly, not all were thought to be excellent or even good musicians; Beecham was called an amateur, Stokowski was widely regarded as a faker, and Koussevitzky an advocate who had to be taught the music he hoped to advance. Even charisma was noticeably lacking in some (Monteux, Reiner, Leinsdorf), while the "leadership" qualities exhibited by conductors in the days before the Musicians' Union, especially by Toscanini, would not be tolerated today. A formula does not exist.

Every musician who harbors a desire to become a conductor should enter the fray. The successful ones will be gifted and intelligent women and men who honor and love the music they choose to perform and will investigate and acquire the necessary technical skills to articulate their musical passions. Most importantly they will regard music and technique as an inseparable entity; the movement of the baton should be a mirror of a conductor's musical soul and heart.

19 The composer-conductor and modern music

MARTYN BRABBINS

With one work, Igor Stravinsky single-handedly transformed the role and function of the conductor. The rhythmic complexities of *Le sacre du printemps* immediately increased the dexterity and technical skill required from conductors. It is remarkable that today, most self-respecting orchestras will expect a competent conductor to produce an acceptable performance of this towering masterpiece of orchestral invention in a single three-hour rehearsal. With amateur orchestras and even schoolchildren able to play this shattering work, it is little wonder that composers have felt free to demand more and more from performers. Without *Le sacre*, it is difficult to imagine the complex scores of Boulez, Stockhausen, Berio, Birtwistle, Carter, Takemitsu, Ferneyhough, or Dillon ever emerging. Without it too, orchestral technique would not have developed at the rate that is has. This technical progress has also meant that first-rate performances of difficult twentieth-century works regularly feature in the programs of all professional orchestras. This is a cause for great rejoicing; *Le sacre* has raised both the demands on and the abilities of modern conductors. It has thus ensured a rich supply of conductors able and willing to conduct new music, often even more demanding than Stravinsky's masterpiece.

The return of composer-conductors

Until the eighteenth century, composers were usually involved in the performances of their own music. The nineteenth century saw the rise of conductors who specialized in leading the music of others: while some composers were capable conductors, others could now turn their scores over to other musicians for performance.[1] Today, however, it is rare to find composers who have *not* actually conducted their own music. While conducting requires special skills (especially with complex modern scores) many musicians will attest to the very particular kind of "magic" even the most technically ill-equipped composer can bring to the performance of his or her own music. The spirit of music is often more important than technical perfection; as Charles Ives said, "forget the notes, play the music."

From recordings it is often possible to experience the unique musical potency of a composer. Sergey Rakhmaninov (1873–1943) recorded as both a pianist and conductor and his unsentimental, somewhat muscular approach to his own symphonic output is instructive. He adheres very closely to the written text, never crossing the bounds of good taste with excessive rubato or self-indulgence: a model interpreter of his own music. Other composers who brought real personality, vibrancy, and individuality to performances of their music include Prokofiev, Strauss, Copland, Hindemith, and Lutosławski. Of course many composers have not been strong advocates: Schumann, Tchaikovsky, Debussy, and Shostakovich, to name but four. Mahler was an exceptional conductor, but made no orchestral recordings and left only piano rolls of his own work.[2] In England, however, three exceptional composer-conductors also left superb and comprehensive recordings of their major works.

Edward Elgar (1857–1934) was the first composer wholly to embrace the idea of gramophone recording. During his later years, when his powers of composition appeared to have somewhat diminished, he conducted both concerts and recordings, perhaps as an alternative outlet for his creativity. Between 1911 and 1912, he was the principal conductor of the London Symphony Orchestra, with his great friend W. H. (Billy) Reed as the concertmaster. Recordings of his own compositions show the true Elgar spirit, lithe, energetic, tautly dramatic, and intensely emotional, and reveal none of the pomp and Empire that Elgar's music is often said to represent.

William Walton (1902–83) had a very distinguished recording career, beginning in 1929 and ending in 1968. He began conducting his own music when it became apparent to him that other conductors were not able or willing to conduct the music themselves. His recordings reveal an authoritative, skilled conductor and, judging from the enthusiastic playing of the orchestra, a man who commanded both the respect and affection of his players. A comment Walton made during rehearsals for the British premiere of his *Partita* for orchestra suggests that he understood well both the complexity of the conductor's art, and his own shortcomings: "Pay no attention to me," he said, "I've got out . . . I'm only an amateur conductor, you know."

Benjamin Britten (1913–76), one of the few truly great composers that England has ever produced, was also a respected pianist and conductor. He began his conducting activities early in his career, conducting the many film scores he created while an employee of the General Post Office Film Unit in the 1930s. At the outbreak of World War II in 1939, Britten left for the United States, where he continued conducting, partly for financial reasons. There is a fine recording from 1941 of *Les illuminations* conducted by the composer, with tenor Peter Pears and the CBS Symphony Orchestra. After his return to England, Britten was instrumental in founding the English Opera Group and the Aldeburgh Festival, where he continued to conduct.

Like Stravinsky, Britten left recordings of virtually all his major works, but also made distinguished recordings of a wider repertoire. As the composer Colin Matthews has written:

> Britten's recorded legacy is of particular importance because his remarkable abilities as performer and conductor, vouched for by everyone who worked with him, mean that the composer's insights into his own music are unimpaired by any technical shortcomings. His interpretations can be listened to in the knowledge that *this* is how the music should sound.[3]

One of the most interesting moments from Britten's recorded legacy is the fifty minutes of *War Requiem* rehearsal that the Decca producer John Culshaw surreptitiously recorded. This was then presented to Britten as a fiftieth birthday gift from the recording company. The composer was "appalled" at this undercover taping of what was, to Britten, a very private process, and Britten felt that his own and the performers' privacy had been rudely invaded. This unique recording is now publicly available and is essential listening for anyone interested in Britten's music or in the concept of the composer conducting his own music. Britten proves himself not only to be an impassioned advocate of his own music (and, therefore, of the pacifist message contained within it), but also a wonderful rehearser, cajoling, encouraging, and reproaching the large forces present. That the Britten recording of the *War Requiem* is of such brilliance is no surprise when one has heard the composer's keen ear for detail, coupled with his concern for the overarching design and impetus of the music.

Bernstein and Boulez

The two foremost composer-conductors of the second half of the twentieth century were undoubtedly Leonard Bernstein (1918–90) and Pierre Boulez (b. 1925). Bernstein was an enormously gifted composer in various styles, although outside the United States he is still perceived as a conductor who composed rather than as a composer who conducted. This is possibly not how he would have wished to be remembered, but despite regular airings of his concert pieces, these works struggle to retain a place in the repertoire of symphony orchestras.

In his inspiring television concerts and lectures, he reveals a sharp intellect coupled with a deft "common touch." His presence at Tanglewood, the summer home of the Boston Symphony Orchestra and international center for summer music courses, had a powerful and profound effect on the student conductors who worked with him. As a student of Bernstein's in 1985,

Grant Llewellyn remembers Bernstein as a caring, inspiring, and demanding teacher. Although Bernstein was aware of his iconic status at Tanglewood, he took pains never deliberately to intimidate or embarrass his students, in what Llewellyn recalls could be fairly chaotic teaching sessions![4]

The Bernstein personality, larger than life, energetic, dynamic, and intelligent, fully informed his conducting style. He was a performer who gave of himself without reservation, and with this level of commitment, whatever music he performed was inflected in the unique Bernstein way.

Pierre Boulez possesses many of these same gifts and inspires great respect, affection, and loyalty from the musicians with whom he works. Bernstein and Boulez also share a passionate desire to communicate through their music, words and physical gestures. Boulez has also exerted an enormous influence on both conductors and composers since the 1950s. At the same time, as the founder of the Ensemble Intercontemporain, and of the prestigious Institut de Recherche et Coordination Acoustique/Musique in Paris he has given composers access to performances, and to research facilities unmatched anywhere in the world.

His earliest conducting experiences with the Domaine Musical in the late 1940s and early 1950s coincided with his emergence as a leading avant-garde composer. Boulez conducted much contemporary repertoire at this time and admits to having learnt a great deal from the experience. His own early pieces were very difficult to play (and to listen to) and the performances were very unpredictable. As Boulez says, "if after numerous rehearsals one has only a 30 or 40 percent chance of playing the work as written it's better to write in a different manner and have an 80 or 90 percent possibility of success."[5] This statement, typical of the penetrating logic and practicality of his thinking, reveals that the experience of conducting his own, and other, complex music informed, in a positive and creative way, the music Boulez himself wrote.

Boulez only began conducting in order to establish ways of performing his own works and those by his equally radical contemporaries, Stockhausen, Nono, Berio, and Pousseur. Toward the end of the 1950s, however, he began to expand his conducting activities. It is surely no coincidence that with the acquisition of "fluency in conducting," as he called it, many orchestras were keen to work with Boulez. He eventually found himself as Chief Conductor for the BBC Symphony Orchestra and then the New York Philharmonic, where he did not program his own music excessively. (Perhaps he felt that by leaving out his own music he would be more able to leave out music by other living composers.)

His repertoire includes some standard repertoire, but is focused on the twentieth century, especially Bartók, Debussy, Stravinsky, Schoenberg, Berg, Webern, and Ravel. The symphonies of Mahler also feature, as does his own music and compositions by some of his contemporaries and by his teacher, Olivier Messiaen. A composer who conducts is not always a conductor. A composer cannot seriously be considered to be a conductor unless he successfully performs music of other composers and from different eras and Boulez excels in technically demanding music of many types.

Boulez performances are distinguished by their attention to detail, textual clarity, and rhythmic precision; essential facets of performances of music from whatever period. Boulez achieves much with very minimal physical gestures. His economy of gesture is the fruit of long preparation of scores, and of his passionate concern to avoid superfluous movements. His goal is to perfect a well-conceived geometric system of gestures, which will convey the beat and the place in the bar clearly.

He never uses a baton. Pierre Monteux once asked him why and Boulez replied that he felt more comfortable without one, to which Monteux retorted: "You'll come round to it." Boulez has not come round, and there seems little likelihood of him ever doing so. Working without a baton may have resulted from his first conducting experiences with small ensembles, where there really is no need for a baton. Boulez believes that a style of conducting will develop which does not need a baton and there are already several new-music conductors who operate very effectively without a baton, many directly influenced by Boulez's example.

There are, inevitably, critics of Boulez the conductor. It was felt by some that during his time with the BBC he conducted too little music by British composers. Notable among the critical voices was the late Hans Keller, who accused Boulez of being unable to phrase, of confusing rhythm with meter, and of ignoring the harmonic rhythm of tonal music:

> What the habitual non-phraser does . . . is to replace phrasing by pace (everything too fast), and rhythm by "beat," by motivic pseudo excitement. The result is that while you can hear things which you shouldn't, you can't hear things which you should.[6]

For most critics, however, a Boulez reading of even the most familiar piece is bound to reveal something new.

Boulez readily acknowledges how composing and conducting interact with each other. Being a composer makes one more exacting as a conductor. The composer-conductor appreciates more fully the effort involved in composing and has more respect for the composer's text. With this respect, there has to be a degree of pragmatism, which enables the conductor to make changes where required, be it a simple misprint, or new dynamics in order to achieve clarity of texture. This is a duty incumbent upon all conductors, of whatever music: to give the most accurate and honest performance of a given work.

Example 19.1a 2/16 with one triplet per beat

Example 19.1b 2/4 with one triplet per beat

As one would expect, Boulez is clear in his appreciation of the composer-conductor phenomenon. The problem with most of his colleagues who conduct, he says, is that conducting is simply not their profession, and they are not going to learn by conducting their own music once or twice a year. Composers who are less experienced conductors often find themselves getting too emotionally involved while conducting their own music. Without the necessary professional detachment, their passion can get the upper hand, often with embarrassing consequences: "It's as if you were cutting a windowpane: either you do it properly with a diamond, or you don't know how to go about it and you use your fist. You'll hurt yourself, and the pane will be cut badly, that's all."[7]

Some of the best composer-conductors working today include John Adams, James MacMillan, Esa-Pekka Salonen, Oliver Knussen, and George Benjamin. Able to give technically flawless, well-paced performances, with every detail in clear focus, they are excellent advocates for their own music.

Preparation: notation

Notation is the essential interface between composer and performer and conductors spend much more time studying scores than they do in rehearsal or performance. For many modern works, the conductor must also assimilate a new notation and then teach it to the orchestra. It is incumbent upon the composer to be as clear as possible, so that the musicians can accurately and efficiently realize the music. Unfortunately, modern notation can be unnecessarily frustrating to rehearse and perform.

Many composers still use overly small note values as the basic unit of pulse: using 2/16 or 5/16 for instance, so the conductor's beat must correspond to a sixteenth. This adds unnecessary lines and confusion. Why write a triplet with three lines (Ex. 19.1a) when one line will do (Ex. 19.1b). This forces the players to spend valuable rehearsal time assimilating the notation instead of the music.

While most composers use the standard layout of an orchestral score with woodwinds at the top and strings at the bottom, I recently conducted a score with a variety of layouts which gave the following reasoning: "The layout changes in each section according to which instruments play together."[8] While the composer was attempting to be helpful, it was not. With experience, the conductor's eye develops the ability to see which groups of instruments in a score are functioning as a unit – providing the conventions of score layout are observed. Any straying from the conventions simply confuses, adds to learning time, and worst of all, can lead to problems in performance. Things do occasionally go wrong in live music-making. When they do, the conductor wants to get information from a quick glance at a logically and consistently notated score.

At the opposite extreme, when a composer gives too little information, the performers are left in a frustrating state of limbo, unable to be sure if what they are rehearsing in any way resembles what the composer was intending. A brief, clear, description of intentions can help enormously.

A posthumous premiere is especially tricky. I conducted the London Sinfonietta, in Schnittke's *Fragment*, which the Sinfonietta had commissioned, but was left unfinished at the time of his death in 1998. I had to take decisions in all three movements concerning tempi, balance, dynamics, and articulation, as the score was virtually bare apart from pitches and rhythms. While these are everyday decisions for the conductor, in the case of a posthumous premiere, one's sense of responsibility for taking the appropriate decisions is greatly increased. In order to make such decisions it is the duty of the conductor to be conversant with the general style and language of a composer.

When confronted with exceptionally complex notation, such as that found in *Transit* by Brian Ferneyhough, musicians struggle and practice, to be as precise and accurate as possible. In this case, however, the composer stated that what mattered most was not perfect rhythmic precision and total pitch accuracy, but rather the shape of the musical gesture. Players often have to read between the lines as well, and musical playing is generally more important than simple accuracy.

Preparation: beat patterns

The more complex the music, the greater the burden of responsibility on the conductor to be technically secure and reliable in execution. One of the most common problems in modern scores is the irregular number of beats in each bar. Beating irregular bars, and combinations of bars of differing lengths and different tempi, is not a simple task. Practicing patterns is the

Example 19.2 Richard Causton's *Notturno* (Oxford University Press, 1998)

conductor's equivalent to scales and arpeggios; the more physically drilled the conductor is in preparation for this task the better. Conducting modern music requires additional time with the score, often simply to determine what beat patterns to use, followed by practice sessions, to make sure they are technically secure.

Again, composers often make things more confusing than need be. A common complaint from orchestral players is that some composers write complex rhythms within the beat, and then add to each note a specific articulation, a crescendo, an *espressivo* indication, and then expect them to watch the conductor for a rallentando! One case of the over-helpful composer concerned pairs of bars, one of 5/16, the other of 5/8 (see Ex. 19.2).

At first glance, these three bars look as though they will be conducted in two beats (short/long). The eighth-note pulse, however, was very slow, so the 5/16 bar was in two while the 5/8 was in five. There was much shaking of heads from the players followed by vigorous crossing-out in the parts. It falls to the conductor to assimilate the notation ahead of time and determine what patterns to beat.

The score for Morton Feldman's *violin and orchestra* is sizable: more than 1,500 bars in one continuous span, containing the most eccentric sequences of time signatures I have witnessed. A particular favorite of mine is: 3/32, 1/8, 5/32, 3/16, 7/32, 2/8, 9/32, 10/32, 11/32, 12/32, 13/32, 14/32. The eagle-eyed reader will have noticed that each bar increases in duration by one thirty-second-note. The twelve bars comprised a sequence of three-part trombone chords, one per bar. We tried several alternative patterns, but my counting thirty-seconds and beating only once per bar worked the best. Always look for the simplest and safest solution.

I was to conduct this piece with the young German violinist Isabelle Faust as the soloist. She had performed the piece once before and as we discussed the piece via the telephone, it became clear I would need to beat the irregular bars in the way she was used to from previous performances. I had no reason not to agree with this as I was conducting the piece for the first time. Why cause a soloist unnecessary difficulties? Peter Rundell had conducted the previous performance in Munich and graciously sent me his marked score. Still, I was required to explain to the orchestra how I would beat each bar. Even though the parts had been used before, there were inconsistencies, mistakes and omissions in many of the parts. I must have spent over an hour simply talking through each section of the piece before we got round to playing it!

Many conductors in this volume advocate beginning rehearsals with a read-through. While this is generally possible with a piece everyone knows, it is virtually impossible when working on a new work. The parts for the standard repertoire are mostly clean and free from errors and virtually all of them can be conducted with the basic beat patterns. Neither of these is true for modern works, and conductors and orchestras should expect to spend much more time talking, both to explain and fix. This challenge, however, can also lead to greater collaboration as it is impossible for the conductor to try most things in advance. The conductor and orchestra must often experiment together to find solutions to unusual and complex problems.

Preparation: physical demands

I was preparing Morton Feldman's *violin and orchestra* for an all-Feldman concert with the BBC Symphony Orchestra which also included his *Rothko Chapel* for double choir, viola, percussion, and celeste, and *Coptic Light* for orchestra. The order of the programme was easy; *Rothko Chapel* was obviously to be the still centre of the concert, with the two larger orchestral pieces on either side of it. As *violin and orchestra* is almost an hour long, we decided that this alone should make up the first half. A major stage reshuffle would be required during the intermission to allow the front of the platform to accommodate the forty singers in the double choir, while the rear of the platform had to be prepared for *Coptic Light*, which requires a very different percussion set-up to that of *violin and orchestra*.

One aspect of contemporary music concerts that can be extremely tiresome and frustrating is the inordinate amount of time some stage changes can take. (Everyone has heard the one about the contemporary music concert where the music lasted one hour and ten minutes, but the concert lasted three hours!) It is crucial that the stage-management team is as professional, well prepared and expert at their job as the players are. Detailed planning and preparation are an absolute requirement and the stage management should ideally involve the conductor; the alert and experienced conductor will often foresee problems. Conductors should communicate all concerns to orchestral management during the rehearsal period, to ensure a concert focused only on the music.

Preparation: technical demands

One undeniable feature of music in the twentieth century is that it has placed ever greater demands upon players, both in terms of instrumental technique and of assuming leading solo roles. Conductors should expect that players will not only require more time between rehearsals to practice, but that rehearsals themselves may be demanding.

In his piece *Coptic Light*, Feldman does a superb job in creating the illusion of the piano sustain-pedal – sounds merging or overlapping, emerging or disappearing, echoing or foreshadowing. The net result for the players, however, is that they have very little extended rest in the thirty-one-minute piece. The conductor must be sensitive to the physical stress required to play such music. It is unreasonable to expect the string players, who play continuous long tones, to put themselves into situations of extreme physical discomfort (and even risk the possibility of permanent physical injury) until the actual performance of the music. So in rehearsals, as long as the majority within the section are playing at any given moment, the conductor can be satisfied, and the players will react well to this concern for their well-being.

For new repertoire and pieces with multiple soloists, like Mark-Anthony Turnage's *Dispelling the Fears* for two solo trumpets and orchestra, and Thea Musgrave's *Echoes of Time Past* for cor anglais, trumpet, and orchestra, it is useful (and quite common) to draw soloists from within the orchestra. The physical demands for modern concerti are likely to be as great or greater than those from the standard repertoire and, of course, new concerti must also be learned. Solo playing by principal players of symphony orchestras is very beneficial to the performance quality of the individual player, and ultimately, to the quality of the whole ensemble, but rehearsal schedules should be carefully planned to allow soloists from within an orchestra to have enough preparation time preceding and recovery time following a concerto performance. One of my regrets concerning the commissioning and performance of new music is the lack of commitment shown by the majority of so-called "star" performers.

Working with composers

There is a school of thought that a composer's own performance is an extension of the creative process. While certainly an authentic performance (using authentic in its traditional sense of genuine as opposed to the impossible historical "authenticity"), a composer's performance is not always the ideal model. Which of Stravinsky's quite different recorded versions of *Le sacre*, for example, should one take as the authentic interpretation?[9] While he did record most of his sizable output, and there are many vivid recordings of great insight and individuality, Stravinsky restricted his activities as both pianist and conductor largely to the performance of his own works. Even when dealing with a technically accomplished conductor, it is impossible to know all of the circumstances of a performance (a wrong note may simply be a mistake), and caution should be exercised before slavishly following all the details of any previous performance.

Many composers have chosen instead to work closely with a single conductor and the combination of a professional conductor with the presence of the composer can be an ideal one. Stravinsky supervised many recordings conducted by Robert Craft, and Seiji Ozawa and Kent Nagano have both worked closely with Messiaen to create recordings. For a composer, few things are more important than the advocacy and support of a trusted performer. Once a conductor has developed an understanding of and insight into the mind and music of a composer, both performer and creator can share in the process of recreation in a spirit of mutual respect.

Bringing a new work before the public is a tremendously exciting process, but it requires the development of a relationship between the performers and the composer.[10] Composers today, although using a language removed, sometimes distantly, from the language of the great masterpieces of the past, still hold an intense desire to reach, to touch, and ultimately to move audiences. Composers have also invested much in their work and can be sensitive to changes. Having the composer at hand can make it easier to fix problems, but it can also make it harder as some composers do not have a crystal-clear idea of how the music should sound, and it is thus possible to be on the receiving end of conflicting advice in rehearsal. The conductor, of course, listens to all advice, but ultimately has to forge a personal interpretation of any given work.

If a composer is willing to allow the conductor to collaborate in the creation of a new piece, it is possible that the conductor can play a helpful and positive role in the creative process. Piers Hellawell was commissioned by the BBC Promenade Concerts to write a piece which I would conduct during the 1999 Proms season. The composer writes:

> My concerto *Inside Story* involved intermittent "en route" collaboration with its three principals – violin, viola, and conductor. It had been a definite "alliance" from the start – in fact I conceived the piece to unite this team – so it was in any case not just the usual management fix-up. While the soloists' discussions were on expected territory, the conductor had less obvious bounds of discussion. My attitude is that few composers have sufficient access to orchestras or commissions from them to learn the myriad angles "in the field" on a regular basis, which is exactly what the conductor does – so that any input from Martyn based on such solid experience (which extended to advice on individual players and venues, in this case) was pure gold, and not to be dismissed. I tell students that the smart composer welcomes advice, whether acting upon it or not: pride is no use in composition.[11]

The creation of a successful operatic premiere is an even more demanding undertaking. In an effort to help and support the composer, the management of English National Opera have developed the very enlightened policy of budgeting for rehearsals of scenes of commissioned works, as the composer completes them, but well in advance of the beginning of the normal rehearsal period. When David Sawer was commissioned to write *From Morning to Midnight*, he had the benefit of having been present at rehearsals and runthroughs, usually recorded, of each scene. Then in the privacy of his own studio, he was able to cut, extend and modify as necessary. Members of the orchestra, the chorus, principals, and I as conductor were able to make observations on any aspect of the score, and even to propose modifications and changes. Being a part of the creative process was an immensely fulfilling experience, and helped, of course, to turn us all into advocates long before opening night.

There is no doubt that working with contemporary works is more demanding in every way for players, audience, and conductor, but it is also a wonderful opportunity to reinvent and refine your technique, work collaboratively with other musicians, make a name for yourself, and give something back to your musical community. Many composers will no doubt continue to conduct their own works, out of either necessity or vocation, but conductors of all interests can and should find worthwhile modern work to conduct.

20 Managers and the business of conducting

STEPHEN WRIGHT

I started in the business in 1971, at the age of twenty-five, when a well-known US manager told me he was opening a European office. The conductors were not particularly well known, but with youthful enthusiasm I worked night and day for them. I had gathered experience for this largely at the Royal Festival Hall, where, as a student, I always bought the cheapest seats behind the orchestra in order to watch the conductor. Through observation, I came to learn how physical gestures and eye contact conveyed musical structure, excitement, and internal balance to an orchestra. I also collected records of all the major conductors of the past and present, so although I was completely green about managing conductors, I had acquired a system of aural and visual evaluation about the conductor's art. I have experienced the artist/manager relationship, the elements needed to build an artist's career, and the changes to both over the last thirty years. These reflections are offered in the hope that future conductors will be better prepared for what may lie ahead of them.

From impresarios to managers

In the nineteenth century, conductors managed their own careers. Conductors tended to stay in permanent positions for ten to fifteen years or even more. Faster travel opened up more opportunities and created the notion of a conducting "career," which then led to the need for more administration and planning.

At the turn of the century, the people who "represented" artists were impresarios, something quite different from managers. Impresarios put on concerts at their own risk to earn money. In the early twentieth century, there was profit to be made from presenting and promoting classical music concerts, but this gradually changed. With the expansion of the classical music business and the introduction of public subsidy, the basic economics of classical music changed dramatically. Over the years, the artistic costs of orchestras and artists have risen at a higher rate than potential box-office income, and reliably large audiences have become more difficult to secure. Managers came to represent and recommend conductors to orchestras and opera houses rather than promote them directly.

One of the first managers of conductors of this kind was Arthur Judson, founder of Columbia Artists in the 1920s. In a way that is difficult for us to understand today, he developed his conductors' roster whilst remaining the General Manager of both the Philadelphia and New York orchestras, thus ensuring a remarkable hold on arranging the music-director choices of major American orchestras. All this was broken up in the 1930s since it was judged, rightly, as a basic conflict of interests.

While the function changed, these representatives continued to be called impresarios until the 1960s. Two mid-century examples were the Englishman Harold Holt and the Russian-American Sol Hurok. These were larger-than-life figures who still risked their own money. Hurok, for example, discovered Arthur Rubinstein for the US market and offered him a guaranteed fee for multiple engagements. He then sold each engagement at a marked-up figure, and thereby made a profit. He took the risk that he would indeed get the engagements, and so could earn far in excess of what a manager would make today by taking their pre-agreed and fixed commission on the fees negotiated.

Since then, the business has changed radically, mostly due to the huge increase in the number of potential candidates chasing the increased international opportunities. Conductors like Walter, Toscanini, and Klemperer accepted that there was a certain learning curve and that experience was needed that took time "out of the mainstream" to acquire. It was once thought that a decade or more in a regional opera house was required to learn the trade. Today, the increased competition has added pressure to capitalize on any success immediately. There is also felt to be such a shortage of outstanding young conductors that if the word goes around that there is someone exceptional, a whole host of orchestras will want to book immediately. This climate tends to over-promote talent that is not yet ripe for the top level of engagement, and has shortened the time a conductor has to train. Tight budgets have reduced the "try-out" opportunities; orchestras needing to keep up attendances now tend to need a surefire draw every week. The recent collapse of the supportive system of recordings has hurt too. Ironically, one could argue that all this has led to an increase in quantity, but with a decrease in quality.

A variety of skills

Today's conductors come with a wider range of styles, personalities, and skills, and the manager needs to understand how to manage the lot. The conductor's craft includes communication skills, physical technique, the ability to adjust orchestral sonority and balance, an understanding of the music's structure, and so on. There are conductors who are wonderful musicians, but appear to do very little in physical terms. The audience then wonders how the orchestra sounds so good with such an apparently awkward visual spectacle in front of them. Instrumentalists who have later turned to conducting can sometimes tend to be of this kind. On the other hand, you have physically flamboyant and brilliant-looking conductors for whom the orchestra often play indifferently, or with little musical depth. Since conducting is both a visual and musical activity, the manager must have the ability to distinguish the different elements that make up the overall impression.

The difference between such "conductor conductors" and "conductor musicians" was sharply illustrated to me when I was in a London hotel room with three Russian conductors. They were watching a very distinguished Western conductor on the television and were all amused throughout his performance, simply because they regarded him as technically incompetent. Russian conducting technique is widely regarded as the best in the world – the abilities of Russian conductors in terms of beat, rhythm, and skills in communicating through their hands and eyes to an orchestra are unparalleled – but at the same time, from a Western point of view, Russian conductors' interpretations of the classical repertoire of Haydn, Mozart, Beethoven, or Schubert often seem as questionable, despite their superb technique, as Western conducting technique often does to the Russian school.

Finding management

The best possible way to interest a manager is to be seen in action. There is no substitute – even if it is with an amateur orchestra – to being seen and heard live. If the manager is musical and competent, signs of emerging talent are easy to spot. A concert with a good student orchestra can be an excellent forum for your skills, because these are often of a high standard, and contain that essential spirit of unspoilt, committed music-making. Young conductors should also build up a decent repertoire list and make good-quality audio or video recordings of concerts.

So for both musical and career advancement, it should be obvious that the key "engine-room oil" for a conductor is practice. Unlike other musicians who can easily acquire an instrument, the conductor can only gain experience through conducting amateur orchestras, creating a new orchestra, or following the traditional path of finding an assistant job with a professional orchestra: all ways of familiarizing yourself with what actually comes out of the orchestra when you bring your baton down. Going to professional conductors' rehearsals is also very useful, but nothing replaces the experience of trying to do it yourself.

Managers also listen to word-of-mouth recommendations from other artists in their agency and note the winners of competitions. A personal meeting can make an impression too; sitting down with a manager, and talking about your background, education, aims, and interests in music, can encourage a manager to come and hear you. There is also no harm in starting the process of interesting a manager from an early age, even if this does not lead to being taken on immediately. Following a young conductor's career from college through concerts with amateur orchestras, through a concert or two with a professional orchestra, can be a good process for both sides. The manager observes the progress being made and the talent being realized, while the conductor feels a relationship being built. The manager may also offer general advice and help, long before any formal commitment.

Choosing a manager

The range of conductor needs and personalities require different management styles. Some conductors are self-confident and want a manager to perform the purely professional functions of advising them on choice of orchestra, finding engagements, and negotiating good fees and conditions. For a manager, these are the easy relationships because they tap into our purely professional competencies. But there are few of this type, for although a conductor in front of an orchestra must outwardly display total confidence, most of them are prone to the normal insecurities all of us have.

I was once told by a very senior manager that the manager is supposed to be even more of a chameleon than an ideal wife has been said to be in the past: he said the cocktail of abilities needed to look after a conductor includes the roles of lawyer, business manager, musical companion, accountant, financial advisor, nurse, psychiatrist, doctor, brother/sister, and friend. All these qualities can sometimes be called upon in just one meeting. So a conductor should look not only for knowledge and experience, but for the ability to focus on you as an artist and a human being, and to be sensitive and understanding of your particular needs and character.

In technical terms, the manager's role involves the overall management of a conductor's career. This includes a knowledge and strategic understanding of symphony orchestras, opera houses, and festivals, including their standards, strengths, and weaknesses, and the constantly changing nature of these institutions throughout the world. It also involves securing and negotiating individual dates, concerts, rehearsal conditions (both orchestral and operatic), record, audio-visual contracts, and repertoire. An intimate knowledge of the repertoire, from Bach through Adès, is essential. A manager advises on suitable programming, understanding the conductor's strengths, but also the orchestra's strengths and weaknesses, and what key repertoire has already been covered by the music director. When looking for a music directorship, it is the manager's job to know whether that conductor's particular repertoire "spread" will marry up well with the orchestra's expectations and needs.

The conductor should also understand that in many good agencies, there are further and considerable benefits to a manager being part of a larger network of contacts and information. The agency can then take on some of the burden of providing the normal administrative and logistical services which justify the commission: i.e. reliable contracting, sorting out of hotel, travel, accounting and legal advice, and making sure that the technical aspects of an orchestral engagement all run smoothly.

Good managers should ideally speak, or at least understand, a few languages and have a flexible attitude and the experience to do business in a wide variety of countries. Artists in former Communist countries were "managed" by state organizations who viewed the individual as an artistic servant for the state (which had paid for their education and now expected a political "return"). Standard fees per concert could be as low as £100 with the balance going to the state as a "profit" on that conductor's activities. These conductors had to be gently educated about Western freedoms and what a manager could deliver. So in addition to all the qualities mentioned above, an understanding of political systems and variations in national character is also useful.

The professional advice a manager should bring to a conductor is very sensitive. Most conductors want an authoritative review of how they conducted that night with that orchestra. While most do not want a manager who quotes bar numbers where their beat was not clear, they do want a general and intelligent opinion as to whether the orchestra played its best or transformed its sound for the conductor; knowledge of the usual performance standards of orchestras is another function of the manager. Another area of partnership is at what pace the conductor best functions. There are conductors who need to work under pressure, so planning in four months of free time for such an artist would make no sense. A manager needs to develop a schedule that supports the conductor's best work/rest/learn rhythm.

The most important element, therefore, is trust; a conductor must trust that the manager understands the business and is able to offer the very best advice. You need a manager who really understands what you want from your music career and what conducting is really all about. The last part is very tricky, because what conductors think they are capable of achieving is often different from either what the manager judges they are achieving, or the orchestras judge them to have achieved. One of the manager's critical functions is to advise a conductor on what has gone wrong. This touches the heart of the manager/conductor relationship: conductors need managers to believe in them.

Belief does not mean uncritical support; it is in the interests of neither conductor nor manager to give this if something has gone wrong. Conductors will often interpret critical comments as a lack of support, so managers often risk their own relationships with the conductor by entering this terrain. This might include, for instance, advice to the conductor to turn down an offer and to wait for the right opportunity. For a productive long-term relationship, with its inevitable ups and downs, both sides must trust each other.

Trust and honesty work on the manager's side as well. A good manager will have built up a series of close professional relationships with the key people in the profession who can engage conductors. If these critical people trust your manager for reliable recommendations you will short-circuit the time and effort needed to secure engagements from the key musical institutions. Classical music is still a small business and the reputation of a manager for fair and honest assessment is your most important link to a wider career.

The responsibilities of the conductor

There is a popular misconception (mostly amongst critics) that managers are Svengalis who push their artists into unsuitable careers and commercial decisions, against the true needs and wishes of the artists themselves. In a proper conductor/manager relationship, nothing should be further from the truth. The role of the manager is first to understand and evaluate the conductor's goals, and then to work to achieve them. When a conductor has taken on too much, the first person to warn him or her to cut down (as should be the case) is the manager. But while it is the manager's role to point out the consequences of decisions, it must be the conductor who decides. What you see, more often than not, is the reflection of what the artist, following advice and discussion, has decided to do (or not to do).

The role of the manager is therefore often overestimated, underestimated, or misunderstood. At their best, the manager functions behind the scenes, giving experienced and considered advice that enables the conductor to rehearse or perform under the best possible circumstances. A good manager wants to nurture talent and create a rewarding and successful long-term relationship where both sides gradually reach a common understanding of the conductor's needs, the manager's role, and what they can achieve together.

In this context, there is also a return trust factor that the manager has a right to expect from the conductor. There is a common saying that when a young conductor needs a manager, the manager does not need him, but when a conductor has become well known, it is the conductor who feels that they do not need the manager. Once established, it is easy for a conductor to forget or leave a manager who has invested time, advice, and experience in guiding them onwards and upwards. Conductors often decide to leave an agency for greener pastures or decide they "no longer need a manager." A well-known conductor can technically obtain his or her own engagements, but it seems to me that every conductor, at whatever career stage, continues to need trusted and objective outside advice.

Planning a conducting career

The first thing to establish – and this deserves a chapter in itself – is what the conductor wants from a life and career in this business. Strategic planning takes years, and may involve conversations now about a possible move in ten years' time, since concerts and music directorships are planned between two and four years in advance. The manager is responsible for evaluating if a conductor has the necessary skills and perseverance for the desired career, and delicately communicating this information. Both parties need to understand that aims, ambitions and skills change every few years, so there must be a constant process of review and evaluation applied to career planning.

On the assumption that the manager and conductor can mutually agree aims for the next five years, the manager must then explain what steps the agency will take to realize these plans. There should be realistic expectations on both sides. This moment is difficult for the young conductor who is likely to be relatively naive and sensitive to early setbacks, which are inevitable and unimportant from the manager's point of view, providing the talent is there. The manager needs to be reassuring, but the unpredictability of building a career is an essential message to get across at this stage. In other words, as a manager you want to prepare your conductor, to some degree, for the reality of the conducting profession and its many-layered complexities.

Orchestra relations and the re-invitation

The vagaries of a professional conducting career and the need for trust are exemplified in the feedback on a guest-conducting engagement. A conductor typically wants to know if it went well and if there will be a re-invitation. Even for an experienced manager, the answer to these questions is often shrouded in mystery. When you stand in front of 110 individuals to weld them into a cohesive unit reflecting your interpretive desires, the occasions on which all of them will agree on what you are doing (and whether you are doing it well) are rare. Opinions are, therefore, often as divided as the number of people involved. With the break-up of the old system of powerful autocratic conductors, the views of the individual musicians in this democratic ensemble have become even more important. There are now plenty of occasions when the general manager says the concert went well, and confirms that a re-invitation is fine in principle – only to say a few weeks later: "I am sorry, it turns out that the orchestra didn't like him/her after all." When you ask why, or in what particular way, the answer is often vague or inconclusive or along the lines of, "You know how it is with orchestras . . ."

Even when the initial post-concert evaluation is that the concert did not go well, the reasons (which could potentially be useful to the conductor) are often imprecise or personal. Comments such as "They didn't like his rehearsal technique" are useless to the manager unless a more exact definition is given, and although people say that music is a universal language, the personalities of conductors (particularly if they are not speaking their own language) can often rub up an orchestra the wrong way and give a mistaken impression of the conductor's character and style. When one adds to this complex mixture that a number of orchestras deliberately "test" conductors from their first rehearsals onward (to see whether they can "break" them through unhelpful or obstructive reactions to their musical requests) a complex picture emerges where it is difficult to give the simple and clear picture a conductor inevitably wants.

This is a profession of smoke and mirrors; things are so often not the way they first appear and there are no rules and no certainties. For instance, conductors must be aware – and beware of – the language in which they are addressed by the people who hire them. Generally, artistic directors and managers of orchestras are either in awe of conductors or treat them with exaggerated reverence and deference. As a result, the tenor of the remarks addressed directly to the conductor tends to be of a welcoming and adulatory nature: "The orchestra adore you!" "That was a wonderful performance!" "We would love to have you back any time!" What general managers say to the much less important manager of the conductor is often quite different and

Figure 20.1 Stephen Wright in discussion with Sir Colin Davis

indeed contradictory: "The orchestra were actually very divided, so I can't be sure when I could persuade them to have your conductor back." "I enjoyed the performance very much myself, but since the orchestra was divided, my opinion doesn't count." All of this generally leads up to: "I don't know whether or when we can invite your conductor back." There is a great deal of hypocrisy in the business in terms of treating the conductor with reverence and respect, but talking a completely different language to the manager. The great problem here is that conductors would obviously much prefer to believe the adulatory words of artistic directors or general managers rather than their own managers!

Trust again is central. If you do not trust that your manager is working in your best interests in passing on the reality of the situation, it will be hard to know whom to depend upon. Accepting the truth in such situations is disappointing but simply part of the nature of this business.

Reviews

Being judged publicly in print by music critics has always been a source of potential problems for conductors and managers. There are only two sensible rules that a manager can suggest: (1) Don't read reviews. (2) If you must read your reviews, then do not attach any more value to the good ones than to the bad ones.

Critics, like all listeners and members of orchestras, have completely different criteria when writing about music and performers to what was the case in the past. The standards of orchestra playing have steadily increased and audiences now have the sound of the finest recorded performances easily at hand. Everyone in the music business (with the obvious exception of the critics themselves) agrees that, with the perceived downturn in the general public's interest in classical music, critics are under enormous pressure from their editors to sensationalize, and therefore often trivialize, their reactions to performances and conducting personalities. Under these conditions, reviews cannot and should not always be taken seriously. Recent books on the classical music business have also completely distorted the position of the conductor. (Some of these accounts are so far removed from the actual experiences of those who practice these professions as to be unrecognizable.) It is essential that conductors, and managers, are not affected in the pursuit of their common aims by commentators who may have completely different agendas, or very little understanding of the real issues involved.

The music director

The pinnacle of a conducting career is becoming the music director of an orchestra and making it your own. Toscanini's NBC Symphony, Koussevitzky's Boston Symphony, Szell's Cleveland Orchestra, Mengelberg's Concertgebouw, and Karajan's Berlin Philharmonic were all perceived as one man's artistic and musical personality being expressed through the sound and interpretations of "his" orchestra. These relationships required decades of autocratic power which is no longer possible in today's more democratic and collaborative climate. While the new climate may or may not be desirable (a Russian conductor said to me recently, "democracy is all very well, but not in music"), the great musical partnerships of the last century were between orchestras and longstanding music directors – and to be a music director remains the most desirable goal of a conductor's career.

The position of music director, however, has radically changed. In this new era of co-operation, the conductor is involved in many aspects of the orchestra beyond rehearsing and making music, for example in contractual, personnel, discipline, and union matters. A conductor without the personnel and management skills (separate from the purely musical abilities) to deal with these questions will not be a suitable candidate for contemporary music-director positions. Furthermore, the finances of an orchestra now come from multiple and complicated sources, and music directors are expected to raise money from governments and businesses and to spend time with sponsors, volunteers, committees, and boards that underpin the maintenance of the institution. Today's music director has a plethora of non-musical responsibilities, and so orchestras now choose conductors for more than their purely musical abilities.

Another factor in today's music-director appointments is the commitment and the length of time that it realistically takes to achieve first-class results. Most of the great conductors mentioned above typically spent between sixteen and twenty weeks a year with their orchestras. Nowadays that would be regarded, both by the conductor and the orchestra, as too long or not necessary. But the pendulum has swung too far the other way. With all the attractive guest-conducting or operatic engagements conductors can get, orchestras have come to accept fewer weeks with their resident music director. Some orchestras have settled for as little as nine weeks a year, which everyone in the profession agrees is too little time to achieve the kind of closely identified style of interpretation and playing which was once the case. With the notable exceptions of orchestras such as Vienna, Berlin, the Concertgebouw, and St. Petersburg, this limited time with the music director has contributed to a more uniform orchestral sound around the world. So while the ease and speed of international travel has allowed music directors more varied musical experiences as guest conductors, and even the ability to fulfill two music-director posts at once, the shorter periods of commitment and shorter contracts can leave both orchestra and conductor dissatisfied with the results achieved.

Over the last fifty years, the partners, to whom managers represent conductors, have changed from being artistic directors at the head of musical institutions (with whom the dialogue about the artist's talents was therefore a natural one), to general managers much more oriented towards business, administration, and finance. This means, in turn, that the methods and language used in representing a conductor's qualities no longer find a naturally informed partner; instead of musical talent, the discussion is much more likely to focus on box-office pull, public appeal of personality, name recognition, with a polarization of the best candidates at either end of the age spectrum – such people tend to look either for brilliant young new stars or for venerable and aged maestros. General managers, therefore, often overlook the most musically qualified conductors whom the orchestra might need or desire. For the manager this means that new techniques of selling and representing conductors, who do not easily conform to these new norms, have to be found.

From the manager's point of view, the best parts of the job are enjoying the musical experiences of some of the most talented young conductors around today, having an ongoing involvement with the future careers of such people, and helping conductors to feel secure and well advised in what they are doing. When combined with a reciprocal trust, this results in a rewarding and successful partnership.

21 The future of conducting

LEON BOTSTEIN

When Hans Keller set about debunking musical professions he considered "phoney," his "hit list" was predictable: opera producers, music critics, musicologists, and of course, violists and conductors.[1] These professions were new to his generation as independent full-time activities; they were consequences of a historical process in Western Europe sociologists once termed "rationalization." During the second half of the nineteenth century, professions became more bureaucratized along lines of ever more narrowly defined specialties. These in turn demanded the creation of targeted processes of training and certification. Expertise, particularly in medicine and science, but in the arts as well became more competitive on a massive international scale justifying discrete divisions and narrow fields.

Music critics once did something else as professionals. They were composers (Schumann, Berlioz, Tchaikovsky, Debussy, and Virgil Thomson), teachers (Richard Wallaschek, Robert Hirschfeld, Eduard Hanslick, and Paul Henry Lang) or writers (consider Max Kalbeck, Ludwig Speidel, and, in the extreme George Bernard Shaw and Ezra Pound). Musicology became an autonomous academic field relatively late, and only in the generation of Guido Adler and Hermann Kretzschmar did music history emerge as a distinct branch of scholarship. In Keller's world (he trained in Vienna as a violinist and was forced to flee to England in 1938) great violists were actually violinists; no one set out to become a violist. Opera producers, in the contemporary sense, were entirely unknown.

Conducting as a profession

When Keller came of age, very few conductors only conducted and viewed conducting as their sole activity as a musician. Arthur Nikisch was the first major conductor to establish himself exclusively (unlike Hans von Bülow, who was a famous pianist and even composed) at a young age as a famous conductor. Nikisch more than anyone else shaped the image of the modern conductor, including an international career, a cult of personality, particularly in his primary venue, Leipzig, replete with a reputation for looks, charm, and charisma. Yet even Nikisch started out as a composer and violinist of promise and accomplishment. In the generation after Nikisch, Serge

Koussevitzky had been a sensational bass virtuoso; Wilhelm Furtwängler, Paul Kletzki, and Otto Klemperer composed in earnest. Arturo Toscanini once played the cello, and trained for that task. Eugene Ormandy was a violinist, as was Charles Munch. George Szell, like Bruno Walter, harbored ambitions to become a composer and continued to play the piano magnificently in public. Sir Georg Solti maintained a discrete public presence as a pianist, as has James Levine. Ernest Ansermet was a mathematician and wrote tracts about music, as did Hermann Scherchen, including the subject of conducting. They both were distinguished public intellectuals. Fritz Reiner trained as a pianist even though he quickly focused, Nikisch-style, exclusively on his career as a conductor. But he may have been the proverbial exception that proves the rule.

Keller's critique of conducting as a profession was characteristic of many of the key figures from a musical and cultural world obliterated by the rise to power of the Nazis and the ensuing war. Franz Schmidt, Arnold Schoenberg, and Igor Stravinsky hated conductors, Schmidt because he suffered under one (Mahler) and the other two because they harbored ambitions to become one. For them the only legitimate route to conducting was composition, which explains in part Anton von Webern's ambitions and frustrations with respect to conducting. Keller absorbed an attitude best articulated by Schoenberg; the emergence of a radical musical modernism seemed to coincide with the unfortunate evolution of conducting as a separate profession. Consider the notorious confrontation Schoenberg recounted with a conductor whose response to the Op. 9 Chamber Symphony was that the score was incomprehensible. Schoenberg mused, "Why did he have to pick on me in this sudden burst of wanting to understand."[2]

Keller's critique of conducting as a profession assumes that conducting does indeed require a distinct technique. But it must emerge as a subsidiary of some other solid musical achievement and training, either in performance or composition. For Keller, the modern profession of conducting is a consequence of the unreasonable highlighting of the centrality and glamour of the role. This happened in the era of Toscanini and Furtwängler. The glorification of the conductor flourished coincidentally with the first truly successful commercial recordings; it reached its peak with the nearly parodistic cult of Karajan and Bernstein sixty years later, in the 1980s. Larger-than-life expectations came to surround conducting and were underscored by its elevated public status as a distinct profession. This in turn destroyed the orchestra by turning orchestral playing into "an unmusical profession."

The source of that disaster was that the conductor had been anointed in the public imagination as the overriding source of a great performance. Professional conductors assumed the trappings of Nikisch-style "charisma," as well as the power and responsibility for leading a first-class orchestra in a context in which all concerned – conductor, orchestra and the public – assumed that the conductor had to be "at every given moment, more musical, more intelligent, more knowledgeable than every single player he conducts."[3] On these terms the professional conductor is bound to fail. Therefore "he has no artistic right to overrule" players who frequently know more, and are often indeed more musical, if not more experienced. Indeed no conductor, no matter how well trained, can fulfill the expectations Keller associated with conducting – not even Lorin Maazel and Pierre Boulez, who are perhaps the most musically skilled conductors working today. The modern professional conductor ends up either faking or criticizing musicians unreasonably, creating a disastrous morale. The cultivation of conducting as a profession has legitimated mannerisms and institutionalized habits of authority that exacerbate the natural tensions between orchestra musicians and maestros.

The conductor as musician

Keller's point, that conductors needed to do something else successfully and publicly in addition to conducting, remains valid. The artistic relationship between a conductor and a professional orchestra can survive only if the conductor is perceived by the musicians in the orchestra as contributing to music beyond the podium. The obvious collateral activities are composing (e.g. Mahler, Bernstein, and André Previn) and instrumental performance (e.g. Daniel Barenboim, Christoph Eschenbach, and in the past, Eugène Ysaÿe). As shown by the "early" music movement, there is now a third option, scholarship in the field of music, particularly if related to performance practices (e.g. William Christie). All conductors, even the instrumentalists and scholars, must have tried composition and be able to think like a composer. If composition and fundamental instrumental competence remain minimum prerequisites, then a high level of command of the history of music has become a third necessary attribute. Only with an active musical identity independent of conducting can the conductor, over time, command respect and lead with sufficient authority without having always to know better than the players on stage. A conductor's musical growth and distinguished musical personality must not be entirely dependent on orchestral musicians functioning as the conductor's subordinates.

The musical work that is not conducting should preferably be an activity orchestral musicians neither wish to nor can emulate, but consider useful to the conductor's role. One reason so many pianists become successful as conductors is that so few of the players in an orchestra ever claim to be as good a pianist. The same holds true for composition. The enterprise the conductor does apart from conducting must be outstanding. If it turns out to have been in the past, as in the case of Charles Munch's little-known career as a fine violinist (he had been concertmaster of the Leipzig Gewandhaus) it should have been visibly competitive. However, as the often disappointing conducting careers of former principal players in orchestras have shown, it is not enough to have been once as good as one of the players in front of you. Players in the orchestra help a conductor and engage in rehearsal if they sense a distinct contribution they themselves cannot make; they will give what they can in exchange for what a conductor uniquely provides. They do so not because the conductor is, in Keller's words "more musical and more intelligent," but because he or she has something special to offer.

The conductor must have the technical skill to conduct in order to communicate his or her distinct contribution. That is not always the case. Conducting demands the acquisition of technique that requires time and training to develop. Aaron Copland, like so many other composers and dozens of great solo instrumentalists, remained a mediocre conductor despite his great achievements. But once one attains the requisite technique, one should not live out one's professional life just as a conductor. The relevance of this idea could not be greater than in the current situation in which the symphony orchestra and classical musical culture, from concert life to recording, composition, and broadcasting find themselves.

A key practical consequence of the self-image of conducting as an autonomous self-sufficient profession is misleading advice derivative of particular images of "professional" behavior. Does one arrive as a guest conductor with one's own parts for works of the standard repertory except in exceptional circumstances? The answer is no.[4] In each city, orchestra, and venue the acoustic conditions and playing habits are different. Listen first, and do not presume to anticipate the outcome. The orchestra one encounters has its own experience making all the variety of sounds and articulations and balances any conductor might seek; the players may know how to adjust, particularly to an acoustic with which they are far more familiar. What the conductor needs to know, after listening, is how to ask for and make changes as a result of what he or she hears. Articulation and balances can be achieved using several different means. Furtwängler frequently stopped in rehearsal, even with his own orchestra in his own hall, and mused silently about what the orchestra or a soloist in the orchestra had just done before deciding whether he thought he needed to adjust it or not.

One needs to respect what the players are prepared to provide in response to one's physical technique as a conductor. Then one can define changes in sound, using different bowings or fingerings, for example. In the "fast" metronome markings in Beethoven, old bowings and fingerings will not work. But the players must participate in finding their means to achieve the articulations the conductor seeks. When the string sound in cantabile is not *semplice* enough and the playing is in high positions, a suggestion of a simpler fingering suffices; one does not need to say precisely which fingering works best. There is no universally valid way to achieve a particular effect, appropriate to all spaces and places. Vibrato is a perfect case in point; general rules collapse under the weight of differentials in the quality and type of instruments and the varying traditions of string playing. The same point applies to bow use. Orchestras that rely on the left hand for color and shading quickly adjust to suggestions focused on bow speed and placement. Marking the parts can be counterproductive and reduce a cadre of well-trained players with pride in their professionalism into passive-aggressive skeptics.

Perhaps as a result of access to a staggering diversity of recordings and a sophistication regarding interpretation and texts, musicians no longer accept the rhetoric and ideology of "the one and only correct way" to perform a work. Gunther Schuller still assumes an anachronistic adherence to a Toscanini-era modernist prejudice that there is objectively a "right" way to perform a work. A conductor needs today to be respected as a musician beyond conducting because a mood of collaboration in rehearsal toward fashioning an interpretation must be generated. One cannot rely any longer on an outdated and reductive notion of truth-telling, or its dubious descendants visible among today's conductors: narcissism and authoritarian mannerisms. As the case of Schuller reveals, when someone of his prodigious talent and exceptional accomplishment outside of conducting (as horn player, composer, writer, scholar, editor, arranger, teacher, administrator, and advocate) steps on a podium, the orchestra will go much farther than expected to accommodate him. They will tolerate nasty and harsh outbursts and even limited technical prowess in terms of baton technique, because they respect his musicianship, interpretative choices, and accomplishment.

Since the need for real conducting technique combined with a collateral musical activity is today reinforced by a cultural context that legitimates interpretative pluralism, it is sad that so many truly great musicians (ranging from Dietrich Fischer-Dieskau to Mstislav Rostropovich) have had only limited success as conductors. They never came to grips with the technique conducting requires. Gary Bertini tells of his experience with Arthur Rubinstein and the Jerusalem Symphony in Israel during the 1970s. Before a scheduled sound check, Rubinstein (then in his mid-eighties) confessed to always having wanted to try his hand at conducting. It was arranged that he would be given one hour to conduct his favorite piece. He chose Brahms's Symphony No. 3. He began and things quickly fell apart; he tried again with no luck. Rubinstein went to the piano and played the opening as he wanted it to sound. He returned to the podium and again a train wreck occurred, at which point Rubinstein put the baton down and smiled, saying "Now I finally understand."[5] Conducting looks deceptively easy.

New standards

The professional image of conductor as absolute dictator and authoritarian presence stemmed from the reputation of Mahler. The conductor as tyrant was, according to some critics, a model also deliberately cultivated by Toscanini. In Mahler's case, his legendary temper and dictatorial manner derived from an intensity and fanaticism that reflected the fact that he, like several of his near contemporaries, including Nikisch, Bülow, and Toscanini, were path-breaking representatives of new standards of public performance. They possessed an aesthetic ambition novel to most nineteenth-century orchestras. The ensemble Mahler inherited in Vienna in 1897 from Hans Richter (no less) was truly without discipline in the modern sense. One reason the tradition of the professional conductor as dictator had become out of date by the time Keller wrote is the remarkable progress in the professionalism of orchestral playing. We forget how astonished critics were at the level of precision and refinement when Hans von Bülow traveled to Vienna with his Meiningen Court Orchestra in the 1880s. The generation of Mahler and Toscanini dramatically improved discipline, particularly in the opera house, and pioneered new standards of public performance.

A widespread increase in higher standards of performance has been made permanent and universal by recording. Today's orchestras, even in the provinces of Europe and North America, are filled with exceptional players and musicians, who play accurately and with subtlety. Their skills are enviable even by comparison with late-nineteenth-century standards in major cities. The tone set by Toscanini with the NBC Orchestra, emulated by Rodzinski (who is said once to have brought a revolver to a rehearsal), Szell, and Reiner, became increasingly out of step with the character, education, training, and capacities of the players they themselves recruited. That generation of conductors established standards of performance with means no longer compatible with sustaining those standards. The conductor of the present and future will face technical prowess and a level of general musical skill in an orchestra far higher than ever previously existed. This is why individuals, even rank amateurs, without any talent or technique, seem to deliver respectable performances when they conduct. At no other time in history could orchestras of quality sustain the careers of so many undisciplined but theatrically alluring personalities on the podium.

As Keller predicted, there remains the chronic issue of morale. The problem of orchestral discipline remains unsolved. At least the famous dictators of the past were great. The new aspirants to the cult of personality or the dictatorial manner (and there are some) are less compelling. Morale has deteriorated as orchestras increasingly face the so-called professional conductor who cannot command the respect of the players. Ironically, the economics of today's orchestras and opera houses demand more technique and not less. More has to be accomplished in, by any reasonable historical comparison, severely restricted rehearsal time. Sergiu Celibidache's attitude notwithstanding, standard rehearsal allotments usually suffice with modern orchestras for most programs.

Given the remarkably high individual standard of competence among instrumentalists, it has become increasingly frustrating for string players to be in a section of an orchestra; the newest members in the back of a section play far better than their predecessors. Even wind players, who generally derive more personal satisfaction from orchestral work, often resent having to bend their will and adjust phrasing to the judgment of a conductor, should the conductor have a judgment and the capacity to control it. There is an acquired reluctance to play at one's best unless either forced or inspired to, in most if not all orchestras, since there is a conflict between the inherent artistry of the individual player and the routine lack of individuality demanded by orchestral playing. From the perspective of modern orchestras, the quality of performances has become too tied to conductors whose skills, preparation, and personality are so often suspect, and for good reason. The exceptions in terms of morale are those orchestras that are self-governing and autonomous; the London Symphony Orchestra, and the Berlin and Vienna Philharmonics, for example, select who conducts them. These ensembles take a pride in setting their own exacting minimum standards of performance, no matter who is on the podium.

The morale problem inherent in modern orchestras poses a special challenge to the contemporary conductor. Conductors who refuse to lead by dictatorial imposition or the display of superior knowledge at all times often discover that in some orchestras, poor intonation or wrong notes will not be corrected unless the conductor publicly points them out, even though the players know they have occurred. Orchestras can unwittingly deteriorate into acting like high-school students faced with a substitute teacher. If the conductor does not object, either he does not care or does not hear what is wrong. Why then fix it, even if it means a poorer performance? The contribution the conductor must make is to lead colleagues to work together to invest themselves in communicating as best they can through musical performance; this in turn requires appropriate psychological strategies. An atmosphere of technical collaboration must be cultivated in rehearsal, including the encouragement of questions and the querying of details. In a recent recording session, for example, a few players thought, as they should have, that perhaps a passage in a Strauss opera where C naturals were pitted against C sharps revealed an error in the parts. It created the opportunity to explain the unusual but striking compositional idea. The assertion of authority would have been more efficient, but far less effective. Intonation in winds and brass must be monitored by players on stage, who know one another's habits, not from the podium. A conductor can tune a single chord, but sustaining intonation over the course of a single work is a matter of habit controlled internally. Players must adjust to one another. A music director can solve the problem over time, but a guest must rely on the players after offering an opinion about what is wrong, given the voicing and scoring. Even with perfect pitch, intonation is relative. The violinist Roman Totenberg used to complain that perfect pitch was frequently a hindrance. He had to adjust because his pitch sense was invariably slightly higher or lower than the orchestras with which he played. Being flat or sharp is frequently a matter of perspective, even when being out of tune is undeniable.

Conductors should not be alone on the look-out for misprints and other errors as they rehearse. They should reward the active engagement of the members of the orchestra. The modern conductor must create an atmosphere in rehearsal in which section members feel able to raise questions, perhaps about bowing, articulation, or even notes, even proffering an opinion of how something might be improved. The conductor also has to be quick to recognize and disarm illegitimate intransigence or habitual rebelliousness. Orchestras know their own personnel and admire the conductor who handles the predictable arrogance or incompetence with finesse. Without a sense of common purpose and common responsibility a great performance is impossible. The modern marketing of the conductor, the mannerisms and style of self-promotion, and the undue public and journalistic fascination have made it hard to generate the requisite atmosphere of collaboration.

What has to change given the high quality of instrumental playing now in evidence is indeed the way conducting is practiced and conductors are trained. In this sense Keller's critique is helpful. Crucial as well is the reorganization of orchestras, creating opportunities for small ensemble performances for all players within the season, and allowing rotation in seating, solo and teaching opportunities, and player participation in programming. Likewise the perception of symphony concerts must change so that the players are not constantly reminded of their relative anonymity and disenfranchisement. The musicians on whom all orchestral performances depend should not be encouraged to withdraw from the deep professional identification with their work with which they began their careers. One key reason for an endemic spirit of resentment and resistance among first-class players in ensembles that could sound ten times as good as they routinely do is indeed the way conducting is practiced and viewed as a profession. The final reading of a work will in the end always be the conductor's responsibility. Therefore, the conductor has to bring to the podium something that holds the attention of the players, some value added. That special contribution to interpretation and performance quality will not come from the experience of conducting alone, no matter how much one does it. The manner in which conductors now have their careers advanced by more conducting of the same repertoire is misguided. The public, and ultimately conductors themselves, have allowed themselves to be deluded as to the role and autonomy of conducting in music and performance. Conducting must remain, as it originally was, part of a composite career in music.

The contemporary predicament

The challenges facing the contemporary conductor are unprecedented. First, classical concert music has drifted to the periphery of contemporary culture. Its cultural and political significance has atrophied. Orchestras and the tradition of composition for the orchestra were, in the nineteenth century, central aspects of national identity; at a minimum, they were socially and politically significant to civic life, even in America, where classical music has always suffered from its origins as European and not quintessentially American. During the Cold War, orchestras and orchestral composition were priorities in Communist regimes, as hallmarks of the successful democratization of high culture to the masses and internationally visible symbols of state prestige. That unique system of support has disappeared. By the late twentieth century, audiences seemed visibly older and were declining all over Europe and North America. Concerts appeared no longer to attract young people. A universal decline (with the exception perhaps of the Far East) in general musical education and amateurism has been observed, ironically coincident with the notable increase in the production of highly skilled professional instrumentalists. But for whom will they play?

Second, as classical music's larger role in culture was diminished, in favor of a vibrant and commercially viable array of popular cultural forms, the demand for and interest in an ongoing tradition of new music for the orchestra have also diminished. Blame has been placed on the mid-twentieth century, in which a radical modernism in music seemed to dominate. But it is not clear that modernism was ever so powerful. The fact is that today, there are no careers to be made through composition of concert music to the extent that was possible in Copland's generation. There are exceptions in every nation (e.g. John Adams and Philip Glass in the United States) but as the music-publishing industry will attest, new music for orchestras, of any kind, has become a fringe enterprise. The introduction of new music no longer rivals the attention and importance given new works in New York in 1893, Munich in 1910, or Paris and Vienna in 1913. In these years and places the premieres of Dvořák's "New World" Symphony, Mahler's Symphony No. 8, and works by Stravinsky and Alban Berg were controversial and highly significant public events. With the decline in the importance of new music, a link between present and past that has always been decisive to the conductor's task as interpreter has been severed. No conductor prior to the mid-1960s made a career as an interpreter of music from the past without a profound commitment to contemporary music. For Toscanini it was Puccini. For Reiner it was Strauss, Bartók and Weiner. For Koussevitzky and Stokowski, it was Stravinsky, Berg, Copland, and practically everyone else. For Walter it was Mahler and Pfitzner. For Munch and Monteux it was their French contemporaries. For Mravinsky it was Shostakovitch. The engagement with a contemporary aesthetic has been a key defining influence on the way the history of music was presented by conductors in performance. Nikisch's capacity to redeem the reputation of the then new Tchaikovsky Symphony No. 5 was influenced by direct encounters with new music and its authors (Wagner and Bruckner). These experiences shaped Nikisch's view of Beethoven, just as Wagner's compositional habits defined, for many generations, the manner in which Beethoven was idealized in performance. For those conductors who compose (Maazel, Previn, and Esa-Pekka Salonen), the relative irrelevance of new classical music is daunting. If the concert repertory is no longer going to expand through the addition of new works at the rate it once did in the years between 1820 and 1920, what can replace the role played by new music in sustaining a vital musical imagination in the interpretation of the music of the past?

Third, the economics of symphonic music have become dire; subsidy and patronage for orchestras and symphony concerts are more needed than ever before. In the post-World War I era, radio broadcasting capitalized on the increased market of educated individuals: classical music still retained its prestige as a widespread symbol of culture. Recording was the next boom industry and it helped carry the day well into the 1960s. In the early twenty-first century, broadcasting and the recording of symphonic music are economically moribund. They will not revive. The relative costs have far outweighed the capacity to earn a profit in either concerts or recordings. Just as classical and symphonic music have lost their centrality and cultural and political importance, their need for state support and philanthropy have increased. Yet the capacity and inclination to respond, in both North America and all of Europe, are understandably diminished. We are still in the grip of a reaction against the welfare state and notions of government subsidy, particularly of culture; the marketplace reigns supreme, with its criterion of competitive commercial viability. Furthermore only a so-called "elite" seems really concerned. In democracies, it is the majority that influences government spending. In the private sector, those with new money, insofar as they seek public recognition through cultural philanthropy, are more interested in the visual arts from painting to the movies; their tastes rarely tend to classical music. There are no parallels to the robber-baron generation that formed the major orchestras as civic contributions in American cities. Meanwhile, Europe has little if any tradition of private philanthropy; there is no evident surrogate to compensate for declining state support in the face of the rising costs of maintaining orchestras. Austria can justify subsidy of concert life in Vienna and Salzburg because classical music, packaged like Mozart candies, is a central part of the Austrian tourist industry. But elsewhere, who cares about a costly cultural institution with little if any audience or broad significance?

Fourth, technology and the attendant changes in the conduct of modern life in North America and Europe have conspired to render the crisis of the modern orchestra severe. With the advent of the compact disc, a relatively stable and indestructible format for recording exists. There will be ongoing improvements in sound recording, but they will not revive the economics of recording for orchestras. Any individual who can afford to attend concerts can buy a myriad of recordings as permanent possessions. No matter how often they are used, they won't scratch, melt, bend, or require fastidious care to help them survive. The CD format has permitted the vast expansion of the recorded library. Every conceivable work of music is recorded, albeit often by obscure ensembles and poorly. The massive archive of recorded sound – from the backlists of record companies from the 1950s, on to the radio archives of Europe, East and West, including Russia – is now available in CD format. One can buy literally dozens and dozens of versions of all the works in the standard repertory, conducted by old-timers and new faces. Major orchestras still record, using subsidies and fulfilling contract obligations with their players, although the rate of new recording has declined to a trickle. Reissues flourish. One can get on CD everything Reiner and Toscanini released, and everything they did not, including live broadcasts and pirate recordings.

All this can be listened to at home with fantastic high fidelity. Who wants to hear some unknown conductor, particularly not with one of the leading orchestras of the world, perform Beethoven, when, in the comfort of one's home, one can listen to Toscanini, even Oskar Fried, Mengelberg, and Mravinsky or Roger Norrington and Carlos Kleiber (if not also his father Erich)? The existence of the extensive library of recorded performances, combined with the atrophy in the role of new music, has wreaked havoc on how conductors today approach the standard repertory. Too many interpretative choices are made in reaction to recordings. The quest for originality of the late Giuseppe Sinopoli (1946–2001) was artificial and distorted, in large measure because a seemingly complete range of interpretative solutions had already been documented and he lacked a new source for himself. The public has fallen under the sway of nostalgia, helped by critics and record labels; we are told that the era of great conducting has passed, just as the great era of violinists, pianists, sopranos and everything else. Recordings have created a deceptively dangerous source for new conductors, as a potential short-circuit of the task of framing an interpretation for performance.

For the potential audience, the seat at home is more comfortable and one can even pause to get a snack. But classical radio is dying because even this allure of home listening is itself a declining habit. For all the richness of what can be bought on CD, no one is buying any more because no one wants to listen. It is estimated that in the United States, there are not more than a hundred thousand individuals who buy more than one classical CD a year, and that statistic covers albums featuring famous opera stars singing Christmas carols.[6] The average time spent listening to classical radio is fifteen minutes per day. The marketing research shows that the audience seeks something it already knows. No one sits by the CD player, or the radio, and listens to an hour-long work, much less a concert or opera recording. With the extension of more rapid and adequate Internet access, individuals will be able to access and download high-fidelity audio and video directly, including live performances from anywhere in the world: we will be able to attend and document concerts from a remote location. Yet with all these possibilities, do we not still have something to offer through the tradition of public concerts, that might make more of our contemporaries inclined to attend and listen to live symphonic music?

Creating a concert community

The sad fact, however, is that the social impetus behind concert attendance has disappeared. The audience for concerts before 1914, and still, albeit to a lesser degree, before 1950, was a coherent social grouping. Audience members knew one another. The concert was a place to be seen and to greet if not converse with one's peers. With the advent of suburbia, the enviable democratization of education, and the fluidity of demography, there is far more anonymity in concert audiences. The social elite whose predecessors were loyal to the symphony concerts would now rather be seen and meet in galleries, museums, and Hollywood events. The result is that ticket buyers to concerts do not expect to meet someone or to socialize except with the one person that may go with them. The concert now seems like an isolating event. One won't know who one's neighbor will be, and few will be friendly.

Nothing about the concert asks the individual to become acquainted with other audience members. The audience is silent and passive. For someone flirting with the idea of going to a concert, the prospect is daunting since the atmosphere is intimidating. The unsophisticated attendees are stared at if they clap at the wrong time, make noise, or speak when the music is playing. Kurt Masur stared down a New York audience for making too much noise, but he missed the point. He failed to realize that the concert ritual we have inherited cannot be preserved as a sterile, quasi-religious event that forces the listener into submission. In the late eighteenth century, audiences applauded in the middle, as in a jazz concert. We need to find ways of making the concert more inviting in a manner that brings audience members to life and offers them a new platform of shared experience.

The orchestra concert must, in most cities, seek to fashion, in the best sense, a community of common commitment, bereft of snobbery. Classical music, particularly the orchestral concert, has been victimized by its defenders. Reading music and skilled amateurism are rare among concert-goers. They have been replaced by record collecting as the means by which an individual becomes expert. Classical music today seems to demand more prior knowledge and training than it really does. Otherwise educated and curious individuals who have finished college, but never encountered orchestral music, have become scared off and say "But I don't know anything about classical music." A parallel absence of expertise does not prevent them from going to movies, the theatre, or museums and galleries. The naive but intelligent listener is not welcomed by symphony orchestras. Yet the untrained art-watcher or movie-lover have been embraced by comparable institutions and industries in the visual arts. No doubt instrumental music is not as accessible as those art forms with words and images, and requires either training or some mediation. Finding that mode of mediation is a major challenge in itself. One crucial disappointment has been the role played by scholars and teachers of music in the university. Instead of strengthening the tradition of music appreciation in undergraduate teaching, the experts in the American academy have taken the opposite direction. The place once occupied by basic music classes has been supplanted by courses on film and art history.

The most convenient solutions have been resounding failures, including so-called crossover concerts, popularizing the repertoire, or trying to spice up the concert with entertainment gimmicks. The worst of the ineffective attempts to enliven the concert have been those that explicitly "dumb down" the experience, particularly talking to the audience in either an offhand or humorous manner by conductors who actually have very little to say beyond platitudes. The problem of how to make a nineteenth-century ritual, in spaces either built a century ago or designed in imitation of them, alluring to a contemporary audience remains unsolved. However, a crucial clue to the solution is the fact that classical music faces the largest and best-educated potential audience in its history, with the most leisure time, most disposable income and the longest lifespan. They also, despite the widespread illiteracy in music, have the easiest access to learning the repertoire, new and old, through listening and reading about it. To exploit this potential, old tricks will not work. Since classical music and the symphony orchestra have receded in relative importance and economic significance, the efforts at marketing the new face and good looks of the next "star" have become ineffective. These are the harsh realities the modern conductor faces, not only at every concert, but particularly when he or she becomes a music director of an orchestra. There are no careers to be made the way Karajan and Bernstein did, because the infrastructure and context have changed so profoundly since the immediate post-World War II decades when their fame was established. Yet there are literally thousands of orchestras – professional, semi-professional and community orchestras – around the world, and many aspiring conductors. How can they address the current predicament?

Rethinking concerts

There are no glib answers. Yet there are helpful basic principles that can lead the conductors to develop responses to the challenges. At every concert the conductor must have a defined reason for conducting the music chosen for that particular audience: the demands of the specific time and place must be addressed. The conductor must forge a construct of meaning that confronts the reality that every concert is a civic and political event. The word politics is used here in its ancient Greek meaning of the "polis." People have gathered at a concert for a reason. That reason may seem mere habit, unarticulated tradition, or as in some cases, the belief that concerts and listening to live music are a refuge from everyday politics, a distraction, or an opportunity to experience art defined as a higher realm than the mundane. In each case the conductor must figure out how to respond. One cannot conduct thoughtlessly, as if in some abstract universal time and space, with an imaginary ideal audience in mind. The definitions of entertainment and boredom are not normative or stable; they are different in different places. The era of the travelling, jetsetting music director, who spends eight weeks a year in a city and has no profound link to the community, are numbered if not gone. Sir Simon Rattle set an example of how this problem can be solved during his tenure in Birmingham, as Leonard Slatkin (b. 1944) did in St. Louis. However will Sir Simon, now elevated to superstar status, grasp the needs of a unified Berlin, in a new Germany, in a shifting European

Community, to reinvent the role of the Berlin Philharmonic? The model of Karajan no longer works, as it did not for Claudio Abbado. Will Slatkin forge a new place for an orchestra in America's capital city? Few orchestras have so much untapped opportunity.

Whatever the results, the music director of the future must create and develop a civic and cultural purpose for the orchestra's home audience. Likewise the guest conductor has to ask the question, "Why this repertoire at this time to this audience?" well before formulating the musical interpretation. These "extra-musical" questions (if there is genuinely such a category) help determine the "musical" decisions. If one is invited to conduct in a place with a sense of its own traditions, particularly with respect to repertoire and performance practice, then a decision to counter them may be in order. Nothing can be more satisfying than rehearsing a first-class American orchestra, who came of age trusting the so-called "authentic" manner of performing Bach that evolved between 1960 and 1980, in the arrangements of Bach by Mahler and Stokowski. The rubato, *portamento*, vibrato, languorous tempos, and gradual dynamic shifts are foreign to the players and shocking to the audience. One must resist a reductive nationalism that claims that Czech orchestras play Dvořák and Janáček best, Hungarian Bartók, Polish Szymanowski, Viennese Bruckner, and American Copland. Alternatively, accept a guest invitation if the program justifies the individual conductor's presence as representative of a culture or tradition. The meaning of the concert and certainly the meaning of the orchestra as a whole in its community are profoundly influenced by non-musical and local factors that conductors must study, contemplate and engage. Conductors must become public intellectuals even more than Bülow, Toscanini, Mahler, Mengelberg, Furtwängler, and Bernstein were, for better or worse. The declining fortunes of symphonic music demand that conductors engage the issues in the world in which the symphonic music tradition seeks a place, much like those few conductors of the past who faced the challenge of fascism and dictatorship, either as collaborators or opponents.

In order to accomplish this, the conductor must know something more than music, narrowly defined. And in the field of music, the minimum knowledge of music history and repertoire, including techniques of research, must be far greater than in the past. Furthermore, it is important to remember that there never has been a great conductor who did not possess a sophisticated knowledge of literature, painting, and history. Too often the training of professional musicians and the atmosphere of competition renders the ambition of becoming generally articulate and literate irrelevant, but it is not. Great music-making derives its source not only from musical texts, but from constructed meaning that depends on the so-called extra-musical. The conductor of the future must be an intellectual in the best sense. Furthermore the remnants of the corrupted simplification of the concept of music, derived from absolutist aesthetics, must be put to rest. It has become widely held that music is somehow abstract, with purely self-referential meaning. This idea stems from Eduard Hanslick's 1854 tract *On the Beautiful in Music,* with its legendary notion of music as "tonally moving forms."[7] Hanslick did not maintain a consistent position and might have been horrified at subsequent elaborations of his idea. Music is never entirely detached from meaning understood in terms of words and images. The conductor of the future must recognize that music must be an indispensable form of life and human expression, with connections to life, either intentional on the composer's part or forged in the act listening. These connections are not merely self-referential, but relate to intimacy, psychology, biography, memory, and then to all aspects of thought, including other art forms. There is, in the end, some narrative the conductor must create through interpretation. That construct is determined not only by a reading of the score but the context of performance. The performance of Szymanowski in Poland by the same conductor will be something different for musical and extra-musical reasons from one in England. Likewise, performing Charles Ives outside of America must necessarily influence interpretative decisions, if for no other reason than that one cannot communicate Ives with non-American audiences the same way one does in America; yet Ives can be enthusiastically received in novel ways, and played differently.

Concert programming must change. Concerts should be curated the way museums curate exhibitions. No museum hangs a Da Vinci next to a Mondrian with a new work by a young artist to the side.[8] The assumption needs to be abandoned that any three works go together. The conductor has to have an explanation of a concert program design that is more than "I want" or "I like." The audience needs to sense an illuminating and enlightening logic. This has been termed "thematic" programming. The theme however cannot be subjective taste per se, unless a concert is personalized like a shirt and explicitly billed "Maestro X's favorites." Finding a valid underlying theme applies even to single-work concerts. The ideal concert season presents the audience with groupings, ongoing explorations of several approaches and ideas, concurrently and perhaps over a number of years.

Themes can be historical. One can develop concerts around the history of music, starting with biography: the composer and the historical context of his or her work. There are several approaches within the history of music, from influence and reaction, to context. Beyond music history there are formal issues in music that generate themes. These can be quasi-historical or purely formalistic. The most potent thematic rubrics are those that connect music with art, literature, politics, history, philosophy, and religion. This strategy also provides opportunities to forge alliances and collaboration with other cultural institutions in a city or region, from museums and libraries to community centers, schools, and universities. Themes that have powerful musical components sufficient to define many concerts include parallels to the history of art, connections to particular writers, responses to historical events and figures, relationships between music and ideas, and images of national identity. The list is endless and is in part determined by the specific location. Thematic rubrics are not always transportable. They have to fit local circumstances. Some thematic structures travel well but always require adjustment to local musical culture and habits.

Thematic programs, however, must fulfill three indispensable criteria. First, thematic programs have to be designed primarily by the conductor, not by a special brand of "artistic" personnel or programming staff; performance cannot be separated from the selection of repertoire. This is why the intellectual training of the conductor, particularly in history, is so crucial. Second, programs cannot be didactic in a simplistic manner. Third, the theme has to be comprehensible, clearly legitimate, and not intrusive. Effective thematic programs tend to have underlying historical justification. The theme has to offer the audience an evident linkage that does not determine how or for what to listen. There have been notorious thematic programs designed by individuals who wish to teach an audience that there are connections between works on the program. This is offensive. As in a good exhibition, the program must be constructed so that quite divergent responses are possible, including the possibility that the individual can ignore the overriding theme. As Thomas Bernhard's great monologue novel *Old Masters* makes clear, the Tintoretto painting, *Man with the White Beard*, which the protagonist returned to gaze at nearly every day for over thirty years, was hung by the Kunsthistorisches Museum in Vienna in a room defined by historical and regional criteria. The classification did not intrude in the individual's capacity to think for himself. So it should be at a concert.

There is after all, no neutral program. The standard potpourri system is arguing a weak case. Its argument is that music should not be organized like other art forms, and that subjective taste of the performer and presumed audience is sufficient. The mixed concert that offers a new or recent work, usually brief, a concerto with a soloist and a major work to close is a recent convention. The programs of a century ago were quite different, if for no other reason than that they included much more contemporary music.

What has driven programming in recent years is the growing masterpiece mania. As audiences have become less reliable if not less numerous, the conventional wisdom, bolstered by market research, has been that repertoire sells. The repertoire that sells is well known and famous. Since audiences are said to dislike contemporary music, a work in Romantic style written by a composer long dead whose name is not familiar (e.g. Josef Suk) is rejected because the audience will think it is a new work. If one wants an audience, we are told, give them Beethoven, Mozart, Mahler, Chopin, and a few chestnuts by composers whose other work is never played, like Bartók, Dukas, or Elgar. Even critics and veteran music-lovers have come to the bizarre conclusion that everything played has to be compared to some few greats. If one plays Hans Rott's symphony, someone is going to say it isn't Mahler, just as someone who encounters a symphony by Chadwick or Myaskovsky will respond that it isn't Brahms or Shostakovich.

Only in music is such nonsense tolerated. We see, buy, and hang art without accusing it of not being the *Mona Lisa*. We read and reread books without damning them for not being *Mrs. Dalloway*. And we certainly see movies without comparing them to a few movie classics. We all go enthusiastically to see painters from the past we have not considered before and read authors of the past whose reputations have come and gone. If we treated art the way we treat the history of symphonic literature from Haydn to the present, 90 percent of the collection hanging in museums would be relegated to storage, leaving three rooms open in the Louvre and the Hermitage, and bookstores would be empty.

Conductors are sitting on a treasure trove of music, most of it composed during the last hundred and fifty years, that lies unperformed or underperformed. This includes orchestral music, concertos, oratorios, choral music, and opera. Some of it is by famous names and some not. Curiously enough, every composer, not only Mahler or Wagner (and including quite obscure ones), seems to have if not a society then a band of dedicated advocates determined to propagate that composer's music. Most of this music from the past was once highly regarded and is quite stunning and more than deserving of performance, several times. Some of it loses its allure even after a few concerts, but the list of works, including concertos, that sustain interest over time, is massive. The problem is that soloists are reluctant to learn works for just one concert. Elmar Olivera had no success programming the Joachim "Hungarian" Violin Concerto despite two successful concert performances, including one in London and a recording. Yet the work is beautiful and thrilling. The same can be said for the violin concertos of Othmar Schoeck, Nikos Skalkottas, and Roberto Gerhard.

Once one abandons repeating the same works, it becomes clear that simple thematic rubrics invite the inclusion of less-performed wonderful works. And for those who never seem to tire of the same few works, nothing is so refreshing as performing them in a new context, surrounded with their own contemporaries, or works that influenced that favorite piece. The most dramatic consequence of opening up the full range of historical repertoire is that it offers the conductor a legitimate and fresh perspective towards the challenges of interpretation. The neglected repertoire holds keys to new insights on the limited list of masterpieces.

Combining under-represented repertoire from the past with a logic for programming concerts can restore a sense of purpose to live concerts. Something happens in such concerts that cannot be captured on records. A dynamic of interest and collective engagement, marked by curiosity and surprise, is generated within the audience. A welcome context is created for performing specially commissioned new music and recently composed works. Above all, the place of the symphony concert is redefined along the lines of a vibrant museum. The history of music can be systematically, controversially, and provocatively represented, with a serious, even scholarly critical and explanatory apparatus, replete with an educational function. A replacement for the "playbill" program and traditional program notes is long overdue. The civic importance of the orchestra as an institution should no longer be justified merely as a species of entertainment, but as a living museum, a cultural and educational enterprise that extends into the field of contemporary art. The sad fact is that the constant repetition of the same repertory, relieved by the occasional premiere, is not only false conventional wisdom, it has helped render the concert and the orchestra marginal even in terms of these goals. To lead the orchestra and realize its promise, the conductor of the future, apart from having impressive technical and musical achievements, must possess the necessary general education and the will to reconnect our vital tradition of musical expression to the culture, society, and politics of our time.

Notes

1 The technique of conducting

1. Discussion of the rise of conducting technique and of the disagreements about technique and training can be found in chapter 6 (The rise of conducting), chapter 17 (Conducting early music), and chapter 18 (Training conductors).

2. Henry Wood, *About Conducting* (London: Sylvan Press, 1945), p. 70.

3. John Barbirolli, "The Art of Conducting," *Penguin Music Magazine* 2 (1947), p. 17.

4. Max Rudolf, *The Grammar of Conducting* (New York: G. Schirmer Inc., 1950), p. 3.

5. Jean Vermeil, *Conversations with Boulez: Thoughts on Conducting* (Paris, 1989); tr. Camille Naish (Portland: Amadeus Press, 1996), p. 65.

6. Leopold Stokowski, *Music for Us All* (New York: Simon and Schuster, 1943), p. 216.

7. Bruno Walter, *Von der Music und vom Musizieren* (Leipzig: S. Fischer Verlag, 1957); *Of Music and Music-Making*, tr. and ed. Paul Hamburger (New York: W. W. Norton, 1961), p. 88.

8. Walter, *Of Music*, pp. 88–9.

9. Leonard Bernstein, "The Art of Conducting," in *The Joy of Music* (London: Weidenfeld and Nicolson, 1960), p. 150.

10. *Conversations with Klemperer*, ed. Peter Heyworth (London: Faber and Faber, 1985), p. 111.

11. Wilhelm Furtwängler, *Furtwängler on Music*, ed. and tr. Ronald Taylor (Aldershot: Scolar Press, 1991), p. 19.

12. Bernstein, "The Art," p. 150.

13. Private conversation with the author, London, 1979.

14. Richard Strauss, *Recollections and Reflections*, ed. Willi Schuh, tr. L. J. Lawrence (London: Boosey and Hawkes, 1953), p. 44.

15. Hermann Scherchen, *Lehrbuch des dirigierens* (Leipzig: J. J. Weber, 1929); *Handbook of Conducting*, tr. M. D. Calvocoressi (London: Oxford Unversity Press, 1933), pp. 187–8.

16. Richard Wagner, *My Life*, tr. Andrew Gray, ed. Mary Whittall (Cambridge: Cambridge University Press, 1983), p. 283.

17. Stokowski, *Music for Us All*, p. 214.

18. Walter, *Of Music*, pp. 132–3.

19. *The Art of Conducting: Great Conductors of the Past* (Teldec Video 4509–95038–3, 1994).

20. Adrian Boult, *Boult on Music* (London: Toccata Press, 1983), pp. 103–4.

21. Richard Osborne, *Conversations with Karajan* (Oxford: Oxford University Press, 1989), p. 105.

22. Ibid.

23. See chapter 7 for more on this subject from the players' point of view.

24. Walter, *Of Music*, p. 131.

25. Ibid.

26. William R. Trotter, *Priest of Music: The Life of Dimitri Mitropoulos* (Portland: Amadeus Press, 1995), p. 112.

27. Ibid.

28. Barbirolli, "The Art," pp. 17–18.

29. Walter, *Of Music*, pp. 83–4.

30. Barbirolli, "The Art," p. 18. See chapter 18 (Training conductors) for an argument against this thesis.

31. Bernstein, "The Art," p. 151.

2 Conductors in rehearsal

1. Both the *New Grove Dictionary of Music and Musicians*, second edn., 29 vols., ed. Stanley Sadie and John Tyrrell (London: Macmillan, 2000), and Vincent H. Duckles and Michael A Keller, *Music Reference and Research Materials: An Annotated Bibliography* (New York: Schirmer Books, 1994), often referred to simply as "Duckles," can direct conductors to the sources (often other printed editions or copies of manuscripts) of the printed editions available.

2. The *Journal of the Conductors' Guild* often publishes such lists. They are invariably the result of the practical experience of their working members.

3. Some publishing houses, having acquired scores under odd circumstances, appear to have disfigured them with error in order to cover their tracks. There is a rather famous twentieth-century score, widely performed, which is available at a cheap price. It contains more than sixty obvious blunders, all of which must be corrected before it can be played. Even an audience of hearing-impaired rock stars would know something was wrong. One can only wonder how (and why) such obvious errors came to exist.

4. *Allgemeine musikalische Zeitung*, supplement of December 17, 1817.

5. Chapters 1 and 21 contain suggestions about varying approaches to space and type of orchestra.

6. George Houle, *Meter in Music, 1600–1800: Performance, Perception, and Notation* (Bloomington: Indiana University Press, 1987).

7. Muti's rehearsals of Dvořák's Symphony No. 5 with the Bavarian RSO in 1993, and of Spontini's *La Vestale* at La Scala in the same year, are especially outstanding examples of this rehearsal technique. These films are not commercially available, but may be viewed in the Conductors on Film Collection at the Stanford University Archive of Recorded Sound.

8. Go first to Furtwängler's astonishing Brahms Symphony No. 1, recorded with the Berlin Philharmonic, Titania Palast, February 10, 1952 (DGG 415.662–2, among other releases).

9. Daniel Gillis, *Furtwängler Recalled* (Zürich: Atlantis Verlag; New York: Meredith Press, 1965) p. 65.

10. Ibid.

11. See, for example, Elizabeth A. H. Green, *Orchestral Bowings and Routines*, second edn, rev. and enl. (Ann Arbor, MI: Ann Arbor Publishers, 1957), a standard entry-level text, and Murray Grodner (ed.), *Concepts in String Playing: Reflections by Artist-Teachers at the Indiana University School of Music* (Bloomington: Indiana University Press, 1979). For younger players, investigate Dorothy A. Straub et al., *Strategies for Teaching Strings and Orchestra* (Reston, VA: Music Educators' National Conference, 1996).

12. Further discussion of when and how to mark parts can be found in chapters 1, 4, 5, 6, 7, 18, 19, and 21.

13. Study the film originally broadcast as *One Man's Triumph*, Bell Telephone Hour, 1966 and now marketed as *The Cleveland Orchestra: A Portrait of George Szell* (Kultur, 1393). The Stanford Collection also includes a private copy of Szell rehearsing Brahms's Symphony No. 3 at Severance Hall in 1957, originally filmed by WEWS-TV.

14. See chapter 17 for a further discussion of conducting early music.

15. There is further discussion in chapter 3 of seating and the ways in which the studio provides ways to overcome the acoustic and physical compromises necessary in the concert hall.

16. More on conductors who talk in rehearsal can be found in chapters 7 and 21.

17. This video, made in 1965, was produced by Unitel Deutsches Grammophon, DGG 440.072.291-3, and is commercially available at the time of writing.

18. This film, made in 1970 with RSO Stuttgart, is not commercially available, but may be viewed at Stanford.

19. See his rehearsal film at Lincoln's Inn, and his conversations with Sir Peter Brook on this subject (*Sir Thomas Beecham at Lincoln's Inn*, Granada Television program, 1958, with the Royal Philharmonic Orchestra). Excerpts were included in the *Art of Conducting*, IMG/BBC television documentary, January 1994, still commercially available on video and laserdisc (Teldec, 4509-95038-6).

20. In the Stanford collection, we have a remarkable film of Stokowski, at age eighty-eight, rehearsing his American Symphony Orchestra in the Rakhmaninov *Rhapsody on a Theme of Paganini*, with Jerome Lowenthal. This document is not commercially available at this writing.

21. The same advice is elaborated upon from the player's perspective in chapter 7.

22. He describes this himself in chapter 6.

23. For a superb example of this art, see Pierre Monteux in 1961 conducting the Chicago Symphony (VAI 69604) in Berlioz's *Roman Carnival* Overture. Or examine the discreetly economical but deeply musical accompaniment he provides to Rudolph Firkusny in Beethoven's Piano Concerto No. 3, with the London Symphony Orchestra in the same year. This film, made in London on October 24, is not commercially available but may be viewed at Stanford.

5 Choral conducting

1. In conversation with Margaret Hillis, Conductor, Chicago Symphony Chorus, c.1969. William Byrd is responsible for another great quote: "Since singing is so good a thing, I wish all men would learn to sing," from the "Preface" to *Psalms Sonnets and Songs* (London: Thomas East, 1588).

2. With the *Virtuose Musik* (EMI, 1971) and *Europaische Chormusik aus fünf Jahrhunderten* (EMI, 1972), reissued 1994, reissued by Collegium USA (Clarion, 2002), for example, Eric Ericson made the choral world aware not only of his chorus, but of Scandinavian choral music. Gary Anderson in the *International Choral Bulletin* 22/2 called it "The Swedish choral culture" (January, 2002). The Dale Warland Singers have spread that culture throughout the US with their performances and recordings.

3. Christoph Wolff, *Bach, The Learned Musician* (New York: W. W. Norton, 2000), pp. 170–1. Wolff discusses Bach's personal development in contrapuntal writing, and the influence of

Vivaldi's Italian Concertos in bringing about changes in his musical thinking, language and design, from which he created a genuinely personal style.

4. Julius Herford, workshop on *Ein deutsches Requiem*, fourth movement, San Diego State University, 1955. There is also an analysis of the first movement in Julius Herford and Harold Decker, eds., *Choral Conducting, A Symposium*, second edn, (Englewood Cliffs, NJ: Prentice-Hall, Inc., 1973), pp. 217–24.

5. Vance George, San Francisco Symphony Chorus, 2001.

6. For a useful analysis of each vocal line see Walter Gray, *The Sacred Motets of William Byrd*, Ph.D., dissertation, University of Wisconsin, pp. 89–91.

7. Robert Craft, *Dialogues* (Berkeley: University of California Press, 1982), p. 46.

8. Robert Shaw in rehearsal, Blossom Festival School of the Cleveland Orchestra, at Kent State University, Ohio, 1971–8. Singing pitches and counting rhythms simultaneously was a device Shaw used throughout his life.

9. John Moriarty, *Diction* (Boston: Schirmer, 1975). Part I is published for choruses, including vowels and consonants in four languages with eighty-one exercises. Another fine reference is David Adams, *A Handbook for Diction for Singers* (Oxford: Oxford University Press, 1999) covering Italian, German, and French.

10. This is an exercise and concept from Paul Salamunovich, former Director of the Los Angeles Master Chorale, used in workshops and rehearsals.

11. James Fankhauser, "Choral/Orchestral Balance," *Choral Journal* (August 1969), pp. 5–7.

12. Robert Page often used the term "in the hum" with his Cleveland Orchestra Chorus (1973–82). It is effective in creating a warm, hushed effect.

13. Bobby McFerrin used this metaphor for hushed singing in a Chorus America Convention in Denver, Colorado on June 7, 2002.

14. The brackets, slurs, accents, and pauses help the eye group the patterns, and the "d" consonants, and crescendos and decrescendos help the voice articulate those patterns. These articulation concepts are a combination of Baroque keyboard techniques and vocal ideas Robert Shaw used for Bach's Mass in B minor in 1962.

15. Robert Page in rehearsal, Cleveland Orchestra Chorus, 1975–83.

16. Robert Shaw in rehearsal, Kent, Ohio, 1971.

17. Robert Shaw in rehearsal, Kent, Ohio, 1971.

18. See Robert W. Demaree Jr. and Don V. Moses, *The Complete Conductor* (Englewood Cliffs: Prentice-Hall, Inc., 1995), pp. 109–15, for advice on auditions. This is perhaps the best book on the myriad aspects of conducting in print. It is comprehensive, detailed and full of information for all conductors.

19. For more exercises, see K. Phillips, *Teaching Kids To Sing* (New York: Schirmer Books, Macmillan Inc., 1992)

20. Margaret Hillis, *At Rehearsals* (Barrington, IL: American Choral Foundation, The Letter Shop, 1969). This booklet contains standard markings and language guides. Tip: to sound authentically German use an "ee" [i] tongue position, the middle of the tongue arching to the middle of the upper teeth, the tip of the tongue resting on the inside of the lower teeth. German is spoken with a floating tongue. English speakers who relax the tongue flat on the floor of the mouth will sound under pitch, not genuinely German. This is helpful for the choral chamber music of Schubert, Schumann, and Brahms.

21. There is considerable advice on bowing, balance, part marking, and working with orchestras in chapters 1, 2, and 5 of *The Complete Conductor*. Don V. Moses, Robert W. Demaree, Jr., and Allan F. Ohmes, *Face to Face with an Orchestra* (Princeton, NJ: Prestige Publications, Inc., 1987) is currently out of print but a second edition is in preparation. It includes excellent discussions of choral/orchestra issues and ideas for preparing Handel's *Messiah*, Bach's *Magnificat* and Vivaldi's *Gloria*.

22. Igor Markevich in conversation with Otto Werner-Mueller, Head of Conducting Department, Curtis Institute of Music. Marking of parts is also discussed in chapters 1, 2, 4, 6, 7, 18, 19, and 21 of this volume.

23. See Demaree and Moses, *The Complete Conductor*, pp. 115–16, for more ideas on seating singers and seating arrangements for orchestra.

24. Thomas Lloyd, "When the Orchestra Arrives," *Choral Journal* (December 1999), pp. 35–45. "An imaginary plane across the middle of your body" comes naturally to most conductors. This and many other ideas regarding choral/orchestral preparation are clearly expressed in this article.

25. See Demaree and Moses, *The Complete Conductor*, pp. 278–82, for examples.

8 The rise of conducting

1. Professor Murchard, "Discovery of Ancient Greek Tablets Relative to Music," *Harmonicon* 3 (April–May 1825), pp. 56, 76; cited from Elliott W. Galkin, *A History of Orchestral Conducting in Theory and Practice* (New York: Pendragon Press, 1986), pp. 245, 487–8.

2. See Pierre Bourdelot and Pierre Bonnet, *Historie de la musique et de ses effets* (1715) in Othmar Wessely, ed., *Die grossen Darstellungen der Musikgeschichte in Barok und Aufklärung*, 4 vols. (Graz: Akademische Druck, 1966), vol. III, pp. 175–6.

3. This practice is known as cheironomy (from the Greek *cheir:* "hand") and was practiced in ancient Egypt, India, China, and Israel. See Curt Sachs, *The Rise of Music in the Ancient World: East and West* (New York: W. W. Norton and Co., 1943), p. 216.

4. The melodic formulas used by Jews to chant the Bible were initially indicated with right-hand signals (*Talmud*, Berakhot 62a), which became the basis for the symbols added to the written text by the Masorites (AD 500–1000). See Abraham Zvi Idelsohn, *Jewish Music and Its Historical Development* (New York: Schocken Books, 1967); rept. (New York: Dover, 1992), p. 67. The Christian transition to neumes (from the Greek *neuma:* "gesture") is harder to document since the practice of cheironomy did not survive.

5. It became standard to conduct choral works with orchestra using a baton, but the use of the baton also indicates that the orchestra conductor, and not the choir master, is the real leader. In chapter 5 of this volume, Vance George encourages all choral conductors to use a baton.

6. Heinrich Christoph Koch, *Musiklexikon* (Frankfurt am Main: August Hermann dem Jungern, 1802), *s.v. Niederschlag* (Greek: *Thesis*) (downbeat). "This beat has been named 'down-beat,' because one moves the hand downward when one is to give the beat in this part of the measure."

7. Jean-Jacques Rousseau, *Dictionnaire de musique* (Paris: Chez la veuve Duchêsne, 1768), *s.v. "frappe"* (downbeat).

8. Thomas Balthasar Janowka, *Clavis ad Thesaurum Magna Artis Musicae* (Prague: In Magno Collegio Carolino Typis Georgij Labaun, 1701), *s.v. tactus.*

9. Galkin gives examples from Westminster to Rome from the sixteenth through the nineteenth century. Galkin, *History of Orchestral Conducting*, pp. 437–9. France seems to be an exception where divided leadership was used in church.

10. Carl Philipp Emanuel Bach, *Versuch über die wahre Art das Clavier zu spielen* (Berlin, 1753–62); tr. William J. Mitchell (New York: W. W. Norton, 1949), pp. 34–5.

11. See Johann Joachim Quantz, *Versuch einer Anweisung die Flöte tranersière zu spielen* (Berlin: J. F. Voss, 1752), *s.v. Anführer*, and Leopold Mozart, *A Treatise on the Fundamental Principles*

of Violin Playing, tr. Editha Knocker (London: Oxford University Press, 1948), pp. 216, 224.

12. The French violin-bow conductors, including François-Antoine Habeneck (1781–1849), and the unusual audible time-beating at the opera are both covered in chapter 10 (The French tradition).

13. Wilhelm Joseph von Wasielewski, *Aus siebzig Jahren: Lebenserinnerungen* (Stuttgart: Deutsche Verlags-Anstalt, 1897), p. 92.

14. In describing the Gewandhaus before Mendelssohn, for example, Wilhelm Adolf Lampadius makes no mention at all of these conductors and reports only that "the symphonies had always been directed by the first violinist standing at his desk." Wilhelm Adolf Lampadius, *Felix Mendelssohn-Bartholdy. Ein Gesammtbild seines Lebens und Wirkens.* (Leipzig: F. E. C. Leuckart, 1886), p. 207.

15. Richard Wagner, *Mein Leben* (Munich: Paul List Verlag, 1963), p. 72; *My Life*, tr. Andrew Gray, ed. Mary Whittall (Cambridge: Cambridge University Press, 1983), pp. 56–7.

16. In practice, the composer was often given this honor. Hiller reports that Ferdinand David allowed him to conduct his G minor concerto in 1843, even though it was still David's duty. Ferdinand Hiller, *Felix Mendelssohn-Bartholdy, Briefe und Erinnerungen* (Cologne: M. Du Mont-Schauberg'schen Buchhandlung, 1874); second edn. (Cologne, 1878), pp. 187.

17. See Charles Burney, *An Account of the Musical Performance in Westminister Abbey, and the Pantheon in Commemoration of Handel* (Dublin: n.p., 1785), pp. 10–11. As was the French practice for large ensembles, three *chefs d'attaque* were also used as deputy conductors.

18. See H. C. Robbins Landon, *The Symphonies of Joseph Haydn* (London: Universal Edition and Rockliff, 1955), pp. 435–551.

19. George Hogarth, *The Philharmonic Society of London* (London, 1862). Cited from Miles Birket Foster, *The History of the Philharmonic Society of London, 1813–1912* (London: John Lane, The Bodley Head, 1912), p. 6, and Robert Elkin, *Royal Philharmonic: The Annals of the Royal Philharmonic Society* (London: Rider and Company, 1942), p. 15.

20. Orchestras and conductors have always battled over the number of rehearsals. While Mendelssohn often got additional rehearsals from his players, two rehearsals remained standard at the Gewandhaus until the twentieth century. Fürtwangler, being unable to get more rehearsals in 1922, simply gave fewer concerts. From 1875 on, one of the Gewandhaus rehearsals became open to the public. Reinecke writes, that from then on there was "really no

longer a concert with two rehearsals, but a rehearsal with two concerts." Cited from Fritz Hennenberg, *The Leipzig Gewandhaus Orchestra* (Leipzig: Veb Edition, 1962), p. 19.

21. See the *Spectator* (London) July 2, 1842, which complains that "the bills of the present season are not only, substantially, those of the last, but of every season for the last twenty years."

22. Chorley is comparing the Philharmonic to the Paris Conservatoire orchestra under Habeneck. Henry F. Chorley, *Music and Manners in France and Germany*, 3 vols. (London: Longman, 1841); repr. (New York: Da Capo, 1984), vol. III, p. 66.

23. Spohr's three accounts are (1) a letter to Wilhelm Speyer, April 14, 1820, in E. Speyer, *Wilhelm Speyer, der Liedercomponist, 1790–1878* (Munich, 1925), which seems to indicate that he bowed to tradition (see Adam Carse, *The Orchestra from Beethoven to Berlioz* [Cambridge: W. Heffer and Sons Limited, 1948]; repr. [New York: Broude Brothers, 1949], p. 319), (2) an article published a few months later, "Musikalische Notizen/ gesammelt von Louis Spohr während seines Aufenthalts in London vom Ende Februars Juny 1820," *Allgemeine musikalische Zeitung* 22/31 (Leipzig, 1820), col. 524, and (3) the longest account written decades later in his autobiography, Ludwig Spohr, *Selbstbiographie* (Kassel and Göttingen, 1860–1); tr. Anon., *Autobiography* (London: Longman and Green, 1865), vol. II, pp. 82–3. The story was sanctioned by George Hogarth, who was also the Society Secretary from 1850–64 and wrote an official history of the Society: *The Philharmonic Society of London* (see note 19 above). Hogarth, though, did not arrive in London until 1830 (when he became a prominent critic). The passages about Spohr's introduction of the baton, however, are directly quoted in Foster's and Elkin's histories of the Philharmonic (also cited in note 19). From the mention of F. Ries as the conductor, in Spohr's longest version, Adam Carse deduced that the date must have been May 8, and not April 10. When Arthur Jacobs found no supporting evidence, he decided it was all "the failing memory of an aging man." Arthur Jacobs, "Spohr and the Baton," *Music and Letters* 21/4 (1950), p. 307.

24. Spohr, *Autobiography*, vol. II, p. 83.

25. Ignaz Moscheles, *The Life of Moscheles with selections from his Diaries and Correspondence*, tr. A. D. Coleridge, 2 vols. (London: Hurst and Blackett, 1873), vol. I, p. 76.

26. Letter from London, May 26, 1829. Sebastian Hensel, *Die Familie Mendelssohn*

(Berlin: 1879); 14th edn. (Berlin: Verlag von Georg Reimer, 1911), vol. I, p. 209; *The Mendelssohn Family (1729–1847): Letters and Journals*, tr. Carl Klingemann (New York: Harper and Brothers, 1882), vol. I, p. 184. This letter to his sister Fanny, written after he made his London debut on May 25, 1829, includes the information that Mendelssohn had his white stick "made for the purpose (the maker took me for an Alderman and would insist on decorating it with a crown)." This confirms that the baton was viewed primary a symbol of authority and not a musical instrument.

27. *Morning Post* (London), May 27, 1829. The *Morning Post* critic probably overstates the case a bit. In 1829 many continental orchestras still had some form of divided or alternating leadership.

28. John Ella recalls the "frowns of the Fiddlers, whose authority Mendelssohn's baton so completely usurped." Supplement to *Musical Union Record* (London), June 11, 1867.

29. The history of English conducting from this point is continued in chapter 13: The English tradition.

30. George R. Marek, *Gentle Genius: The Story of Felix Mendelssohn* (New York: Funk and Wagnalls, 1972), p. 219. Marek claims this is a recent discovery.

31. Johannes Forner, et al., *Die Gewandhauskonzerte zu Leipzig 1781–1981* (Leipzig: VEB Deutscher Verlag für Musik, 1981), p. 68.

32. Carse, *The Orchestra*, p. 297.

33. Charles Hallé, *The Autobiography of Charles Hallé with Correspondence and Diaries*, ed. Michael Kennedy (London: Paul Elek Books, 1972); (New York: Barnes and Noble, 1973), p. 116.

34. Robert Schumann's review of Mendelssohn's first concert at the Gewandhaus, October 4, 1835. Schumann, *Schumann on Music: A Selection from the Writings*, tr., ed. and annot. Henry Pleasants (New York: Dover Publications, Inc., 1988), p. 66.

35. Ercole Bottrigari, *Il Desiderio, or Concerning the Playing Together of Various Musical Instruments*, tr. Carol MacClintock (Rome: American Institute of Musicology, 1962), p. 58; also in *Women in Music: An Anthology of Source Readings*, ed. Carol Neuls-Bates, rev. edn. (Boston: Northeastern University Press, 1996), p. 46.

36. H. Bertram Cox and C. L. E. Cox, *Leaves from the Journals of Sir George Smart* (London: Longmans Green and Co., 1907); (New York: Da Capo, 1973), p. 212.

37. Letter of November 12, 1838. Moritz Hauptmann, *The Letters of a Leipzig Cantor*

being the Letters of Moritz Hauptmann to Franz
Hauser, Ludwig Spohr, and Other Musicians,
2 vols., ed. Alfred Schöne and Ferdinand Hiller,
tr. and arr. A. D. Coleridge (London and New
York: Novello, Ewer and Co, Richard Bentley
and Son, 1892); repr. (New York, 1972), vol. I,
p. 189.

38. England sent eight music critics from as
many papers and Mr. Robertson drew for the
Illustrated London News. Even more were sent to
cover the visit of Queen Victoria and Albert to
Germany. Many other musicians, like Smart,
Hallé, and Berlioz, attended and left memoirs.
The collected reports of Spohr's and Liszt's
conducting are forthcoming in Bowen, "Reports
of the Bonn Beethoven Festival."

39. Musical World (London), September 4,
1845, p. 422.

40. Cox, Smart, p. 312.

41. "Notes on the Beethoven Festival," The
Athenaeum (London), August 16, 1845, p. 815,
and "Beethoven Festival at Bonn," Morning Post
(London), August 15, 1845. While both are
unsigned, Chorley wrote in the Athenaeum and
Morris Barnett corresponded for the Post.

42. Max Maria von Weber [son of Carl], Carl
Maria von Weber, Ein Lebensbild (Leipzig: E.
Keil, 1864); tr. J. Palgrave Simpson, Carl Maria
von Weber, the Life of an Artist (London:
Chapman and Hall, 1865), vol. I, p. 354.

43. Cox, Smart, p. 140.

44. Berlioz, Hector, Mémoires, (Paris, 1870); tr.
and ed. David Caivns, (New York: W. W. Norton
and Co., 1975), p. 306.

45. Letter from Weber to Ferdinand Praeger,
"About the Interpretation of Euryanthe." Anton
Schindler says this letter was published in the
Berliner MusikZeitung, No. 28, 1827. (Anton
Schindler, Beethoven as I Knew Him, tr.
Constance S. Jolly and annot. Donald W.
MacArdle from the 3rd edn. of 1860 [Chapel
Hill: The University of North Carolina Press,
1966], p. 410.) It is cited most often from Felix
Weingartner, On Conducting, tr. Ernest Newman
(New York: Edwin Kalmus, 1934), p. 35, but is
cited here from a longer passage in Carl
Bamberger (ed.), The Conductor's Art (New
York: McGraw-Hill, 1965), pp. 19–20.

46. Bamberger, Conductor's Art, p. 20. For more
on the history of the ideology of interpretation
and its relationship to tempo, see José Bowen,
"The Conductor and the Score; The Relationship
between Interpreter and Text in the Generation
of Mendelssohn, Berlioz and Wagner," Ph. D.
dissertation, Stanford University, 1994.

47. Moritz Hanemann, Aus der Musikerwelt
(Berlin, 1875), p. 90, cited from Carse, The
Orchestra, p. 345.

48. Richard Wagner, "Erinnerungen an
Spontini," Gesammelte Schriften, 14 vols., ed.
Julius Kapp (Leipzig: Hesse & Becker Verlag,
1914), vol. V, p. 116; Prose Works, 8 vols., tr.
William Ashton Ellis (London: Routledge and
Kegan Paul Ltd., 1892), vol. III, p. 130.

49. Wagner, "Spontini," p. 134.

50. J. T., "Notes of a Musical Tourist,"
Harmonicon 8 (Jan. 1830), p. 5. "J. T." is the only
indication of authorship for this article.

51. Footnote to J. T., "Notes of a Musical
Tourist."

52. Daniel J. Koury, Orchestral Performance
Practices in the Nineteenth Century (Ann Arbor:
UMI Research Press, 1986), p. 35.

53. "The Oratorios," Harmonicon 40 (Apr.
1826), p. 85.

54. Eduard Devrient, Meine Erinnerungen an
FMB und Seine Brief an mich (Leipzig: J. J.
Weber, 1869), p. 63; My Recollections of FMB and
His Letters to Me, tr. Natalie Macfarren (London:
P. Bentley, 1869), p. 59. See also Ferdinand
Hiller, Felix Mendelssohn-Bartholdy, Briefe und
Erinnerungen (Cologne: M. Du
Mont-Schauberg'schen Buchhandlung, 1874);
second edn. (Cologne, 1878), vol. I, p. 134, and
Charles Salaman, "Pianists of the Past: Personal
Recollections by the late Charles Salaman,"
Blackwood's Edinburgh Magazine 170/1031
(Sept. 1901) (Edinburgh: William Blackwood;
London: T. Cadell and W. Davis, 1817–1905),
p. 308.

55. Cox, Smart, p. 310.

56. See Koury, Orchestral Performance Practices,
p. 80.

57. Carse, The Orchestra, p. 345.

58. Wagner, "Spontini," p. 124.

59. Devrient, Meine Erinnerungen an FMB,
p. 71.

60. Berlioz, Mémoires, p. 297.

61. Elise Polko, Erinnerungen an Felix
Mendelssohn-Bartholdy (Leipzig, 1868), p. 78.

62. Athenæum (London), May 18, 1844.

63. Morning Post (London), May 14, 1844.

64. Wilhelm Adolf Lampadius, Felix
Mendelssohn-Bartholdy. Ein Gesammtbild seines
Lebens und Wirkens (Leipzig: F. E. C. Leuckart,
1886), p. 373; tr. W. L. Gage, The Life of Felix
Mendelssohn-Bartholdy (Boston: Oliver Ditson,
1887), p. 329.

65. Spectator (London), May 18, 1844.

66. The "treatise" is actually an appendix, L'Art
du chef d'orchestre, which Berlioz added to the
second edition of his Grand Traité
d'instrumentation et d'orchestration modernes in
1855; tr. Mary Clarke, A Treatise of Modern
Instrumentation and Orchestration to which is
appended The [sic] Chef d'orchestre (London and

New York: J. L. Peters, 1858); rev. edn. Joseph Bennett (London and New York: Novello, Ewer and Co., 1882), p. 246. Berlioz the conductor is discussed in chapter 10.

67. Berlioz, *Chef d'orchestre*, p. 245.

68. *Times* (London), March 25, 1852.

69. *Illustrated London News*, June 18, 1842.

70. Letter, April 3, 1835. Moritz Hauptmann, *The Letters of a Leipzig Cantor being the Letters of Moritz Hauptmann to Franz Hauser, Ludwig Spohr, and Other Musicians*, 2 vols., ed. Alfred Schöne and Ferdinand Hiller, tr. and arr. A. D. Coleridge (London and New York: Novello, Ewer and Co, Richard Bentley and Son, 1892); repr. (New York, 1972), vol. I, pp. 123–4.

71. Franz Liszt, "The *Perseus* of Benvenuto Cellini," letter from Florence, November 30, 1838, *Revue et Gazette musicale de Paris*, January 13, 1839, pp. 14–15; *Lettres d'un bachelier ès musique 1835–1841*; tr. and annot. Charles Suttoni as *An Artist's Journey* (Chicago and London: University of Chicago Press, 1989), p. 156.

72. David Lloyd-Jones, "Borodin on Liszt," *Music & Letters* 42 (1961), p. 118.

73. *Morning Post* (London), June 7, 1824, cited from Adrian Williams, *Portrait of Liszt by Himself and His Contemporaries* (Oxford: Clarendon Press, 1990), p. 18.

74. Letter to Pierre Wolff, May 2, 1832 in Franz Liszt, *Briefe*, ed. La Mara [Marie Lipsius]. (Leipzig: Breitkopf & Härtel, 1893]; *Letters of Franz Liszt*, tr. Constance Bache, 2 vols. (New York: Charles Schribner's Sons, 1894); repr. (New York: Greenwood Press, 1969), vol. I, pp. 8–9.

75. John Knox Laughton, *Memoirs of the Life and Correspondence of Henry Reeve, C.B., D.C.L.*, 2 vols. (London: Longmans, Green and Co., 1898), p. 49.

76. Wilhelm von Lenz, *Die grossen Pianoforte-Virtuosen unserer Zeit* (Berlin, 1872); tr. Madeleine Baker, *The Great Piano Virtuosos of our Time* (New York: G. Schirmer, 1899); rev. edn. tr. Philip Reder (London and New York: Regency Press, 1971), p. 7.

77. Franz Liszt, full score of *Die Legende von der Heiligen Elisabeth* (Leipzig, C. F. Kahnt, 1870), p. 69.

78. *Figaro* (Berlin), February 18, 1843, cited from Peter Raabe, *Franz Liszt: Leben und Schaffen*, 2 vols. (Stuttgart, 1931); rev. edn. in one vol. (Tutzing: Hans Schneider, 1968), p. 254, fn. 165.

79. Franz Liszt, "Letter on Conducting," to Richard Pohl, November 5, 1853, cited from Ernst Burger, *Franz Liszt: A Chronicle of his Life in Pictures and Documents*, tr. Stewart Spencer

(Princeton: Princeton University Press, 1989), p. 341.

80. Ibid. "Nous sommes pilotes, et non manoeuvres."

81. Hermann Uhde writing after he saw Liszt conduct Beethoven's Ninth in 1870, *Musica sacra* 11 (1910), p. 131, cited from Raabe, *Franz Liszt*, p. 255, fn. 165; the translation is adapted from Hugh Macdonald's in his "Liszt the Conductor," *Journal of the American Liszt Society* 38 (July–December 1995), p. 85. It appears in the original language along with many other contemporary reports in José Bowen, "The Missing Link: Franz Liszt the Conductor," *Basler Jahrbuch für Historische Musikpraxis* 24, 2000 (Basel: Schola Cantorum Basiliensis, 2002), pp. 125–50.

82. *Illustrated London News*, June 12, 1852.

83. Richard Wagner, *Briefe an Uhlig von Zürich*, February 13, 1852, in *Selected Letters of Richard Wagner*, tr. and ed. Stewart Spencer and Barry Millington (London: J. M. Dent and Sons Ltd., 1987), p. 250.

84. Richard Wagner, "Über Schauspieler und Sänger," in vol. XII of *Gesammelte Schriften*, p. 376.

85. Wagner, *Uhlig*, p. 250.

86. Richard Wagner, *Über das Dirigieren*, in vol. IX of *Gesammelte Schriften*, p. 164; "On Conducting," in *Three Wagner Essays*, tr. Robert L. Jacobs (London: Ernst Eulenburg Ltd., 1979), p. 57.

87. See José Bowen, "Mendelssohn, Berlioz and Wagner as Conductors: The Origins of 'Fidelity to the Composer,'" *Performance Practice Review* 6/1 (Spring 1993), pp. 77–88; rept. *Journal of the Conductors' Guild* 18/2 (Summer/Fall 1997), pp. 76–84.

88. Wagner, *Dirigieren*, p. 66.

89. *Morning Post* (London), March 13, 1855.

90. *Musical World* (London), March 17, 1855.

91. Wagner, *Dirigieren*, pp. 77 and 67.

92. Mr. Gericke cited in Anton Seidl, *On Conducting* (New York, 1899), p. 68. (This would be an enormous change and nothing recorded in the twentieth century comes close.)

93. *Sunday Times* (London), June 17, 1855.

94. *Sunday Times* (London), June 3, 1855. For more on the living tradition of slowing for cantabile themes, see José Bowen, "Tempo Duration and Flexibility: Techniques in the Analysis of Performance," *Journal of Musicological Research* 16/2 (July 1996), pp. 111–56.

9 The Central European tradition

1. Christopher Fifield, "Conducting Wagner: the Search for Melos," in Barry Millington and

Stewart Spencer (eds.), *Wagner in Performance* (New Haven and London: Yale University Press, 1992), p. 4.

2. Felix von Weingartner, *Buffets and Rewards*, tr. Marguerite Wolff (London: Hutchinson, 1937), p. 162.

3. Richard Strauss, *Recollections and Reflections*, tr. L. J. Lawrence (London: Boosey and Hawkes, 1953), p. 118.

4. A more detailed history and analysis of the performance styles of Bülow and other conductors considered in this chapter is given in Raymond Holden, *The Virtuoso Conductor: A Central European Tradition* (New Haven and London: Yale University Press, forthcoming).

5. Weingartner, *Buffets*, p. 135.

6. Ibid.

7. Bruno Walter, *Theme and Variations*, tr. James Galston (London, 1947); (Knopf: New York, 1968), p. 210.

8. Walter Damrosch is discussed in chapter 12.

9. Christopher Fifield, *True Artist and True Friend: A Biography of Hans Richter* (Oxford: Clarendon Press, 1993), p. 60.

10. Much of his famous *Parsifal* was captured by Columbia and HMV (1927–9) and reissued as Opal CD 9843.

11. The implications of this legacy for American conducting are considered in chapter 12.

12. The basis for these reforms are set out in Possart's article, "Ueber die Neueinstudierung und Neuinszenierung des Mozart'schen Don Giovanni (Don Juan) auf dem kgl. Residenztheater zu München" (Munich, 1896).

13. Cf. Bernhard Paumgartner, *Gustav Mahlers Bearbeitung von Mozarts "Così fan tutte" für seine Aufführungen an der Wiener Hofoper* (Kassel: Bärenreiter, 1968).

14. Felix von Weingartner, *Ratschläge für Aufführungen der Symphonien Beethovens* (Leipzig: Breitkopf und Härtel, 1906); *On the Performance of Beethoven's Symphonies*, tr. Jessie Crossland (London, 1907); repr. in *Weingartner on Music and Conducting* (New York: Dover Books, 1969), pp. iii–viii.

15. *Famous Composers Playing Their Own Works*, sleeve notes (Teldec CD 4509–95354–2, 1971, Ⓟ 1971, © 1994).

16. The Introduction's opening speed ($\varepsilon=96$) is linked to that of the first movement's second subject ($\eta.=48$) and the overall tempo of the last movement ($\theta=144$). Further, the speed of the Introduction at bar 21 ($\varepsilon=104$) is linked to both the first movement's first subject ($\eta=52$) and the tempo of the second movement's bridge passage ($\varepsilon=104$). Cf. Raymond Holden, "Richard Strauss: The Mozart Recordings," *Richard Strauss-Blätter* 35 (Vienna, June 1996),

pp. 39–56, and Raymond Holden, "Richard Strauss, an Organised Mozartian," *Richard Strauss-Blätter* 46 (Vienna, December 2001), pp. 119–84.

17. Raymond Holden, "Recording *Don Juan*: The Composer's Perspective," *Richard Strauss-Blätter* 40 (Vienna, December 1998), pp. 52–70.

18. Arthur Schnabel, *My Life and Music* (New York: Dover, 1988), pp. 154–5.

19. Klaus Kropfinger, "Gerettete Herausforderung: Mahlers 4. Symphonie – Mengelbergs Interpretation," in R. Stephan (ed.), *Mahler-Interpretation: Aspekte zum Werk und Wirken von Gustav Mahler* (Mainz and London: Schott, 1975), pp. 111–75.

20. Bruno Walter, *Von der Music und vom Musizieren* (Leipzig: S. Fischer Verlag, 1957); tr. Paul Hamburger, *Of Music and Music-Making* (London: Faber and Faber, 1961); reprint edn. (New York: Norton, 1961), pp. 76–7.

21. Daniel Gillis, *Furtwängler Recalled* (Zürich: Atlantis-Verlag, 1965); (New York: Meredith Press, 1965), p. 57. For an empirical study of tempo fluctuation on recordings see José Bowen, "Tempo Duration and Flexibility: Techniques in the Analysis of Performance," *Journal of Musicological Research* 16/2 (July 1996), pp. 111–56.

22. Walter, *Of Music*, pp. 136–8.

23. Ibid., p. 140.

24. Otto Klemperer, *Minor Recollections* (London: Dobson, 1964), p. 26.

25. Wilhelm Furtwängler, *Notebooks 1924–1954*, tr. Shaun Whiteside, ed. Michael Tanner (London: Quartet Books, 1989); repr. (London 1995), pp. 46–7.

26. Beethoven's Symphony No. 5 (1937), Bach's Brandenburg Concerto No. 3 (1929), Strauss's *Till Eulenspiegel* (1930), Mozart's *Eine kleine Nachtmusik* (1936–7), and Tchaikovsky's Symphony No. 6 (1938).

27. Karajan joined the Nazi Party twice, at Aachen on April 8, 1933 and, again, at Ulm in May 1933, and not in 1935 as he claimed. See R. Vaughan Moor, *Herbert von Karajan: A Biographical Portrait* (London: Weidenfeld and Nicolson, 1986), and Fred K. Prieberg, *Kraftprobe: Wilhelm Furtwängler im dritten Reich* (Wiesbaden: F. A. Brockhaus, 1986), and Prieberg, *Trial of Strength*, tr. Christopher Dolan (London: Quartet Books, 1991); (Boston: Northeastern University Press, 1994) for extensive evidence about this Nazi record.

28. Bernard Holland, "How von Karajan Sees His Conducting Success" *New York Times*, October 22, 1982.

29. Erich Leinsdorf, *The Composer's Advocate: A Radical Orthodoxy for Musicians* (New Haven

and London: Yale University Press, 1981), p. 201.

30. Until recently, the story of American conducting has been largely one of immigrants, and their activities are described fully in Chapter 12.

10 The French tradition

1. Cited from D. Kern Holoman, "The Emergence of the Orchestral Conductor in Paris in the 1830s," in *Music in Paris in the Eighteen-Thirties*, ed. Peter Bloom, vol. IV of *Musical Life in 19th-Century France* (Stuyvesant, NY: Pendragon Press, 1987), p. 390, fn. 6.

2. *Berliner allgemeine musikalische Zeitung*, June 27, 1829, repr. in *La Critique musicale d'Hector Berlioz, 1823–1863*, ed. H. Robert Cohen and Yves Gérard, vol. I (Paris: Editions Buchet/Chastel, 1996), pp. 29–30.

3. *The Letters of Mozart and His Family*, tr. and ed. Emily Anderson (London: Macmillan, 1938); rev. edn. (London: Macmillan, 1985), pp. 557–8.

4. David Cairns, "The Operas of Berlioz," in Alan Blyth (ed.), *Opera on Record 2* (London: Hutchinson, 1983), p. 162: a review of the mutilated, two-disc version of Berlioz's *Les Troyens* conducted by Georges Prêtre (1965), with Régine Crespin and the orchestra and chorus of the Paris Opéra.

5. *Notes de musique*, (Paris: Charpentier et Cie 1875), p. 63.

6. "Ce bufle de Pasdeloup." See *Correspondance générale d'Hector Berlioz*, vol. VII, ed. Hugh Macdonald (Paris: Flammarion, 2001), p. 681.

7. In *The World*, January 13, 1892; repr. in *Shaw's Music*, ed. Dan H. Laurence (London: Max Reinhardt, The Bodley Head, 1981), vol. II, p. 519.

8. Though frequently disputed, the incident is attested by independent witnesses.

9. See Jean-Michel Nectoux, "Trois Orchestres Parisiens en 1830," in Bloom, *Music in Paris* p. 480.

10. Repr. "Dixième Soirée" in Hector Berlioz, *Les soirées dans l'orchestre* (Paris: Michel Levy Frères, 1852).

11. Hector Berlioz, *Grand Traité d'instrumentation et d'orchestration modernes: nouvelle édition augmentée de l'Art du chef d'orchestre*, (Paris: Schonenberger [1855]), p. 308.

12. Edouard Marie Ernest Deldevez, *L'Art du chef d'orchestre* (Paris: Firmin-Didot, 1878), pp. 3, 76.

13. Georges Kastner, "Des qualités à exiger des artistes d'un orchestre, et d'un chef lui-même," supplement to Kastner's *Cours d'instrumentation* (Paris, rev. 1844).

14. Deldevez, *L'Art* pp. 140–1.

15. Letter to Zelter, Feb. 15, 1832, *Felix Mendelssohn Bartholdy Briefe*, ed. Rudolf Elvers (Frankfurt/Main: Fischer Taschenbuch Verlag GmbH, 1984).

16. See D. Kern Holoman, *The Société des Concerts du Conservatoire (1828–1967): Chronicle of the Paris Conservatory Orchestra after Documents in its Archive* (Berkeley: University of California Press, forthcoming).

17. Cited from Holoman, *Société des Concerts*.

18. Antoine Elwart, *Histoire de la Société des Concerts du Conservatoire Impérial de Musique* (Paris, 1860), pp. 5, 12.

19. Richard Wagner, *Über das Dirigieren* (Leipzig: Breitkopf und Härtel, 1869); *Gesammelte Schriften*, 14 vols., ed. Julius Kapp (Leipzig: Hesse & Becker Verlag, 1914), vol. IX, pp. 163–4.

20. Mikhail Glinka, *Memoirs*, tr. Richard B. Mudge, (Norman, OK: University of Oklahoma Press, 1963), p. 192.

21. See Louis Engel, *From Mozart to Mario* (London, 1886), vol. I, p. 68.

22. Cited from David Cairns, *Berlioz: Servitude and Greatness* (London: Allen Lane, The Penguin Press, 1999), p. 407.

23. *Life and Letters of Sir Charles Hallé* (London: Smith, Elder and Co, 1896), pp. 64, 68.

24. Cited from Vladimir Stasov, *Selected Essays on Music*, tr. Florence Jonas (London: Barrie and Rockliff, The Cresset Press, 1968), p. 166.

25. See *Correspondance générale d'Hector Berlioz*, ed. Pierre Citron (Paris: Flammarion, 1978), vol. III, p. 138.

26. *Briefwechsel zwischen Franz Liszt und Hans von Bülow*, ed. La Mara (Leipzig, 1898), pp. 76–9.

27. Paul Smith, "Revue de l'année 1850," in the *Revue et gazette musicale* (Jan. 5, 1851).

28. See Cairns, *Servitude*, p. 776 (Cornelius), pp. 289–90 (Griepenkerl), p. 522 (Singakademie ladies).

29. Charles Gruneisen in the *Illustrated London News* (May 15, 1852).

30. *Musical World*, June 5, 1852.

31. Romain Rolland, *Musiciens d'aujourd'hui*, ninth edn. (Paris: Librairie Hachette, 1921), p. 237.

32. The Monteux and Munch Boston years are discussed in chapter 12.

33. Holoman, *Société des Concerts*.

34. See Roger Nichols, *The Harlequin Years: Music in Paris 1917–1929* (London: Thames and Hudson, 2002), p. 46.

35. Boulez and his conducting of modern music are also discussed in chapter 19.

36. See for example *Illustrated London News,*
May 15, 1852, where Gruneisen recalls that the
choral part of Beethoven's Ninth was always
"very deficiently done" at the Conservatoire
concerts.

11 The Italian tradition

1. Charles de Brosses, *Lettres familières sur
l'Italie,* ed. Yvonne Bezard, 2 vols. (Paris:
Firmin-Didot, 1931), vol. II, pp. 357 and 356.
2. Johann Wolfgang von Goethe, *Italian
Journey,* tr. W. H. Auden and Elizabeth Mayer
(London: Collins, 1962), pp. 67–8.
3. Charles Santley, *Student and Singer* (London:
Edward Arnold, 1892), p. 100.
4. De Brosses, *Lettres familières,* vol. II,
pp. 337–8.
5. Louis Spohr, *Autobiography,* tr. Anon., 2 vols.
(London: Longman, Green, Longman, Roberts
and Green, 1865), vol. I, p. 259.
6. Spohr, *Autobiography,* vol. II, p. 13.
7. Hector Berlioz, *Mémoires* (Paris: 1870); tr.
David Cairns, second edn. (London: Gollancz,
1977), p. 196.
8. Felix Mendelssohn, *Letters from Italy and
Switzerland,* tr. Lady Wallace (London:
Longman, Green, Longman and Roberts, 1862),
p. 150.
9. Henry Wood, *My Life of Music* (London:
Gollancz, 1938), p. 82.
10. Stendhal, *Life of Rossini,* tr. Richard N. Coe
(London: John Calder, 1956), p. 289.
11. *Rivista teatrale* (Rome) 1834, cited from
David Kimbell, *Italian Opera* (Cambridge:
Cambridge University Press, 1991), p. 422.
12. Spohr, *Autobiography,* vol. I, pp. 308–9.
13. Guido Zavadini, *Donizetti, vita, musiche,
epistolario* (Bergamo: Istituto italiano d'arti
grafiche, 1948), p. 343.
14. Spohr, *Autobiography,* vol. I, p. 258.
15. *Musical World* (London), April 18, 1846,
p. 179.
16. John Rosselli, *Music and Musicians in
Nineteenth Century Italy* (London: Batsford,
1991), p. 51.
17. For Spontini's activities in Berlin see chapter
8, The rise of conducting.
18. For which see chapter 13, The English
tradition.
19. Ignaz Moscheles, *The Life of Moscheles with
Selections from his Diaries and Correspondence,*
tr. A. D. Coleridge, 2 vols. (London: Hurst and
Blackett, 1873), vol. II, p. 202.
20. *I copialettere di Giuseppe Verdi,* ed. Gaetano
Cesari and Alessandro Luzio (Milan, 1913),
p. 256, note.
21. James W. Davison, *From Mendelssohn to
Wagner* (London: Wm Reeves, 1912), p. 30.

22. Bernard Shaw, *London Music in 1888–89*
(London: Constable, 1937), p. 191.
23. Angelo Mariani, ms autobiography, cited in
Frank Walker, *The Man Verdi* (London: J. M.
Dent, 1962), p. 291.
24. Antonio Ghislanzoni, "Angelo Mariani," in
Libro serio (Milan: Tip. Ed. Lombarda, 1879),
p. 30.
25. Walker, *Man Verdi,* p. 339.
26. Ghislanzoni, "Mariani," p. 45.
27. Franco Abbiati, *Giuseppe Verdi,* 4 vols.
(Milan: Ricordi, 1959), vol. III, p. 249.
28. "Lettres inédites de G. Verdi à Léon
Escudier," *Rivista musicale italiana* 35 (1928),
p. 526.
29. *Copialettere di G. Verdi,* p. 256, note.
30. *Copialettere di G. Verdi,* p. 256–7.
31. Santley, *Student,* p. 236.
32. Cited from Kimbell, *Italian Opera,* p. 573.
33. Notices in *La patrie* and *Le Gaulois,* cited
from Raffaello de Rensis, *Franco Faccio e Verdi*
(Milan: Treves, 1934), p. 163.
34. Shaw, *London Music,* p. 161.
35. Walker, *Man Verdi,* p. 342.
36. Toscanini's work in America is discussed in
chapter 12.
37. Wilhelm Furtwängler, *Notebooks 1924–1954*
(London: Quartet Books, 1989), pp. 45–6.
38. Alma Mahler, *Gustav Mahler, Memories and
Letters,* ed. Donald Mitchell (London: Murray,
1968), p. 146.
39. Bernard Shore, *The Orchestra Speaks*
(London: Longmans and Green, 1938), p. 165.
40. *Conductors in Conversation,* ed. Robert
Chesterman (London: Robson, 1990), pp. 137
and 135.
41. Ibid., p. 73.

12 The American tradition

1. Richard Crawford, *America's Musical Life: A
History* (New York: W. W. Norton and Co.,
2001), pp. 272–81, and Margret Hindle Hazen
and Robert M. Hazen, *The Music Men: An
Illustrated History of Brass Bands in America,
1800–1920* (Washington, DC: Smithsonian
Institution Press, 1987), p. 118.
2. W. Porter Ware and Thaddeus C. Lockard Jr.,
*P. T. Barnum Presents Jenny Lind: The American
Tour of the Swedish Nightingale* (Baton Rouge:
Louisiana State University Press, 1980), p. 54.
3. Joseph Horowitz, *Understanding Toscanini: A
Social History of American Concert Life*
(Berkeley: University of California Press, 1987),
p. 28, and Howard Shanet, *Philharmonic: A
History of New York's Orchestra* (Garden City,
NY: Doubleday, 1975), pp. 35–7, 109–10.
4. John H. Mueller, *The American Symphony
Orchestra: A Social History of Musical Taste*

(Bloomington: Indiana University Press, 1951), p. 25.

5. Theodore Thomas, *A Musical Autobiography*, ed. George P. Upton, 2 vols. (Chicago, 1905), vol. I, pp. 24–5, cited from Lawrence W. Levine, *Highbrow Lowbrow: The Emergence of Cultural Hierarchy in America* (Cambridge, MA: Harvard University Press, 1988), p. 113. Levine called this process of separation and purification of the orchestral world "sacralization."

6. H. Earle Johnson, *Symphony Hall, Boston: With a List of Works Performed by the Boston Symphony Orchestra, Compiled by Members of the Staff of Symphony Hall* (Boston, 1950), pp. 47, 52, cited from Levine, *Highbrow Lowbrow*, p. 137.

7. Mueller, *The American Symphony Orchestra*, p. 24.

8. For more on Jullien, see chapter 13 or Adam Carse, *The Life of Jullien, Adventurer, Showman, Conductor* (Cambridge: Heffer, 1951).

9. Ezra Schabas, *Theodore Thomas, America's Conductor and Builder of Orchestras, 1835–1905* (Urbana: University of Illinois Press, 1988), pp. 36–8.

10. Theodore Thomas, "Musical Possibilities in America," *Scribner's Monthly* 21 (March 1881), pp. 777–8, 780; *Theodore Thomas: A Musical Autobiography*, ed. George P. Upton (Chicago: McClurg, 1905); (Da Capo, 1964).

11. M. A. Dewolfe Howe, *The Boston Symphony Orchestra, 1881–1931* (Boston, 1931), pp. 62–6, cited from Levine, p. 125.

12. Howe, *The BSO*, pp. 62–6, Mueller, *The American Symphony Orchestra*, p. 363, and Levine, *Highbrow Lowbrow*, 125.

13. Muck's European career is discussed in chapter 9.

14. Monteux's earlier French career is discussed in chapter 10.

15. The orchestra was founded in 1891 as the Chicago Orchestra. In 1905, it changed its name to the Theodore Thomas Orchestra, in honor of its founding director. In 1913, it assumed its present name, the Chicago Symphony Orchestra.

16. For more on symphony choruses, see chapter 5.

17. See Herbert Kupferberg, *Those Fabulous Philadelphians: The Life and Times of a Great Orchestra* (New York: Charles Scribner's Sons, 1969).

18. Olga Samaroff Stokowski, *An American Musician's Story* (New York: Norton, 1939).

19. Mueller, *The American Symphony Orchestra*, p. 128.

20. Even today, the orchestra touts its status as the city's "Premiere International Ambassador": "Such performances remind listeners throughout the world each year of the Orchestra's renowned 'Philadelphia Sound' while also bringing attention to the ensemble's hometown." http://www.philorch.org/fs_poa.htm. Accessed on Nov. 15, 2002.

21. Roland Gelatt, *The Fabulous Phonograph, 1877–1977* (New York: Collier Books, 1977), p. 230.

22. See Horowitz, *Understanding Toscanini* (and other articles) for the argument, and Harvey Sachs, "Misunderstanding Toscanini," in *Reflections on Toscanini* (New York: Grove Weidenfeld, 1991) for the counterargument.

23. Mortimer H. Frank, *Arturo Toscanini: The NBC Years* (Portland: Amadeus, 2002), p. 16.

24. Toscanini's life and work are discussed at length in chapter 11.

25. See, for example, Harvey Sachs, *Letters of Arturo Toscanini* (New York: Knopf, 2002), p. 200.

26. Howard Taubman, *The Maestro: The Life of Arturo Toscanini* (New York: Simon and Schuster, 1951), p. 231.

27. William R. Trotter, *Priest of Music: The Life of Dimitri Mitropoulos* (Portland: Amadeus, 1995), pp. 401–22.

28. Humphrey Burton, *Leonard Bernstein* (New York: Doubleday, 1994), pp. 390–7.

29. Bernstein is often credited with reviving Mahler's music, and more recently with not deserving that accolade. In truth, Walter, Klemperer, and Mitropoulos, among others, performed Mahler well before Bernstein did. But he was the first to record all nine of the composer's symphonies, which he regularly programmed in concert as well, and his fame certainly brought greater exposure to the Viennese composer.

13 The English tradition

1. George Bernard Shaw (unsigned), "Vocalists of the Season: Sir Michael Costa," *The Hornet*, August 1, 1877. Cited from *Shaw's Music: The Complete Musical Criticism of Bernard Shaw*, 3 vols., ed. Dan H. Lawrence (London: Bodley Head, London, 1981), vol. I, p. 169.

2. *Shaw's Music*, vol. I, p. 170.

3. Ralph Vaughan Williams, "Conducting," in *Grove's Dictionary of Music and Musicians* (London, Macmillan, 1906), vol. I, p. 587.

4. Shaw (*Shaw's Music*, vol. I, p. 170) describes Costa "presumptuously reinforcing the brass parts with trombones" in Beethoven, while Berlioz writes that "In London you hear *Don Giovanni, Figaro,* and *The Barber of Seville* with additional parts for bass drum, trombones and

ophicleide supplied by Costa." Hector Berlioz, *Mémoires*, (Paris: 1870); tr. David Cairns (London: Gollancz, 1969), p. 92.

5. Gerald Norris, *Stanford, the Cambridge Jubilee and Tchaikovsky* (Newton Abbot: David and Charles 1980), p. 117.

6. Ignaz Moscheles, *Recent Music and Musicians*, ed. Charlotte Moscheles, ed. and tr. A. D. Coleridge (New York: Henry Holt and Co, 1873), pp. 291–2.

7. A. H. W. (Mrs. Edmond Wodehouse), "Jullien," in *Grove's Dictionary* (1906), vol. II, p. 552.

8. J. A. Fuller Maitland, "Charles Hallé," in *Grove's Dictionary* (1906), vol. II, p. 276.

9. Ralph Vaughan Williams, in *Grove's Dictionary* (1906), vol. I, p. 588.

10. Richard Wagner, "On Conducting," *Prose Works*, 8 vols., tr. William Ashton Ellis (London: Routledge and Kegan Paul Ltd., 1892), vol. IV, pp. 306–7.

11. George Bernard Shaw, "Herr Richter and his Blue Ribbon," *The Dramatic Review*, February 8, 1885. Cited from *Shaw's Music*, vol. I, pp. 208–9.

12. Hubert Parry, Diary, May 4, 1877, cited from Christopher Fifield, *True Artist and True Friend: A Biography of Hans Richter* (Oxford: Clarendon Press, 1993), p. 123.

13. Shaw, "Herr Richter and his Blue Ribbon."

14. Arnold Bennett, *The Journal of Arnold Bennett* (London, 1933), October 24, 1899.

15. Claude Debussy, "London Letters: 29 April 1903," cited from *Debussy on Music*, tr. and ed. Richard Langham Smith (London: Secker and Warburg, 1977), p. 189.

16. Vaughan Williams, *Grove's Dictionary* (1906), vol. I, p. 588.

17. Cited from Arthur Jacobs, *Henry J. Wood Maker of the Proms* (London: Methuen, 1994), p. 136.

18. Jacobs, *Wood*, p. 142.

19. Adrian Boult, *Boult on Music* (London: Toccata Press, 1983), p. 108.

20. Bernard Shore, *The Orchestra Speaks* (London: Longmans Green, 1938), p. 189.

21. Boult, *Boult on Music*, p. 111.

22. Neville Cardus, *Sir Thomas Beecham: A Memoir* (London: Collins, 1961), p. 71.

23. Ibid., p. 106.

24. *Beecham Stories*, ed. Harold Atkins and Archie Newman (London: Robson, 1978), p. 49.

25. *Beecham Stories*, p. 59.

26. Charles Reid, *Thomas Beecham: An Independent Biography* (London: Gollancz, 1962), p. 240.

27. Cardus, *Beecham*, p. 83. Cardus calls this remark "rich."

28. Shore, *Orchestrd*, pp. 39.

29. Ibid., pp. 116–17.

30. Reid, *Beechan*, p. 192.

31. Thomas Russell, *Philharmonic* (London: Hutchinson, 1942), p. 60.

32. Reid, *Beecham*, p. 195.

33. *Morning Post* (London), October 23, 1930, cited from Nicholas Kenyon, *The BBC Symphony Orchestra (1930–1980)* (London: BBC Publications, 1981), p. 55. Kenyon quotes four other reviews, and notes their "rare unanimity." The critic of the *Daily Mail* also praises the performance of the National Anthem!

34. Boult, *Boult on Music*, p. 95.

35. From 1930 to 1942 Boult combined the functions of chief conductor of BBC Symphony Orchestra and director of music for the BBC.

36. Shore, *Orchestra* p. 59.

37. Harold C. Schonberg, *The Great Conductors* (London: Gollancz, 1968), p. 299.

38. *Beecham Stories*, p. 61.

39. The orchestra was reformed the same year as a self-governing body, under Klemperer's direction, as the "New Philharmonia Orchestra." Klemperer is also discussed in chapter 9.

40. *Conversations with Klemperer*, ed. Peter Heyworth (London: Gollancz, 1973), pp. 111–12.

41. *Times* (London), December 6, 1960, cited from Peter Heyworth, *Otto Klemperer: His Life and Times* (Cambridge: Cambridge University Press, 1996), vol. II (ed. John Lucas), p. 287.

42. Stephen Johnson. "Music We Thought We Knew," interview in *Gramophone* (April 1989), p. 1553. It is arguable that something of this Beechamesque spirit has been a part of the British historical performance movement from early on. In his seminal study *The Interpretation of Music* (London: Hutchinson, 1954), harpsichordist and musicologist Thurston Dart (1921–71) gave this advice to scholar-performers: "Perhaps the best present-day examples of mannered performance may be found in jazz music . . . The student of the history of performance will find much to interest him here; many of these devices are debased or improved versions of the mannered styles used in 'classical' music at various stages of its development" (p. 78, fn.).

43. Cited from Roy Jenkins, *Churchill* (London: Macmillan, 2001), p. 743.

44. Cited from Nicholas Kenyon, *Simon Rattle: From Birmingham to Berlin* (London: Faber, 2001), p. 321.

14 The Russian tradition

1. Alexander Serov, quoted from Nikolay Andreyevich Rimsky-Korsakov, *My Musical Life*,

ed. Carl van Vechten, tr. Judah A. Joffe (New York: Alfred A. Knopf, 1923); rept. (London: Faber and Faber, 1989), p. 102 (fn. 9).

2. Vladimir Stasov, "Musical Events of the Year 1847," in *Selected Essays on Music*, tr. Florence Jonas (London: Barrie and Rockliff, 1968), p. 25.

3. Hector Berlioz, letter to Ernest Reyer, January 23, 1868, quoted in David Cairns, *Berlioz: Servitude and Greatness* (Berkeley and London: University of California Press, 1999), p. 766.

4. Richard Wagner, letter to Josef Standhartner, February 15, 1863, quoted in Rosamund Bartlett, *Wagner and Russia* (Cambridge: Cambridge University Press, 1995), p. 21.

5. Pyotr Tchaikovsky, letter to Nadezhda von Meck, March 28, 1879, quoted in Bartlett, *Wagner and Russia*, p. 23.

6. Tchaikovsky quoted in Alexandra Orlova, *Tchaikovsky: A Self-Portrait* (Oxford: Oxford University Press, 1990), p. 321.

7. Ibid., p. 87.

8. Sergey Prokofiev, letter to his father, December 14, 1902, quoted in Prokofiev, *Avtobiografya* (Moscow: Sovietskii Compositor, 1973), pp. 125–6.

9. Prokofiev, letter to Vasily Morolev, July 28, 1907, quoted in *Prokofiev by Prokofiev: A Composer's Memoir*, tr. Guy Daniels (New York: Doubleday and Co., 1979), p. 205.

10. Nikolay Medtner, quoted in Sergey Bertensson and Jay Leyda, *Sergei Rachmaninoff: A Lifetime in Music* (London: Allen and Unwin, 1965), pp. 108–9. Martyn Brabbins makes much the same point about Rakhmaninov's conducting of his own work in chapter 19.

11. Nikolai Malko, *A Certain Art* (New York: William Morrow and Co., 1966), p. 79.

12. Koussevitzky's years in Boston are discussed in chapter 12.

13. *Prokofiev by Prokofiev*, p. 218.

14. Nicolai Malko, *The Conductor and his Baton* (Copenhagen: Wilhelm Hansen, 1950).

15. Sergey Prokofiev, *Soviet Diary 1927 and Other Writings*, ed. and tr. Oleg Prokofiev (London: Faber and Faber, 1991), p. 16.

16. David Nice, "Russian Opera," interview with Valery Gergiev, *Gramophone* 70 (June 1992), p. 32.

15 The conductor as artistic director

1. Arthur Jacobs, *Henry J. Wood Maker of the Proms* (London: Methuen, 1994), p. 355.

2. Nicholas Kenyon, *Simon Rattle: From Birmingham to Berlin* (London: Faber and Faber, 2001).

3. The reduced residency of modern conductors is discussed in chapter 20, Managers and the business of conducting.

4. See chapter 8.

5. See José Bowen, "The Missing Link: Franz Liszt the Conductor," *Basler Jahrbuch für historische Musikpraxis* 24, 2000 (Schola Cantorum Basiliensis: Basel, Switzerland, 2002), pp. 125–50, and Alan Walker, *Franz Liszt, Volume 2: The Weimar Years* (Ithaca: Cornell University Press, 1989), pp. 270–99. More on both Mendelssohn and Liszt as conductors can be found in chapter 8.

6. Two contrasting and noteworthy exceptions, Leonard Bernstein (New York Philharmonic, 1957–69) and Pierre Boulez (New York Philharmonic, 1971–8), are discussed in chapter 19.

7. Robert Sunter, *International Journal of Arts Management* 2/1 (HEC Montréal, 2000).

8. Richard Turner, principal harp, Winnipeg Symphony Orchestra, Canada, interview with the author, 2002.

9. Sir Adrian Boult, *My Own Trumpet* (London: Hamish Hamilton, 1973).

10. Leon Botstein also discusses programming and curating in chapter 21.

11. Interview with Joan Peyser, *New York Times*, January 12, 1969, quoted in Joan Peyser, *Leonard Bernstein: A Biography* (New York: Ballantine Books, 1987). Incidentally, Humphrey Burton re-quotes Peyser (whose book was loathed by Bernstein) in his biography *Leonard Bernstein* (New York: Doubleday, 1994). Both authors include a tasteless story where Bernstein, attempting to keep the orchestra's attention during rehearsal, holds a limerick competition beginning "There was a composer named Babbitt/Who had the peculiar habit . . ." The personal style of Boulez (who succeeded Bernstein in 1971) would have been a refreshing antidote to this kind of atmosphere.

12. Hector Berlioz, *Mémoires*, Paris: 1870; *Memoirs of Hector Berlioz*, tr. David Cairns (New York: W. W. Norton, 1975).

13. Walt Whitman, "Passage to India," in *Complete Poetry and Selected Prose and Letters* (London: Nonesuch Press, 1967), p. 372.

14. This relationship is further discussed in chapter 19.

16 Women on the podium

1. Elias Canetti, *Masse und Macht* (Hamburg: Claassen, 1960; also Munich: Carl Hanser, 1960); tr. Carol Stewart, *Crowds and Power* (New York: The Viking Press, 1962), p. 394.

2. Christine Battersby, *Gender and Genius: Towards a Feminist Aesthetics* (Bloomington: Indiana University Press, 1990); Norman Lebrecht, *The Maestro Myth: Great Conductors in Pursuit of Power* (New York: Birch Lane Press

Book published by Carol Publishing Group, 1991).

3. Christopher Porterfield, "At the Juilliard, Conducting Course Plays Molto Vivace," *Smithsonian* 15 (September 1984), Expanded Academic ASAP [online database].

4. Andrea Quinn quoted by Malcolm Hayes, "Future of Music: Women Conductors: Waving, Not Drowning," *Classic CD* 108 (Feb. 1999), p. 26.

5. The description is cited in chapter 8 (fn. 35), Ercole Bottrigari, *Il Desiderio, or Concerning the Playing Together of Various Musical Instruments*, tr. Carol MacClintock (Rome: American Institute of Musicology, 1962), p. 58, also in *Women in Music: An Anthology of Source Readings from the Middle Ages to the Present*, ed. Carol Neuls-Bates rev. edn. (Boston: Northeastern University Press, 1996), p. 46.

6. Felix Mendelssohn-Bartholdy, *Reisebriefe von Felix Mendelssohn Bartholdy aus den Jahren 1830 bis 1832*, ed. Paul Mendelssohn Bartholdy (Leipzig: Verlag von Hermann Mendelssohn, 1862), [vol. 1], p. 297; Françoise Tillard, *Fanny Mendelssohn*, trans. Camille Naish (Portland: Amadeus, 1996), pp. 203–4. The German phrase Felix used to describe her conducting is "*mit Umsicht*," which seems less glowing in its evaluation than Tillard's translation. Further, Tillard unjustifiably assumes that Felix's comment indicates that "her conducting was precise and effective, like her brother's, with no showy effects" (p. 206).

7. *Fanny Mendelssohn: Italienisches Tagebuch*, ed. Eva Weissweiler (Darmstadt: Luchterhand, 1985), p. 11, as quoted in translation by Tillard, *Fanny Mendelssohn*, p. 328. Kinkel led the Bonn Gesangverein as a young woman and re-established the chorus after her return to Bonn from study in Berlin (Ann Willison Lemke, "Kinkel, Johanna," *The New Grove Dictionary of Music Online*, ed. Laura Macy, http://www.grovemusic.com [accessed July 26, 2002]).

8. Sebastian Hensel, *The Mendelssohn Family (1729–1847) from Letters and Journals*, second rev. edn., tr. Carl Klingemann (1882); rept., (New York: Greenwood Press, 1968), vol. II, p. 334, or *Die Familie Mendelssohn. 1729–1847. Nach Briefen und Tagebüchern* (Berlin: B. Behr's Verlag, 1888), vol. II, p. 376.

9. Material for this paragraph from Carol Neuls-Bates, "Steiner, Emma Roberto," *The New Grove Dictionary of Music Online*, ed. Laura Macy, http://www.grovemusic.com (accessed August 1, 2002); Christine Ammer, *Unsung: A History of Women in American Music* rev. edn. (Portland: Amadeus, 2001), pp. 196–8. Steiner's

death date is clearly established by the obituary in the *New York Times* (February 28, 1929, p. 27); however, according to Ammer, her birth date and other biographical details are inconsistent in the sources (p. 335, n. 11).

10. "Leginska to Retire from Concert Stage," *New York Times*, Apr. 22, 1926, p. 23.

11. Beth Abelson Macleod, *Women Performing Music: The Emergence of American Women as Instrumentalists and Conductors* (Jefferson NC: McFarland, 2001), p. 117.

12. *Antonia: A Portrait of the Woman*, codirected by folk singer Judy Collins [a former student of Brico] and Jill Godmilow, 1973.

13. Macleod, *Women Performing Music*, p. 132.

14. Olin Downes, "Music in Review: Brico and Musicians' Symphony," *New York Times*, Feb. 8, 1933, p. 17.

15. Transcription from interview on "Instrumental Women: Conducting Business," produced by Public Radio International (PRI) by Lauren Rico; first broadcast on Mar. 4, 2002; hour 1 at 3:20. http://music.mpr.org/features/instrumentalwomen/rafiles/iw2002_2.ram. See also http://www.ktamarkin.com

16. The first woman performer joined the New York Philharmonic in 1966.

17. Founded by Leopold Stokowski in 1962, this orchestra included a significant number of women, African-Americans and members of other minority groups (Ammer, *Unsung*, p. 250).

18. H. T., "Women's Group in Recital," *New York Times*, Nov. 5, 1935, p. 33.

19. Howard Klein, "4,500 Hear Concert at Riverside Park," *New York Times*, June 25, 1963, p. 23.

20. Raymond Ericson, "Federique Petrides Conducts Orchestral Concerts in the Park," *New York Times*, July 30, 1975, p. 17.

21. Jeanice Brooks, "Nadia Boulanger and the Salon of the Princesse de Polignac," *Journal of the American Musicological Society* 46/3 (Fall 1993), p. 421. In "*Noble et grande servante de la musique*: Telling the Story of Nadia Boulanger's Conducting Career," *Journal of Musicology* 14/1 (Winter 1996), pp. 92, 97, Brooks clarifies that the Royal Philharmonic is the standing orchestra of the Royal Philharmonic Society. Boulanger's recording is reissued on CD, EMI Classics Import CDH 61025 (2001), and was previously available on Pearl GEMM CD 9994 (1992), where Monteverdi was paired with the Brahms *Liebeslieder Walzer*, Op. 52, with Boulanger and Dinu Lapatti at the piano.

22. Brooks, "*Noble et grande servante*," p. 93.

23. The origins of the baton as a symbol of power are discussed in chapter 8.

24. Brooks, "*Noble et grande servante*," p. 108.

25. Lucien Mainssieux, *République de l'Isère*, March 1936, cited in translation from Brooks, "*Noble et grande servante*," p. 115.

26. Brooks, "*Noble et grande servante*," p. 114.

27. See http://www.marinalsop.com for additional information.

28. See J. Michele Edwards, "Conductor's Profile: Congratulations to JoAnn Falletta!" *IAWM Journal* 4/3 (Fall 1998), pp. 16–7, which includes a discography and biographical material.

29. Although ASOL includes a few Canadian and other international members, none of those orchestras have had a woman as music director or principal conductor.

30. For information on the orchestra's recent financial difficulty, see Tom Buckham, "Success Isn't Enough, Financially," *Buffalo News*, July 4, 2002.

31. See, for example, Geoffrey Norris, chief music critic of London's *Daily Telegraph*, on Alsop as quoted by M. S. Mason, "Conducting Energy," *Christian Science Monitor*, Apr. 19, 2002, and Daniel Cariaga on Falletta in "A Masterful Season Opener by the Long Beach Symphony," *Los Angeles Times*, Oct. 18, 1999, p. F5.

32. Mark Swed has called Ben-Dor "a star on the rise and very much ready for prime time" in "A Big-Time Opener for Little Festival," *Los Angeles Times*, Jan. 12, 1998, p. F3. See http://www.giseleben-dor.com for much relevant information.

33. See Sharon McDaniel, "Check Your Preconceived Ideas at the Door," *Palm Beach Post*, Nov. 25, 2001, p. J1.

34. Fiona Maddocks, "May the Forceful Conductor Be with You: The Star Wars Look Does Figaro Few Favours – but Jane Glover Overcomes All Obstacles," *The Observer* (London), Nov. 11, 2001, review pages, p. 11.

35. Niki Sommer, "Jetzt geben Frauen den Takt an," *SonntagsZeitung*, Feb. 8, 1998, p. 61.

36. Norman Lebrecht, "A Maestro Need Not Be a Mister: The Treatment of Female Conductors is Unfair, Counterproductive and Must Stop," *Daily Telegraph* (London), June 29, 2000, p. 26.

37. Interview by Sara Jobin, "Maestra: Five Female Orchestral Conductors in the United States," (BA honors paper, Harvard University, 1992), p. 114.

38. Stefan Siegert, "Der Kampf um den Taktstock," [The battle over the baton], *Die Woche*, May 12, 2000, Kultur, p. 54.

39. Ibid., author's translation.

40. Laurie Neeb, "An Interview with Germany's Only Woman Conductor," *The School Musician* 53/8 (Apr. 1982), pp. 38–9.

41. *Swan Flight*, Finlandia 8573–89876. See Christopher Thomas, *Classical Music Web*, June 2002, http://www.musicweb.uk.net/classrev/2002/Jun02/Swan_Flight.htm (accessed Aug. 1, 2002).

42. Anthony Tommasini, "Music Rarity: One Woman Wielding a Baton," *New York Times*, Apr. 9, 1996, p. C13.

43. "Opera Wars," *The Age*, Sept. 18, 2002 http://www.theage.com.au/articles/2002/09/16/1032054745393.html (accessed Sept. 17, 2002); Anne Summers, "'Tis Suits, Not Genius, That Strut the Stage,'" *Sydney Morning Herald*, Oct. 7, 2002, p. 17; Andrew Hornery and Ben Wyld, "Spike: Drumming up a Baton Charge," *Sydney Morning Herald*, Sept. 24, 2002, p. 24; Kathy Marks, "Australian Opera Turned Upside Down by Director's Sacking," *Independent* (London), Oct. 1, 2002, p. 15; www.keepsimone.com

44. Family names appear first in Japanese and Chinese.

45. Artist profile by Kajimoto Concert Management Co., Ltd. http://www.kajimotomusic.com/artists-e/matsuo_yoko-e.html (accessed July 31, 2002); Angela Jeffs, "Conductor Says Yes to Noh Style 'Don Giovanni,'" *Japan Times*, May 28, 2000

46. Biography from the Asia Society http://www.asiasource.org/arts/unbreaksprts/Daughter.cfm (accessed July 31, 2002); "In Xiamen, China, a Fledgling Orchestra Thrives," *Xinhua News Agency*, July 31, 2002, http://www.andante.com/magazine/article.cfm?id= 17879&highlight= 1&timeline=1&highlightterms= woman%7Ccondu%2A&lstKeywords= woman%20conductor (accessed Aug. 7, 2002).

47. "Instrumental Women," hour 2 at 36:30.

48. Gwendolyn Freed, "Semiconductors: Why Are Women Conductors Overlooked at the Top of the Orchestra World?" *Star Tribune* (Minneapolis–St. Paul), Mar. 18, 2001, pp. F1, 16.

49. Ibid.

50. Léonie Rosenstiel, *Nadia Boulanger: A Life in Music* (New York: W. W. Norton, 1982), p. 292.

51. Stephanie von Buchau, "JoAnn Falletta at the Podium of the Women's Philharmonic," *San Francisco Magazine*, Nov. 1987, p. 58.

52. Louis Biancolli, "Boulanger Gives Views on Careers," *New York World Telegram*, Feb. 11, 1939, as quoted in Brooks, "*Noble et grande servante*," p. 103.

53. Jane Glover quoted by Christian Tyler, "Christian Tyler Meets the Conductor Jane Glover," *Financial Times* (London), Feb. 9, 1991, p. 16.

54. Freed, "Semiconductors," p. 16. See also Jonathan Finer, "Study: There's Still Few Women at Top," *Star Tribune* (Minneapolis–St. Paul), Aug. 29, 2002, p. D8, for a report about a study on communication companies that suggests changes for women will not occur without specific action taken by top leadership.

55. Frédérique Petrides, "On Women Conductors," *American Music Lover* 2/3 (July 1936), p. 77. (NB. This journal is often erroneously cited as being from 1935.)

56. Dr. Mary Mattis, who heads the research and advisory division of Catalyst in New York, America's leading nonprofit organization for the advancement of women in business, tracks women's progress in leadership for virtually all fields and has remarked about orchestral conducting: "I can't think of any profession with a more dismal record in the area of women's advancement." Quoted by Freed, "Semiconductors," p. 16.

57. "Instrumental Women," hour 2 at 55:00.

17 Conducting early music

1. James L. Webster, "On the Absence of Keyboard Continuo in Haydn's Symphonies," *Early Music* 18/4 (Nov. 1990), pp. 599–608; Simon McVeigh, *Concert Life in London from Mozart to Haydn* (Cambridge: Cambridge University Press, 1993), p. 212. See chapter 8 for more on early conducting.

2. But see below for a discussion of the experiments of Nikolaus Harnoncourt and Christopher Hogwood.

3. See John Butt, *Playing with History* (Cambridge: Cambridge University Press, 2002), pp. 96–9. The debate about who should mark the parts and how best to do it is actively pursued in this volume in chapters 1, 2, 4, 5, 16 and 21.

4. Butt, *Playing*, chapter 4, discusses many other explanations as well.

5. See, for example, Colin Lawson, *The Early Clarinet: A Practical Guide*, Cambridge Handbooks to the Historical Performance of Music (Cambridge: Cambridge University Press, 2000).

6. See Richard Taruskin, *Text and Act* (Oxford: Oxford University Press, 1997) and Bernard D. Sherman, *Inside Early Music* (New York: Oxford University Press, 1997).

7. John Butt, *Music Education and the Art of Performance in the German Baroque* (Cambridge: Cambridge University Press, 1994), pp. 102–3.

8. Wolfgang Caspar Printz, *Musica Modulatoria Vocalis, oder Manierliche und zierliche Sing-Kunst* (Schweidnitz, 1678), pp. 37–8.

9. Johann Samuel Petri, *Anleitung zur practischen Musik, vor neuangehende Sänger und Instrumentspieler* (Lauban, 1767), p. 45.

10. Butt, *Music Education*, p. 103. The 1779 booklet by "Biedermann" (a pseudonym for an anonymous writer) lends support to this speculation: "Where an orchestra is arranged so that its members can all see and hear one another, where it is staffed with virtuosos, where the composer has included performance indications in the parts, and where there are sufficient rehearsals, then no further direction is necessary: the piece plays itself like a clock that has been wound up and set running." "Biedermann," *Wahrheiten die Musik betreffend*, translation cited from Adam Carse, *Orchestra in the Eighteenth Century* (Cambridge: Cambridge University Press, 1940), pp. 98–9. Further bibliographic details are unavailable, even after "extensive research," says Elliott W. Galkin in *A History of Orchestral Conducting in Theory and Practice*, (New York: Pendragon Press, 1988), pp. 447–8.

11. David Charlton, " 'A maître d'orchestre . . . conducts': new and old evidence on French practice," *Early Music* 21 (1993), pp. 340–53, quotation on p. 346.

12. Neal Zaslaw, *Mozart's Symphonies* (Oxford: Oxford University Press, 1989), p. 508.

13. Letter of 1774; in Werner Neumann and Hans-Joachim Schulze, *Bach-Dokumente* (Leipzig, 1972), vol. III, p. 801 (and cited in chapter 8).

14. There is some debate about whether this was typical. See Joshua Rifkin, "Performance Questions in Bach's Trauerode," in *Bach Studies II*, ed. Daniel Melamed (Cambridge: Cambridge University Press, 1989) and Laurence Dreyfus, *Bach's Continuo Group* (Cambridge, MA: Harvard University Press, 1987).

15. In Leipzig, the organ faced away from the ensemble. (See Dreyfus, *Bach's Continuo Group*, pp. 31–2.) Also, Bach's transposed organ parts, which would not have been necessary if he had been playing the instrument. See Rifkin, "Performance Questions," p. 148, n. 111.

16. Dreyfus, *Bach's Continuo Group*, p. 31.

17. Johann Matthias Gesner (1738) in *Bach-Dokumente*, vol. II, no. 432; tr. from *The New Bach Reader*, ed. Hans T. David and Arthur Mendel, revised and expanded by Christoph Wolff (New York, 1999), entry 328. Dreyfus believes that Bach was leading from a harpsichord (*Bach's Continuo Group*, p. 28) while Rifkin disagrees firmly (Rifkin,

"Performance Questions," p. 147, n. 104).

18. The 1750 obituary of J. S. Bach by Carl Philipp Emanuel Bach and Johann Friedrich Agricola, *Bach-Dokumente*, vol. III, p. 666; trans. in *The New Bach Reader*, entry 306, p. 305.

19. Dreyfus, *Bach's Continuo Group*, pp. 28–30.

20. Mattheson complains about "useless stamping, din and pounding with sticks, keys, and feet" used in conducting, in his 1739 Hamburg treatise *Der Volkommene Kapellmeister*, tr. Ernest C. Harriss (Ann Arbor: UMI, 1981), p. 866; (facs. edn.: Basel, 1954). Mary Sue Morrow also argues that later eighteenth-century reports of foot-tapping and hand-waving by conductors may have reflected "the inadequacy of the system" of directing from the violin, in her *Concert Life in Haydn's Vienna* (Stuyvesant, NY: Pendragon, 1989), pp. 182–3.

21. Uri Golomb, personal communication; interview conducted for a doctoral thesis, in progress at Cambridge University.

22. Galkin, *Orchestral Conducting*, p. 475.

23. Leon Botstein, "Conducting (2)," in the *New Grove Dictionary of Music and Musicians*, second edn., 29 vols., ed. Stanley Sadie and John Tyrrell (London: Macmillan, 2000), vol. X, p. 270.

24. Clive Brown, *Classical and Romantic Performing Practice: 1750–1900* (Oxford: Oxford University Press, 1999), p. 389.

25. Carl Spazier, "Hints and Rules for Leaders of Music in Concerts," *Berlinische Musikalische Zeitung* (1793); tr. Mary Sue Morrow in *Concert Life in Haydn's Vienna*, p. 182.

26. Dreyfus, *Bach's Continuo Group*.

27. See chapter 19 or Botstein, "Conducting," p. 270. Bach's music does not demand the ability to beat three meters at once, as Fritz Reiner could do – and Furtwängler or Toscanini could not.

28. Robert Philip, *Early Recordings and Musical Style: Changing Tastes in Instrumental Performance* (Cambridge: Cambridge University Press, 1992).

29. Leon Botstein discusses how reduced rehearsal time in recent decades has led to more precise conducting technique; see his "On Conducting," *The Musical Quarterly* 81 (1997), pp. 9–10; "Conducting," p. 271. It may be worth noting that this is a rare counterexample to William Baumol's well-known argument that performing arts cannot generally increase productivity, at least as measured by person-hours.

30. Sherman, *Inside Early Music*, pp. 283–4 and Monika Mertl, *Vom Denken des Herzen: Alice und Nikolaus Harnoncourt, Eine Biographie* (Salzburg, 1999), p. 36.

31. See F. G. Wegeler and Ferdinand Ries, *Biographische Notizen über Beethoven* (Coblenz, 1838), p. 77. and David Levy, *Beethoven: The Ninth Symphony* (New York: Schirmer Books, 1995), pp. 122–62.

32. Anton Schindler, *Biographie von Ludwig van Beethoven* (Münster, 1840), pp. 237–9.

33. George Barth, *The Pianist as Orator* (Ithaca, NY: Cornell University Press, 1992).

34. Anton Schindler, *Biographie von Ludwig van Beethoven*, (Münster: Aschendorff'schen Buchhandlung, 1871); repr. (Hildesheim: Georg Olms Uerlag, 1970), pp. 242–4. Ignaz von Seyfred independently reported that Beethoven, when rehearsing an orchestra, "was very meticulous with regard to expression, the more delicate shadings, an equable distribution of light and shade, and an effective tempo rubato." In Oscar G. Sonneck, ed., *Beethoven: Impressions by His Contemporaries* (New York: Dover, 1926), p. 41.

35. Nicholas Cook, *Beethoven: Symphony No. 9* (Cambridge: Cambridge University Press, 1993), pp. 44–7. See also Levy, *Beethoven: The Ninth Symphony*, pp. 122–62.

36. "An Interview with H. C. Robbins-Landon and Sir Charles Mackerras"; booklet notes to Mackerras's recording of *Le Nozze di Figaro*, Telarc 80388 (Cleveland, 1995), p. 31.

37. Sherman, *Inside Early Music*, p. 327.

38. A. E. M Grétry, *Mémoires, ou Essais sur la musique* (Paris, 1789; facsimile of 1797 edn., New York, 1971), vol. I, pp. 40–1. Cited from Charlton, "A maître," p. 342.

39. Butt, *Playing*, p. 211. See also Laurence Dreyfus, "Early Music Defended against Its Devotees," *Musical Quarterly* 69 (1983), pp. 297–322.

40. Sherman, *Inside Early Music*, p. 284.

41. Butt, *Playing*, p. 9.

42. Allan Kozinn, "It's 30 Now, and Still Faithful to Its Mission," *The New York Times*, Oct. 19, 2002.

43. Clive Brown is one of the few to revive dual direction in opera.

44. Butt, personal communication, August 17, 2002.

45. Indeed, Daniel Barenboim likes to lead Mozart concertos from the keyboard for reasons opposite to Levin's: he says it allows for more unified phrasing. Daniel Barenboim, *A Life in Music* (London: Weidenfeld and Nicolson, 1991), p. 91. The term "noticeable," by the way, is Butt's.

46. Taruskin, "The Crooked Straight and the Rough Places Plain," *Opus* (Dec. 1986), pp. 42–3; reprinted in *Text and Act*, pp. 316–20.

47. Rifkin, quoted in Sherman, *Inside Early Music*, p. 380.
48. See, Malcolm Bilson, "Interpreting Mozart," and Eric Van Tassel, "Interpreting Mozart, a Reply," in *Early Music* 12/4 (1984), p. 519.
49. Golomb, "Modernism, Rhetoric and (De-) Personalisation in the Early Music Movement," King's College Seminar paper, August 1998; online at http://homepages.kdsi.net/~sherman/golomb1.htm
50. See ibid., and Van Tassel, "Interpreting Mozart."
51. Rifkin in Sherman, Inside Early Music, p. 380. Botstein argues that to communicate meaning through instrumental music to modern audiences – as composers hoped would happen with their audiences – may require different interpretative means than those used by the composer for period audiences. "On Conducting," p. 8.
52. Leon Botstein, "Sound and Structure in Beethoven's Orchestral Music," in Glenn Stanley, ed., *The Cambridge Companion to Beethoven* (Cambridge, 2000), p. 182.
53. Eric Van Tassel, "What Jazz Teaches Musicians," *Early Music America* 63 (Fall 2000), pp. 23–9.
54. Mackerras, "Handel," in Phelan, *Charles Mackerras: A Musician's Musician* (London, 1987), p. 306.
55. Clive Brown, "Joachim's Violin Playing and the Performance of Brahms's String Music," in Michael Musgrave and Bernard D. Sherman, *Performing Brahms* (Cambridge: Cambridge University Press, forthcoming).
56. Lydia Goehr, *The Imaginary Museum of Musical Works: An Essay in the Philosophy of Music* (Oxford: Clarendon Press, 1992); Butt, *Playing*, p. 217.

18 Training conductors

1. There were also experiments in leading with musical sound (by playing). The wide range of early time-keeping is discussed in chapter 8.
2. *The Memoirs of Hector Berlioz*, tr. David Cairns (New York: Knopf, 1969); cited from Harold C. Schonberg, *The Great Conductors* (New York: Simon and Schuster, 1967), p. 82.
3. Thomas Baltazar Janoka, *Clavis ad Theasaurum Magna Artis Musicae* (Prague: In Magno Collegio Carolino Typis Georgij Labaun, 1701) *s.v.* "Tactus."
4. Louis Spohr, *Grand Violin School*, ed. and tr. U. C. Hill (Boston: Oliver Ditson, 1851), and Hector Berlioz, *L'Art du chef d'orchestre* (Paris, 1855). A modern version of these beat diagrams is given in chapter 1. The graphic representations that appear in all modern textbooks have been only marginally updated, and the technique seems virtually unchanged.
5. Heinrich Christoph Koch, *Musiklexikon* (Frankfurt am Main: August Hermann dem Jungerin, 1802), *s.v.* "Kapellmeister." Koch also confirms that duties varied by genre, revealing that Kapellmeisters beat time during choral music, but play the figured bass during the opera. When there is a concertmaster, Koch says the Kapellmeister concentrates on the singers.
6. Hector Berlioz, *L'Art du chef d'orchestre* (Paris, 1855). The treatise proved so popular it was soon reprinted in the new edition of the *Grand traité d'instrumentation et d'orchestration modernes*, first printed in 1843 and reprinted in several languages including Mory Clark's English translation as *A Treatise on Modern Instrumentation and Orchestration to which is Appended the Chef d'Orchestre* (London and New York: Novello, Ewer, 1856).
7. In his proposal, "A Music School for Munich," Wagner mentions conducting only in reference to the piano course which, in addition to the occasional virtuoso, would aim to produce good piano teachers and "good orchestra and choral conductors." Richard Wagner, *Prose Works*. 8 vols., tr. William Ashton Ellis (London: Routledge and Kegan Paul Ltd., 1892); rept. edn., (New York: Broude Brothers, 1966), vol. IV, p. 198.
8. *Editor's note*: In some ways, the exclusion of conducting technique was also a product of more general attitudes toward musical education in the nineteenth century. Advanced conservatories specifically excluded instrumental technique from their curricula and concentrated on "artistic" training. In his Munich proposal, Wagner writes: "As with the orchestral instrument, we relegate the learning of sheer technique of the pianoforte to private tuition, and only to the already finished technician would the school stand open for instruction in the higher art of rendering" (Wagner, "School," p. 198). Despite having the greatest technique of his day, Liszt also refused to teach technique and taught only interpretation. His students are unanimous on this point. See, for example: "Of plain technic [sic] he said little or nothing. Why should he have done so? Anyone requiring instruction in technic did not belong here. Those who came to him had sufficiently mastered technic." Carl Valentine Lachmund, *Living with Liszt, Diary of Carl Lachmund: An American Pupil of Liszt, 1882–1884*, ed. Alan Walker (Stuvesant NY: Pendragon Press, 1995), p. 14. So while they recognized the importance of technique, Wagner and Liszt, at least, saw it as a preliminary stage and never considered the

paradox of learning to conduct which, unlike the piano, ends rather than begins with technique.

9. Hermann Scherchen, *Lehrbuch des dirigierens: Mit zahlreichen notenbeispielen* (Leipzig: J. J. Weber, 1929); (Mainz: B. Schott's Sohne, 1956); *Handbook of Conducting*, trans. M. D. Calvocoressi (London: Oxford University Press, 1933), repr. 1989.

10. Max Rudolph, *The Grammar of Conducting* (New York: Schirmer, 1949); second edn. (1980); third edn. (New York: Maxwell Macmillan, 1994).

11. Rudolf, first edn., p. ix.

12. Ibid., p. 299.

13. Harold C. Schonberg, *New York Times*, unidentified clipping.

14. Carl Flesch, *The Memoirs of Carl Flesch*, tr. H. Keller, (New York: Macmillan, 1958), cited from Schonberg, p. 23.

15. I have known two remarkable teachers who have the gift of creating meaningful conducting technique. One is Daniel Lewis, retired from USC in California, and the other is Jorma Panula, still teaching in Finland.

16. A more detailed discussion of this topic can be found in Harold Farberman, *The Art of Conducting Technique: A New Perspective* (Los Angeles: Warner Brothers, 1997).

17. Erich Leinsdorf, *The Composer's Advocate: A Radical Orthodoxy for Musicians* (New Haven and London: Yale University Press, 1981), p. 167.

19 The composer-conductor and modern music

1. The history of this change is discussed in chapter 8.

2. The conducting of both Mahler and Strauss is discussed in chapter 9. Table 9.1 gives the tempos Strauss used in the three recordings of his *Don Juan*.

3. Colin Matthews in the "Introduction" to the CD booklet for Benjamin Britten's *Les Illuminations, Sinfonia da Requiem, Seven Sonnets of Michelangelo*, Benjamin Britten Archive Series (London: NMC Recordings, NMC D030, 1995), p. 3.

4. Grant Llewellyn in conversation with the author (summer 2002). More on Bernstein's career as a conductor can be found in chapter 12.

5. Jean Vermeil, *Conversations with Boulez: Thoughts on Conducting* (Paris: Calmann Lévy; Portland: Amadeus, 1989), p. 33.

6. Hans Keller, *1975 (1984 minus 9)* (London: Dobson, 1975); *Music, Closed Societies and Football* (London: Toccata Press, 1988).

7. Vermeil, *conversations*, p. 135.

8. Rebecca Saunders, *G and E on A for Orchestra and 27 Music Boxes*, (Peters Edition, 1996–7).

9. Robert Fink examines the performance materials and discusses both the Stravinsky recordings and the other early performances (Koussevitsky, Monteux, Stokowski and Ansermet) in his " '*Rigoroso*': *The Rite of Spring* and the Forging of a Modernist Performing Style," *Journal of the American Musicological Society* 52/2 (Summer 1999), pp. 299–363.

10. Bramwell Tovey further discusses the commissioning of new works in chapter 15.

11. Letter from Piers Hellawell to Martyn Brabbins, 2002.

21 The future of conducting

1. Hans Keller, *Criticism* (London: Faber and Faber, 1987), pp. 21–7.

2. Arnold Schoenberg, "My Public" (1930), in *Style and Idea*, ed. Leonard Stein (London: Faber and Faber, 1975), p. 97. See also p. 28.

3. Keller, *Criticism*, p. 23.

4. Both complementary and conflicting opinions are given in chapters 1, 2, 4, 5, and 16.

5. Gary Bertini, personal communication, Detroit, fall 1982.

6. Statistics courtesy of Sound Scan Reports 2000, USA.

7. Eduard Hanslick, *Vom Musikalisch-Schönen: ein Betrag zur Revision der Ästhetik der Tonkunst*, eighth edn., (1891); *On the Musically Beautiful: A Contribution towards the Revision of the Aesthetics of Music*, tr. and ed. Geoffrey Payzant (Indianapolis: Hackett Publishing Co., 1986).

8. See chapter 15 for a further discussion of curating concerts.

Bibliography

1. Books on conducting

This is an alphabetical and largely comprehensive list of books about conducting technique, skills or training from 1800 to the present in the most common European languages. It also includes several important treatises on conducting (even if they are only pamphlets, letters or chapters in larger books).

Adey, Christopher, *Orchestral Performance: A Guide for Conductors and Players* (London: Faber, 1998)

Ansermet, Ernest, *Der Dirigent* (Zürich: Verlag der Arche, 1965)

Ansermet, Ernest, *Les fondements de la musique dans la conscience humaine et autres écrits* (Paris: Robert Laffont, 1989)

Badal, James, *Recording the Classics: Maestros, Music, and Technology* (Kent, OH: Kent State University Press, 1996)

Bailey, Wayne, *Aural Skills for Conductors* (Mountain View, CA: Mayfield, 1991)

Bakaleinikoff, Vladimir, *Elementary Rules of Conducting for Orchestra, Band, and Chorus* (New York: Boosey and Hawkes, Belwin, 1938)

Bamberger, Carl, ed., *The Conductor's Art* (New York: McGraw-Hill, 1965)

Barbirolli, John, "The Art of Conducting," *Penguin Music Magazine* 2 (1947)

Berg, David Eric, *Early and Classic Symphonies and the Functions of a Conductor* (New York: The Caxton Institute, 1927)

Berlioz, Hector, *Grand traité d'instrumentation et d'orchestration modernes: nouvelle édition augmentée de l'Art du chef d'orchestre* (Paris: Schonenberger, 1855); *A Treatise of Modern Instrumentation and Orchestration to which is appended The Chef d'orchestre*, tr. Mary Clarke (London and New York: J. L. Peters, 1858); *The Art of Conducting* (New York: Carl Fischer, 1936); *Berlioz's Orchestration Treatise: A Translation and Commentary*, ed. Hugh Macdonald (Cambridge: Cambridge University Press, 2002)

Bernard, D., *Le Chef d'orchestre* (Paris, 1989)

Bernstein, Leonard, "The Art of Conducting," in *The Joy of Music* (London: Weidenfeld and Nicolson, 1960)

Blackman, Charles, *Behind the Baton* (New York: Charos Enterprises, 1964)

Blitz, Eduoard, *Quelques considérations sur l'art du chef d'orchestre* (Leipzig and Brussels, 1887)

Bodegraven, Paul van, *The School Music Conductor* (Chicago: Hall and McCleary, 1942)

Boult, Adrian, *Handbook on the Technique of Conducting* (Oxford and London: Hall, H. Reeves, 1921, 1949); (London: Paterson's, 1968)

Boult, Adrian, *Thoughts on Conducting* (London: Phoenix House, 1963); (London: Hamish Hamilton, 1973)

Boult, Adrian, *Boult on Music* (London: Toccata Press, 1983)

Bowles, Michael, *The Art of Conducting* (New York: Doubleday, 1959); (New York: Da Capo Press, 1975)

Bowles, Michael, *The Conductor: His Artistry and Craftsmanship* (London: G. Bell, 1961)

Braithwaite, Warwick, *The Conductor's Art* (London: Williams and Norgate, 1952); (New York: McGraw-Hill, 1965)

Busch, Fritz, *Der Dirigent* (Zurich: Atlantis, 1961)

Cahn-Speyer, Rudolf, *Handbuch des Dirigierens* (Leipzig: Breitkopf and Härtel, 1909)

Carnett, Ellis, *The Technique of Conducting* (Nashville: Broadman, 1948)

Carse, Adam, *Orchestral Conducting* (London: Augener, 1935); (Westport, CT: Greenwood Press, 1971)

Carse, Adam, *The Orchestra from Beethoven to Berlioz: A History of the Orchestra in the First Half of the 19th Century, and of the Development of Orchestra Baton-Conducting* (Cambridge: W. Heffer and Sons Ltd., 1948)

Coward, Henry, Sir, *Choral Technique and Interpretation* (London: Novello, 1914); supplement, *"C.T.I." The Secret: "Les nuances bien indiquées"* (London: Novello, 1938)

Cox-Ife, William, *The Elements of Conducting* (New York: J. Day, 1964)

Croger, Thomas Rudolfus, *Notes on Conductors and Conducting* (London: "Nonconformist Musical Journal" Office, [1899]); second rev. edn. (London: William Reeves, 1903); sixth edn. (1938); (reprint service, 1991)

Curtis, Larry, and Kuehn, David, *A Guide to Successful Conducting* (Dubuque, IA: Brown and Benchmark, 1992)

Dechant, Herman, *Dirigieren* (Vienna: Herder, 1985)

Deldevez, Edouard Marie Ernest, *L'Art du chef d'orchestre* (Paris: Firmin-Didôt, 1878)

Del Mar, Norman, *Conducting Beethoven: Vol. I, The Symphonies* (Oxford: Clarendon Press, 1992)

Del Mar, Norman, *Conducting Beethoven: Vol. II, Overtures, Concertos, Missa Solemnis* (Oxford: Clarendon Press, 1993)

Del Mar, Norman, *Conducting Brahms* (Oxford: Clarendon Press, 1993)

Del Mar, Norman, *Conducting Berlioz* (Oxford: Clarendon Press, 1997)

Del Mar, Norman, *Conducting Elgar*, completed and ed. Jonathan Del Mar (Oxford: Clarendon Press, 1998)

Del Mar, Norman, *Conducting Favourite Concert Pieces*, ed. Jonathan Del Mar (Oxford: Clarendon Press, 1998)

Demarer, Robert W. Jr, Moses, Don V., and Ohmes, Allan F., *Face to Face with an Orchestra* (Princeton, NJ: Prestige Publications, Inc., 1987)

Demarer, Robert W. Jr., and Moses, Don V., *The Complete Conductor: A Comprehensive Resource for the Professional Conductor of the Twenty-First Century* (Englewood Cliffs, NJ: Prentice-Hall, 1995)

Diestel, Hans, *Ein Orchestermusiker uber das Dirigieron* (Berlin: Edition Adler GmbH, 1931)

Dubois, Anthony, *Étude sur la direction d'orchestre* (Anvers: Lachisse, 1899)

Earhart, Will, *The Eloquent Baton* (New York: Witmark and Sons, 1931)

Farberman, Harold, *The Art of Conducting: A New Perspective* (Miami: Warner Brothers, 1997)

Fétis, Francois Joseph, *Manuel des compositeurs, directeurs de musique, chefs d'orchestre et de musique militaire* (Paris: Schlesinger, 1837); tr. Wellington Guernsey (London, 1870); *Harmony and Instrumentation: A Manual for Composers, Musical Directors, Orchestral Leaders and Bandmasters*, rev. S. Victor Balfour (London: J. R. Lafleur and Son, 1922)

Finn, William Joseph, *The Conductor Raises His Baton* (New York, London: Harper Brothers, 1944)

Fuchs, Peter Paul, *The Psychology of Conducting* (New York: MCA Music, 1969)

Furtwängler, Wilhelm, and Abendroth, Walter, *Gespräche über Musik* (Vienna and Zurich: Atlantis Verlag, 1948); *Concerning Music*, tr. L. J. Lawrence (London: Boosey and Hawkes, 1953)

Furtwängler, Wilhelm, and Abendroth, Walter, *Notebooks 1924–1954*, ed. Michael Tanner, tr. Shaun Whiteside (London: Quartet Books, 1989)

Furtwängler, Wilhelm, *Furtwängler on Music: Essays and Addresses,* tr. Ronald Taylor (Aldershot: Scolar Press, 1991)

Galkin, Elliott W., *A History of Orchestral Conducting in Theory and Practice* (New York: Pendragon Press, 1988)

Gehrkens, Karl W., *Essentials in Conducting* (Boston: Oliver Ditson, 1919)

Gehrkens, Karl W., *Twenty Lessons in Conducting* (Boston: Oliver Ditson, 1930)

Gielen, Michael and Paul Fiebig, *Beethoven im Gesträch: Die Neun Sinfonien* (Stuttgart: Metzler, 1995)

Goldbeck, Frederik, *The Perfect Conductor: An Introduction to His Skill and Art* (New York: Pellegrini and Cudahy, 1951); (London: Dobson, 1960)

Green, Elizabeth A[dine] H[erkimer], *The Modern Conductor: A College Text on Conducting Based on the Technical Principles of Nicolai Malko as Set Forth in his The Conductor and his Baton* [see below] (Englewood Cliffs, NJ: Prentice-Hall, 1961); (sixth edn., 1997)

Green, Elizabeth A[dine] H[erkimer], *The Conductor and His Score* (Englewood Cliffs, NJ: Prentice-Hall, 1975)

Green, Elizabeth A[dine] H[erkimer], *The Dynamic Orchestra* (Englewood Cliffs, NJ: Prentice-Hall, 1987)

Grosbayne, Benjamin, *A Bibliography of Works and Articles on Conducting and Related Fields in Various Languages from the Sixteenth Century to the Present Time* (New York: Brooklyn College mimeographed, 1934)

Grosbayne, Benjamin, *Techniques of Modern Orchestral Conducting* (Cambridge, MA: Harvard University Press, 1956); (second edn., 1973)

Haberlen, John, *Mastering Conducting Techniques* (Champaign, IL: Mark Foster Music, 1977)

Hillis, Margaret, *At Rehearsals* (Barrington, IL: American Choral Foundation, The Letter Shop, 1969)

Hoesen, Karl Duane van, *Handbook of Conducting* (New York: Appleton Century Crofts, 1950)

Holmes, Malcolm Haughton, *Conducting an Amateur Orchestra* (Cambridge, MA: Harvard University Press, 1951)

Hölzl, P., *Die Technik des Dirigierens* (Vienna, 1989)

Hubbard, Thomas, *A Baton for the Conductor* (Boston: Houghton Mifflin, 1958)

Hunsberger, Donald, and Ernst, Roy, *The Art of Conducting* (New York: Knopf, 1983); second edn. (New York: McGraw-Hill, 1992)

Inghelbrecht, Désiré-Emile, *Le Chef d'orchestre et son équipe* (Paris: René Juilliard, 1949); *The Conductor's World*, tr. G. Prerauer and S. Malcolm Kirk (London and New York: Peter Nevill, 1953); (New York: Library Publishers, 1954); (Encore Music Editions, 1979)

Inghelbrecht, Désiré-Emile, *Le Chef d'orchestre parle au public* (Paris, 1957)

Jacobson, Bernard, *Conductors on Conducting* [Levine, Davis, Haitink, Boult, Harnoncourt, Mackerras, Serebrier, Giulini] (Frenchtown, NJ: Columbia Publishing, 1979)

Jakobi, Theodor, *Die Kunst des Partiturspielens* (Berlin: Hesse, 1956)

Jungheinrich, Hans-Klaus, *Der Musikdarsteller: Zur Kunst des Dirigenten* (Frankfurt am Main: S. Fischer, 1986)

Junker, Karl Ludwig, *Einige der Vornehmsten Pflichten eines Kapellmeisters oder Musikdirektors* (Winterthur: Steiner, 1782)

Kahn, Emil, *Conducting* (New York: Free Press, 1965)

Kahn, Emil, *Workbook for Conducting* (NewYork: The Free Press, 1965); second edn., *Conducting Guide to Selected Scores* (New York: Schirmer, London: Collier Macmillan, 1976)

Kinyon, John Leroy, *The Teacher on the Podium* (New York: Alfred Publishing, 1975)

Klemperer, Otto, *Klemperer on Music: Shavings from a Musician's Workbench*, ed. Martin Anderson (London: Toccata Press, 1986)

Kling, Henri, *Der Vollkommene Musik-dirigent* (Hanover: Oertel, 1890)

Kohut, Daniel, and Grant, Joseph, *Learning to Conduct and Rehearse* (Englewood Cliffs, NJ: Prentice-Hall, 1990)

Kolisch, Rudolph, *Rudolph Kolisch, Zur Theorie der Aufführung* (Munich: Text + Kritik, 1983)

Kondrashin, Kyril, *Die Kunst des Dirigierens* (Munich, 1989)

Koury, Daniel, *Orchestral Performance Practices in the 19th Century* (Ann Arbor: UMI Research Press, 1986)

Krips, Josef, *Ohne Liebe kann man keine Musik machen. Erinnerungen* (Vienna: Boehlau Verlag, 1994)

Krone, Max Thomas, *Expressive Conducting* (Chicago: Neil A. Kjos, 1945)

Krueger, Karl, *The Way of the Conductor: His Origins, Purposes, and Procedures* (New York: Scribner's, 1958)

Kufferath, Maurice, *L'Art de diriger l'orchestre* (Paris: Fischbacher, 1891); third edn. (Paris, 1909)

Labuta, Joseph A., *Basic Conducting Techniques* (Englewood Cliffs, NJ: Prentice-Hall, 1982)

Lara, Francisco Navarro, *Nueva Técnica de Dirección de Orquesta, Coro y Banda* [NB: At Nov. 2002, this book existed on the web only, and may be downloaded at www.ari.es/franav/navarrolara.zip]

Leinsdorf, Erich, *Lesen Sie Musik oder "aimez-vous Beethoven?"* (Frankfurt: Litolffs Verlag, 1976)

Leinsdorf, Erich, *The Composer's Advocate, A Radical Orthodoxy for Musicians* (New Haven: Yale University Press, 1981)

Leinsdorf, Erich, *Erich Leinsdorf on Music* (Portland: Amadeus Press, 1997)

Liebert, Georges, ed., *L'Art du chef d'orchestre* (Paris: Hachette Pluriel, 1988)

Liebert, Georges, ed., *Ni empereur, ni roi, chef d'orchestre, Découvertes. Musique 87* (Paris: Gallimard, 1990)

Lindenberg, Edouard, *Comment lire une partition d'orchestre* (Paris: Heugel, 1952)

Linton, Stanley, *Conducting Fundamentals* (New York: Prentice-Hall, 1982)

Liszt, Franz, "Letter on Conducting" to Richard Pohl in Dresden, from Weimar, Nov. 5, 1853. Original written in French to Pohl: Franz Liszt, *Briefe*, ed. La Mara [Marie Lipsius] (Leipzig: Breitkopf & Härtel, 1893), vol. I, pp. 142–5, letter no. 104); it first appeared in Pohl's German translation in his pamphlet *Das Karlsruher Musikfest im Oktober 1853 unter Liszts Leitung* (Leipzig: Bruno Hinze, 1853), published under the pseudonym "Hoplit."

Long, Gerry, *The Conductor's Workshop: A Workbook for Instrumental Conducting* (Dubuque, IA: W. C. Brown, second edn., 1977)

Lualdi, Adriano, *L'arte di dirigere l'orchestra* (Milan: Hoepli, 1940); second edn., (1949); third edn. (1957)

Lumley, J[ohn] S[tuart] P[enton], and Nigel Springthorpe, *The Art of Conducting: A Guide to Essential Skills* (London: Rhinegold, 1989)

McElheran, Brock, *Conducting Technique for Beginners and Professionals* (New York: Oxford University Press, 1966); rev. edn. (1989)

McKelvy, James, *Music for Conducting Class* (Champaign, IL: Mark Foster Music, 1988)

Malko, Nicolai, *The Conductor and His Baton* (Copenhagen: Wilhelm Hansen, 1950); see also Green, Elizabeth

Mason, William, *Touch and Technic; or, The Technic of Artistic Touch* (Philadelphia: T. Presser, 1897)

May, Robin, *Behind the Baton* (London: Muller, 1981)

Meek, Charles J., *Conducting Made Easy for Directors of Amateur Musical Organizations* (Metuchen, NJ: Scarecrow Press, 1988)

Melichar, Alois, *Der Vollkommene Dirigent* (Munich: Langen-Müller, 1981)

Mengelberg, Willem, *De Taak en de Studie der Reproductieve Toonkunst* (Amsterdam: Munster, 1934)

Mikorey, Franz, *Grundzüge einer Dirigierlehre: Betrachtungen über Technik und Poesie des modernen Orchester-Dirigierens*, 2 vols. (Leipzig: Kahnt, 1917)

Moe, Daniel, *Problems in Conducting* (Minneapolis: Augsburg, rev. 1973)

Morales, Olallo, *Handbok i Dirigering* (Stockholm: Nordiska Musikförlaget, 1946)

Norlind, Tobias, *Dirigeringskonstens Historia* (Stockholm: Nordiska Musikförlaget, 1944)

Noyes, Frank, *Fundamentals of Conducting* (Dubuque, IA: W. C. Brown, 1954)

Otterstein, Adolph William, *The Baton in Motion* (New York, Boston: C. Fischer, 1942)

Pappoutsakis, Ippocrates, *Diagrams of Basic Movements in Conducting* (Boston: Birchard, 1943)

Pembaur, Josef, *Uber das Dirigieren* (Leipzig: Leuckart, 1892)

Pisa, Agostino, *Breve Dichiarazione della battuta musicale*. Fl. 1611. rept. (Bologna: Forni, 1969)

Prausnitz, Frederik, *Score and Podium: A Complete Guide to Conducting* (New York: Norton, 1983)

Previtale, F. *Guida allo Studio della Direzone d'Orchestra* (Rome: De Santis, 1951)

Ross, Allan A., *Techniques for Beginning Conductors* (Belmont, CA: Wadsworth, 1976)

Rozhdestvensky, Gennady, *Dirizherskaya Applikatura* [Conductor's Lessons] (Leningrad, 1974)

Rudolph, Max. *The Grammar of Conducting* (New York: Schirmer, 1949); second edn. (1980); third edn. (Maxwell MacMillan, 1994)

Sacchi, Filippo, *The Magic Baton* (London: Putnam, 1957)

Saminsky, Lazare, *Essentials of Conducting* (London: Dobson, 1958)

Scaglia, C., *Guida allo studio della direzione d'orchestra* (Milan, 1929)

Scaramelli, Giuseppe, *Saggio sopra i doveri di un primo violino directtore d'orchestra* (Trieste, 1811)

Schenker, Heinrich, "Konzertdirigenten" (1894), "Bülow-Weingartner"" (1896), "Die Jungen Dirigenten" (1896); rept. *Heinrich Schenker als Essayist und Kritiker*, ed. Hellmut Federhofer (Hildesheim: Olms, 1990)

Scherchen, Hermann, *Lehrbuch des dirigierens: Mit zahlreichen notenbeispielen* (Leipzig: J. J. Weber, 1929); (Mainz: B. Schott's Sohne, 1956); *Handbook of Conducting*, tr. M[ichael] D[imitri] Calvocoressi (London: Oxford University Press, 1933); repr. edns. (1946, 1989): *Manuale del direttore d'orchestra* (Milan: Curci, 1966)

Scherchen, Hermann, *Vom Wesen der Musik* (Zürich: Mondial Verlag, 1946)

Scherchen, Hermann, *Musik für Jederman* (Winterthur: Mondial Verlag, 1950)

Schmid, Adolf, *The Language of the Baton* (New York: Schirmer, 1937)

Schröder, Karl, *Katechismus des Dirigierens und Taktierens: Der Kapellmeister und sein Wirkungskreis*, 2 vols. (Berlin, 1889); rev. edn. (Leipzig: Max Hesse's Verlag, 1900); *Handbook of Conducting*, tr. J. Mathews (London: Augener, 1889)

Schubert, Franz Ludwig, *Der Praktische Musik-Direktor oder Wegweiser für Musik-Dirigenten* (Leipzig: Merseberger, 1873)

Schuller, Gunther, *The Compleat Conductor* (London: Oxford University Press, 1994)

Schünemann, Georg, *Zur Geschichte des Dirigirens* (Leipzig: Breitkopf and Härtel, 1913); (Hildesheim: Olms, 1965)

Seidl, Anton, *Moderne Dirigenten* (Berlin, 1902); *On Conducting* (New York, 1899)

Sellers, Ernest, *Elements of Musical Notation and Conducting* (Nashville: Broadman, 1938)

Sendrey, Alfred, *Dirigierkunde* (Leipzig: Breitkopf and Härtel, 1932)

Shore, Bernard, *The Orchestra Speaks* (London: Longmans, Green, 1946)

Stoessel, Albert, *The Technique of the Baton* (New York: Fischer, 1920)

Swarowsky, Hans, *Wahrung der Gestalt* (Vienna: Universal Edition, 1979)

Swift, Frederick Fay, *Fundamentals of Conducting* (Rockville Centre, NY: Belwin, 1961)

Szendrei [also Sendrey], Alfred, *Dirigierkunde* (Leipzig: Breitkopf and Härtel, 1932)

Thienemann, Alfred Bernhard, *Die Kunst des Dirigierens* (Potsdam: Bonness and Hachfeld)

Thomas, Kurt, *Lehrbuch der Chorleitung*, vol. I (Leipzig: Breitkopf and Härtel, 1935); twentieth rev. edn. (1982); rev. A. Wagner (1991); vol. II (Leipzig: Breitkopf and Härtel, 1937); fifteenth rev. edn. (1982); vol. III (Leipzig: Breitkopf and Härtel, 1948); eleventh rev. edn. 1983); abridged as *The Choral Conductor: The Technique of Choral Conducting in Theory and Practice*, ed. and tr. Alfred Mann and William H. Reese (New York: Associated Music Publishers, 1971)

Vermeil, Jean, *Conversations de Pierre Boulez sur la direction d'orchestre* (Paris: Editions Plume, 1989); *Conversations with Boulez: Thoughts on Conducting*, tr. Camille Naish (Portland: Amadeus Press, 1996)

Wagar, Jeannine, ed., *Conductors in Conversation Fifteen Contemporary Conductors Discuss Their Lives and Profession* [Blomstedt, Comet, Davies, von Dohnanyi, Dutoit, Herbig, Hillis, Kiesler, Masur, Mata, Norrington, Previn, Skrowaczewski, Slatkin, de Waart] (Boston: G. K. Hall, 1991)

Wagner, Richard. *Über das Dirigieren* (Leipzig: Breitkopf and Härtel, 1869); "About Conducting," *Richard Wagner Prose Works*, tr. William Ashton Ellis, second edn., 8 vols. (London: Kegan Paul, Trench, Trübner and Co. Ltd., 1895), vol. IV, p. 314; "On Conducting," *Three Wagner Essays*, tr. Robert L. Jacobs (London: Ernst Eulenburg Ltd., 1979); *On Conducting (Ueber das Dirigiren): A Treatise on Style in the Execution of Classical Music*, tr. Edward Dannreuther (London: William Reeves, 1887), rept. *Wagner on Conducting* (New York: Dover Publications, 1989)

Waldorf, Jerzy, *Diably i anioly* (Warsaw: Wiedza Powszechna, 1994)

Walter, Bruno, *Von der Musik und vom Musizieren* (Leipzig: S. Fischer Verlag, 1957); *Of Music and Music-Making*, tr. Paul Hamburger (New York: W. W. Norton, 1961)

Waltershausen, Hermann, *Die Kunst des Dirigierens* (Berlin, 1942)

Waters, Fred Elbert, *The Music Conductor's Manual* (Elkhart, IN, 1929)

Waters, Fred Elbert, *Practical Baton Technique for Student Conductors* (Chicago: Gamble Hinged Music, 1939)

Weingartner, Felix, *"Über das Dirigieren," Neue Deutsche Rundschau* (Berlin); first book edn. (Berlin: 1895); second edn. (1869); third edn. [with substantial revision] (1905); *On Conducting*, tr. Ernest Newman; rev. (Leipzig and Berlin: Breitkopf and Härtel, 1925); (New York: Edwin Kalmus, 1934); (New York: Dover, 1969)

Weingartner, Felix, *Ratschläge für Aufführungen der Symphonien Beethovens* (Leipzig, 1906); third rev. edn., *Ratschläge für Aufführungen klassischer Symphonien, i; On the Performance of Beethoven's Symphonies*, tr. Jessie Crosland (1907); *On The Performance of Beethoven Symphonies* (New York: Kalmus, 1934); rpt. edn. *Weingartner on Music and Conducting* (New York: Dover Publications, 1969)

Weingartner, Felix, *Ratschläge für Aufführungen klassischer Symphonien, iii: Mozart* (Leipzig, 1923); trans. Theodore Albrecht, "On the Performance of the Symphonies of Mozart," *Journal of the Conductor's Guild* 6/3 (Summer 1985), pp. 66–78.

Weisberg, Arthur, *Performing Twentieth-Century Music* (New Haven: Yale University Press, 1993)

Wilson, Robert B., *The Technique of Orchestral Conducting* (London: The Macmillan Company, 1937)

Wood, Sir Henry, *About Conducting* (London: Sylvan Press, 1945); (St. Clair Shores, MI: Scholarly Press, 1972)

Wooldridge, David. *A Conductor's World* (London: Barrie and Rockliff, 1970)

Zopff, Hermann, *Der Eingehende Dirigent* (Leipzig: Merseberger, 1881)

Zurletti, Michelangelo, *La direzione d'orchestra* (Rome: Ricordi, 1985)

2. Books on conductors

Since books about conductors and their lives are quite common (and of varying quality), this is a greatly abbreviated list. (A complete list is forthcoming.) Books in English are given some priority as are books by conductors. While it is not always possible to distinguish between memoirs that ruminate on life and those that offer more practical advice on conducting, where that happens (as with Nicolai Malko or Bruno Walter for example) the technical manual is listed above and the biography is listed here. The list is limited to books, with the exception of several chapters, dissertations and articles on women conductors graciously provided by J. Michele Edwards.

Ammer, Christine, *Unsung: A History of Women in American Music,* rev. edn. (Portland: Amadeus, 2001)

Ansermet, Anne, *Ernest Ansermet, mon père* (Lausanne: Payot, 1983)

Antek, Samuel, and Hupka, Robert, *This Was Toscanini* (New York: Vanguard, 1963)

Appert, Donald L., *Berlioz the Conductor* (DMA dissertation, University of Kansas, 1985)

Ardoin, John, *The Furtwängler Record* (Portland, OR: Amadeus Press, 1994)

Assenbaum, Elisabeth, *Dirigentinnen Heute. Versuch einer musiksoziologischen Aufarbeitung* (Düsseldorf: Tokkata-Verlag, 1991)

Atkins, Harold, and Cotes, Peter, *The Barbirollis: A Musical Marriage* (London: Robson, 1983)

Atkins, Harold, and Newman, Archie, *Beecham Stories* (London: Robson Books, 1978)

Bachmann, Robert, *Karajan, Anmerkungen zu einer Karriere* (Düsseldorf: Econ Verlag, 1983); *Karajan: Notes On A Career,* tr. Shaun Whiteside (London: Quartet, 1990)

Barenboim, Daniel, *A Life in Music* (London: Weidenfeld and Nicolson, 1991)

Batagova, Tatiana, *Veronika Dudarova* (Moscow: Muzyka, 2001)

Batiz, Enriqué, *Enriqué Batiz* (Mexico City: Universidad Autonoma Metropolitana-Azcapotzalco, 1984)

Batley, Thomas, ed., *Sir Charles Hallé's Concerts in Manchester, 1858–1895* (Manchester: Sever, 1896)

Bebbington, Warren A., *The Orchestral Conducting Practice of Richard Wagner*, Ph.D. dissertation, State University of New York, 1984

Beecham, Thomas, *A Mingled Chime: Leaves from an Autobiography* (London: Hutchinson, 1944); (London: Columbus Books, 1987)

Beecham, Thomas, *Beecham Stories: Anecdotes, Sayings and Impressions of Sir Thomas Beecham,* compiled and ed. Harold Atkins and Archie Newman

(London: Robson, 1978); (New York: St. Martin's Press, 1979); (London: Future
Publications, 1979); (London: Warner, 1993) second rev. edn. (London: Robson,
2001)

Berlioz, Hector, *Les Soirées dans l'orchestre* (Paris: Michel Lévy Frères, 1852);
Evenings in the Orchestra, tr. and ed. Jacques Barzun (New York: Alfred A. Knopf,
1956); rpt. edn. (Chicago: University of Chicago Press, 1973)

Berlioz, Hector, *Mémoires* (Paris: 1870); *Autobiography*, tr. Rachel and Eleanor
Holmes, 2 vols. (London: Macmillan, 1884); *Memoirs of Hector Berlioz,
1803–1865*, tr. and rev. Ernest Newman (New York: Alfred A. Knopf, 1932);
rpt. (Dover, 1966); *Memoirs*, tr. David Cairns (New York: W. W. Norton, 1975)

Bertenssen, Sergei, and Leyda, Jay, *Sergei Rachmaninoff: A Lifetime in Music*
(London: Allen and Unwin, 1965)

Biancolli, Louis, and Peyser, Herbert, *Masters of the Orchestra* (New York: Putnam's,
1954)

Bing, Rudolph, *5000 Nights at the Opera* (New York: Doubleday, 1972)

Blackman, Charles, *Behind the Baton* (New York: Charos Enterprises, 1964)

Blackwood, Alan, *Sir Thomas Beecham: The Man and His Music* (London: Barrie and
Jenkins, 1994)

Blaukopf, Kurt, *Grosse Dirigenten* (Teuffen: Verlag Arthur Niggli, 1957); (London:
Arco, 1955)

Blyth, Alan, *Colin Davis* (London: Shepperton, 1969); (London: Ian Allen, 1972)

Bogdanov-Berezovsky, V., *The Soviet Conductor Mravinsky* (Leningrad, 1956)

Böhm, Karl, *Ich erinnere mich ganz genau* (Zürich: Diogenes Verlag, 1968); *A Life
Remembered*, tr. John Kehoe (New York: Marion Boyars, 1992)

Bookspan, Martin, and Yockey, Ross, *Zubin: The Zubin Mehta Story* (New York:
Harper and Row, 1978); (London: Hale, 1980)

Boulez, Pierre, *Notes of an Apprenticeship*, tr. Herbert Weinstock (New York: Knopf,
1968)

Boult, Adrian, *My Own Trumpet* (London: Hamish Hamilton, 1973)

Bowers, Jane M., and Tick, Judith, eds., *Women Making Music: The Western Art
Tradition, 1150–1950* (Urbana: University of Illinois, 1986)

Briggs, John, *Leonard Bernstein* (New York: World Publishing, 1961)

Brook, Donald, *Conductors' Gallery* (London: Rockliff, 1945)

Brook, Donald, *International Gallery of Conductors* (London: Rockliff, 1951)

Brown, Clive, *Louis Spohr: A Critical Biography* (Cambridge: Cambridge University
Press, 1984)

Bülow, Hans von, *Briefe und Schriften*, 8 vols. (Leipzig: Breitkopf and Härtel, 1899);
The Early Correspondence of Hans von Bülow, tr. Constance Bache (New York:
D. Appleton and Co., 1896)

Burghauser, Jarmil, *Slavní Cestí Dirigenti* [*Great Czech Conductors*] (Prague: Státní
hudební vydavatelství [State Art Publishers], 1963)

Burton, Humphrey, *Leonard Bernstein* (New York: Doubleday, 1994)

Burton, William Westbrook, ed., *Conversations about Bernstein* (London: Oxford,
1995)

Busch, Fritz, *Pages from a Musician's Life*, tr. Marjorie Strachey (London: Hogarth,
1953)

Cardus, Neville, *Sir Thomas Beecham* (London: Collins, 1961)

Carse, Adam, *The Life of Jullien, Adventurer, Showman, Conductor* (Cambridge: Heffer, 1951)

Chasins, Abram, *Leopold Stokowski* (London: Dutton, 1979)

Cheng, Marietta Nieh-hwa, "Women Conductors: Has the Train Left the Station?" *Harmony: Forum of the Symphony Orchestra Institute* 6 (1998), pp. 81–90

Chesterman, Robert. *Conversations with Conductors* [Ansermet, Bernstein, Boult, Klemperer, Stokowski, Walter] (London: Robson Books, 1976); (New York: Robson Books, 1976)

Chotzinoff, Samuel, *Toscanini: An Intimate Portrait* (London: Hamish Hamilton, 1956)

Christensen, Lance Eugene, *I Will Not Be Deflected from My Course: The Life of Dr. Antonia Brico*, M.H. thesis (University of Colorado at Denver, 2000)

Christopoulo, Maria, *Dmitri Mitropoulos: His Life and Works* (Athens, 1971)

Cowden, Robert, *Concert and Opera Conductors: A Bibliography of Biographical Materials* (New York: Greenwood, 1987)

Damrosch, Walter, *My Musical Life* (New York: Scribner's, 1923); rev. edn. (1935)

Daniel, Oliver, *Stokowski: A Counterpoint of View* (New York: Dodd, Mead, 1982)

Deck, Marvin L. von, *Gustav Mahler in New York: His Conducting Activities in New York City, 1908–1911*, Ph.D. dissertation (New York University, 1973)

DePriest, James, *Au fûr et à mesure* (Saint-Lambert, Québec: Editions Heritage, 1980)

Dickson, Harry Ellis, *Gentlemen, More Dolce Please!* (Boston: Beacon Press, 1974)

Dickson, Harry Ellis, *Directory of Conductors in Canada* (Toronto: Association of Canadian Orchestras, 1977)

Dickson, Harry Ellis, *Arthur Fiedler and the Boston Pops* (Boston: Houghton Mifflin, 1981)

Dickson, Harry Ellis, *Beating Time: A Memoir* (Boston: Northeastern University Press, 1994)

Dobrin, Peter, "A Woman's Hand on the Baton: Four of the Few Women Who Work as Conductors Gather to Talk of Prejudices, Perceptions and Prospects," *Philadelphia Inquirer*, June 30, 2002

Dohnanyi, Christoph von, *Christoph von Dohnanyi* (Frankfurt: Litolff, 1976)

Dorati, Antal, *Notes of Seven Decades* (London: Hodder and Stoughton, 1979)

Durham, Lowell M., *Abravanel!* (Salt Lake City: University of Utah Press, 1989)

Dyment, Christopher, *Felix Weingartner: Recollections and Recordings* (Rickmansworth: Triad Press Bibliographical Series No. 5, 1976)

Endler, Franz, *Karl Böhm* (Hamburg: Hoffmann and Campe, 1981)

Endler, Franz, *Karajan* (Hamburg: Hoffman and Campe, 1992)

Ewen, David. *The Man with the Baton* (New York: Thomas Crowell, 1936)

Ewen, David. *Dictators of the Baton* (Chicago: Alliance Books, 1943)

Ewen, David. *Famous Conductors* (New York: Dodd, Mead, 1966)

Ewen, David. *Musicians since 1900: Performers in Concert and Opera* (New York: H. W. Wilson, 1978)

Fifield, Christopher, *True Artist and True Friend: A Biography of Hans Richter* (Oxford: Clarendon Press, 1993)

Finck, Henry Theophilus, ed., *Anton Seidl: A Memorial By His Friends* (New York: Scribner's, 1899)

Fomin, Vitalii, *Mravinsky Conducts* (Leningrad: Muzyka, 1976)

Fomin, Vitalii, *Evgenii Aleksandrovich Mravinskii* (Moscow : Muzyka, 1983)

Freedland, Michael, *André Previn* (London: Century, 1991)

Gartenberg, Egon, *Mahler: The Man and His Music* (New York: Schirmer, 1978)

Gavoty, Bernard, *Igor Markevitch* (Monaco: R. Kister, 1954)

Gavoty, Bernard, *André Cluytens* (Geneva: R. Kister, 1955)

Gavoty, Bernard, *Wilhelm Furtwängler* (Geneva: R. Kister, 1956)

Gavoty, Bernard, *Herbert von Karajan* (Geneva: R. Kister, 1961)

Gavoty, Bernard, *Carl Schuricht* (Geneva: R. Kister, 1961)

Gavoty, Bernard, *Bruno Walter* (Geneva: R. Kister, 1961)

Geissmar, Bertha, *The Baton and the Jackboot* (London: Hamish Hamilton, 1944)

Geissmar, Bertha, *Two Worlds of Music* (New York: Da Capo Press, 1975)

Geitel, Klaus, *Grosse deutsche Dirigenten: 100 Jahre Berliner Philharmoniker* (Berlin: Severin and Siedler, 1981)

Gerboth, Christopher B., *An Inventory of the Papers of Dr. Antonia Brico Collection Number 1457: A Holding of the Library of the Colorado Historical Society* (Denver, CO: The Colorado Historical Society, 1990)

Gillis, Daniel, *Furtwängler Recalled* (Zürich: Atlantis-Verlag, 1965); (New York: Meredith Press, 1965)

Gillis, Daniel, *Furtwängler and America* (New York and Palo Alto: Maryland Books, 1970)

Gilman, Lawrence, *Arturo Toscanini and Great Music* (New York: Farrar and Rinehart, 1938)

Gilmour, John D., *Sir Thomas Beecham: The Seattle Years 1941–1943* (Aberdeen, Washington: World Press, 1978)

Godfrey, Daniel Eyers, *Memories and Music: Thirty Five Years of Conducting* (London: Hutchinson, 1924)

Goosens, Eugene, *Overture and Beginners: A Musical Autobiography* (London: Methuen, 1951)

Gradenwitz, Peter, *Leonard Bernstein: The Infinite Variety of a Musician* (New York: Berg, 1987)

Greenfield, Edward, *André Previn* (London: Ian Allen, 1973)

Greer, David, ed., *Hamilton Harty: His Life and Music* (New York: DaCapo Press, 1980)

Groh, Jan Bell, *Evening the Score: Women in Music and the Legacy of Frédérique Petrides* (Fayetteville: University of Arkansas Press, 1991)

Gruen, John, *The Private World of Leonard Bernstein* (New York: Viking Press, 1968)

Haggin, B. H., *The Toscanini Musicians Knew* (New York: Horizon Press, 1967)

Hallé, Charles, *The Autobiography of Charles Hallé with Correspondence and Diaries*, ed. Michael Kennedy (London: Paul Elek Books, 1972)

Handy, Antoinette, *Black Conductors* (Metuchen, NJ: Scarecrow Press, 1997)

Hart, Philip, *Conductors, A New Generation* (New York: Scribner's, 1979); (London: Robson Books, 1980)

Hart, Philip, *Fritz Reiner: A Biography* (Evanston, IL: Northwestern University Press, 1994)

Harty, Hamilton, and Freer, David, eds., *Hamilton Harty, Early Memories* (Belfast: Queen's University Press, 1979)

Henahan, Donal, "Prodigious Sarah [Caldwell]," *New York Times* (October 5, 1975), pp. 93–8.

Henschel, George, *Musings and Memories of a Musician* (1919); (New York: Da Capo Press, 1979)

Herzfeld, Friedrich, *Wilhelm Furtwängler, Weg und Wesen* (Leipzig: Goldmann, 1941)

Herzfeld, Friedrich, *Herbert von Karajan* (Berlin: Rembrandt Verlag, 1962)

Heyworth, Peter, ed., *Conversations with Klemperer* (London: Gollancz, 1973)

Heyworth, Peter, ed., *Otto Klemperer, His Life and Times*, vol. I. (Cambridge: Cambridge University Press, 1983); vol. II (1996) [ed. John Lucas]

Ho, Allan, and Feafanov, Dmitry, *Biographical Dictionary of Russian/Soviet Composers* (New York: Greenwood Press, 1989)

Holmes, John, *Conductors on Record* (London: Gollancz, 1982)

Holmes, John, *Conductors on Composers* (Westport, CI: Greenwood Press, 1993)

Horowitz, Joseph, *Understanding Toscanini: How He Became an American Culture-God and Helped Create a New Audience for Old Music* (New York: Knopf, 1987)

Horowitz, Joseph, *Wagner Nights: An American History* (Berkeley: University of California Press, 1994)

Hughes, Spike, *The Toscanini Legacy: A Critical Study of Arturo Toscanini's Performances of Beethoven, Verdi and Other Composers* (New York: Dover Publications, 1959)

Hunt, John, *Furtwängler and Great Britain* (London: Furtwängler Society, 1985)

Hunt, John, *Musical Knights: Wood, Beecham, Boult, Barbirolli, Goodall, Sargent: 6 Separate Discographies* (London: self-published, 1995)

Jacobs, Arthur, *Henry J. Wood: Maker of the Proms* (London: Methuen, 1994)

Jagow, Shelly M., "Women Orchestral Conductors in America: The Struggle for Acceptance – An Historical View from the Nineteenth Century to the Present," *College Music Symposium* 38 (1998), pp. 126–45

Jefferson, Alan, *Sir Thomas Beecham* (London: Macdonald and Jane's, 1979)

Jobin, Sara, "Maestra: Five Female Orchestral Conductors in the United States," B.A. honors thesis (Harvard University, 1992)

Johnson, Edward, *Stokowski: Essays in Analysis of His Art* (London: Triad Press, 1973)

Jungheinrich, Hans-Klaus, *Die grossen Dirigenten: die wichtigsten Interpreten des 20. Jahrhunderts* (Düsseldorf: Econ, 1986)

Karajan, Herbert von, and Endler, Franz, *My Autobiography*, tr. Stewart Spencer (London: Sidgwick and Jackson, 1989)

Keller, Hans, and Milein, Cosman, *Stravinsky at Rehearsal* (London: Dobson, 1962)

Keller, Hans, and Milein, Cosman, *Stravinsky Seen and Heard* (London: Toccata Press, 1982); (New York: Da Capo, 1986)

Kempe-Oettinger, Cordula, *Rudolf Kempe, Pictures of a Life* (London: Robson Books, 1980)

Kennedy, Michael, *Barbirolli* (London: Hamish Hamilton, 1971)

Kennedy, Michael, *Barbirolli, Conductor Laureate* (London: MacGibbon and Kee, 1971)

Kennedy, Michael, *Richard Strauss* (London: Dent, 1976)

Kennedy, Michael, *Adrian Boult* (London: Hamish Hamilton, 1987)

Kenyon, Nicholas, *Simon Rattle: The Making of a Conductor* (London: Faber and Faber, 1987); rev. edn., *Simon Rattle: From Birmingham to Berlin* (London: Faber and Faber, 2002)

Klemperer, Otto, *Minor Recollections* (London: Dobson, 1964)

Kosloff, Doris Lang, "The Woman Opera Conductor: A Personal Perspective," in *The Musical Woman: An International Perspective, vol. I, 1983*, ed. Judith Lang Zaimont (Westport, CT: Greenwood Press, 1984), pp. 235–43

Kuna, Milan, *Václav Talich* (Prgue: Panton, 1980)

Kurnick, Judith, *Riccardo Muti: Twenty Years in Philadelphia* (Philadelphia: Univ. of Philadelphia Press, 1992)

Lang, Klaus, *Lieber Herr Celibidache* (Zürich: M&T, 1988)

Lang, Klaus, *The Karajan Dossier*, tr. Stewart Spencer (London: Faber, 1992)

Lawson, Kay, "Women Conductors: Credibility in a Male-Dominated Profession," in *The Musical Woman: An International Perspective, vol. III, 1986–1990*, ed. Judith Lang Zaimont (New York: Greenwood Press, 1991), pp. 197–219.

Lebrecht, Norman, *The Maestro Myth: Great Conductors in Pursuit of Power* (New York: Birch Lane, 1991); (London: Simon and Schuster, 1991)

Legge, Walter, *On and Off the Record* (New York: Scribner's, 1982)

Lehmann, Lotte, *Five Operas and Richard Strauss*, tr. Ernst Pawel (New York City: Macmillan, 1964)

Leichtentritt, Hugo. *Serge Koussevitsky, the Boston Symphony Orchestra and the New American Music* (Cambridge: Harvard University Press, 1946)

Leinsdorf, Erich L., *Cadenza: A Musical Career* (New York: Houghton Mifflin, 1976)

LePage, Jane Weiner, *Women Composers, Conductors, and Musicians of the Twentieth Century* (Metuchen, NJ: Scarecrow Press, 1980); vol. II (1983); vol. III (1988)

Levine, James, and Marsh, Robert C., *Dialogues and Discoveries* (New York: Scribner's, 1997)

Lewis, Laurance, *Guido Cantelli: Portrait of a Maestro* (San Diego: A. S. Barnes, 1981)

Lourié, Arthur, *Serge Koussevitsky and His Epoch*, tr. S. W. Pring (New York: Knopf, 1931)

Lucas, John, *Reggie: The Life of Reginald Goodall* (London: Random House, 1983)

Macleod, Elizabeth A., *Women Performing Music: The Emergence of American Women as Classical Instrumentalists and Conductors* (Jefferson, NC: McFarland, 2001)

Malko, Nicolai, *A Certain Art* (New York: William Morrow and Co., 1966)

Markevitch, Igor, *Être et avoir Été* (Paris: Gallimard, 1980)

Marsh, Robert Charles, *Toscanini and the Art of Conducting*, rev. edn. (New York: Collier Books, 1962)

Martin, George, *The Damrosch Dynasty: America's First Family in Music* (Boston: Houghton Mifflin, 1983)

Martyn, Barrie, *Rachmaninoff: Composer, Pianist, Conductor* (Aldershot, Hants.: Scolar Press, 1990)

Matheopoulos, Helen, *Maestro* (London: Hutchinson, 1982)

Matthews, Denis, *Arturo Toscanini* (Tunbridge Wells: Midas/Hippocrene, 1982)

Mengelberg, Willem, *Gedenkboek, 1895–1920* (Gravenhage: Martinus Nijhoff, 1920)

Mitropoulos, Dmitri, and Katsoyanis, Katy, *A Correspondence: 1930–1960* (New York: Martin Dale, 1963)

Monteux, Doris, *It's All in the Music: The Life and Works of Pierre Monteux* (London: William Kimber, 1966)

Monteux, Fifi, *Everyone is Someone* (New York: Farrar, Straus, and Cudahy, 1962) [Fifi was a poodle owned by Doris and Pierre Monteux]

Munch, Charles, *I Am a Conductor*, tr. Leonard Burkat (Oxford: Oxford University Press, 1955)

Mundy, Simon, *Bernard Haitink: A Working Life* (London: Robson, 1987)

Mussulman, Joseph, *Dear People: Robert Shaw* (Bloomington: Indiana University Press, 1979)

Myers, Paul, *Leonard Bernstein* (Phaidon Press: New York, 1998)

Nicotra, Tobias, *Arturo Toscanini* (New York: Knopf, 1929)

Olivier, Philippe, *Charles Munch* (Paris: Belfond, 1987)

Opperby, Preben, *Leopold Stokowski* (Tunbridge Wells: Midas Books, 1982)

Osborne, Richard, *Conversations with von Karajan* (New York: Harper and Row, 1989); (London: Oxford University Press, 1991)

Osborne, Richard, *Herbert von Karajan: A Life in Music* (London: Chatto and Windus, 1998)

Parrott, Jasper, *Ashkenazy beyond Frontiers* (London: Collins, 1984)

Pendle, Karin, ed., *Women and Music: A History* (Bloomington: University of Indiana Press, 1991)

Perone, James E., *Howard Hanson: A Bio-Bibliography* (New York: Greenwood Press, 1993)

Peyser, Joan, *Boulez: Composer, Conductor, Enigma* (London: Cassell, 1977); (New York: Schirmer, 1978)

Peyser, Joan, *Bernstein: A Biography* (New York: Ballantine Books, 1987)

Phelan, Nancy, *Charles Mackerras: A Musicians' Musician* (London: Gollancz, 1987)

Pirie, Peter, *Furtwängler and the Art of Conducting* (London: Duckworth, 1980)

Porges, Heinrich, *Wagner Rehearsing the 'Ring:' An Eye-Witness Account of the Stage Rehearsals of the First Bayreuth Festival*, tr. Robert Jacobs (Cambridge: Cambridge University Press, 1983)

Pound, Reginald, *Sir Henry Wood: A Biography* (London: Cassell, 1969)

Praeger, Ferdinand, *Wagner as I Knew Him* (New York: Longmans, Green, 1893)

Previn, André, *No Minor Chords: My Days in Hollywood* (New York: Doubleday, 1991)

Prieberg, Fred K., *Trial of Strength*, tr. Christopher Dolan (London: Quartet Books, 1991); (Boston: Northeastern University Press, 1994)

Procter-Gregg, Humphrey, *Sir Thomas Beecham* (Windermere: Procter-Gregg, 1973)

Procter-Gregg, Humphrey, *Sir Thomas Beecham, Conductor and Impresario, As Remembered by His Friends* (London: Duckworth, 1976)

Rasmussen, Tenesa, *Antonia Brico and the New York Women's Symphony Orchestra: 1934–1939*, M.M. thesis, Southern Methodist University, 1997

Reid, Charles, *Thomas Beecham: An Independent Biography* (London: Gollancz, 1962)

Reid, Charles, *Malcolm Sargent* (London: Hamish Hamilton, 1968)

Reid, Charles, *John Barbirolli* (London: Hamish Hamilton, 1971)

Reis, Claire R., *Composers, Conductors, and Critics* (New York: Oxford University Press, 1955)

Riess, Curt, *Wilhelm Furtwängler: A Biography*, tr. Margaret Goldsmith (London: Frederick Muller, 1955)

Rigby, Charles, *John Barbirolli: A Biographical Sketch* (London: John Sherratt, 1948)

Rimsky-Korsakov, Nicolai, *My Musical Life*, tr. Judah A Joffee (London: Faber, 1989)

Robinson, Paul, *The Art of the Conductor: Karajan* (London: MacDonald, 1975); (New York: Vanguard, 1976)

Robinson, Paul, *The Art of the Conductor: Stokowski* (London: MacDonald, 1977)

Robinson, Paul, *Solti* (Toronto: Lester and Orpen, 1979); (New York: Vanguard, 1979)

Robinson, Paul, *The Art of the Conductor: Bernstein* (London: MacDonald, 1982)

Rodzinski, Halina, *Our Two Lives* (New York: Scribner's, 1976)

Russell, Charles Edward, *The American Orchestra and Theodore Thomas* (New York: Doubleday, 1927)

Russell, John, *Erich Kleiber: A Memoir* (London: André Deutsch, 1957); (Da Capo, 1981)

Sacchi, Filippo, *Magic Baton: Toscanini's Life for Music* (New York: G. P. Putnam, 1957)

Sacchi, Filippo, *Toscanini* (Milan: Longanesi, 1988)

Sachs, Harvey, *Toscanini* (Philadelphia: Lippincott, 1978); (London: Weidenfeld and Nicolson, 1978)

Sachs, Harvey, *Reflections on Toscanini* (New York: Grove Weidenfeld, 1991)

Schabas, Ezra, *Theodore Thomas: America's Conductor and Builder of Orchestras* (Urbana: University of Illinois Press, 1989)

Schonberg, Harold, *The Great Conductors* (New York: Simon and Schuster, 1967); (London: Gollancz, 1968)

Schönzeler, Hans-Hubert, *Furtwängler* (Portland: Amadeus, 1991)

Secrest, Meryle, *Leonard Bernstein: A Life* (New York: Knopf, 1994)

Shirakawa, Sam H., *The Devil's Music Master: The Controversial Life and Career of Wilhelm Furtwängler* (Oxford and New York: Oxford University Press, 1992)

Shore, Bernard, *The Orchestra Speaks* (London: Longmans, Green, 1938)

Simeone, Nigel and Mundy, Simon, *Sir Adrian Boult, Companion of Honour* (Tunbridge Wells: Midas, 1980)

Simon, Charnan, *Seiji Ozawa: A Symphony Conductor* (Chicago: Children's Press, 1992)

Smith, Moses, *Koussevitsky* (New York: Allen, Towne, and Heath, 1947)

Smith, William Ander, *The Mystery of Leopold Stokowski* (Cranbury, NJ: Association of University Presses, 1990)

Smyth, Ethel, *Beecham and Pharoah* (London: Chapman and Hall, 1935)

Sollitt, Edna, *Mengelberg and the Symphonic Epoch* (New York: Washburn, 1930)

Solti, Georg, *Memoirs* (New York: Knopf, 1997)

Spohr, Louis, *The Musical Journeys of Louis Spohr,* tr. & ed. Henry Pleasants
(Norman, OK: University of Oklahoma Press, 1961)

Stambaugh, Sonja A., *Women Instrumental Conductors in the United States: From
Pioneers to the Present Day*, M.Mus. Ed. thesis, Indiana University, 1993

Stanley, Patricia, "Dr. Antonia Brico and Dr. Albert Schweitzer: A Chronicle of Their
Friendship," in *Literary and Musical Notes: A Festschrift for William A. Little,* ed.
Geoffrey C. Orth and William A. Little (Bern: P. Lang, 1995), pp. 185–203

Stebbins, Lucy, and Stebbins, Richard, *Frank Damrosch: Let the People Sing*
(Durham, NC: Duke University Press, 1945)

Stefan, Paul, *Toscanini* (New York: Viking, 1936)

Stefan, Paul, *Bruno Walter* (Vienna, 1936)

Stoddard, Hope, *Symphony Conductors of the USA* (New York: Thomas Y. Crowell,
1957)

Stokowski, Leopold, *Music for All of Us* (New York: Simon and Schuster, 1943)

Stokowski, Olga Samaroff, *An American Musician's Story* (New York: Norton, 1939)

Taubman, Howard, *The Maestro: The Life of Arturo Toscanini* (New York: Simon and
Schuster, 1951)

Thomas, Michael Tilson, and Seckerson, Edward, *Michael Tilson Thomas: Viva Voce*
(London: Faber, 1994)

Thomas, Rose Fay, *Memoirs of Theodore Thomas* (New York: Moffat, Yard, 1911)

Thomas, Theodore, *Theodore Thomas: A Musical Autobiography*, ed. George P.
Upton, (Chicago: McClurg, 1905); (Da Capo, 1964)

Toscanini, Arturo, *The Letters of Arturo Toscanini*, tr. and ed. Harvey Sachs (New
York: Knopf, 2002); (London: Faber, 2002)

Trotter, William, *Priest of Music: The Life of Dimitri Mitropoulos* (Portland:
Amadeus, 1995)

Ueland, Brenda, *Mitropoulos and the North High Band* (St. Paul: The Schubert Club,
1984)

Ursuleac, Viorica, *Singen für Richard Strauss* (Vienna: Doblinger, 1986)

Vaughan, Roger, *Herbert von Karajan: A Biographical Portrait* (London: Weidenfeld
and Nicolson, 1986)

Valenti Ferro, Enzo, *Los Directores* (Buenos Aires: Ediciones de Arte Gaglianone,
1985)

Voss, Egon, *Die Dirigenten der Bayreuther Festspiele* (Regensburg: Gustav Bosse
Verlag, 1976)

Waleson, Heidi, "Music, Maestra, Please," *New York Times*, April 16, 1989, sect. 2,
pp. 1, 36.

Walter, Bruno, *Gustav Mahler*, tr. James Galston (London: Kegan Paul, 1937)

Walter, Bruno, *Theme and Variations: An Autobiography*, tr. James Galston (New
York: Knopf, 1947)

Weingartner, Felix, *Lebenserinnerungen* (Vienna, 1923); rev. edn. (1928–9); *Buffets
and Rewards: A Musician's Reminiscences,* tr. Marguerite Wolff (London:
Hutchinson and Co., 1937)

Wilson, Carol Green, *Arthur Fiedler: Music for the Millions* (New York: Evans
Publishing, 1968)

Wolfe, Rinna Evelyn, *The Calvin Simmons Story; or, Don't Call Me Maestro* (Berkeley, CA: Muse Wood Press, 1994)

Wood, Sir Henry, *My Life of Music* (London: Gollancz, 1938)

Wood, Jessie, *The Last Years of Henry J. Wood* (London: Gollancz, 1954)

Young, Percy, *World Conductors* (London: Abelard-Schuman, 1966)

Zaimont, Judith Lang, "Equal Opportunity – Assessing Women's Presence in the Exxon/Arts Endowment Conductors Program: An Interview With Jesse Rosen," in *The Musical Woman: An International Perspective. Vol. II 1984–1985*, ed. Judith Lang Zaimont (Westport, CT: Greenwood Press, 1987), pp. 91–119

Index

Cambridge Companions to Music

Topics

The Cambridge Companion to Blues and Gospel Music
Edited by Allan Moore

The Cambridge Companion to Conducting
Edited by José Antonio Bowen

The Cambridge Companion to Grand Opera
Edited by David Charlton

The Cambridge Companion to Jazz
Edited by Mervyn Cooke and David Horn

The Cambridge Companion to the Musical
Edited by William Everett and Paul Laird

The Cambridge Companion to the Orchestra
Edited by Colin Lawson

The Cambridge Companion to Pop and Rock
Edited by Simon Frith, Will Straw and John Street

The Cambridge Companion to the String Quartet
Edited by Robin Stowell

Composers

The Cambridge Companion to Bach
Edited by John Butt

The Cambridge Companion to Bartók
Edited by Amanda Bayley

The Cambridge Companion to Beethoven
Edited by Glenn Stanley

The Cambridge Companion to Benjamin Britten
Edited by Mervyn Cooke

The Cambridge Companion to Berg
Edited by Anthony Pople

The Cambridge Companion to Berlioz
Edited by Peter Bloom

The Cambridge Companion to Brahms
Edited by Michael Musgrave

The Cambridge Companion to Bruckner
Edited by John Williamson

The Cambridge Companion to John Cage
Edited by David Nicholls

The Cambridge Companion to Chopin
Edited by Jim Samson

The Cambridge Companion to Debussy
Edited by Simon Trezise